BLACK DAHLIA
AVENGER
II

Presenting the Follow-Up Investigation and Further
Evidence Linking
Dr. George Hill Hodel to Los Angeles's Black Dahlia and
other 1940s
LONE WOMAN MURDERS

By

STEVE HODEL

Thoughtprint Press

Los Angeles, California

Copyright ©2012 by Thoughtprint Press
Los Angeles, California
Published in the United States of America
Visit our Web site at www.thoughtprintpress.com
ISBN-978-0-9830744-4-1

Author Website at www.stevehodel.com

For the victims, living and dead

CONTENTS

INTRODUCTION

Twelve years and three months have now passed since I received that fateful 1:00 a.m. phone call from my stepmother on May 17, 1999.

"Steve, this is June in San Francisco. Your father is dead! The paramedics are here. Come down now."

As a career homicide cop with LAPD, most of my three-hundred plus murder investigations began with a call just like that, but, always from the Hollywood Watch Commander.

Not in my wildest dreams could I have imagined that a personal "Death Notification" would become the most difficult murder investigation of my career.

But, it did and it has.

Since the spring of '99, seemingly, each month has brought a new twist to the investigation. New witnesses have surfaced, new cold case victims were discovered, and new evidence was found.

It has taken over a decade for the public perception of the investigation to transition from "strong circumstantial" to—**CASE SOLVED**.

The Black Dahlia murder, has, for obvious reasons, stood out as the most challenging criminal investigation in my forty-three years of working cases.

Surprisingly, my biggest challenge did not come from within; *that is, from being confronted with the fact that the prime suspect I was pursuing—was my father.*

No, rather, it came from without. From finding myself in the position for the first time in my career of having to—DECONSTRUCT THE EVIDENCE!

What do I mean?

Prior to the Black Dahlia, without exception, all of my previous murder investigations had always been a *tabula raza*—a clean slate. You start with a blank field notebook and move forward as you begin to build your case.

Not so with the Dahlia. As I began my investigation, I discovered that the "facts" of the case were a briar patch of misinformation, constructed from fifty-years of legend and lore.

Never was the oft quoted cinematic line from the 1962 classic, *The Man Who Shot Liberty Valance*, truer than in the Black Dahlia murder:

"This is the West, sir. When the legend becomes fact, print the legend."

As if to underscore this, within three short years from the time of her murder, we have Elizabeth Short's legend appear *on-screen, as a laugh line*, in the 1950 Hollywood classic, *Sunset Boulevard*. [Ironically, the words are spoken by a young Jack Webb, who, the following year, will begin his career in his new television show, *Dragnet*, starring as LAPD Sergeant Joe "Just the Facts" Friday.]

In *Sunset Boulevard*, Webb plays the part of Artie Green, a young film producer, who, at his New Year's Eve party, introduces his writer friend, Joe Gillis [William Holden] to the guests with the following line:

"Fans, you all know Joe Gillis, the well-known screenwriter, uranium smuggler, and Black Dahlia suspect." [Much laughter]

With the publication of this, my third book on Elizabeth Short and the related *1940s Los Angeles Lone Woman Murders*, I believe that I have been able to replace most of the hype and *faction* [hack writers' hyperbolic mix of fact and fiction] with the truth as documented in my accessing of the official Los Angeles District Attorney's Black Dahlia secret files.

These records, besides providing their own factual accounts contained many of the original LAPD summaries from the 1947 Black Dahlia investigation.

Here, in *BDA II, I present separate chapters detailing the Black Dahlia's three major myths.* Those being: (1) "The Black Dahlia was a standalone crime," (2) Elizabeth Short had a "missing week" and (3) "The case was never solved."

None of these "urban legends" were ever true and I present the evidence which proves them false.

In explaining and exposing the third myth, "The case was never solved," I now have confirmation coming from within the LAPD–from most of its top commanders, *past* and *present.*

The last "official word" from LAPD on the Black Dahlia case status came from self-professed gatekeeper, Detective Brian Carr, who, before exiting stage-right and retiring in May 2009, informed the public:

"I don't have time to prove or disprove Hodel's investigation. All the physical evidence from the Dahlia investigation has disappeared, so we can't do any DNA and so we can't solve the case."

On my side of the law enforcement ledger, I now have the following officers who were and are all in agreement that the Black Dahlia murder "is solved."

They include *four of the original top ranking command staff:* two former LAPD police chiefs, as well as the original DA's investigators; a LASD under sheriff, an LASD commander, and the 2004 LAPD chief of detectives.

Also voicing his strong support was a then active head deputy district attorney, who, in 2003 and again in stronger terms in 2006, informed the public that based on the evidence—and were George Hodel still living and the witnesses available—he would have filed two murder counts [Elizabeth Short, Black Dahlia, and Jeanne French, Red Lipstick Murder] and believed he "would win a conviction in both cases in a jury trial."

The names and reasons for these separate law enforcement officers' opinions, as well as the source of their statements, are all summarized in Chapter 13, **CASE SOLVED.**

But, it is *you, my readers,* who have followed my ongoing investigations and served as dedicated jurors in the *Court of Public Opinion,* that have been my biggest supporters.

My unofficial tally, based on the many letters and thousands of e-mails I have received from you over the past decade, indicates that most of you [about 90 percent] have found the evidence not just compelling, but "beyond a reasonable doubt," which of course meets the legal criteria for establishing a "guilty" verdict.

Within the following chapters, you will find much that is new.

In my chapter on "Maganda," which deals with the controversy of the photographs found in my father's private album, I was able to "prove myself wrong" [by following the evidence] on what I formerly believed was solid forensic evidence. It was not. And by following the truth of it, and self-correcting the error, it led me to new and important proofs.

That is what truth does. It opens doors and keeps on opening them until the case is *made.*

In a criminal investigation, one of the surest signs that one may well be on the wrong track and in pursuit of the wrong suspect, is when the doors start to close and no more open. Generally speaking, when one hits that dead-end, it is advisable to either turn around or to back out and drive down another alley.

Probably, the most dramatic new investigative finding came in 2008 with the discovery and linkage of physical evidence to the actual Black Dahlia crime scene. However, I'll leave that revelation for you to discover on your own.

Finally, there is the *Huston Letters*—private, highly personal correspondences between my mother and her former husband, famed film director/writer/actor, John Huston.

They span the years 1948-1957 and give us a real-time understanding of the absolute terror and horror my mother was suffering as she struggled to keep us together—just to survive. Her struggle was literally, week by week, during those dangerous post-Dahlia months from 1948 to 1950. The reading of those letters, which contained her desperate pleas to John for help, leave NO DOUBT that our father was a psychological time bomb, about to explode.

I have included all of the letters not only because of my mother's dramatic first person descriptions of the desperate conditions at the Franklin house, but also because, in the later years, they documented an exchange of ideas between John and Dorothy that many readers, as well as historians and cinephiles, will find of interest.

On a personal note, [which has only been revealed to me through the discovery of these hitherto unknown and unpublished letters] I have, since reading them, become exceedingly grateful to John upon learning of his overwhelming generosity.

Time and time again, as demonstrated in my mother's letters, John repeatedly sent emergency dollars which kept the sheriff at bay and fed and housed us during those difficult *gypsy years*.

In the writing of this third book, I would like to acknowledge a few close friends who have been of tremendous help. First, as always, there is Roberta McCreary who has been my confidant and with me from the start, and remains constant and true. Also, much thanks goes to my good friend, Hermann H., for providing encouragements and suggestions, and to Dennis Effle, my resident Hollywood historian, amigo, and researcher extraordinaire! Kudos to Kevin Knoblock for his many suggestions and critique. And, finally a sincere "well done" to all the staff at *Accurance Author Partner's* for their outstanding professionalism in helping me to cross all the t's, dot the i's as well as design and format the book.

Steve Hodel
Los Angeles, California
November 22, 2011

Chapter 1

Madi Comfort, Duke Ellington's Original "Satin Doll"

"We all knew that he (Dr. George Hill Hodel) had done it. There was no doubt!"
—Madi Comfort June, 2003

The year was 1942. The "cigarette girl" at the Hollywood Casino Club on the Sunset Strip was a knockout. Just eighteen, she had a perfect figure, soft satin skin, and jet-black hair. Mattie Hodge (she would later, at Duke Ellington's suggestion, change the spelling to Madi) was the bar crowd's favorite. A few whispered complaints may have come from the chorus-line girls who knew they couldn't compete with Mattie's natural beauty.

From the contacts she made on The Strip, Mattie's public persona would go on to include: model, singer, film actress, and, later in life, she would school herself in painting and become an accomplished artist.

Mattie also had a secret—a big one! A secret so big that all of Los Angeles wanted to know it. For fifty-five years, she kept it hidden and planned to take it with her to the grave. But, in the final ten days before her death, Fate or Happenstance jumped on board and whispered in her ear, telling her to "Share it." She did. This is the story of that secret—Madi's secret.

The Lead

I've been a detective all my adult life. Born and raised in Los Angeles, I am sixty-eight, and this is my forty-seventh year in conducting criminal investigations. Working LAPD's Hollywood Division Homicide in the 1970s, my hot leads came to me in one of three ways: (1) from a jailhouse snitch, (2) someone "dropping a dime" and calling me with information, or (3) a "walk-in" where the witness would come to the police station with a "Here's what I know...."

Detective work is much different today. Twenty-first century witness tips now generally come to me by way of "e-mails." That's how this one arrived. It was from Lynelle Lujan, the office-manager at the Whittier Historical Society Museum. It read:

August 20, 2010

"Dear Mr. Hodel,

I don't know if you remember me. I sent you a *Whittier Daily News* article about 3 months ago. I'm writing you today for a different reason however. While lending my boss [Myra Hilliard, the Museum's Executive Director] your first book, she recognized Madi Comfort's name, whom she knew briefly before her death.

We have since made contact with Madi's longtime companion and mentioned your book and the connection of your father with Madi. His name is George and he is willing to meet with you. He remembers the time that your father died, and that Madi made several phone calls and seemed agitated.

If you would like to meet with George, we can offer the Whittier Museum as a private meeting place, perhaps before or after your October 12th speaking engagement at the Whittier Public Library.

Sincerely,

Lynelle Lujan

Madi Comfort—Her Backstory

Madi returned to her roots, Whittier, California, in 1970. The small town, which lies just twelve miles southeast of Los Angeles, was originally a Quaker community and is now famous for its "urban forest," magnificent tree lined parkways, providing a country lifestyle for its city dwellers.

Madi has been featured in a number of local articles over the years, and former Whittier mayor, Allan Zolnekoff, proclaimed February 3,

2002 to be "Madi Comfort Day." The honor read in part, "...for the historical precedent set by her family of pioneering African-Americans to settle in Whittier and overcoming racial unwelcome; her achievements as an artist, her contributions to the Whittier Community, and her dedication to the arts and music in Whittier."

Madi, at age seventy-nine, suffered a heart attack and died in Whittier on June 20, 2003. For those not familiar with Madi, here is a brief biography on this exceptionally talented lady.

Her birth name was Mattie Hodge, born November 19, 1923. Her mother, not wanting to raise her newborn daughter, had agreed to allow her to be adopted by Whittier's first ever black residents, Mr. and Mrs. Mark Huff. When time came to turn the child over, her mother informed the Huff's that she had changed her mind and decided to keep her daughter, but would honor them by giving the child Mrs. Huff's given name, "Mattie."

Mattie's mother was abusive, and the child's growing up years were difficult ones, compounded greatly by the otherwise hard times of the Great Depression.

As a young woman, Madi's natural charm and exceptional beauty drew her west, from Whittier to Hollywood, where in 1942, at age eighteen, she was offered a job as a "cigarette girl" at a nightclub on the Sunset Strip. Her popularity at the club and regular contact with Hollywood celebrities brought her modeling jobs, some singing gigs, and a few small parts in films.

Madi met and fell in love with Joe Comfort, a young soldier who would become a well-known LA bass player in the 1940s and 1950s. Joe later joined with Lionel Hampton and Nat King Cole, and played on many of the classic Sinatra/Nelson Riddle records that Capitol made in the 1950s. Joe and Madi were married in Los Angeles on May 13, 1943. She was just nineteen. Madi soon found herself in an abusive relationship with Joe and ended the marriage several years later.

3

Madi and Joe Comfort, Wedding Day, May 1943
Dancing at the Plantation Club, 108th and Central, Watts

Madi as Ebony Magazine's 1955 Cover Girl—*Kiss Me Deadly*

Madi's most memorable film role was a small part in the 1955 film noir, *Kiss Me Deadly*. Madi plays a blues singer working in an LA Jazz Club. In this Mickey Spillane adapted classic, hard-boiled P.I. Mike Hammer (played by actor Ralph Meeker) comes into the bar for a few drinks as she was singing, *"I'd Rather Have the Blues than What I've Got."* In the film, Madi lip-syncs the song which was actually sung by popular Central Avenue vocalist, Kitty White. The film's producer would later tell Madi, "If I'd known you sang as well as you do, I'd have had you sing the piece in our picture."

**Screen shots from the 1955 film noir, *Kiss Me Deadly* – Left: Madi singing
Right: Madi with star of film, Ralph Meeker and unidentified male**

One of Madi's major claims to fame was that she was the original, "*Satin Doll*" from the song of the same name. Duke Ellington, along with Billy Strayhorn and Johnny Mercer, wrote the song which became a major hit in 1956.

Ellington, Madi's one-time boyfriend, named her his "Satin Doll" as well as suggested that she change the spelling of her name from Mattie to Madi, telling her, "My Dear, you should really spell your name M A D I, because you really are the Mad One, you know." She followed his advice.

The following additional information and excerpt on Mattie Comfort was recently e-mailed to me by a friend familiar with the LA music scene of the 1950s. It gives us a fascinating look into that time, along with a Madi anecdote.

MF wrote:

The attached excerpt is from a book about Charlie Mingus, another bass player. The incident about Mattie apparently took place around 1960. "Knepper" in the book is Jimmy Knepper, who was Mingus's trombonist.

From: *Myself When I Am Real: The Life and Music of Charles Mingus* by Gene Santoro (2001, Oxford University Press):

> One night during the Hollywood gig, Mingus started riding Knepper onstage in front of women friends. One of them was one of Duke Ellington's girlfriends, Mattie Comfort, wife of Mingus's Watts friend and fellow bassist Joe Comfort. Mattie looked like Lena Horne, and was sitting with Pat Willard, a white Duke fan, in the front row.
>
> Mattie called out, "Hey, Mingus, leave that white boy alone, he loves you." He rasped, "You're not black enough to talk to me like that." She said coolly, "You're lighter than I am, Mingus."
>
> Mingus spotted Knepper with the women in the lobby. When Mattie left to get her car, he followed her into the parking lot, then took out a thick pen filled with a charge to shoot pepper. He had no pepper, just charges. He had taken to firing it off in the club during his shows, but now he shot it off in her face.
>
> Mattie was still shaking when she picked up the other two. In the rearview mirror, she watched Mingus follow them up Sunset Boulevard in the Cadillac. She turned right on Vine, right on Hollywood, and headed for the police station. No cops, no cop cars, and Mingus was right behind them. So she made a right on N. Bronson and ran a red light at Sunset, where a police cruiser parked there stopped them.
> To the puzzled cop, Mattie explained that Knepper worked for Charles Mingus, who was chasing them. When the cop looked up, the limo wheeled into a U-turn and sped off. The cop shrugged, and let Mattie off with a warning. Relieved, they drove to Pat Willard's house and listened to Ellington records.

The DA Secret Files

Black Dahlia Avenger originally published in April 2003. As a result of the heavy print and television coverage of my story, NBC's *Dateline*, CBS *48 Hours Mystery*, *A&E Court TV*, and Bill Kurtis', *Cold Case Files* would all subsequently produce full hour television shows. Los Angeles District Attorney Steve Cooley gave *Los Angeles Times* columnist Steve Lopez an interview, along with granting him permission to examine some previously secret DA files, which had been locked in the county vault and unexamined for over fifty-years.

Within days of the original publication, reporter Lopez, in two separate back to back *LA Times* articles, revealed some of the contents of these never-before-seen DA files. To the absolute shock of both LAPD and Angelenos in general, the reports fully documented the DA's separate investigation into the original Black Dahlia murder and *named Dr. George Hill Hodel as the prime suspect*. This was huge news because it was a totally independent and external confirmation of my own findings.

A month later, in mid-May, I approached DA Steve Cooley and requested permission to view the secret files. To his credit, Mr. DA granted my request and I would spend a full day copying all the relevant *Hodel-Black Dahlia Files*. The DA investigation related to my father and the Black Dahlia investigation totaled approximately 600 pages. None of it had ever been seen or reviewed *by anybody* since it had been locked away in the DA vault in 1950!

It took me several months to thoroughly review the material, most of which has now been included as new evidence in two updated chapters of *Black Dahlia Avenger*, added to the July 2006 HarperCollins paperback publication.

In the "Aftermath" chapter of that book, I included the DA's 1950 investigation which documented in detail *the detective's electronic surveillance and actual physical "bugging" of Dr. Hodel's Hollywood residence.*

Those files revealed that on February 15, 1950, DA detective, Lt. Frank Jemison and his partner arranged an appointment for my father to meet and be interviewed by them at their office in the downtown Hall of Justice.

While they detained him for questioning, separate officers from both the LAPD and the DA's sound lab went to Dr. Hodel's private residence, gained entry by shimming the front door, *and installed microphones inside the walls in the living room/home office and the master bedroom*. A hard line was then run from the basement of our home, outside to the street, and connected to *Pacific Bell Telephone* lines. These pole lines were then strung to the basement of the *Hollywood police station*, a distance of about two miles, where the live conversations could be monitored and recorded by detectives around the clock. [It is important to understand that these microphones were picking up "live conversations" and were not simply phone bugs.]

A taskforce of eighteen (18) detectives, which included officers from both the DA's Office and LAPD, conducted the stakeout 24/7. This audio surveillance lasted forty days.

As a result of their efforts, detectives obtained over forty spools of wire tape recordings *which included statements from my father admitting to killing the Black Dahlia.*

The DA tapes also contained admissions by George Hodel to committing the 1945 barbiturate overdosing of his personal secretary, Ruth Spaulding. That crime, while originally listed as an undetermined death and possible "suicide," was actively investigated by LAPD as a suspected murder some eighteen months before the Dahlia crime. The Spaulding investigation was suspended when Dr. Hodel temporarily left the country in February 1946 to become chief medical officer in Hankow, China while working for the United Nations. He would unexpectedly return to Los Angeles and resume his medical practice in September 1946, four months before the murder of Elizabeth Short.

Several weeks later, one of the surveillance tapes captured Dr. Hodel admitting to performing abortions at his privately owned VD clinic in downtown Los Angeles. The taped transcripts also record him informing a confederate, "This is the best payoff between law enforcement agencies that I've ever seen. You do not have the right connections made. I'd like to get a connection made in the DA's office." Later he brags, "I'm the only person who knows how all these things fit into the picture."

The detectives staked out in the basement of the Hollywood police station, and, while listening to the conversation in real time, overheard a woman crying as she attempted to call the telephone operator. The monitoring detectives heard George and a second man walk downstairs to the basement. The sounds of a pipe striking an object were heard. The woman cried out, more blows, she cried out again, and then went silent. Words were heard discussing "not leaving a trace"—then nothing but silence. Inexplicably, these two on duty officers, listening to what is obviously a serious felony assault, or worse, an actual murder in progress, were just two miles away and TOOK NO ACTION.

Much more is contained in the 146-page transcripts, which I have attached unaltered, and in their entirety, as an addendum to this book.

The stakeout was terminated in late March 1950, only because George Hodel had been informed by Dorothy [his ex-wife and my mother] that the detectives had some damning evidence and photographs, and she was sure that he was about to be arrested. Armed with that information, my father immediately left town.

Sample page of DA Transcript of Surveillance Tapes (1 of 146 pages)

LAPD Hollywood Division Basement. Detectives are monitoring live conversation from the Hodel residence, 5121 Franklin Ave, Hollywood, California. DA investigators Hronek & McGrath on duty. Verbatim transcript of Spool #2:

February 18, 1950

7:35 pm- Conversation between two men. Recorded. Hodel and man with a German acent [sic] had a long conversation; reception was poor, and conversation was hard to understand. The following bits of conversation, however, were overhead.

Hodel to German:

"This is the best payoff I've seen between Law Enforcement Agencies. You do not have the right connections made. I'd like to get a connection made in the DA's office."

...

"Any imperfections will be found. They will have to be made perfect. Don't confess ever. Two and two is not four." Much laughter. "Were just a couple of smart boys." More laughter.

Hodel to German:

"Supposin I did kill the Black Daliah. [sic] They couldn't prove it now. They can't talk to my Secretary anymore because she's dead."

Madi Comfort—The DA's Secret Black Dahlia Witness

As I continued my careful review of the never before released 1950 DA Hodel-*Black Dahlia Files*, a new name surfaced. A name that had never appeared in any police reports, newspaper account, or the volumes of lore and mythology—*Mattie Comfort.*

Background

During the 1950 investigation and before installing any microphones at my father's Frank Lloyd Wright Jr.-built home in Hollywood, DA Lt. Frank Jemison and his partner, Lt. Sullivan, contacted a young ex-navy man by the name of Joe Barrett.

They picked-up the twenty-five-year-old Navy veteran from his day job and brought him to their office for questioning. At the time of the interview, Barrett, discharged from the Navy in 1946 was a struggling artist. In 1948, he started renting a room at the north-end of our home. It was large and open, with great lighting that served as both his residence and art studio.

As Barrett would tell me in a 1999 interview, "Lt. Sullivan laid it on the line with me. He came right out and said, 'We think Dr. George Hodel killed the Black Dahlia. You live there and we need your help. We want you to be our eyes and ears.'" Simply put, they wanted Joe

Barrett to be their *mole*–their informant. With his free access on the INSIDE, he would be invaluable. Joe agreed to try and help.

With that as background, let's examine a scanned excerpt from the police report exactly as found in the DA files

Actual scan of original DA documents referencing Mattie Comfort

```
Camarillo.  Joe Barratt, a roomer at the Hodel residence cooperated as
an informant.  A photograph of the suspect in the nude with a nude
identified colored model was secured from his personal effects.  Under-
signed identified this model as Mattie Comfort, 3423-1/2 South Arlington,
Republic 4953.  She said that she was with Doctor Hodel sometime prior
to the murder and that she knew about his being associated with victim.
```

Short and to the point. We learned that detectives obtained several photographs of Dr. Hodel. But, not just any portraits. In these, he is seen completely naked in the company of a "nude colored model," later identified as MATTIE COMFORT. But, the critical information can be found in the last sentence which reads, "She [Mattie Comfort] was with Doctor Hodel sometime prior to the murder and that she knew about his being associated with victim. [Elizabeth "Black Dahlia" Short.]

In this document, we discovered that in 1950 detectives interviewed a new and critically important witness *who actually placed Dr. George Hill Hodel and the victim, Elizabeth Short, as being together!* Or did she?

Take a closer look at the scanned police report and you will see what I first discovered back in 2003. Some unknown writer at an unknown date and time *has altered the report by inserting the word "nothing" within the text of that sentence. This simple act was obviously an attempt to reverse the meaning of the statement which now reads,* "She said that she was with Doctor Hodel sometime prior to the murder and that she knew **nothing** about his being associated with victim."

Enlargement showing word "nothing" inserted by hand

Based on Lt. Jemison's report, what we do know for sure is that Mattie Comfort and George Hodel were on intimate terms sometime in the 1940s.

Was this document deliberately altered years or possibly decades later? Clearly, Lt. Jemison would not have allowed his typed final investigative report to be filed away uncorrected. Who changed it and when? What was the truth of it?

Lt. Jemison interviews Dorothy Hodel—"On the Record"

Dorothy Huston Hodel 1946   Later photo of Madi Comfort, circa 1954

On March 22, 1950, while the stakeout and bugging continued at my father's home, Detective Jemison, accompanied by a DA stenographer, proceeded to my mother's separate residence at an apartment located on Santa Monica Pier and conducted a follow-up.

This six-page interview was transcribed and placed in the secret files and only came to light upon my examination of the records in 2003, some fifty-three years later. I should note that while my mother, my two brothers, and I continued to live on-and-off with my father at the Franklin house well into 1950, my parents had been legally divorced in 1944.

While there is much of interest in the Lt. Jemison, Dorothy Hodel Q&A transcript, I will just include in here those portions that relate to the separate photographs which Lt. Jemison showed to Dorothy. It should also be noted that at the time of this interview, Lt. Jemison had seemingly not yet identified the photo of the "nude colored model" as Mattie Comfort. And it became apparent in his interview that he was hoping to obtain a name identification from Dorothy Hodel. (I will attach the complete interview as addendum.)

Excerpts from Lt. Jemison/Dorothy Hodel 3.22.50 Interview transcripts: Page-2

Lt. Jemison:	I will now show you a photograph of Beth Short, Santa Barbara No. 11419 and ask you whether or not you have ever seen that young lady in your life?
Dorothy:	No, I never have.

Elizabeth Short "Black Dahlia" booking photo shown to Dorothy Hodel

Lt. Jemison: Did you have a conversation with Dr. Hodel about the murder of Beth Short?

Dorothy: No, unless we mentioned it when it was in the papers, but I don't like to read about things like that. I can't say for sure that I have never mentioned her name to him, but it may have been in passing.

Lt. Jemison: Did he ever tell you, "They can't pin that murder on me?"

Dorothy: No, to the best of my knowledge he didn't and doesn't know her.

Lt Jemison: On or about the date of her murder, January 15, 1947 do you remember being out until 4:00 in the morning with George Hodel and coming in slightly intoxicated? Now, that's three years ago.

Dorothy: Well, I think I explained before we never went on drinking parties because I don't drink because of certain tendencies to drink too much and particularly if I were near him I would not drink because from a medical point of view he does not approve of my drinking and I don't know that I understood that question.

Page 3-

Lt. Jemison: Well, the information that I have is that he was quite intoxicated himself and at that time on that occasion stated that they couldn't pin the Black Dahlia murder on him. [Note: In Lt. Jemison's follow-up investigation and final report prepared in 1951, he corrected George Hodel's quote to read, "They will never be able to prove I did that murder."] [Black Dahlia]

Dorothy: No. No, that isn't true.

Lt. Jemison: Do you remember ever telling Tamar that? [Note: Tamar was my then twelve-year-old half-sister and George Hodel's daughter by another woman.]

Dorothy: No.

Lt. Jemison: Did you ever tell Tamar that Dr. George Hodel was out the night before the murder with Beth Short at a party?

Dorothy: No, I was living at my brother's house at the time. We were not living at the same house. I wouldn't know what he was doing.

Page 5-

Lt. Jemison: Now in view of the fact that the District Attorney's office is interested in contacting all persons that might know something about whether or not Dr. Hodel had anything

	to do with this murder, I now show you a photograph of a nude girl and ask you if you recognize who that girl is. In other words, we want to know her name and where we can contact her?
Dorothy:	There is something familiar about her face. I think she may have been some model or something.
Lt Jemison:	Would you say she is a colored girl or half Indian, do you know?
Dorothy:	No.
Lt. Jemison:	I show you another photograph of the same girl with a man. Do you recognize that man in that photograph?
Dorothy:	I would say that was Dr. Hodel.
Lt. Jemison:	Do you know the person who owns the cat that they are holding between them?
Dorothy:	No, I don't.
Lt. Jemison:	In other words, I am sincerely interested in contacting this girl for information.
Dorothy:	No, I don't know her I have seen her face. I have seen photographs that George has of her.
Lt. Jemison:	Would you have any idea where we could find her?
Dorothy:	No.
Lt. Jemison:	I show you the third picture. Dr. Hodel and the colored girl. You still can't place any person that might know where I can find her?
Dorothy:	No, I don't know. I can't think.
Lt. Jemison:	**Let me advise you that we do have information that he [George Hodel] did associate with Beth Short... [Emphasis mine]**

Entries by detectives in the surveillance transcripts reveal that, immediately, following this interview, my mother went directly to George's home the very next day and informed him of being questioned by Lt. Jemison, as well as providing him with all the questions asked of her, and, most importantly, that she was *shown photographs of both Elizabeth Short and Mattie Comfort*. While my parents' actual conversation was apparently out of range of the microphones and not recorded, we do know that she told him everything based on the following conversation, THAT WAS RECORDED.

DA Transcripts—Franklin House

March 23- 7:45 pm- Hodel came in with Dorothy. (Phone rang, recorded)
...

March 25 11:10 pm
Hodel and Baron (man with accent) came in talking low (can't hear) ...Sounded like Hodel said something about Black Dahlia. Baron said something about F.B.I. Then talked about Tibet. Sounds like Hodel wants to get out of the country. Mentioned passport. Hodel giving Baron dope on how to write to Tibet. Hodel talking about Mexico. Going down and take pictures and write a story. Hodel seems afraid about something. Hodel says his Sanitarium, if he gets it started in Mexico would be "Safe".

March 26 12 a.m. (spool 39)
Spool ran out. Changing. Talking about woman. Hodel says "he wants money and power. "Talking about China. Talking about selling some of Hodel's paintings or something. Hodel talking about picture police have of him and some girl-thought he had destroyed them all- (wire quit at 50-new one going on) Not much talk.

This was the final night of the surveillance tapes. The next day, George Hodel left town, leaving the DA and LAPD detectives in the lurch, literally sitting there with their microphones up his walls. Lt. Jemison was forced to terminate the stakeout.

As summarized in the transcripts in the final hours before George Hodel left LA, he had conversed with Dorothy Hodel and obviously was made aware that the police now had photographs of Mattie Comfort ["I thought I had destroyed all of them"]. And despite Mother's best efforts at withholding her name, the cops were sure to discover it in short order. The stakeout detectives referenced that "Hodel seems afraid of something." Hodel mentioned the "Black Dahlia," "the FBI," and, the following day, he is "in the wind."

In reading the Jemison/Dorothy Hodel transcripts for the first time, I knew my mother was lying and stonewalling Lt. Jemison. I knew that Mother was close friends with Mattie Comfort. On one occasion in the 1970s, my mother had called me up and asked if I could give her a ride out to the Sunset Strip. She wanted to go to a party being held by some friends. I drove her out and accompanied her to an apartment house. At the door, Mother briefly introduced me to a beautiful woman, simply saying, "Steven, this is Mattie, a good friend from the old days. Mattie, meet Steven." The beautiful "Satin Doll" smiled at me. We shook hands, and I turned and left. But Mattie Comfort's face is not a face that one forgets—it was her!

The Whittier Meeting

In my responding e-mail to Lynelle Lujan and Myra Hilliard, I had requested that they contact Madi's boyfriend, "George," and see if he was available to meet with us at their office at the Whittier Historical Museum on September 11th at 10:00 a.m. He was. "George" is George Parkington. I found him to be a gentle intelligent soul, with the look and manner of an artist. He is a carpenter. George had met Madi in 1997. The two of them had become very close and spent the last six years together before her death in 2003.

As the four of us sat down to talk, George opened up the conversation with these words:

> I want to say something to you right away. When your book came out, there was a big article and photos of you in *People Magazine*. Madi always read *People*. And as soon as she read the piece, she called me. She was so excited. I couldn't believe it. Madi said, "George, you've got to come home right now." I drove home immediately, and she was ecstatic...thrilled because this [the Black Dahlia connection] was a secret she'd always held inside her. And now it was in the open.

In the week after my book published, *People Magazine* interviewed me, and, on June 2, 2003, ran a feature story complete with photospread. It was entitled, *"Accusing His Father: An ex-L.A. cop uncovers a painful answer to the notorious 1947 Black Dahlia slaying."* Madi Comfort never got to read my book as she died from a sudden heart attack on June 20, 2003, *just eighteen days after reading the magazine article.*

My first question to George was the obvious one. "Did Madi ever discuss with you what she knew about the Black Dahlia murder? Did she ever provide any specifics?"

George responded:

Here's what I will tell you. Madi told me that she and everybody else were sure that it was your father that killed the Black Dahlia. They had NO DOUBT. She told me, "We all knew that he had done it." Now, who the "we" was I'm not sure, but there are some people still around from way back then. I'll try and dig on that a little bit and see if there is someone you can speak with. Most of the people I know were more like from the fifties, so I'm not sure there is anybody I can locate from that exact era.

As Lynelle, Myra, and I listened to George as he shared his memories of Madi, it was obvious that the man had been deeply devoted to her. When he spoke her name, his words were filled with a deep love and a great sense of loss.

A half-hour into our talk, George reached into his briefcase and removed a stack of papers. Handing them to me he explained:

Madi has written a book. It's in rough form and unpublished and runs about twelve-hundred pages. It's her autobiography. The title is: *MADI COMFORT: THE ORIGINAL SATIN DOLL.* I think Madi started writing it sometime in the seventies or maybe later. In it she mentions and writes about both your father and mother. What Madi writes about them is explicit, but I thought you would want to have everything about them. There may be other references because her writings are scattered, and she jumps back and forth in time. But, for now, I wanted you to have these pages that talk about your parents.

I reached for the papers and asked, "Had Madi mentioned Elizabeth Short in her book?" George replied:

I don't think so. I don't think, even all of these years later, that she wrote about that. That is why she was so excited when your book came out. My sense of it was that she was still protecting people she cared about even though they were dead. She would have been like your mother. She would have protected anybody she cared about. She would have protected even somebody that she didn't care about.

Our meeting lasted nearly two hours. It ended with a handshake and the assurance that the four of us would keep in touch. George and I exchanged contact numbers with the hope and promise to together try and search deeper into the mystery of Madi, which connected her to my father, Dr. George Hill Hodel, now known and identified as the "Black Dahlia Avenger."

Dorothy Huston Hodel—"Dorero"

George Parkington had warned me that Madi's writings about my parents were "explicit." Well, after reading what she has written, I can certainly confirm he was "spot on" in that observation.

Perhaps before opening the pages of Madi's manuscript, and for those who have not read *Black Dahlia Avenger*, a little background and brief bio on my mother is in order.

Dorothy Jean Harvey was born in New York (Central Park West) on April 15, 1906. Her parents moved to Los Angeles sometime in the teens. They had two children, Dorothy and her younger brother, Eugene. Dorothy was exceptionally precocious, as well as strikingly beautiful—a dangerous combination! Ever the free spirit, she was named Elysian Park's, "Queen of the May" in 1917. As a teen in high-school, she dabbled in acting and began double-dating. Dorothy dated a teenager by the name of George Hodel, who, though only *fifteen* had a stratospheric IQ (186) and was enrolled and attending Pasadena's prestigious Caltech University. The other couple who dated with them was a beautiful young woman by the name of Emilia Lawson, who worked at the newly opened Los Angeles Public Library. Her boyfriend was a lean and lanky young man by the name of John Huston, the son of one of Hollywood's brightest film stars, Walter Huston.

At some point in their double-dating, John and George switched partners. John and Dorothy discovered that they were in love. In about 1926, they found a Justice of the Peace who married them. Then the teens eloped to New York and decided to play house in Greenwich

Village. There they began socializing with a very Bohemian crowd of intelligentia-artists, actors, and musicians—free spirits all. John and Dorothy partied with George and Ira Gershwin and many of the Algonquin Round Table types. Lots of drinking, lots of love making. Being twenty in the '20s, they were in full roar.

Stage and screen star, Walter Huston, meeting his son, John and new bride, Dorothy at LA train station, circa 1926. Photo on right, Dorothy Harvey Huston, age eighteen, circa 1924.

John and Dorothy returned to Los Angeles and both became screenwriters for the film studios. Bohemian New York and its red wine were traded in for the Hollywood cocktail crowd and martinis—very dry.

By 1934, after seven years of a very bumpy marriage, John and Dorothy had become serious alcoholics and both were sleeping with pretty much anything that moved.

In about 1936, Dorothy, with her beautiful actress-lover, Greta Nissen in arm, took a cruise to Europe where she continued to drink and play. (In his well-researched book, *The Hustons* (Charles Scribner's Sons, NY 1989) Lawrence Grobel gave a fine account of how John went to England, rescued Dorothy from an almost certain death from alcoholism, and got her back to the US where she made a full, albeit temporary, recovery.)

For the most part, Dorothy was very open about her bisexuality. She was proud of what she called her "paganism" and pretty much wore it on her sleeve in defiance of conventionality.

Circa 1937, Dorothy reunited with her former boyfriend, George Hodel, who had graduated from medical school. After completing his internship at *San Francisco General Hospital,* he was hired as a logging camp surgeon in Arizona and then took a temporary appointment as a US Health Department physician, doctoring in the Southwest to the Hopi and Navaho Indian reservations.

George and Dorothy were now both "back in love." George returned to LA where Dorothy immediately got pregnant. My older brother, Michael, was born in July 1939. They married in Mexico in 1940 and my twin, "John," and I were born in 1941, followed by my younger brother Kelvin's birth just eleven months later.

Our father was hired by the LA County Health Department, specializing in the treatment of venereal disease. He was quickly promoted to become the chief VD officer for all of LA County.

Father, ever a believer in the importance and symbolism of names, christened his new wife, "Dorero," replacing her given name of "Dorothy." To all who would listen, he explained that his inspiration came from combining two words: "Dor," meaning "a gift of" and "Eros," the God of sexual desire. Hence, "Dorero"—a gift of sexual desire.

This quick overview brings us to about the point in time when, according to Madi's manuscript, she met my parents. So, I will let her take over the narrative from here with her own very unique perspective.

With the exception of some minor spelling corrections, I am going to present Madi Comfort's writing and words here exactly as they appear in her manuscript. I have changed NOTHING. These are her verbatim descriptions, written some twenty or thirty years past. I have, however, inserted in bold my own comments to assist the reader in understanding or to clarify a specific person, place, etc.

One further explanation is needed. What we are reading here are Madi's personal reflections as dictated directly into a tape recorder and then transcribed to paper. So, they are not actually her "writings" so much as they are a conversational storytelling of her life, which was then transcribed into a 1200-page rough draft manuscript. The following excerpted pages, which directly relate to Madi's association and memories of my parents, George and Dorero Hodel, were provided to me by her boyfriend, George Parkington.

Madi Comfort: The Original Satin Doll—(Rough draft)

Page 28 (bottom):

Well, I was introduced to Dr. George and Dorero [**Dorothy**] Hodel by Suzette Harbin, who was one of the chorus girls in the show. Dorothy posed for the great photographer Man [**The artist, Man Ray, a close personal friend of my parents and our family photographer**] with Suzette. What a beautiful photograph! Dorero's white delicate face profile together with Suzette's rich beautiful brown skin was such a beautiful contrast, yet there was such a oneness.

Page 29-

George and Dorero lived in this tremendous mansion in Pasadena. Once entering the driveway one would wind, in this case I would wind with George and Dorero in their ... [**in their car up the driveway**]...last to be made after or before the war. It was a gorgeous black Lincoln Continental convertible with a wheel on the back. It was pure gorgeous. Round and round and up and down for what seemed like blocks to this four-story mansion. The top floor was a ballroom; the third floor was a nursery for their three gorgeous children. The second was their bedroom quarters. I guess I should say playground because that's where we played. They were both completely sensuous. George a very handsome polished tall lean born rich man indulged and adored by his father. George had beautiful black hair with a sophisticated wave in front, a classic nose with a perfectly trimmed mustache and very nice lips. George would smile at a person with such charm and sweetness as well as elegance in his perfect clothes with such sincerity. George could turn around and be as cold as ice, yet complete composure in his superior authoritative voice, become this strange distant in charge person. He was a doctor.

George and Dorero led me gracefully and pleasurably, into sharing their joys in many exciting ways of the art of making love. It was all done so tastefully and made us very close friends. We liked very much bringing such joy and pleasures to one another's life, yet we all maintained our dignity and self-respect.

Dorero's first husband had been John Huston. Her father-in-law, Walter Huston. Dorero had been a writer. She once told me that John and George and she were good friends. George stole her away from John. Dorero was so soft and lovely as well as feminine. I loved the way she pronounced words. Her father told me she had once been a schoolteacher. Her father also told me her name was Dorothy. She certainly had her own style.

George and Dorero had me over to their home for dinner quite often. They would take me out, come all the way to Willowbrook to pick me up. ... Dorero was having guests for dinner who had arrived from New York. They had both been put under contract. Their names were Van Heflin and Vincent Price. Actually we were having hors d'oeuvres and cocktails at their [the Hodels] home first then we were going to Chinatown for dinner afterwards. Chinatown was fairly new (remodeled) then and quite fancy and intriguing. It was a fun evening. Van and Vincent were both very charming and witty and they talked about New York and the theater. I just mostly remember what nice down-to-earth gentlemen they were.

One morning around ten a.m. or so I was lying in bed and I hear this crash and Dorero crying. I ran into the bathroom. Dorero was in the bathtub, crying. George cool as you please explains to me Dorero is an alcoholic and has "sneaked a drink." He was reprimanding her for her own good. I'm protesting. "You could break her neck! George I cannot stand to see you knocking poor Dorero around like this. Please don't treat her like this." Meanwhile, I'm busy trying to pull Dorero out of the tub. We were all stark naked.

Madi Comfort's two lovers—George and Dorothy ("Dorero")

Dorero Hodel 1942   **George Hodel circa 1950**

The photo on left was taken in October/November 1942. It shows Mother holding her newborn son, my younger brother, Kelvin, as I look on while standing on the fencepost. Based on the timing, this photo would have been taken at the hilltop "tremendous mansion" described earlier by Madi. (I have no memory of this location, but my half-sister, Tamar, recalls the home, and specifically remembers seeing our father "physically abusing Dorero by pulling her around by her hair in the large open driveway."

Page 31-

I truly enjoyed my job, and loved walking around meeting people, being constantly complimented. I shared the dressing room when I changed with the chorus girls. ... Here comes Joe Comfort on his first furlough from Camp Rucker, Alabama. What a thrill. ...Joe proposed marriage. I naturally said, "Yes." There was a problem.

One had to wait three days after getting your license at City Hall plus the blood test. Well, Dr. George Hodel solved that problem for me. He pulled strings at City Hall and we got our marriage license in one day. Off we went with my sister, and Joseph's sister, Laura, as witnesses, to the preacher.

Page 39-

I married him [Joe Comfort] on May 13, 1943. I missed him so much when he left and went back to Alabama. I couldn't sleep. I cried most of the time. They said, "You can't go to the South with all its prejudices." ...George and Dorero Hodel bought me a ticket and put me on the train. Dorero gave me some advice about pleasing my new husband. She suggested that I should before kissing and sucking Joe's penis, I should gargle or drink some very hot water so my mouth would be steaming hot. She said that would drive Joe crazy. She said, better yet for me to chew some of those red, dried chili peppers and that would really send Joe into pure ecstasy. ...When I tried to kiss Joe's penis he had a pure fit. He snatched his penis out of my mouth and asked, 'Where did you learn that?' I told him Dorero had told me about it, and Dorero had said, 'you'd be in pure heaven.' 'Well, I'm not in pure heaven. I don't want my wife doing things like that.'...

Some Final Thoughts

Madi's unpublished manuscript with its candid and highly explicit narrative is a remarkable historical find. Because it surfaced posthumously, there is no breach of Madi's personal code of silence, only CONFIRMATION. Madi's excited call to her boyfriend, George, came on June 2, 2003—the very day the *People Magazine* article informed the world that George Hodel was the Black Dahlia killer

The day and the time it became public knowledge, permitted her—in Madi's mind—to reveal to George Parkington her fifty-six-year-old secret. She could now finally, in good conscience, relieve herself of a terrible burden and tell her closest friend her darkest secret, "We all knew that he had done it."

Two weeks later, she was gone. But look at what she has left us. Madi's memoirs, written decades ago, just like the DA's secret "Hodel Black Dahlia Files," have now in the twenty-first century presented us with new evidence and new confirmations into what the DA and the LAPD knew back then.

Madi Comfort's boyfriend, George Parkington at a 2010 meeting with author at Whittier Museum

MONDAY, SEPTEMBER 27, 2010

WHITTIER DAILY NEWS

Whittier woman connected to Black Dahlia

Singer had ties to suspect in murder case

By Sandra T. Molina *Staff Writer*

WHITTIER — Madi Comfort, a jazz singer and model who appeared on the cover of *Life* magazine, is Whittier's connection to one of the country's most infamous crimes — the Black Dahlia murder.

Elizabeth Short was found mutilated, her body severed at the waist, on Jan. 15, 1947, in Leimert Park in Los Angeles.

The local papers dubbed it the Black Dahlia murder.

Short's friends had come to call her "Black Dahlia," inspired by her dark hair, a penchant for wearing black lacy clothing and the popularity of the films "Blue Dahlia."

Comfort, who died of a heart attack in

June 2003 at age 79, was said to have been seen with main suspect, Dr. George Hodel, before the murder.

"She never talked about her connection to the murder," said former Whittier Mayor Allan Zolnekoff, who was a friend of the late chanteuse, who lived in Whittier for a decade.

He was surprised to find out recently about the link from Myra Hilliard, executive director of the Whittier Museum.

Comfort had known Zolnekoff's father, Red Mitchell, Billie Holiday's bassist.

"She was quite a character," Zolnekoff said. "She told me 'I was known as a bit of a little flirt.'"

COMFORT A4

Madi Comfort, a jazz singer and model, is Whittier's connection to one of the country's most infamous crimes — the Black Dahlia murder. Comfort, shown here in the 1940s, lived in Whittier for the last decade of her life. She died in 2003.

Photo courtesy of the Whittier Museum

Whittier Daily News, September 27, 2010, announcing Madi Comfort's connection to the Black Dahlia

Madi passed away in Whittier, California on June 20, 2003, just two weeks after revealing her fifty-six year-old secret to her boyfriend, George Parkington.

Madi Comfort with self-portrait done in acrylic

REST IN PEACE PRETTY MADI COMFORT

Chapter 2

"This anatomical anomaly [identical freckle on left eyebrows] is as distinct as a tattoo, and proves beyond any doubt that they are one and the same woman."

Steve Hodel, 2005, *Black Dahlia Avenger* page 546

Photograph No. 1—"Maganda"

One of the things I enjoy most about being my own P.I. is the fact that in my criminal investigations, I get to wear all the hats. I am the gumshoe "in the field," knocking on doors and taking routine witness statements, as well as being the detective supervisor sitting behind the desk, reviewing his/my own reports for accuracy.

In this chapter, I will present my own reinvestigation and offer direct evidence disproving my initial claim that Elizabeth Short and Photo No. 1 in my father's album (the woman standing by the horse statue) were one and the same person. In other words, by continuing to follow new evidence, I am going to prove that my former assertions relating to the identification of photograph No. 1 as being Elizabeth Short—was incorrect.

For the record, Exhibit 84, [originally presented in the updated chapter: *New Investigation: Hard Evidence and Forensics*] despite the fact that both women have what appears to be an identical freckle in the approximate same location on their left eyebrows, **Photo No. 1, found in my father's album, IS NOT ELIZABETH SHORT.**

Original Exhibit 84

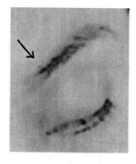
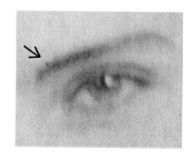

In September 2006, within two weeks of discovering the truth that the woman in my father's photo album *was not Elizabeth Short,* I publically disclosed that fact in a televised interview on CNN News with journalist, Anderson Cooper. The eight-minute interview also discussed the surrealist aspects of my father's crime, as well as Head Deputy DA Steve Kay's reconfirmation that, in his opinion, "the case was solved and the evidence and proofs go way beyond the question of the photographs."

September 18, 2006 CNN AC-360 interview

LA County Head Deputy DA Steve Kay [top-right]

Two weeks later, I was able to conduct an in-person follow-up interview with the woman in the photo and wrote and published an investigative summary of that meeting on my website. In 2006, to protect the woman's privacy, I simply called her, MAGANDA, which in Tagalog (she is Filipina) means, "Beautiful One."

Over the years, many of my readers, while supporting my investigation and agreeing with my conclusions that George Hodel was the killer, have also voiced their disagreement that the two photographs seen in his photo album were the same women. I hereby freely admit—they were and are CORRECT.

As specifically related to *Photo No. 1*, I would now like to personally acknowledge three specific individuals who were correct in that assessment:

First and foremost, my half-sister, Tamar, who stated that she believed the woman in Photo No. 1 appeared to be Asian and felt she may have met or seen her as a child at the Franklin house. (In the story about to unfold, we shall soon learn how and why she remembered the face, even with eyes closed.) Also, my ex-stepmother, Hortensia Starke, who also believed Photo No. 1 was an Asian acquaintance of George Hodel's from the Franklin house days. The third would be Elizabeth Short's living sister, who, apparently in looking at the photograph, told a third party, "that the woman was not Elizabeth, as she never wore flowers in her hair in that fashion." My further investigation, some six years later, has proven each of you correct.

How were these new proofs uncovered?

In September 2006, CBS television network replayed their previously aired program, *Black Dahlia Confidential*. By mere happenstance, a woman was flipping the channels and saw Photo No. 1 displayed and recognized it as being her grandmother! After the show, she contacted both the network and me, which led to my immediate follow-up.

Maganda's Story

(As originally reported on my website in 2006)

On Monday, October 2, 2006, the fog had lifted early, leaving the small coastal community bathed in bright sunlight. As I pulled my Ford Crown Vic into the restaurant parking-lot, I felt high excitement, knowing that the fog surrounding a sixty-year-old *mystery photograph* was also about to be lifted.

Maganda (not her real name, but one I have selected to protect her privacy, means "Beautiful One" in Tagalog, the native language of the Philippines) was seated at a large open table covered with white linens and fine china. Her two granddaughters were seated on either side of her there to protect and support their ninety-one-year-old "nanny."

Polite introductions were exchanged and Maganda's older granddaughter explained to her that I was the author of a book written about Dr. George Hodel, and was also his son. Her eyes brightened as she spoke, "You are the son of Dr. Hodel?" I nodded and smiled. "Oh, give me a hug. It was your father who I have to thank for starting me in my career as an actress."

I would spend the next five hours with Maganda, as she shared her incredible life story. Maganda would tell me about her life in the Philippines, in Manila, where she and her family were held captive in a Japanese prisoner-of-war camp. She told me how, in the mid-1940s, she and her family were freed with the liberation of Manila and hastily escorted directly to a Navy transport ship, which brought them to America.

She narrated how, soon after her arrival in Los Angeles, she met my father, George Hodel, and their five-year association. She also told me how, in the early 1950s, she decided to leave the bright lights of Hollywood and the brand new medium of television so she could devote herself full time to raising her beautiful children.

Now in her nineties, Maganda remains alert and happy. She has been kept strong and nourished with the familial love from both grandchildren, who held "Nanny's" arms as we conversed. After the introductions, Maganda slowly reached into the cardboard box on the table and handed me two large pictures from the group. One was framed, the other was not. She smiled and said, "Here are the two pictures your father took of me at his beautiful home in Hollywood. These pictures were on your father's desk, and they are what got me started in motion pictures."

"Maganda" and author, October 2006

Photos on left (top and bottom) taken by Dr. George Hodel
at the "Franklin house" circa fall or winter, 1945

What follows are selected, relevant excerpts of Maganda's incredible
story, told in her own words.

Early life:

I was born in the Philippines. My mother was Filipina and taught Spanish. My
father was an American missionary. When he first saw my mother, he said, "I'm
going to marry that woman." My parents' romance was love at first sight.

During World War II, my husband, who was American, and I and our children
were kept in a Japanese prison-of-war camp in Manila. We were there almost six
years. Then American soldiers came and freed us. I had my young daughter and
my newborn son. They took us straight to the Navy ship and we boarded and
came to America. The ship was originally going to go to dock at San Francisco,
but there was a world conference, so they came to Los Angeles, to San Pedro
harbor instead. (Note: The San Francisco Conference was held on April 25, 1945.
Delegates from fifty nations met in San Francisco for the United Nations

Conference on International Organization. The delegates drew up the 111-article Charter, which was adopted unanimously on June 25, 1945 in the San Francisco Opera House.)

Meeting Dr. George Hill Hodel

I met your father through a woman that was raising money for the War Chest to send donations to the Philippines after the war had ended. She was connected somehow with the mayor's office, and also owned a modeling agency. The woman knew George Hodel and suggested that he might want to meet and photograph me. She sent Dr. Hodel a note. And later, we met and he photographed me and took these two photographs along with some others. On the one, he had me close my eyes and tilt my head downward. I don't know why?

Your father's home was filled with many of these art objects (Maganda pointed to the Chinese horse statue in the background of photo) and he wanted to photograph me with each separate art piece. There were many such objects, but it never happened and we just photographed this one.

I don't recall how many times your father took photographs of me. It was a number of times, but my husband was always there. He waited in the interior courtyard, or in his car. Your father and my husband liked each other. My husband was chief engineer for a large aircraft company, and your father and he enjoyed talking to each other.

I never attended any parties at your father's house. I was only there during the photographic sessions. Your father was always professional and never said or did anything that would be considered out of line. My husband was always present.

It was because of these two pictures that your father took that I became an actress and got into motion pictures. The pictures were in a frame on a desk at your father's house. Your father had two important men, patients of his, who he was seeing at his house. He was treating them for some illness or something. The men were high up in the government of a foreign country.

They saw the pictures of me and said, "Who is this? She is perfect for a part in the film we are making." George told them that he had taken the pictures and who I was, and the next thing I know; I had a small part in their film. From there, I went on to make many more films and was one of the first actresses to be involved in a television series.

On meeting Tamar Hodel

I never met your mother, or you boys. But, I did meet his daughter, Tamar. She actually stayed with me overnight. It was quite strange. Here is how I recall what happened. Your father called me one night and his voice was quivering. He sounded very upset. He said to me, "Are you alone?" I told him I was. He went on to say, "There has been some trouble and would you mind if my daughter, Tamar, stayed with you for some time?" I told him she could, and he sent her over in a taxi cab.

Tamar was a young girl, maybe twelve or thirteen? She arrived in the cab and was crying. She said, "My daddy was bad to me," but wouldn't tell me what had happened, so I didn't ask anything further.

I asked her if she was hungry and she said, "Do you have any milk?" I gave her the milk and put her to bed. I was rubbing her arm, comforting her on the bed, and she said, "It's nice to have a mommy." And I told her, "Well, I can be your mommy." I told her that anytime she had trouble, she could talk to me."

George called me early the next morning and told me that "Tamar has to go to school" and for me to, "send her to school in a cab." Tamar refused to go to school, so I told George that I was sending her back to him instead. I then sent her home.

Franklin House Connections

I met a few people and recognized some names that you mentioned, but I never really met any other girls at your father's house. Fred Sexton and Joe Barrett sound familiar. There was an artist friend of your father's that gave me a large wooden sculpture of a pelican. He had made it for some important person in Brentwood, but they decided they didn't want it, so he gave it to me. I still have it at home. It is very large, all carved from one piece of wood. It was quite modern. (Note: The artist was most likely Fred Sexton, who as we know, sculpted in wood and carved "The Black Bird" for his friend, John Huston, which John used in *The Maltese Falcon* in 1941.)

I remember that your father had told me that "he had gotten into some trouble and was going on a long trip." I asked him, "Are you going to get out of it?" He told me, "Oh yes, one of these days I will." Shortly after that he left for the Philippines.

The last contact I had with your father was very strange. He called me from Manila. I was still living in Los Angeles. He asked me, "Do you know of any young women here in the Philippines that I could take pictures of?" I told him, "No, I don't." It was a very strange call, and I felt a bit uncomfortable about it. That was the last I ever heard from your father. No, I never was invited to any of the parties. No, I never met Hortensia.

Maganda Identified

More than five-years have passed since my original interview with Maganda and I have decided now to reveal her true identity. I break no confidence since she never asked me to keep her name private and I believe she deserves just credit and recognition for helping us better understand the truth of what occurred in the mid to late 1940s.

Based on Maganda's statements, it became obvious that she had unknowingly become an important witness related to the July 1949 sexual molestation by George Hodel of his then fourteen-year-old daughter, Tamar.

We learned that George telephoned Maganda and told her, "There has been some trouble and would you mind if my daughter, Tamar, stayed with you for some time?" She agreed, and he immediately sent Tamar by taxi to the residence, where, upon arrival, Tamar was crying and immediately told Maganda, "My daddy was bad to me." (Had the DA's office known about these actions and statements, Maganda certainly would have been called to testify as an important prosecution witness at George Hodel's December 1949 criminal trial.)

Maganda's real name is Marya Marco, aka Mary Marco, aka Maria San Marco. Her acting credits include both screen and television. To name just a few of her early films: *Anna and the King of Siam (1946), Song of the Thin Man (1946), Intrigue (1947), Tycoon (1947), Sleep, My Love (1948), and The Clay Pigeon (1949)*

Marya Marco publicity photo from *Intrigue* (1947)
Film starred George Raft and June Havoc

Marya in scene from *Song of the Thin Man* (1947)

Sleep, My Love (1948)
Star Bob Cummings in scene with Marya

George Hodel bought the Sowden/Franklin house in 1945. He likely took the Marya photographs that same year—probably in the spring or winter of 1945—sometime after she arrived in the US and prior to his departure for China in February, 1946.

In my interview with Marya, it became clear that she had no knowledge or suspicions that my father had been the DA's prime suspect in the Black Dahlia investigation, nor did it appear that she was even aware of his 1949 arrest by LAPD for child molestation and incest. Her only reference to George was him telling her just before his departure from the US that he "was in some trouble and was leaving the country and expected one day to get out of it." Then, at the close of our talk, she mentioned that her final contact with my father was "a strange and uncomfortable telephone phone call" she received from him from Manila, where George asked her if she could provide him with the names of any girls in the Philippines that he could photograph.

Dr. George Hill Hodel—One Degree of Separation

During her acting career, Marya Marco came in contact with many well-known actors. One of them was the handsome lead actor, Robert Cummings, who gave her the below autographed photograph circa 1948. As shown in the previous clip, Marya and Bob worked together in the 1948 film, *Sleep My Love*.

"To my dear friend Maria, beautiful, exotic, charming, and I mean very, your friend, Robert Cummings"

As detailed in BDA, Robert Cummings was also friends with actress Jean Spangler, and *was one of the last persons known to have seen her alive.* He had a conversation with Spangler at the studio on October 5, 1949, just two days before her date with an unidentified new boyfriend. Spangler at that time told Cummings, "I have a happy new romance and am having the time of my life." [Note: Refer to BDA, chapter 24, for the linkage of victim Spangler to George Hodel, as being this probable "new boyfriend."]

I showed a photograph of Jean Spangler to Marya, who indicated "she looked familiar," and thought she may well have seen her on the studio lots back in the forties, but did not personally know her.

The new information received from Madi Comfort informed us that George Hodel was personally acquainted with actor Vincent Price, as Madi was present at the Hodel residence when George and Dorero hosted Price and Van Heflin. After which, the five of them went to dinner in Chinatown.

Jean Spangler's last movie, *Champagne for Caesar,* was filmed in Hollywood in 1949, just weeks before she was murdered. One of the stars of that comedy was Vincent Price, George Hodel's acquaintance and former dinner guest. I strongly suspect that Jean Spangler knew and was dating my father in October 1949, and was the same "Jean" whom Duncan, my then [1949] twenty-one-year-old half-brother, met at the Franklin house as one of our father's dates. Duncan described her as, "a drop-dead gorgeous actress by the name of Jean."

What we do now know for sure is that with both the Robert Cummings-Marya Marco and the Vincent Price connections, we again have just one degree of separation between *Lone Woman Murder* victim, Jean Spangler, and George Hodel.

Hollywood's Dirty Big Secret

Who was included in the "we" that Madi Comfort spoke of as knowing that George Hodel had killed Elizabeth Short? Clearly, some were from her inner circle of friends from the late 1940s.

That would include many of Hollywood's literati, as well as actors, artists, dancers, and politicians, many of whom visited George and were entertained at his lavish Frank Lloyd Wright Jr.-built Mayan temple in the heart of Hollywood. Film stars like Walter and John Huston, Tim Holt, the surrealist artist, and our family photographer, Man Ray, writer Henry Miller, beat poet Kenneth Rexroth, along with lesser luminaries, and the beautiful but yet undiscovered wannabes, who, like pilot fish, can always be found swimming close to the larger catch.

Also, in attendance at the Franklin house parties were "the girls," many of them current or ex-patients from George's *First Street* VD clinic, very likely working double shifts on loan from Madam Brenda Allen. Brenda, known as Hollywood's "Queen of Hearts" was the Heidi Fleiss of her day. Before her arrest for pandering in 1948, Brenda had 114 girls working in her stable, and was making sizeable weekly pay offs to LAPD's vice squad and brass.

Dr. George Hill Hodel as the head venereal disease control officer for the entire LA County was powerful and connected. So much so that he was basically, "untouchable." If you were a studio exec [like the two producers Marya told us visited Dr. Hodel at his private residence for medical treatment], a politician, or a cop with a girlfriend "in trouble," Dr. George—as "top dog"—was the go-to guy in 1940s LA, a true bon vivant and a man who could be trusted with any confidence.

Many of Hollywood's elite must have whispered the secret. Power and information go hand in hand. But, it was like a low burning grass fire, which had to be stepped on and smothered before it had a chance to spread. There was simply too much at risk to allow this secret to become public knowledge. This was not difficult in 1947 Los Angeles, which was a real life *LA Confidential,* where corruption was the rule rather than the exception.

Practically, on the very day of the *Black Dahlia* murder, Hollywood novelist turned screenwriter, Steve Fisher, who wrote *I Wake Up Screaming, Destination Tokyo, Song of the Thin Man,* and *Winter Kill* for MGM in 1947, had just finished adapting a screenplay for Raymond Chandler's, *Lady in the Lake.*

One of LA's largest dailies, the *Los Angeles Herald Express,* asked Fisher to contribute his thoughts on whodunit. On February 3, 1947, just over two weeks after the Dahlia murder, in a *Herald Express* article headlined, **"Noted Film Scenarist Predicts 'Dahlia' Killer Will Soon Be in Toils,"** Fisher complied.

He opened the article by saying:

"After writing this I am going to leave town, and I will not return until the killer of the 'Black Dahlia' is under lock and key."

Fisher went on to provide readers with a long running scenario on how the fictional detective, Nick Charles, "The Thin Man," would have conducted the investigation. He suggested:

I'd have him [Sleuth Nick Charles] "rig" a phoney [sic] killer, one the police would give credence to, and have him use the phoney as bait to bring the real culprit in." [Note: Incredibly, the *Herald Express* newspaper took Fisher's suggestion to heart, and, just one week later, "rigged a phoney confessor as bait."]

Their headline in 6" letters read:

"CORPORAL DUMAIS IS BLACK DAHLIA KILLER."

The police, going along with the ruse, initially gave it credence, despite knowing that the false confessor was innocent and had already established that Dumais was on his east coast military base on the date of the murder. Did the *Black Dahlia Avenger* respond by turning himself in? No, but their ploy did provoke him to act. He went out the following night *and killed again*, writing his response in lipstick on his new victim, Jeanne French's strangled and bludgeoned body. It was his direct and very public reply to the press and police department's attempt to try and trap him. In large bold letters, he wrote across her nude torso, **"FUCK YOU - BD."** This savage killing, known as *"The Red Lipstick Murder,"* occurred just three weeks after Elizabeth Short's and is the second murder count that Head Deputy DA Steve Kay indicated he would file against George Hodel, based on the accumulated evidence.

Fisher ended his 1947 piece with these startling comments:

... "I think I know who the killer is, and think the police do also, and in a very short time will have his name. When the killer's name is

published I think a lot of his friends will be very surprised and terrified. ... I believe the police right now have a definite 'line' on the real killer. Look for a thriller finish to this case."

Apparently, Fisher didn't get the "Don't Tell Memo." For those who might wonder just exactly where Fisher would have obtained this "inside information," I would offer the following:

At the time Steve Fisher wrote his article, Dorothy "Dorero" Hodel, a fellow studio screenwriter, though still living with George Hodel, was working for and having an ongoing affair with the iconoclastic writer and rebel film director, Rowland Brown. (*Quick Millions*, *Blood Money*, *The Doorway to Hell*, *What Price Hollywood*, *Angels with Dirty Faces*, *Nocturne*).

Rowland would remain close to Dorero until his death in 1963. Dorero knew George had overdosed his personal secretary, Ruth Spaulding in 1945. And the later DA files revealed that she knew he had killed Elizabeth Short. Obviously, my mother would have shared this knowledge with her then current lover, Rowland.

At that time, Rowland was a close friend of and collaborator with fellow screenwriters Steve Fisher, Ben Hecht, and Gene Fowler. [Brown co-wrote the screenplay of *What Price Hollywood* with Gene Fowler. Fowler's son, Will, was one of the first news reporters to arrive at 39[th]and Norton Ave, and obtained his own private set of photographs of the *Black Dahlia* crime scene, which most certainly would also have also been circulated to many of Hollywood's "insiders."]

In addition to Steve Fisher being a close friend of Dorothy Hodel's then part-time lover, Rowland Brown, we also have a second direct link of Fisher to George Hodel, again, by way of George's friend and actress, Marya Marco. As we have seen from her filmography, Myra had a small part in the 1947 film, *Song of the Thin Man* starring William Powell and Myrna Loy. Who was the screenwriter for that film? STEVE FISHER!

Chapter 3

Marion Herwood Keyes

Marion Herwood Keyes circa 1947
1940s personal secretary to Vincente Minnelli and Dr. George Hill Hodel

Marion Herwood was born in Greenfield, Massachusetts on January 25, 1904, and died in Sequim, Washington on July 4, 2009 at the remarkable age of 105!

In his excellent book, *A Hundred or More Hidden Things: The Life and Films of Vincente Minnelli* (Da Capo Press, 2010) author, Mark Griffin, informs us that in the late 1930s, Marion was personal secretary to Vincente Minnelli. Griffin's research seems to indicate that the Minnelli-Herwood relationship may well have been more than just business.

On pages 30-31 Griffin writes:

Just as Vincente's relationship with Lester Gaba had everybody guessing, so did his association with a striking, modishly attired young woman named Marion Herwood. As Minnelli recalled, "The work at the Music Hall was getting so involved that it was decided that I should have a secretary. I hired Marion.

43

Each time Minnelli made the move from Broadway to Hollywood (first for a brief stint at Paramount in the late '30s, then with MGM for keeps) Herwood went with him. It was during Vincente's second attempt at breaking into the movies that his faithful assistant was dealt a devastating blow. Without explanation, Vincente suddenly shifted his attention from Herwood to MGM's resident showstopper. [Judy Garland]...After Herwood recovered from her broken engagement and the breakdown that followed, she would resume her work as a costumer on such MGM classics as *The Picture of Dorian Gray* and *The Postman Always Rings Twice.* And she would eventually marry an investment banker.

Based on the timing of her breakup with Minnelli, it would appear that Marion was then almost immediately hired by Dr. George Hill Hodel to be his personal secretary at his privately owned, downtown Los Angeles *First Street VD* clinic.

During the war years, Marion was obviously wearing two hats: George Hodel's girl Friday, as well as being a highly talented A-list costumer at the Hollywood film studios.

Marion was a coworker and close friend to Ruth Spaulding, who was also employed as a secretary at the *First Street* clinic. Ruth as we know, in the early to mid-1940s, was very much in love with and having an ongoing intimate affair with George Hodel.

As summarized in the "Aftermath" chapter of *BDA*, we now know that Ruth was the previously "unidentified secretary" that George Hodel admitted to killing in the 1950 DA tape recordings. Here is a partially excerpted section from those original DA transcripts where George was speaking in conversation with his close confidant, "The Baron" in the living-room of the Franklin house:

"Supposin I did kill the Black Dahliah [sic]. They couldn't prove it now. They can't talk to my Secretary anymore because she's dead."

...

"...They [LAPD] thought there was something fishy. Anyway, now they may have figured it out. Killed her. Maybe I did kill my secretary. ..."

That forced overdose occurred in May 1945, just eighteen months prior to the Elizabeth Short *Black Dahlia* murder. And it is believed that Marion Herwood Keyes terminated her employment as George Hodel's secretary shortly after the suspicious "overdose" death of her good friend and coworker, Ruth Spaulding.

Here is a summary of Marion's amazing filmography from the years 1944-1948:

1944: *Gaslight, Mrs. Parkington, The Thin Man Goes Home, Marriage is a Private Affair*. 1945: *Between Two Women, The Picture of Dorian Gray, Keep Your Powder Dry, Without Love, Her Highness and the Bellboy, Weekend at the Waldorf, Adventure, The Clock,* and *The Valley of Decision*. 1946: *Easy to Wed, The Hoodlum Saint, The Postman Always Rings Twice, A Letter for Evie*. 1947: *The Other Love, Body and Soul*. 1948: *No Minor Vices* and *Arch of Triumph*.

Marion Herwood Keyes's last credited film, *Arch of Triumph* (1948) starred Ingrid Bergman, Charles Boyer, and Charles Laughton.

In the secret DA files, I discovered that DA Lt. Frank Jemison had named and interviewed two of Elizabeth Short's personal acquaintances, Ann Toth and Connie Star, both of whom were "extras" and frequently obtained bit parts in films from Hollywood's *Central Casting*. Ann Toth, a part-time actress, was the girlfriend of Mark Hansen, owner of the *Florentine Gardens*, a popular restaurant and "nude girlie revue" nightclub. I am quite certain that my father both knew and frequented Mark Hansen's nightclub on a regular basis. Why? Because (1) he loved burlesque and "nude reviews" [on the DA Bugging Tapes, he bragged about taking some visiting dignitaries from China to a local burlesque house] and (2) Hansen's *Florentine Gardens Club* was located just one mile from the Franklin house.

Connie Star, in her interview with Lt. Jemison, recalled seeing Elizabeth Short with a young boyfriend at Mark Hansen's home, located on Carlos Avenue at the rear of his club, on January 11, 1947, just four days prior to her body being discovered.

Lt. Jemison determined that both Connie Starr and Ann Toth worked together as extras on location at the Hollywood studio set during the filming of *Arch of Triumph*. As noted, Marion Herwood Keyes, George Hodel's former personal secretary, was the costume designer on that film, which means that the three women most certainly would have come in contact with each other during the shoot. Just another example of the seemingly unending one-degrees-of-separation.

The DA Hodel-Black Dahlia files also contained Lt. Jemison's original handwritten notes, including his George Hodel "To Do List." Below is a scan from the files where we discovered that on March 2, 1950, less than two weeks after George Hodel's taped confession referencing his admitted killing of his secretary, that Lt. Jemison *is reopening the original 1945 LAPD Spaulding death investigation with plans to reinterview all the original witnesses.* He listed six items for follow-up on the Hodel investigation, number four being:

"#4- all witnesses – In Re. to Ruth's death- Sec. to Hodel."

Lt. Jemison's reinterviews of all of the original 1945 witnesses would most certainly have included Ruth's then coworker and closest friend, Marion Herwood Keyes.

DA Lt. Jemison   **Section of Note referencing
Dr. Hodel's secretary, Ruth**

Ruth Spaulding—Motives for Murder

On the back of the thick brown envelope, the handwritten note read, "NOT TO BE TAMPERED WITH OR OPENED BY ANYONE EXCEPT ——."

The writer, a young married woman, distraught, with emotion, had sealed the packet in March 1945. She left instructions that it was *not to be opened until after her death.* Sixty years later, the personal and highly confidential contents of this package would find their way to me to help establish, at least in part, the probable motive for my father's murder of his personal secretary, Ruth Spaulding.

We recalled the specifics. Ruth Spaulding was George Hodel's secretary at the *First Street Clinic.* She died of an overdose of barbiturates on May 9, 1945. The facts were suspicious and LAPD investigated George Hodel as her possible killer. LAPD learned that they were having an affair and that George had recently broken up with Ruth. As a woman scorned, Ruth had written detailed information about George Hodel's activities and was about to reveal them. My father, in a late night telephone call from Ruth's apartment, summoned my mother to the residence and gave her Ruth's writings, ordering her "to burn them." LAPD investigated, but the evidence was insufficient to charge him with the crime. Five years later [February 1950] in a confidential conversation with "The Baron," which was captured on the DA surveillance recordings, George Hodel admits to the Spaulding murder. "They thought there was something fishy. Anyway, now they may have figured it out. Killed her. Maybe I did kill my secretary..."

Part of the Spaulding puzzle has been previously examined and discussed. We know that had Ruth survived the forced overdose, she could have most probably linked George Hodel to dating and possibly treating Elizabeth Short as his patient. Hence, his recorded statement, "Supposin' [sic] I did kill the Black Dahlia, they couldn't prove it now. They can't talk to my Secretary [Ruth Spaulding] anymore, because she's dead." But those statements made by my father were *after the fact.* They did not provide the motive for Ruth's 1945 murder. We know that my father killed Ruth to keep her silent, but about what?

Based on the recent receipt of copies of these sixty-year-old private letters and documents, I believe we may well now have the answer!

It appears that Ruth Spaulding was about to expose and make public the fact that Dr. George Hill Hodel, head venereal disease control officer for the Los Angeles County Health Department, and chief-of-staff of his privately-owned *First Street Clinic was fraudulently and intentionally misdiagnosing patients, then billing them for unwarranted laboratory tests, prescriptions, and medical treatment!* What patient in 1945 Los Angeles would even think to question or consider a second opinion after hearing the diagnosis of "syphilis" or "gonorrhea" coming from the mouth of LA's top VD doctor? Imagine the headlines and scandal that would have resulted from Ruth Spaulding's revelations:

"HEAD OF COUNTY HEALTH CHARGED WITH MALPRACTICE"

Here is the back story and documentation.

In 1945, Mrs. X, a married woman, met and fell in love with a dashing young naval officer. They had a brief affair. Mrs. X became concerned that she may have contracted a venereal disease. And her lover, to reassure her, suggested that she go and see Dr. George Hodel at his *First Street Clinic.* Dr. Hodel examined the young woman and ordered lab tests. Shortly thereafter, she was informed by Dr. Hodel that "she has contracted Gonorrhea" and he treated her accordingly. Mrs. X was billed and paid $75.00 in services. [Approximately $750.00 in today's dollars.] Upon returning to her home state, the distraught woman obtained a second opinion and was advised that she never had a gonorrhea infection. Mrs. X contacted Dr. Hodel's clinic secretary, *Ruth Spaulding,* who then rechecked the lab reports and determined that they *"were negative" and confirmed to Mrs. X that she had never contracted a venereal disease.*

Ruth Spaulding sent Mrs. X the laboratory reports, signing the letter with, "cordial personal regards." [Note: This is hardly a business salutation and to my thinking is suggestive that the two women could well have had additional correspondence or personal contacts of which we are unaware.] My father's secretary further personalized her letter by adding an apologetic, "P.S., I am required to send the enclosed bill."

Exhibit A

COPY OF MRS. X 1945 TYPED/SIGNED LETTER TO BE OPENED ONLY AFTER HER DEATH

(I have redacted personal names and identifying information)

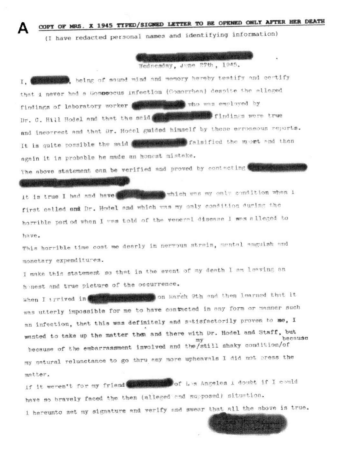

Exhibit B

COPY OF 1945 LETTER THAT RUTH SPAULDING MAILED TO MRS. X

(Dated and signed *just sixty days* prior to Spaulding's death by "barbiturate overdose")

B   COPY OF 1945 LETTER RUTH SPAULDING MAILED TO MRS. X

(Dated and signed *just sixty-days* prior to her death by "barbiturate overdose")

FIRST STREET CLINIC
G. HILL HODEL, M.D., AND STAFF
369 EAST FIRST STREET
LOS ANGELES 12
24-HOUR TELEPHONE: MICHIGAN 2697

March 9, 1945

Dear Mrs. ▓▓▓▓:

The following are the reports which you requested.

3/5/45   Urethral & cervical smears:
　　　　　Moderate amount of pus cells.
　　　　　Moderate amount of gram negative diplococci,
　　　　　extracellular, and diplo-bacillus.
　　　　　No gram negative diplococci seen which are
　　　　　typical of N. gonococcus.
　　　　　Smears are negative for gonorrhea.
　　　　　The culture was grown under reduced oxygen tension.
　　　　　The oxydase reaction was negative.
➡　　　　The culture was negative for gonorrhea.

3/6/45   Urethral and cervical smears:
　　　　　Few pus cells seen.
　　　　　Many gram positive rods.
　　　　　No gram negative diplococci seen.
　　　　　Smears are negative for gonorrhea.
　　　　　The culture was grown under reduced oxygen tension.
　　　　　The oxydase reaction was negative.
➡　　　　The culture was negative for gonorrhea.

Cordial personal regards!

　　　　　　　　Sincerely,
　　　　　　　　Ruth Spaulding
　　　　　　　　Clinic secretary

P.S.   I am required to send the enclosed bill.

50

Exhibit C

Mrs. X's 1945 *First Street Clinic,* billing receipt

Mrs. X's 1945 *First Street Clinic,* billing receipt

C

FIRST STREET CLINIC

G. HILL HODEL, M. D., AND STAFF

369 EAST FIRST STREET

LOS ANGELES 12

24-HOUR TELEPHONE: MICHIGAN 2697

TO

FOR PROFESSIONAL SERVICES   **8/1/45**

Consultation, examination,
and medication

75.00

Paid in full

Exhibit D

Mrs. X's Public Health VD prevention pamphlet provided by George Hodel

Mrs. X's Public Health V.D. prevention pamphlet provided by George Hodel

D

a booklet on the

prevention of **syphilis** and **gonorrhea**

VD Bulletin No. 95
FEDERAL SECURITY AGENCY
UNITED STATES PUBLIC HEALTH SERVICE
WASHINGTON, D. C.

☆   U. S. GOVERNMENT PRINTING OFFICE : 1942   29—26985-2

Price . . . . . 5 cents

for distribution in clinics
and by private physicians

In addition to Ruth Spaulding's knowledge of the above malpractice, I can now add a second, equally compelling reason, why my father would have wanted his personal secretary—dead. In her secret writings and intended expose of my father, it is likely that Ruth had also included her direct firsthand knowledge of the fact that her ex-boyfriend/employer, was *regularly performing illegal abortions at his* downtown *First Street Clinic.*

How do we know this? It came directly from George Hodel's own mouth—from his own recorded statements and admissions. Overlooked in 2005, I discovered them during a careful review of the District Attorney's *1950 Hodel Surveillance Transcripts.*

The date was March 19, 1950. [The thirty-first day of electronic surveillance at the Franklin house.] As we know, the detectives were recording and monitoring the conversations two-miles away in the basement of LAPD's Hollywood Police Station. Below is a scanned copy of page 133 (my numbering). Between 2:00 and 2:30 p.m., George Hodel and "a colored woman" are at the Franklin house, discussing the possibility of the woman being provided a room in exchange for her maid service. Father tells her he is a doctor. They discussed medicine, and she mentioned having had a "currettement" (abortion) in 1944. Father informed her that he owned the *First Street Clinic*, located downtown at First and Central, and incredibly, went on to tell her, "He has done lots of them (abortions)." [Note: The transcript shows the word as "currettement." This is the shortened term for a 1940s abortion procedure known as a "D&C", or dilation and curettage. The patient was first administered an anesthetic and then the physician performed a surgical abortion, where, after dilating the cervix, he used a curette (sharp metal instrument) to scrape the uterus. In modern times, this scraping has been replaced with a suction technique to reduce the chances of heavy bleeding and infection. My half-sister Tamar's 1949 abortion by Dr. Ballard was a "D&C," and, according to Tamar, "resulted in a large amount of blood loss."]

Exhibit E

Dr. Hodel 1950 Electronic Surveillance Transcript page 133

E <u>Dr. Hodel 1950 Electronic Surveillance Transcript page 133</u>

HODEL FILE - 114 / 3 3   133

1:45P	Hodel answers door bell, lets in woman - he talks to her about renting her a room in return he will knock off the rent - any work she does for him such as cleaning and taking care of his quarters. Negro woman has her minor daughter with her.
1:50P	Phone rings - Hodel says "Mrs Hodel is out - I can take message. He said he is going down to the beach about 4 PM today - talks about renting room.
2:00P	Hodel again talking to negro woman. Hodel asks her daughter where she goes to school - the girl says-a catholic school.
2:10P	Colored woman and child leaving. woman is going to think it over - about renting room. Woman then starts talking about Doctor's-Hodel tells her about his clinic at 1st and Central Woman said she had a curettemet (curettement ?) in 1944. Hodel said he has done lots of them. Hodel and woman continue to talk about doctors, sickness, and other medical subjects. (Hodel seems to be acting overly nice to this woman He must be trying to talk her into renting the room, or ?) Hodel tells her that Dr. Hill, a colored Doctor, lives next door.
2:30P	Woman leaves
2:50P	Phone rings 2 times, must have been answered in another room. Hodel moving about desk.
3:15P	Hodel leaves room - all quiet.
3:45P	All quiet.
SPOOL 38 4:00P	Hronek, D.A.'s office, on duty.

Prior to the discovery of these statements, I had speculated that at least part of my father's source of power and influence came from the information he had locked in his *First Street Clinic* VD files—highly sensitive medical charts listing the identity and specific medical treatment of well-connected film, police, and politicians documenting their sexual and moral indiscretions.

Now, with absolute certainty, we can add to it their criminal actions. In 1950, abortion was a felony, punishable by state imprisonment. Anyone (including a police officer, deputy mayor, or film director) who brought his pregnant girlfriend or mistress in for a *quick cure* was guilty as an accessory or accomplice. Once *the procedure* had been performed, that person was beholden to and at the mercy of the individual he had entrusted. From 1938 through March 1950, at least at the *First Street Clinic,* that person was—Dr. George Hill Hodel.

In 2003, LAPD reluctantly confirmed to the press that George Hodel was a suspect in his secretary's overdose. In 1949, the LAPD detectives interviewing my sister, Tamar, at Juvenile Detention also informed her of their suspicions:

> "We [LAPD] found her death [Ruth Spaulding] suspicious, and suspected George Hodel was involved in her overdose, but didn't have enough evidence to prove it."

In May 1945, secretary/girlfriend Ruth Spaulding's secret writings, which were about to reveal George Hodel's malpractice and criminality cost her—HER LIFE.

Five years later, in January 1950, Lillian Lenorak, after perjuring herself a second time at the trial of Dr. Francis Ballard and Charles Smith, made similar threats to George Hodel. She told George that she was "going to the DA and inform him of her twice perjured testimony and that in truth, she had witnessed Tamar's abortion performed by Dr. Ballard and his assistant, Charles Smith." This almost cost Lillian her life. She "got off lucky" and escaped George Hodel's wrath with only an assault, drugging, and his staged "attempted suicide." [He used a scalpel to inflict superficial cuts to her wrists while she lay unconscious.] Father's actions were apparently effective enough to at least temporarily discredit her as being "psychologically distraught."

These latest posthumous revelations from Mrs. X, supported by her original 1945 letters, along with my father's admissions that he "had performed abortions, lots of them" at his *First Street* VD clinic, established powerful motives for the Spaulding overdose-murder and reinforce what my investigation has demonstrated time and time again— in 1950 Los Angeles, Dr. George Hill Hodel was UNTOUCHABLE

Chapter 4

Lillian Lenorak—Update 2011

The Back story

I first introduced Lillian Lenorak to the public in a 2004 updated chapter of BDA after I discovered a letter written by officer Mary Unkefer, a Santa Barbara P.D. policewoman and former acquaintance of Elizabeth "Black Dahlia" Short. The Unkefer Letter—buried deep in the DA secret files—documented, confirmed, and greatly expanded upon a verbal report first made by Joe Barrett.

Joe Barrett, in 1950, was a young artist renting a room at our home in Hollywood. In a 2003 on-camera television interview for ABC's *Date line*, Joe Barrett recounted witnessing an incident in early 1950 involving Lillian Lenorak at the Franklin house. He told of returning home to find an excited Ellen (our maid) warning him that Lillian Lenorak was in George Hodel's bedroom and was threatening to shoot Hodel when he came home.

Barrett entered the bedroom and found a hysterical Lenorak, armed with a rifle belonging to George Hodel. Lenorak was screaming, **"He is going to pay for what he has done. He has to pay for it. I'm going to kill him."** Barrett claims he calmed her down, and removed the rifle from her person. When asked in this interview by reporter Josh Mankiewicz, "What Lenorak was referring to?" Barrett replied, **"It was about the fact that Lillian knew that George had killed Elizabeth Short. Lillian knew Elizabeth and had met her at the house, and said that George had to pay for killing her."**

Barrett went on to say that "When George came home, I told him about what happened, and that Lillian was going to shoot him, and George's response was, 'Why didn't you let her?'" (In the DA Hodel

Bugging transcripts in March 1950, George Hodel confirmed Barrett's account and was overheard saying, "She [Lillian Lenorak] was going to shoot me and then kill herself."

From *Black Dahlia Avenger: A Genius for Murder* page 479:

Unkefer-Short-Hodel-Lenorak Connections

On January 16, 1947, the day "Jane Doe Number 1" was identified by the FBI as Elizabeth Short, Santa Barbara policewoman Mary Unkefer was one of the first important witnesses contacted by LAPD in the Black Dahlia investigation. Why? Because Officer Unkefer had direct and extended contact with Elizabeth Short after Elizabeth's September 1943 arrest for "minor possession." The *LA Daily News* of January 17, 1947, under the headline: **"Identify Victim as Hollywood Resident,"** detailed Officer Unkefer's connections:

She (Elizabeth Short) had been a clerk at the Camp Cooke post exchange near Santa Barbara and was picked up for drinking with soldiers in a cafe there.

Policewoman Mary Unkefer of the Santa Barbara police department took the girl to her own home to live with her for nine days...

"We put her on the train for her home, and several times later she wrote to me from there" Miss Unkefer recalled. One of her letters said: "I'll never forget you. Thank God you picked me up when you did!"

Incredibly, from the information contained in these DA documents, we only now discovered that Officer *Mary Unkefer—who in 1943 had been directly responsible for rescuing Elizabeth Short from a dangerous environment— in January 1950 drove from Santa Barbara to Dr. Hodel's Franklin Avenue residence and there removed another young female victim from harm's way.*

Officer Unkefer, after safely returning the victim—whose name was Lillian Lenorak—to Santa Barbara, typed a letter to Los Angeles DA investigators, describing and informing them of Dr. Hodel's involvement in multiple crimes, including subornation of perjury and felony assault.

Through other DA documents, we knew that Lillian Lenorak, a 1949 defense witness testifying at the Hodel incest trial, was an acquaintance of George Hodel. And when photographs of Elizabeth Short were shown by DA investigators, she identified her as Hodel's girlfriend. Miss Lenorak was preparing to recant her previous sworn testimony and admit that she perjured herself at the incest trial. Lenorak's perjury at the Hodel trial had to do with the fact that she was present at Dr. Ballard's office with Charles Smith when Tamar, George Hodel's fourteen-year-old daughter, was "examined" but no abortion occurred. She was now going to admit the truth that, in fact, an abortion was performed on Tamar.

[Note: It is my belief that the "rifle incident" occurred in late January 1950, and was the event that immediately precipitated my father's "staging Lillian's attempted suicide." Lillian Lenorak, under pressure from George Hodel, had perjured herself twice in the preceding weeks. First, at his incest trial in late December 1949, and then again on January 15, 1950, at the abortion trial of Dr. Francis Ballard and Charles Smith. Lillian testified as a defense witness that she had been present with Tamar at Dr. Ballard's office when she was examined, but lied and informed the court "that no abortion had occurred." Her perjury resulted in Dr. Ballard and Smith being found "not guilty" by the judge hearing the case.]

Lillian Lenorak was now threatening to reveal the truth and to inform the DA that she was present and did witness Tamar's abortion. George Hodel had to either kill her or try to discredit her. With Barrett as a witness, he couldn't kill her. So, he took the next best step—try to set her up as a "mental case." He then drugged her and staged her "attempt suicide" as described in policewoman Unkefer's letter to the DA. We even have the dramatic corroboration from Lillian's three-year-old son, John, who witnessed George Hodel's assault on his mother. In route to Santa Barbara with his mother and officer Unkefer, the child told the policewoman, **"He [Dr. Hodel] hit mommy and knocked her down. He made her cry hard."**

In 2003, with the post-publication discovery and release of the secret DA Hodel Files, we first learned that Lillian Lenorak met with DA Lt. Frank Jemison *and made a positive identification of Elizabeth Short as being a sometime girlfriend of George Hodel.*

Prior to that, Lillian Lenorak's name had surfaced only as an acquaintance of George Hodel and as one of the "defense witnesses" in his December 1949 incest trial. Lillian also appeared as a defense witness three weeks later, on January 15, 1950, on behalf of Dr. Francis Ballard and Charles Smith who had both been arrested by LAPD and were on trial for performing the actual abortion on fourteen-year-old, Tamar Hodel.

After the discovery of the Unkefer/Lenorak Letter, I now know that Joe Barrett was not completely candid with me regarding all of the facts and his further involvement in this late January 1950 Lillian Lenorak Franklin house incident.

Joe withheld all of the critical information that followed in the immediate aftermath of Lillian's confrontation with George at the Franklin house. Joe omitted telling me about his involvement in helping police officer Mary Unkefer transport Lillian to Santa Barbara after she had been drugged and had her wrists superficially cut and bandaged by George Hodel. This staged "attempt suicide" was my father's way of anticipating and going on the offense should Lillian follow through with her threats to inform the DA of her perjured testimony. By branding her "distraught and suicidal" in advance of any allegations she would make against him, he could make anything she said "sound, unreliable." For the most part, it worked!

However, what George Hodel had not anticipated was the Mary Unkefer Letter. The letter written by Santa Barbara police officer Mary

Unkefer to the LADA's Office documented Joe Barrett's, Lillian Lenorak's, and her three-year-old son, John Lenorak's statements of what occurred at the Franklin house in the day(s) and hours immediately following the Franklin house incident.

Here is a brief recap of excerpts from Officer Unkefer's report, which she mailed to Lt. Jemison at the DA's office on January 30, 1950, immediately following her contact with the three witnesses. [For a complete review of the Lenorak-Unkefer investigation, see BDA "Aftermath" chapter, pages 479-484.]

Re. Lillian Lenorak

...She [Lillian] told me she had witnessed an abortion performed on his [George Hodel] little girl [Tamar, age 14] He had threatened to have her child [John Lenorak, age 3] taken away from her if she did not testify in his favor in Court. She said that she had never attempted suicide and that she had never cut her wrists or her hands. She said that the Dr. constantly gave her drugs and that when she wakened the cutting had been done. There were scratches and bruises on her forehead and arms. Lillian stated that she had a very guilty mind after the trial and told Hodel that she was going to tell the DA that she had lied on the witness stand and that Dr. Hodel told her if she squealed that he would name Charles and the other doctor [Smith and Ballard] as being the ones who performed the operation. [Tamar's abortion] Lillian said she would like to tell me all the true facts concerning the doctor's activities, but knew that he [Hodel] would have her done away with as well as her baby. ...she was just PLUMB SCARED to tell for fear he would carry out his threat to have her Boy taken from her and to have her committed to an insane institution.

Re. John Lenorak [Lillian's three-year-old son]

Her three-year-old baby told me that "the doctor knocked his mommie down and made mommie cry hard."

Re. Joe Barrett

He stated emphatically that there was nothing wrong with Lillian except what had been brought on by the cruel treatment received from Dr. Hodel. He stated that he knew Lillian had perjured herself at the trial because the Dr. had her under his influence. He stated that the relations between the Dr. and his Child [Tamar] were terrible and were worse than I had any idea. He stated that Dr. boasted that the $15,000.00 the doctor paid Jerry Giesler [his criminal defense attorney] was used to influence the DA and that was how the doctor was cleared of the charge against him. Barrett described Dr. Hodel as being "A REAL NO GOOD GUY."

Officer Unkefer had originally responded to Dr. Hodel's residence to pick up Lillian and her son, John, *at the specific request of Lillian's mother, Mrs. Hamilton,* a prominent resident of Santa Barbara.

Unkefer, after arriving at the Franklin house, insisted that Dr. Hodel call an adult female friend to accompany Lillian on the ride back home. George Hodel called, Karoun Tootikian, a dance instructor at the Ruth St. Denis Studio, who rode with Joe Barrett and Officer Mary Unkefer to Santa Barbara. [Tootikian would remain with the St. Denis Studio for the next twenty years and eventually become a director and head of the Oriental Dance Dept.]

On their arrival in Santa Barbara, three-year-old John was dropped off at his grandmother's home, and Lillian, due to her drugged and distraught mental condition, was driven by Unkefer to the Psychiatric Evaluation Unit where she was examined and initially admitted for "72-hour observations." [Note: The subsequent hospitalization likely would and could have been avoided had Mrs. Lillian Hitchcock Hamilton been willing to take Lillian into her custody. But due to a "falling out" between mother and daughter, she refused. Mrs. Hamilton died five years later in 1955.]

Officer Unkefer in her January 30, 1950 letter to the DA's Office offers the following additional information:

This morning I went to the hearing at the Psycho Ward and it was determined that she [Lillian] was mentally upset. The Dr. said a great deal of the condition was brought about from the strain of the trial. Both Drs. stated that they felt she should have medical care. So she is to be taken to Camarillo State Hospital for treatment.

My personal opinion is that if the feeling between her and her Mother was not so strained, she might have been given a chance to go home & be taken care of by her Mother. There seems to have never been love between these two. The Mother takes the attitude that she is going to MAKE Lillian do things the way she (Mother) wants them & the Girl seems just as determined that she is not going to be always treated as a Child. Hence there is fireworks between them.

George Hodel (center) December 1949 at the LA Courthouse awaiting trial charged with incest and sexual molestation of his fourteen-year-old daughter, Tamar. Lillian Lenorak will, by her own admissions, provide perjured testimony in behalf of Dr. Hodel, and, just one month later in January 1950, will repeat her perjury at the felony trials of abortionists Dr. Ballard and his assistant, Charles Smith, resulting in the case being dismissed by the judge. Within days of that dismissal, Lillian would confront George Hodel at his Franklin house at gunpoint and threatened to recant her testimony and admit she was present during the abortion. These actions and threats resulted in Dr. George Hodel's drugging her and staging her "attempted suicide," as well as threatening to have her son, John, taken from her, and to harm him should she go to the police.

Lillian Lenorak and Film Director John Farrow

As previously documented in 2003, with the post-publication discovery and release of the secret DA Hodel Files, we learned that Lillian Lenorak met with DA Lt. Frank Jemison *and made a positive identification of Elizabeth Short as being a sometime girlfriend of George Hodel.*

Lillian was an extremely intelligent and attractive woman, as well as a talented dancer with the famed Ruth St. Denis studio.

In the mid-1940s, Lillian met and had an affair with the well-known Hollywood film director, John Farrow, who at that time was married to actress Maureen O'Sullivan. [John Farrow 1904-1963. Credited with directing forty-seven films, including: *Two Years Before the Mast* (1946), *The Big Clock* (1948), *Where Danger Lives* (1950), *Hondo* (1953), *Around the World in Eighty Days* (1956), and many more.]

Out of their relationship was born a son, John, who would, three-years later in January 1950, be the eyewitness to George Hodel's brutal assault on his mother at the Franklin house. [We recalled the boy's statement to Officer Mary Unkefer, in route to Santa Barbara, "He knocked mommie down and made her cry hard."]

In the DA Hodel Surveillance Transcript (page 114), there was a reference to my mother knowing and having met John Farrow. Exhibit F is a scanned extract from that page. The date was March 11, 1950. The police log showed the time to be 1:59 p.m. My mother was at the Franklin house. She dialed and spoke with a secretary, "Elsie," then to a person identified only as, "Bob." She talked about "John getting her a job." [Here she was referring to John Huston, her ex-husband, not John Farrow.] She then went on to mention a story idea for a screen play she thought might interest John Farrow.

Exhibit F

DA Hodel Surveillance transcript (scanned excerpt) page 114

```
DA Hodel Surveillance transcript (scanned excerpt) pg-114
     EX F
1:59P    Woman dials phone. Sounded like she said, "This is Elsie".
         Talked about Vincent Price. Also, about M.G.M. Talked abou
         John getting her a job. "Say Bob", I found a story. A stor
         of a black saint, a negro. Do you know John Farrow? I
         thought of him because of his Catholicism. I met him years
         ago. I have the babies down at the beach. But, I'd love
         to see you. (t must be Dorothy talking) You're at home
         all day. Oh, wonderful darling" then "I'll get to see you"
2:05P    End of conversation.
```

At the same time the DA/LAPD was bugging and staking out on our home, director John Farrow was completing his noir-film, *Where Danger Lives*, to be released in July 1950. The story involved a woman who attempted suicide [Maureen O'Sullivan], a young doctor who falls in love with her [Robert Mitchum], a murder, and their attempt to escape to Mexico. But the irony doesn't stop there. Cast in a bit part in the film was an attractive Eurasian actress by the name of Kiyo Cuddy, the ex-lover of George Hodel and future wife-to-be of then nine-year-old Steve Hodel.

John Lenorak would not discover that his actual biological father was film director John Farrow until adulthood. As the fates would have it, the disclosure did not come from a family member, but rather from his mother's 1940s acquaintance and former Franklin house tenant, Joe Barrett.

The two men had a chance meeting which I believe occurred sometime in the late 1970s. John had no memory and Joe Barrett made no mention of the January, 1950 Franklin house assault by George Hodel on his mother. Their discussion centered strictly on Barrett informing John that he was the son of film director John Farrow.

Subsequent to receiving this information, I was told that John contacted and met his half-sister, Mia Farrow, and was accepted into the Farrow clan. John, after verifying the truth of it, then changed his name to John Lenorak Farrow.

The Palm Springs Murder

Lillian Hamilton Lenorak was murdered on November 8, 1959. She was just forty-two. Here is a summary of what happened. It's short, senseless, and very sad.

Lillian was living in Hollywood and was dating Dr. Frank Back, a wealthy physicist and businessman, with an office at Hollywood's

Crossroads of the World. Dr. Back designed and manufactured movie camera lenses and had become world famous for his development of television's Zoomar Lens.

Frank Back picked Lillian up at her Hollywood home for a weekend getaway on Saturday, November 7, 1959. They drove from Hollywood to his vacation home, two hours away, in the desert community of Palm Springs. They had known each other for about one-year.

After spending the day at Dr. Back's home, the two dressed for dinner, and, at about 8:00 p.m., left to go dine at the Rivera Hotel. In route, an argument ensued in the car, and Lillian, apparently having decided to return to Los Angeles, asked Frank for the keys to his house so she could pick up her clothes. He refused. The quarrel escalated and Lillian demanded that he pull to the side of the road and let her out of the car. He stopped and she got out in front of the El Mirador Hotel and walked away. Dr. Back drove back to his home. And when Lillian failed to return the following morning, he gathered her clothes together and drove himself back to Hollywood.

On Sunday morning, just six-hours after she left Dr. Back's car, a passing motorist found Lillian's body lying just off the highway on the north-side of Palm Springs. The autopsy showed that her skull had been crushed, and she had been bludgeoned to death with the butt of a rifle.

Lillian's identity remained unknown for several days until Dr. Back, having read the article and her description in the newspaper, suspected that it was Lillian and contacted several of her friends who in turn contacted the Palm Springs authorities. Three days later, on November 10, Frank Back returned to Palm Springs and made a positive identification of the body.

Dr. Frank Back and Lillian Lenorak

FRIEND — Dr. Fronk G. Bock, optical physicist, who said he quarreled with desert murder victim.

SLAYING VICTIM — Lillian Lenorak, above, described by a friend as a "girl of many romances," was found beaten to death on a lonely road near Palm Springs, Calif., Sunday morning. Police are seeking some of her many men friends for questioning. (AP Wirephoto.)

Within a week, the mystery of who killed Lillian was solved.

Her killer was Tord Ove Zeppenfield, age twenty-one. Tord, a troubled young man, lived with his mother who owned and ran a motel a short distance from where Lillian got out of the car. Tord saw Lillian walking down the highway and approached her in his car. When she refused to get in, he abducted her at gunpoint and killed her. Here is his excerpted confession of what happened, as printed in the *Los Angeles Times* on November 18, 1959, just eleven-days after the murder:

> "He was sitting in his room when he saw Mrs. Lenorak walk past. ...He followed her in his mother's car and offered her a ride, which she refused.
> He threatened her with a sawed-off rifle and she got into the car. Then he drove to the north limits of Palm Springs, hit her once with the gun, dragged her from the car and struck her repeatedly."

On March 2, 1960, Tord Zeppenfield plead guilty to killing Lillian Hamilton Lenorak. His guilty plea was entered with the understanding that the prosecution would sentence him to life in prison and not seek the death penalty.

Los Angeles Times November 18, 1959

At the time of Lillian's murder, her son, John, was thirteen years-old and attending Elsinore Military Academy.

John and Lillian Lenorak circa 1956

A younger Lillian as a Ruth St. Denis dancer

Larry Harnisch, a copy-editor for the *Los Angeles Times* and a self-appointed "Black Dahlia expert" has, for the last fourteen-years, been claiming to be writing his own theory on "whodunit" with his own "surgeon-suspect." In 2009, using McCarthy-like tactics, Harnisch wrote an article questioning both Lillian's morality and her mental stability. Choosing to post his article specifically on the fiftieth anniversary of Lillian's murder, he went so far as to publicly "blame the victim" and advised his readers to be skeptical of Lillian Lenorak, her three-year-old son, John, and Officer Unkefer's statements as originally reported. Harnisch, appointing himself as a defense witness for Dr. George Hodel and sounding like he belonged right back in the *Sexist Fifties*, had this to say regarding the DA reports and the murder victim, Lillian Lenorak:

> "Keep in mind as you read these letters that this lady [Lenorak] is not a typical, well-grounded middle-class suburban housewife but a chronic patient of mental hospitals and adjust your skepticism accordingly."

How's that for a sexist slam! Apparently, in his mind, any woman who might dare to consider stepping outside the role of "a typical, well-grounded suburban housewife" can forget about being the victim of a crime. Outrageous!

Mr. Harnisch's statement that Lillian was "a chronic patient of mental hospitals" is totally unsubstantiated and has NO BASIS IN FACT.

Other than *the one George Hodel/Franklin house incident, which clearly was "a set-up" to my knowledge, there is no record of Lillian Lenorak ever having been admitted for "mental problems" at any other hospital or psychiatric facility. NONE!*

The fact is that Lillian Lenorak was a bright, fully functioning hard-working mother who loved her son. She was well liked and admired by her co-workers, and, at the time of her murder, was working as a film editor at *General Film Laboratories* in Hollywood.

A single mother, she also worked a second job as an actress using her maiden name of Lillian Hamilton. Her filmography credits show that she worked in both films and television, receiving separate bit parts *every year from 1949 until her untimely death in 1959.*

Lillian Hamilton Filmography:

1950- *Outrage-* Mrs. Walton
1951- *On the Loose-* Miss Druten
1952- *Week-End with Father*
1952- *Phone Call from a Stranger-* Nurse
1952- *The Unexpected* (TV series)
1953- *Sweethearts on Parade-* Mother
1954- *The Pride of the Family* (TV series)
1956- *Storm Center-* Mrs. Banning
1957- *The Joseph Cotton Show-* On Trial (TV series) Mrs. Bagby
1957- *Sheriff of Cochise* (TV series) Mrs. Conley, Bisbee National Bank
1958- *Whirly Birds* (TV series) First Nurse
1960 *Men in Space* (TV series) Mrs. Bennett (filmed in 1959, but aired after her murder in 1960)

In 1949-1950 Lillian worked on the then controversial film, *Outrage*, directed by Ida Lupino, which starred, Mala Powers and Tod Andrews. *Outrage* was one, if not *the* first, of the films to attempt to take an honest and sensitive look at the subject of rape and how it and society's attitudes impact a young rape victim's life. [Prior to making this film, Mala had just completed sharing equal billing with Jose Ferrer in her role as Roxane in the Hollywood film classic, *Cyrano de Bergerac*, which was also released in 1950.]

In *Outrage*, Lillian Hamilton Lenorak plays the mother of the rape victim, Ann Walton (Mala Powers).

Lillian Hamilton Lenorak and Mala Powers in a clip from *Outrage* (1950)

Postscript:

On October 16, 2010, I received an e-mail from Rosanna Wilson Farrow informing me that her husband, John, had passed away the previous Saturday. John was in Fort Bragg, California, and died suddenly from an unexpected heart attack. He left behind his wife, Rosanna Wilson, and their two daughters, Kyla and Acacia.

John passed away at a relatively young age of sixty-four.

Since starting my Black Dahlia investigation in 1999, I had spoken to John Farrow Jr. only twice. It was obvious that he was living and attempting to deal with a tremendous amount of pain, which I assumed was mostly the result of having experienced so much sadness in his youth.

Immediately after learning of Rosanna's loss, I wrote a letter of condolence. She responded, informing me that John, after the major traumas of his childhood, at age nineteen, was called to serve his country in Vietnam. I will let Rosanna's very touching e-mail to me describe those years.

Dear Steve,

Your response about John's sudden death was very touching to me. I agree with you that it takes incredible strength of character for a human being to overcome a tragic past such as his, and especially still become a kind loving and devoted husband, a tender father and a great and fun-loving friend to many. He worked very hard at having some measure of joy and happiness, however, it was not at all an easy journey for him, just so you know, nor always an easy one for us.

As if his sad childhood was not enough....You wrote that you felt you knew him but also knew you didn't, so I want to share this important information about his life that you don't seem to know about John. (Maybe because he did not tell you, or maybe you didn't chose to mention it)

John was a combat veteran in Vietnam, and he was seriously affected with PTSD during his lifetime. He was in receipt of a 100% veterans compensation for severe PTSD, a disability pension that he received 6 years ago, even though he suffered terribly from PTSD most of his adult life starting after his intense service in Vietnam.

He was in and out of vet centers and veterans' counseling offices over the years. However, he did not apply for his benefits that were certainly his due for decades. It was with my encouragement and help that he finally allowed himself to get the help he deserved.

He was drafted in 1965 at age 19, right out of high school. He chose to enlist in the Marine Corps rather than serve in the Army for personal reasons. He was sent to Vietnam right after boot camp, where he experienced a great deal of very hard combat...more than many veterans I've known, because the Marines in his battalion were deployed in more remote regions towards the DMZ, far from the comfort of military bases. John served honorably between1966-1969. He was slightly injured on the outside and seriously injured where it was hidden. He never put in for his Purple Heart because he lost so many friends....brothers...he even lost his very best friend from high school, Steve. When he was discharged he moved back to Santa Barbara, but his was never the same. He was a sensitive..... His nerves were basically shot.

I wanted you to know this because even considering the terrible things that happened to him in his childhood, there was more drama yet to come. More acts of personal bravery as well, and this one was personally most endearing....

After Vietnam John worked at a college bookstore and started to read constantly. He chose political works, biography, commentary, history and black history. He was never college educated prior to the war, though he was a very intelligent man. These readings, the atmosphere of questioning the war on campus, the anger inside him......it all worked on his psyche; after he read the *Autobiography of Malcolm X* he told me he became convinced that the war in Vietnam was wrong....was evil. He became very politicized and he joined VVAW (Vietnam Veterans Against the War) a very outspoken, progressive Veterans' group. He marched with fellow veterans who felt betrayed by their own country and politicians, and spoke out against the war he fought in, while still respecting and honoring those brave men and women who served their country.

There is more to say, but just know that the burdens he endured went beyond his childhood. Oddly enough it was John that made me laugh the most in this crazy life. I don't know how I will cope with the absurdities now.

Rosanna Wilson Farrow

Despite these many psychological hardships, I am informed by Rosanna that John was, "a gentle, loving man, the heart of our family, whom he was so devoted to."

73

It takes great strength of character to overcome the kind of shocks and traumas that we know John suffered, both in childhood and as an adult, and for him to rise out of those ashes and become a loving, nurturing husband and father.

Our hearts go out to his family in this time of loss and sadness.

REST IN PEACE JOHN LENORAK FARROW.

1946-2010

Photo courtesy of Rosanna Wilson Farrow

Chapter 5

"I am confident that the murder [Black Dahlia] occurred in some permanent place of abode, rather than some hotel, rooming house or auto court. It is doubtful that such a crime could be perpetrated in cramped quarters with nearby neighbors."

Captain Jack Donahoe, LAPD Homicide Division
Los Angeles Times, January 23, 1947

Scene of the Crime

Sowden/Franklin house, 5121 Franklin Avenue, Hollywood

The Link

Sixty-two years after they were written, documents preserved at UCLA's *Special Collections Department*, literally establish a "paper trail" connecting Dr. George Hill Hodel to the Elizabeth Short "Black Dahlia" crime-scene, the vacant lot at 3815 S. Norton Avenue.

Background

On January 22, 1947, an inquest hearing into the death of Elizabeth Short was held at the downtown Hall of Justice. The purpose of the hearing was to formally establish a "cause of death." After hearing the testimony of sworn witnesses, as well as the deputy coroner, the jury found that the victim died from "blunt force trauma to the head and face caused by person or persons unknown." Elizabeth Short had been brutally murdered.

One of the witnesses who was called to testify at the coroner's inquest that morning was Lt. Jesse Haskins from LAPD's University Division. He was one of the first officers to arrive at the crime scene.

Lt. Haskins testified in general about the condition of the body and informed the jurors that the murder had been committed elsewhere and that the body parts, after being placed *on top* of a fifty-pound empty paper sack, was then transported by car to the vacant lot. [Apparently, the sack (s) were used to prevent spillage in the car and to then transfer the body parts from the car to the curbside]. These investigative findings, as originally reported and testified to by Lt. Haskins, have never been in doubt and have always remained a part of the factual record, as supported by the original crime scene photographs.

Elizabeth Short crime scene January 15, 1947

[Top] LAPD crime photo showing empty paper sacks used by suspect to transfer body parts from his car to curbside. A portion of victim's upper body is seen posed at bottom of photo. [Bottom] Crime scene enlargement showing blood on paper sack

Lloyd Wright-George Hodel Letters
UCLA Special Collections Library

In October 2008, some five-years after the publication of BDA, I learned that famed architect, Lloyd Wright, had donated many of his personal papers to UCLA's Special Collections Department. I also discovered that within these papers, there was a *Hodel File* containing documents and correspondence between Lloyd Wright and my father, Dr. George Hill Hodel, covering the years, 1945-1947.

Upon learning of their existence, I immediately made an appointment to view and copy the materials. Here is what they established:

1) From 1945-1947, Lloyd Wright was engaged by George Hodel to oversee construction repairs and renovations at the Sowden/Franklin house. [Originally designed and built by Lloyd Wright in 1926 for John Sowden, and later purchased by Dr. Hodel in 1945.] Most of the repair work was to be done during George Hodel's temporary assignment as United Nations chief regional medical officer in Hankow, China [February-September, 1946].

2) In an April 1946 letter from George Hodel to Lloyd Wright, which was sent from China, father advised the architect that he "has made inquiries into the possibility of your being brought to China for city planning work." Father's **letter went on to** provide several names to Wright, suggesting he contact them for potential employment potentials.

3) Included in these papers were receipts showing that cement work and repair was performed at the Hodel residence, *requiring ten (10) fifty-pound bags of cement. The work was completed on January 10, 1947.*

In my opinion, the significance of this document is one of the most important investigative findings to date! *It circumstantially links physical evidence connected to Elizabeth Short's murder directly to George Hodel and the Franklin house, and from there to the vacant lot at 3815 S. Norton Avenue.*

According to LAPD and the DA investigative reports, Elizabeth Short reportedly "disappeared" on January 9, 1947 after meeting a man in front of LA's downtown Biltmore Hotel, at Fifth and Olive, just three blocks from Dr. Hodel's medical office.

Police surmised that the victim was taken to an unknown private residence, held captive, tortured, then bisected by a man "with medical finesse," who, in their (and the coroner's) opinion, was most likely a skilled surgeon.

In a public statement to the press, eight days into the investigation, LAPD Homicide Capt. Jack Donahoe confirmed that the victim had not been slain at the vacant lot, adding:

> "I am confident that the murder occurred in some permanent place of abode, rather than some hotel, rooming house or auto court. It is doubtful that such a crime could be perpetrated in cramped quarters with nearby neighbors."

LAPD confirmed that her body parts were placed on top of *several* fifty-pound empty cement paper sacks and transported by car from the actual murder location to the vacant lot where they were posed, with the cement sacks left nearby the body.

The Cement Sacks

The below document is a scanned copy of the original receipt.

It showed that Lloyd Wright contracted with a Mr. J.A. Konrad and had him perform renovations at Dr. Hodel's Franklin house in January 1947. *The cement work was completed on January 9-10, 1947.*

According to the receipt, the work performed at the Franklin house required a total of ten (10) sacks of cement. Eight (8) were used on January 9, 1947, and two (2) sacks were added on the following day, January 10th.

"J.A. Konrad to Dr. Hodel January 9, 1947
Cement work completed at the above address." [5121 Franklin Ave]

Found in UCLA Lloyd Wright–George Hodel File

In addition to the cement bag linkage, I made a second interesting discovery related to the UCLA Wright-Hodel Letters.

Below is a scan of the envelope mailed to Lloyd Wright by George Hodel from China in April 1946. The address is typed, however, on the envelope. George Hodel has hand printed the word **"Registered,"** which I hereby identify as my father's handwriting.

Note his unusual letter "D" compared to the letter "D" written in lipstick on the body of *LA Lone Woman Murder* victim, Jeanne French, who was slain in February 1947, just three-weeks after the Black Dahlia murder and four-months after George Hodel's return from China.

The same identical characteristics are clearly visible in both. In the letter "D," we see the curved, overextended horizontal lines with the vertical line unconnected to either the top or bottom in both samples. These are some of the same characteristics that Questioned Document Expert Hannah McFarland used to positively identify George Hodel's handwriting in other known samples—as well as in the Jeanne French, "Red Lipstick Murder."

George Hodel envelope mailed to Lloyd Wright from China in 1946

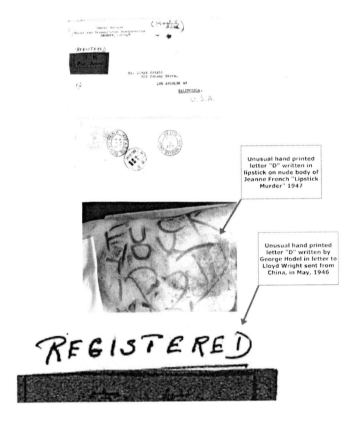

Unusual hand printed letter "D" written in lipstick on nude body of Jeanne French "Lipstick Murder" 1947

Unusual hand printed letter "D" written by George Hodel in letter to Lloyd Wright sent from China, in May, 1946

The envelope contained the below letter written to Lloyd Wright. In it, George Hodel mentioned his "promise" to check out architectural design potentials for Wright while in China.

From this we learned that the two men obviously had some personal discussions prior to George leaving the US for China in February 1946.

We also learned that as of May 1946, it was Dr. Hodel's intention to remain in China at least until, "the spring of 1947." His UN personnel papers in my possession show that just four months later, in September 1946, he suddenly "resigned for personal reasons" and quickly returned to Los Angeles.

We will likely never know his reason for resigning. We can only guess.

Was it under duress for conduct unbecoming? Did he commit a crime in post-war China's Wild, Wild East? Did he receive a letter from Elizabeth Short mentioning or hinting at her suspicions of his possible connections to the 1945 Chicago Lipstick Murders?

The secret DA files documented that Elizabeth was actively investigating those crimes in Chicago in June-July 1946, just a month after George wrote this letter to Lloyd Wright. The DA File went so far as to provide names and addresses of several different Chicago reporters that Elizabeth was sleeping with, apparently, in hopes of obtaining inside information related to the murder investigations.

George Hodel Letter to Lloyd Wright mailed from
China, dated April 20 and postmarked May 5, 1946

UNITED NATIONS

RELIEF AND REHABILITATION ADMINISTRATION

Anlee House,
Sze Wei & Han Chung Roads,
Hankow, China.
20 April, 1946.

Lloyd Wright,
858 Doheny Drive,
Los Angeles 46,
California.

Dear Mr. Wright:

In pursuance of my promise, I have made inquiries as to
the possibility of your being brought to China for city
planning work. I am informed that a firm request has
been made by the Chinese National Relief and Rehabilitation
Administration for at least two city planning experts,
and that the Washington headquarters of United Nations
Relief and Rehabilitation Administration may soon be
recruiting these specialists.

If you are interested, it is suggested that you write
to Franklin Ray, Director, Far Eastern Division, UNRRA,
Dupont Circle Building, Washington, D.C.

It might also be well to write to Ha Shiung-Wen, Vice-Minister,
Ministry of the Interior, Nanking, China. I know Mr. Ha,
but did not discuss your interest in China with him because
I was not aware, during the occasions on which I spoke
with him, that he was in charge of city planning work.

I expect to remain here until the spring of 1947. It would
be a pleasure to hear from you, and I am naturally very
much interested to know how my house is coming along.

With cordial personal regards, I am

Sincerely yours,

G. Hill Hodel, M.D.,
Chief Regional Medical Officer,
Hankow Regional Office, UNRRA.

A Mixed Bag—More Crime Scene Evidence

"Roll Call, Kuster, O'Steen, Mannocchia, Souza, Jones, Everheart ..."

As an occupation, nothing tops police work. It is never routine. Every day brings something new and exciting. Working homicide guarantees that there will always be a new *whodunit* just around the corner. It may come tonight, tomorrow, or next week. You don't know when, but you do know it's coming. (I think my old partner and I still hold the record at Hollywood. We were called in and investigated *three separate unrelated murders* on one weekend standby.)

It's especially good when you're teamed up with a savvy, street-smart partner! During my career, I was luckier than most and had more than my share of "the best."

Since the publication of BDA, I've learned that you don't have to wear a gun or carry a badge to be a good detective.

In the past ten-years, thanks to the power of the Internet, I've heard from scores of "arm chair detectives." Their real day jobs? Secretary, librarian, bus driver, history professor, medical doctor, and electrician— John and Jane Q. citizens all.

Many of these men and women possess an uncanny ability to think like a veteran detective and have provided invaluable insights into my ongoing investigations. Here is just one more example, an e-mail from Tom Davis, a patent-illustrator with a keen eye and photographic memory.

Tom wrote:

Steve,

...

A photo I have seen clearly shows yet another type of empty bag at the body site.

The bag says BANDINI which is a brand of fertilizer. It is just possible that a bit of garden and lawn repair was done to the Franklin property in addition to any architectural work, and this empty bag was discarded on 39th street along with the cement bags.

Tom goes on to say:

And there is yet another little mystery this fertilizer bag may clear up. The autopsy of Elizabeth's body noted a mysterious "green granular material" inside her stomach. Could this stuff have been left over steer manure that she was forced to eat as part of an act of sado-humiliation? It's my personal hunch. Such an ordeal may also have been meant to add a bit of surrealist wit to her death. It was a message: "This woman is was full of bullshit."

As a former art student I learned that the surrealists sometimes expressed visual puns and this would have been a perfect example.

Tom Davis

After reading my June 11, 2009 blog post [*Architect Lloyd Wright Letters at UCLA Links Dr. Hodel to Dahlia Crime Scene*] Tom sent me a new e-mail the following day, which in addition to complimenting me on my newly designed website, pointed to what he believed was an important error on my part, having to do with one specific paper-bag. I quote verbatim from Tom's second e-mail:

"I also found one new exciting detail. On your website you show an enlarged portion of a photograph that you call a cement bag. In fact, if you study this blow-up very carefully you can just make out the letters "URE" as in "MANURE." If I'm correct, and this bag is indeed a FERTILIZER bag, then you now have ABSOLUTE PROOF that BOTH cement AND fertilizer bags were used in the transport of Bette Short's body to the dump site. Please look into this as I think it is of extreme importance. No longer can ANYONE pass the existence of these two types of bags at the scene as coincidence. Taken along with your own research into renovations at the Sowden House, it STRONGLY points to Hodel driving directly from the Sowden House to the dump site."

Let's now reexamine several of the original crime scene photographs in light of what Tom Davis has pointed out.

First, **in the crime scene photos we see** what appears to be three separate paper sacks. The one on the extreme left is enlarged and does appear to read "URE" as in MANURE. This is the sack I originally labeled as Lt. Haskin's "cement sack" which appears to have watery blood stains on it. Based on the evidence before us, it becomes obvious that Tom is correct and this bag contained manure, not cement.

What happened? Reexamination of additional LAPD photographs gave us the answer. The detectives, after photographing the original cement sack lying just inches from Elizabeth Short's extended right hand, then moved it out of the way [collecting it as evidence] and reshot the crime scene from a different angle. Here are the proofs.

The above photograph was obviously taken first and shot from north to south. It shows a different bag, probably, Lt. Haskin's "cement bag" left by the suspect just inches from Elizabeth Short's extended right hand. Seen kneeling on sidewalk are the primary LAPD detectives Finis Brown and Harry Hansen and reporter Will Fowler. [Man on right was not identified. It was possibly criminalist Jones from LAPD Scientific Investigation Division.]

This photo was taken standing south of the body looking north and showed that the original "cement" sack had either been collected as evidence and removed from the scene or was one of the three sacks seen in this photo, which had been moved north, away from the body.

In this third photo, we no longer see three bags above the body, but just two. The third had either been collected or removed from view; or possibly, it was moved eastward and was the sack seen close to the curbside.

Photo above shows an enlarged area to the right of driveway. Clearly visible are the photographer's equipment box and an empty paper bag which appears to read "BANDINI." [Rotated in lower photo for easier readability.] I have also inserted in the photo an *LA Times* display showing a 1947 bag of "Bandini Fertilite."

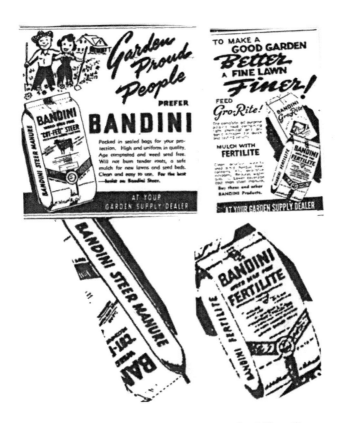

Bandini Steer Manure   Bandini Fertilite

The above display ads were copied from the *Los Angeles Times* newspaper showing pictures of fifty-pound Bandini fertilizer sacks as they appeared for sale in 1947. The Bandini lettering on the side of the bag is similar to the brand labeling seen at the crime scene.

Based on the photographic evidence *we can now confirm that both large cement and Bandini Steer Manure paper sacks were found at the crime scene.* (By my count, at least three separate sacks, possibly more?)

A Second Paper Trail

Included in the UCLA Lloyd Wright-George Hodel Papers were additional receipts for renovation work completed between 1945-1947. Below, we'll find an itemized billing list which includes, "Gardening - $230" and "Flower Box & bank planting- $60.00." [Nearly $300 just for landscaping, a sizable amount equal to approximately $3,000 in today's dollar value.]

Granted, unlike the cement bag receipts, which connected the cement work to the exact time of Elizabeth Short's murder, the below receipts were presented a year earlier in December 1945. However, the gardening needs would have been ongoing and the receipts establish that *there existed a large demand for fertilizer due to the extensive landscaping.*

Lloyd Wright receipts dated November 1945 which include $330.00 for "Landscaping/Planting" expenses at "Dr. Hodel Residence."

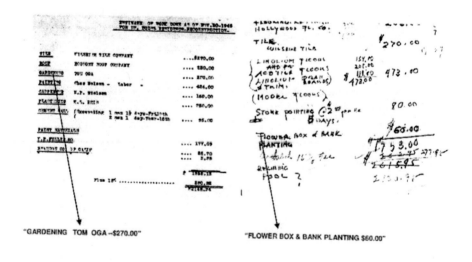

"GARDENING TOM OGA -$270.00"   "FLOWER BOX & BANK PLANTING $60.00"

Photos from a 1949-1950 sales brochure prepared by Dr. George Hodel for the sale of his "SHANGRI-LA," Franklin house. Note the heavily landscaped interior and exterior gardens.

To fully understand the relevancy that in addition to the cement sack (s), George Hodel may have also used empty bags of "Bandini" steer manure to transport the body parts from the Franklin house, we must venture deeper into the absolute horror of this crime.

"LA'S MOST HORRIFIC MURDER EVER"—The Signature of a Master Sadist

The murder of twenty-two-year-old, Elizabeth "Black Dahlia" Short lives in infamy because IT WAS A TORTURE-MURDER OF THE HIGHEST ORDER. HER KILLER WAS A SOPHISTICATED SADIST WHO WENT TO EXTREMES TO MAKE SURE THE PUBLIC WOULD BE BOTH HORRIFIED AND OUTRAGED. HER KILLER WANTED TO INSURE THAT HIS CRIME WOULD BE FOREVER REMEMBERED AS A MASTERPIECE OF THE MACABRE. HE SUCCEEDED.

These specific acts of sadism are so extreme and the signatures so unique that they set this killer totally apart from your "average sexual psychopath."

Below is a list of what we KNOW occurred during the killer's drawn-out ritualistic torture-slaying of Elizabeth Short in the early morning hours of January 15, 1947:

1. Bound feet and hands with rope or wire ligature
2. Strangulation to neck leaving ligature marks
3. Blunt force trauma to face and head
4. Scalpel lacerations [five distinct incisions to her upper lip]
5. Surgically rounded scalpel lacerations to both sides of mouth
6. Tic-tac-toe scalpel cuttings to the right thigh
7. Scalpel laceration/incision (two inches) near the left nipple
8. Scalpel lacerations and some cutting away of pubic hair and insertion of hair into anus
9. Cigar or cigarette burns to the back [at least eight separate burn marks]
10. Incision from umbilicus to supra pubic in imitation of a hysterectomy [four and a half inches]
11. Scalpel incision and removal of large section of left thigh and insertion of it into vagina
12. Surgical removal of right breast. [Not believed recovered at autopsy. Possibly retained by suspect as "trophy."]
13. Sexual anal-rape using unknown object. [Sodomy]
14. Surgical bisection of body [hemicorpectomy] by incision through the intervertebral disks between the second and third lumbar vertebrae. [Note: To date, four separate surgeons have viewed the autopsy photographs and provided their expert opinions that "only a highly skilled surgeon could have performed the bisection without leaving any "hacking" marks and would have known that only by dividing between the second and third lumbar vertebrae can a body be bisected without the use of a saw.]
15. Washing and scrub down of the body parts using a coconut fiber brush

The most shocking act of sadism was revealed in the transcripts of Chief Autopsy Surgeon Dr. Frederick Newbarr's testimony before the coroner's inquest where *he established that the victim was forced to ingest feces.* Here is a quote from his testimony at the coroner's inquest of January 22, 1947:

"The stomach was filled with greenish brown granular material, mostly feces and other particles which could not be identified."

[SKH Note: Some self-professed "Dahlia experts" have claimed that the feces in the stomach was there "due to natural digestion and as a result of her being bisected."]

On this point, I went to Dr. Doug Lyle M.D., a recognized forensic expert, and put the question to him. His response:

True feces is produced in the lower portions of the bowel. And the bowel doesn't move stuff backwards so there is no way feces can get from the colon to the stomach—unless some connection between the two was made at the time of the bisection, but that would be obvious. If the stomach was found intact with feces inside it got there some other way.

Bottom line: Elizabeth Short, during her extended torture, was forced to suffer the ultimate humiliation of having to ingest and swallow feces.

Having reviewed the many acts of known torture, it takes very little imagination to speculatively add to that list the forced feeding of *Bandini Steer Manure* or *Bandini Fertilite* from a nearly empty bag of fertilizer—perhaps recently used by the gardener in the inner courtyard landscaping at the Franklin house.

Certainly, this fertilizer would match the coroner's description of the stomach contents as a "greenish-brown granular material, mostly feces and other particles which could not be identified."

Based on all the previous evidence, which was supported by the crime scene photographs and the Lloyd Wright documents and receipts, it is my firm belief that Dr. George Hill Hodel, in the hours before her death, drugged and held Elizabeth Short captive at the Franklin house.

[*As previously noted, the DA files from 2004 established that father was alone at the house* as my mother and we, three sons, were temporarily staying with her brother, our Uncle Gene, some three miles away in the Silver Lake District of East Hollywood.]

Time Line and Crime Scene Reenactment

January 14, 1947 3:00-4:00 p.m. [approximate]

Based on my interview with LAPD policewoman Myrl McBride, we know that she was the last witness to see Elizabeth Short alive. Officer McBride stopped and spoke with Elizabeth Short on two separate occasions in the hours just prior to her disappearance. The first was at approximately 3:00 p.m. when a frightened Elizabeth ran up to her and claimed, "A man, a former suitor just threatened to kill me." McBride accompanied her back to a bar and the man was gone and Elizabeth retrieved her purse. The second encounter came about one hour later when the officer observed her exit a second bar again in the vicinity of Fifth and Main Street.

Officer McBride informed us that Elizabeth was accompanied by "**two men and a woman.**" McBride asked Elizabeth, "Are you okay? Elizabeth nodded that she was and told McBride she "was going to the Greyhound Bus station to meet her father." [Bus depot at that time was just two blocks away.]

It is my belief that these two males and one female were the same three persons who were looking for Elizabeth at the Dorothy French residence in San Diego just one week earlier. A neighbor reported to the police about seeing three individuals, "two males and a female," on January 7, standing and knocking at Dorothy French's house. After a few moments, the witness saw them run to their parked car and "**hurriedly drove away.**" I believe that one of the males was likely George Hodel, possibly accompanied by either Fred Sexton or the man later described on the DA tapes as "The Baron." So far, we have no clue as to the woman's identity?

January 14-15, 1947—Sowden/Franklin house

The newly discovered physical evidence [the paper sacks], link the Franklin house to the vacant lot and confirm our earlier suspicions that it was the original crime-scene.

The extended torture and subsequent "surgical operation" (a hemicorpectomy), according to several forensic and medical experts, would probably have required a minimum of three (3) hours to complete.

I *suggest* that the murder unfolded along the following lines:

Elizabeth Short was initially drugged either by using chloroform and or by Dr. Hodel injecting her with a strong sedative.

She was then bound and trussed with rope, tortured with non-lethal scalpel cuts to the body, sexually assaulted [sodomized with an unknown object], and then subjected to the ultimate sadistic humiliation of being forced fed with *Bandini* steer-manure.

Franklin House Master Bathroom tub

She was taken to the master bathroom tub, where the torture continued, and she was eventually slain. [Time of death, based on the coroner's estimate, would have been at approximately 2:00-3:00 a.m. in the early morning hours of January 15, 1947. This time is also substantiated by the fact that officers and the deputy coroner at the crime scene at 10:00 a.m. *noted that rigor mortis had not yet begun to set in the body*, which normally *begins* at eight to twelve hours after death.]

The surgical bisection was then performed and the body, drained of blood, was scrubbed with a coconut fiber brush and washed clean. [Fibers from the brush were found on the body during the autopsy.]

The two halves were likely towel-dried and each placed separately on top of a large empty paper sack, which was readily at hand and left over from the recent construction and landscaping work. [Note: Each half, having been drained of fluids, would have weighed no more than approximately fifty-five pounds.]

Franklin House Diagram
[Arrows mark: probable route from master bathroom to car]

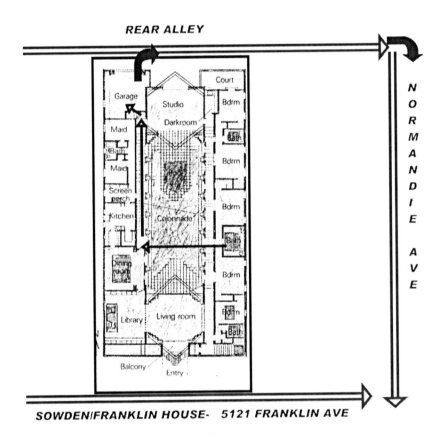

SOWDEN/FRANKLIN HOUSE- 5121 FRANKLIN AVE

The separate victim's body parts were carried from the master bathtub through the house to the rear garage and placed in George Hodel's black sedan. They could have been placed either in the trunk or on the backseat of the car. Additional cement and or fertilizer sacks were likely placed over them to cover and conceal the butchery.

As seen in the above diagram, all of these actions, including placing the body parts in the car, would have been conducted *within the privacy of the home and at no time would George Hodel ever have been exposed to public view.*

On January 16, 2011, I reenacted the drive from the Franklin house garage to 3815 S. Norton Avenue. Departing from the rear alley at 6:00 a.m., I arrived at the location of the vacant lot at 6:32 a.m., which is the same time that witness Robert Meyer claimed he first saw a black sedan pull up and stop at the curbside.

Meyer observed a lone male get out and indicated that the vehicle remained at the location for approximately four minutes. Due to the darkness and the fact that he was across the lot and nearly one-half block away, and his view was partially blocked by grass, it would have been impossible for Mr. Meyer to determine exactly what the suspect was doing.

After waiting four minutes, I then drove from 3815 S. Norton to the 1100 block of south Crenshaw Boulevard, where the suspect had placed Elizabeth Short's purse and shoes atop a trashcan outside of a local restaurant. I arrived at 6:50 a.m. and daylight had just begun to break. [This location is approximately halfway between the vacant lot and the Franklin house.] The drive from Crenshaw Boulevard back to the Franklin house added another twenty minutes, and I arrived back at the rear alley at 7:12 a.m.

I offer the foregoing reenactment not as fact but only as a *possible scenario.*

We will likely never know what exactly occurred. While I suspect that my father was one of the three persons seen leaving the Main Street Bar with Elizabeth, he may not have been. The three could have brought her to the house and then departed.

Another question is: Did George Hodel perform these horrific acts by himself or were others present? Again, we will probably never know the answer. But, in at least one of his taunting mailings to the police after the murder, he did claim to have an accomplice:

... A certain girl is going to get the same as E.S. got if she squeals on us. We're going to Mexico City—catch us if you can.

2K's

[SKH Note: Does the signature "2K's" after the "us" and "we" stand for "Two Killers"?]

As to the WHY we have multiple motives, the most likely being handed to us from inside the DA files.

It would appear that Elizabeth Short may have unwittingly signed her own death warrant by inadvertently making known to her ex-boyfriend, George Hodel, that she had gone to Chicago and was investigating the *1945 Chicago Lipstick Murders*. [I would refer my readers to my sequel, *Most Evil: Avenger, Zodiac and the Further Serial Murders of Dr. George Hodel*, Dutton 2009 for full details of that investigation.]

In a later mailing, the *Black Dahlia Avenger* tells us:

..."Dahlia Killing was justified"

George Hodel Album—Photo No. 2—Friend or Trophy?

Eyewitness misidentification is the single greatest cause of wrongful convictions nationwide, playing a role in more than 75% of convictions overturned through DNA testing.

The Innocence Project

I have no desire to reopen the 2003 George Hodel photo album controversy.

In my 2006 CNN interview, I was personally able to publicly eliminate photograph No. 1 in my father's album as NOT BEING ELIZABETH SHORT. As summarized in Chapter 4, we now know that the Franklin house photo was my father's friend, Marya Marco.

Whether the second photograph in my father's album is or is not Elizabeth Short, no longer matters. Its initial relevance was to address the question of whether George Hodel and Elizabeth Short had ever met.

Thanks to the 2004 post-publication discovery of the secret DA files and transcripts, that question has become a moot point. We now have independent confirmation from both law enforcement documents and new witnesses that George Hodel both KNEW AND ADMITTED TO KILLING ELIZABETH SHORT.

Over the past seven-years, I have received dozens of varying opinions on WHO PHOTO No. 2 might be. Many believe the photo IS Elizabeth Short.

Dr. George Hodel
photo album

Elizabeth Short
crime scene, 1947
(lacerations airbrushed)

Photo No. 2 compared to Elizabeth Short photo at crime scene
[lacerations airbrushed]

Others suggest the photo looks more like the 1949 *Lone Woman Murder* victim, actress Jean Spangler, whose purse was found just a half-mile from the Franklin house. Miss Spangler vanished on October 7, *the day after George Hodel bailed out of jail on the child molestation charges.* Jean was last seen seated at a table at a Hollywood restaurant engaged in a late-night argument with two men, one of them described as "dapper-looking" who closely fit George Hodel's description.

Daily News 1949 Jean Spangler headlines suggesting
killer may be linked to 1947 Black Dahlia Murder

Jean Spangler comparisons to George Hodel's Photo No. 2

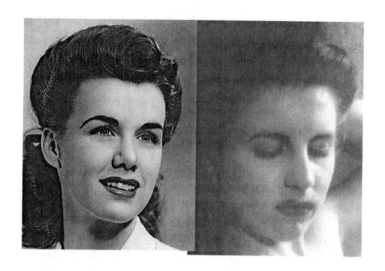

Jean Spangler rt/ear

Hodel photo rt/ear

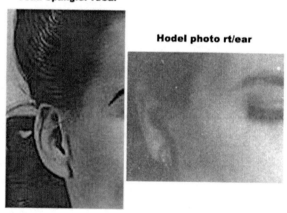

Jean Spangler and Photo #2 enlargement

Jean Spangler

Jean Spangler

Was the "drop-dead gorgeous actress named Jean" who my half-brother, Duncan, recalled was dating our father and who he met at the Franklin house parties in 1948-1949—the same Jean Spangler?

George Hodel photo No. 2 nude compared to "Showgirl" Jean Spangler nude

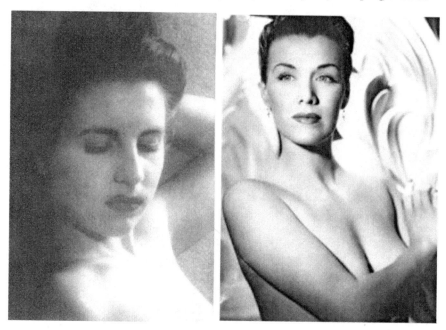

Still others offer the possibility that Photo No. 2 could have been the unidentified woman/victim from the DA transcripts, heard crying and dialing the telephone operator from the Franklin house on February 18, 1950. [Later that same evening, in the transcript, the stakeout detectives described hearing George Hodel and his confidant, "The Baron," go downstairs to the basement. Then beating sounds and blows were heard, which detectives described as "sounding like a pipe striking an object," immediately followed by a woman crying out several times, then silence.]

Setting aside the speculation of *who* the woman in Photo No. 2 might be, let's take a closer look at the actual photo.

In the photograph below we see George Hodel sitting on top of the desk in his home/office/living room. This photo was taken circa February 1950. Displayed on the north wall are forty-nine (49) separate Chinese and Tibetan art objects which GHH, using his "diplomatic immunity," sent to himself from his UNRRA base in China before unexpectedly resigning and returning home in September 1946. Also, note his preference for mixing the old with the new as demonstrated by the modern art painting [enlarged, artist unknown] hanging on the wall behind his desk.

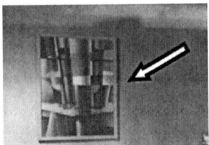

GHH album, Photo No. 2

When I initially viewed this photograph [upper right], I assumed that the woman was lying on a carpeted floor. However, in closer examination, it becomes obvious that she is not.

Based on the downward slope of her breast line, it appears that her head and shoulders are braced against a vertical object, with her left arm bent and propped behind her head.

In the living-room, we see two upholstered chairs. The lower-left photo shows a close-up of the chair material in comparison to the material in Photo No. 2. To my eye, they look similar. I would suggest that the nude woman's back was braced against one of these fabric chairs when this photo was taken.

The woman in the photo, with eyes closed, is either feigning sleep, drugged unconscious, or worse, she is dead! Could this be one of George Hodel's "trophy" photographs?

Her lipstick is heavily applied and appears to have been smeared on as if by another.

Lipstick and lips were a regular and repeating theme seen in many of the surrealist art works of that time period.

In one of Man Ray's later photographs, believed taken shortly before his death, he was seen holding a photograph of a large pair of lips identical to the Photo No. 2 enlargement shown below as he winks directly into the camera. Behind him, hanging on the wall in plain view, we see one of his paintings—a bisected body.

In addition, in Photo No. 2, we also have the suggestion of the surrealist's *Minotaur* theme, with the woman's arm bent at the elbow and extended above her head. Could all of this add up to another George Hodel post-mortem homage to his Dadaist Master and good friend, Man Ray?

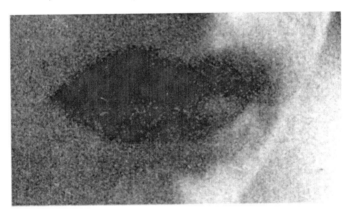

Photo No. 2 lipstick enlarged

Regardless of who this woman was, be she Short, Spangler, the Jane Doe in the basement, or someone else, we cannot discount the very real possibility that she may have been another one of George Hodel's victims, who was drugged, posed, and about to be or had already been slain.

As we know, drugging his victims was an important part of the doctor's M.O.... To date, we KNOW of at least three drugging incidents: Ruth Spaulding, Lillian Lenorak, and his teenage granddaughter, Deborah Hodel [Tamar's daughter], who, after being drugged while having dinner with him, reported awakening to find herself nude and spread-eagled on his hotel room bed with George snapping pictures of her.

The fourth probable drugging, based on a reading of the 1950 DA transcripts, was the Jane Doe victim who was assaulted and possibly slain in the Franklin house basement on February 18, 1950.

Sowden/Franklin House Photos-1969

In August 1969, the National Park Service, Department of the Interior undertook a project to both survey and photograph the Sowden/Franklin house.

This "Historic American Building Survey" CA-1940 and the photographs taken in connection with it were made public and I am here including those 1969 photographs.

George Hodel sold the house in 1950, and while it is believed the new owners initially took up residence, the home, after a few years of occupancy, became and remained vacant during the decades of the 1950s and 1960s. Later, in the early 1970s, the owner's grandson and his wife moved in and were in residence until selling the home in 2002.

[In BDA Chapter 20, "The Franklin House Revisited," I refer to the owners as "Mr. and Mrs. Bill Buck" to protect their privacy.]

These survey photographs show that by 1969, the interior courtyard had become overgrown and the home had fallen into disrepair due to being vacant for more than a decade.

I am including these photographs from the sixties as they have preserved and best captured the look and feel of the Franklin house—AS IT WAS IN 1947.

All one need do is perform a little landscaping of the mind. Manicure the inner courtyard, cut back the cacti, trim the ivy, and YOU'RE THERE.

5121 Franklin Avenue, Hollywood, California.

It is 1947. A warm starlit night and the sweet smell of jasmine fills the air. Imagine you are one of the invited guests, standing on the polar bear rug, sipping an ice-cold gin-and-tonic, as the handsome dapper doctor approaches with a charming smile and his most sincere, "Good evening. So glad you could make it tonight."

Historic American Buildings Survey-
National Park Service
Sowden House Photographs-1969

(Full text and diagrams attached as Addendum)

ENTRANCE, OBLIQUE VIEW

ENTRANCE, AXIAL VIEW

ENTRANCE GATE

ENTRANCE GATE – DETAIL VIEW

LIVING ROOM, DISTANT VIEW, LOOKING WEST TO STUDY

LIVING ROOM, CLOSE VIEW LOOKING WEST TO STUDY

STUDY, FIREPLACE

GLAZED OPENING, LIVING ROOM, LOOKING TOWARDS
COURT

COURT, LOOKING NORTH FROM LIVING ROOM TERRACE

ENTRANCE TO STUDIO AT NORTH END OF COURT, FROM
COURT

CLOSE VIEW, ENTRANCE TO STUDIO AT NORTH END OF COURT

VIEW IN COURTYARD, LOOKING SOUTH TO LIVING ROOM

LIVING ROOM, CLOSE VIEW FROM COURTYARD

COLONNADE, LOOKING THROUGH DOOR

COLONNADE, BEYOND DOOR

BATHROOM, TUB

BATHROOM, SINK

Chapter 6

The DA-Hodel Black Dahlia Transcripts

As you begin to read the following summaries, it is important to understand that the detective's entries that make-up these 146-pages of transcriptions are nothing more than THEIR PERSONAL LOG. In these files, [with a few fortunate exceptions] we are only reading brief "headlines" as to what was contained in each of the separately recorded conversations.

The officers' entries, made in real time, summarized only *bits and pieces* of each conversation. Consequently, we are only receiving a few sentences of a total conversation.

Unfortunately, the actual forty-one wire recordings have "disappeared" from LAPD custody, and, it is almost certain, that the missing recordings containing the complete conversations were destroyed and will never become available.

It is also important to understand that the modern day LAPD had nothing to do with the original investigation *and had no idea that Dr. George Hill Hodel was ever named as a suspect, let alone that he had confessed on tape to committing the crimes. Today's LAPD first learned of both Dr. George Hodel's existence and these transcripts only AFTER the publication of BDA in 2003.*

Today's LAPD had NO KNOWLEDGE that these DA transcripts existed. All of the evidence connecting George Hodel to the crimes, as well as these transcripts, was removed from LAPD files a long time ago, probably in the 1950s or 1960s.

LASO undersheriff James Downey was almost correct when he told his chief of detectives, Gordon Bowers, when speaking about

George Hodel and LAPD solving the case, **"...it will never come out."** It did take fifty-five years!

Also, keep in mind, as you read these transcripts, that we owe their existence solely to one honest [and very cautious] detective.

It was Lt. Frank B. Jemison who was assigned by the 1949 Grand Jury to reinvestigate the Black Dahlia and other *Lone Woman murders.* He did it and he solved it. When he was then ordered by his superiors to "shut it down" and turn over all the files, tape recordings, and transcripts to LAPD's chief of detectives, Thad Brown, he did that too.

But it was Lt. Jemison's final act that ultimately changed the course of history and permitted the public to ultimately discover the TRUTH.

Prior to turning over all the materials to LAPD, as ordered, Lt. Jemison made a copy of his complete investigation, including the Hodel transcripts, and secretly locked all of the documents away in the DA's vault, where they remained unopened and untouched for six-decades. This was his insurance. UNBENOWNST TO ALL THE TOP BRASS IN BOTH THE DA'S OFFICE AND THE LAPD, LT. JEMISON KEPT A SECOND SET OF BOOKS!

Here then—thanks to an honest and careful cop—are those books!

Note: In the pages that follow, I have reduced the 146-pages down to just 15 for easier readability. Included in those pages are extracts of what I consider to be the most relevant statements and admissions.

For historical purposes and the hardcore researchers, [and in case I have missed something that an eagle-eyed armchair detective might find] *I have included the complete unedited Hodel-Black Dahlia transcripts in the "Addendum."*

LOS ANGELES DISTRICT ATTORNEY

BUREAU OF INVESTIGATION

HODEL – BLACK DAHLIA CASE FILE

ELECTRONIC SURVEILLANCE TRANSCRIPTS OF GEORGE HILL HODEL M.D.

DA Case No. 30-1268
Title: Elizabeth Short
Suspect: Dr. George Hill Hodel
Inv. Assigned: Lt. Frank Jemison
Charge: Murder
Case: ACTIVE

The following fifteen-page annotated summary was prepared by retired LAPD homicide detective Steve Hodel. It contains the verbatim statements and entries of both DA and LAPD detectives as found in the original 1950 DA Case File.

The statements and admissions made by Dr. George Hill Hodel are also verbatim, taken from the pages of the DA's transcription of the secret wire-recordings.

The recordings were obtained during a joint DA/LAPD task-force stakeout comprised of eighteen detectives. The electronic surveillance was ongoing 24/7 over a five-week period from February 15, 1950 through March 27, 1950 (1872 man hours) and was terminated only because Dr. Hodel, after being tipped-off, then fled his residence.

As of that date, detectives had recorded forty-one wire spools of Dr. Hodel's personal conversations. The DA's original summary resulted in 146 pages of transcription. In the pages that follow, I have left the original timeline intact and included only those statements that are relevant to criminal activity, payoffs to law enforcement, and which make specific references to the Black Dahlia Murder investigation. *The complete and unedited 146-page transcript is included as an addendum to this book.*

ELECTRONIC SURVEILLANCE INSTALLATION
DR. GEORGE HILL HODEL RESIDENCE —5121 FRANKLIN AVE, HOLLYWOOD
2/15/50

D.A. Hodel/Black Dahlia File
"INVESTIGATOR'S PROGRESS REPORT"

The handwritten report (above) is a copy of the one found in the DA Hodel-Black Dahlia File.

The verbatim typewritten copy at the right includes all spellings and punctuations as they appear in the above original.

Case No. 30-1268 Date: 2/27/50
Title: Short, Eliz.
Suspects: Dr. Geo. Hill Inv.
Assigned Jemison
Charge: Murder
THIS CASE IS: ACTIVE
BRIEF STATEMENT AS TO RESULTS TO DATE: (Indicate present status if being brought to trial at this time.)

"On Feb. 15, 1950 the undersigned investigator, working with Sgts Stanton & Guinnis from the LAPD crime lab, installed two microfones in the home of Dr. Geo. Hodel.
The microfones were connected to a wire recorder located in the basement of the Hollywood Station of the LAPD thru telephone lines leased from the Pac. Tel. & Tel. Co. Trouble was not rectified until approx. 2:00, Feb. 18. No intelligible conversation was heard over the system until that time."

Signed—David E. Bronson

DA/LAPD MICROPHONE INSTALLATION LOCATIONS

Two microphone (M) "bugs" installed in main level walls of Dr. Hodel's residence.
Based on surveillance transcripts we know they were hidden in the West Office
Library, and Master Bedroom. Because of its placement. the bug in George Hodel's
bedroom was able to pick-up and record the Feb. 18 assault and possible murder
that occurred in the basement. Below floor plan diagrams basement which was
located directly below the Master bedroom.

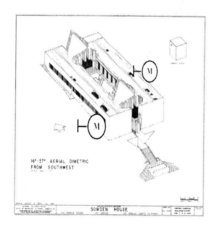

16'-57° AERIAL DIMETRIC
FROM SOUTHWEST

SOWDEN HOUSE

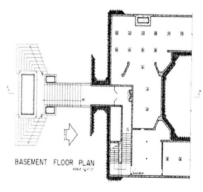

BASEMENT FLOOR PLAN

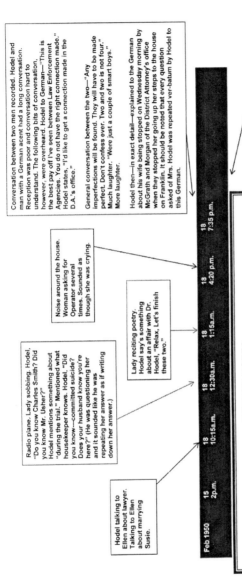

Conversation between two men recorded. Hodel and man with a German accent had a long conversation. Reception was poor and conversation hard to understand. The following bits of conversation, however, were overheard. Hodel to German—"This is the best pay off I've seen between Law Enforcement Agencies. You do not have the right connection made." Hodel states, "I'd like to get a connection made in the D.A.'s office."

General conversation between the two—"Any imperfections will be made to be found. They will have to be made perfect. Don't confess ever. Two and two is not four." Much laughter. "Were just a couple of smart boys." More laughter.

Hodel then—in exact detail—explained to the German about his wife being stopped on Wednesday morning by McGrath and Morgan of the District Attorney's office when they stopped her going up her steps to the house on Franklin. It should be noted that every question asked of Mrs. Hodel was repeated ver-batum by Hodel to this German.

He (Hodel) then began to explain to the German about his recent trial—making statements that, "Ther'e out to get mo. Two men in the D.A.'s officer were transferred and demoted because of my trial." Hodel then explained about his being questioned at the D.A.'s office on Wednesday morning and told in great detail as to questions perpounded to him at that time. One statement made to the German was as follows: "Supposin' I did kill the Black Daliah. They couldn't prove it now. They can't talk to my Secretary anymore because she's dead.... One point of the conversation was also, "Have you heard from Powers."

Noise around the house. Woman asking for Operator several times. Sounded as though she was crying.

Radio plane. Lady sobbing. Hodel, "Do you know Charles Smith? Did you know Mr. Usher?" Hodel mentions something about "during the trial." Mentioned what housekeeper knows. Hodel. "Did you know—committed suicide? Does your husband know you're here?" (He was questioning her and it sounded like he was repeating her answer as if writing down her answer.)

Lady reciting poetry. Hodel say's something about an affair with Dr. Hodel. "Relax, Let's finish these two."

Hodel talking to Ellen about lawyer. Talking to Ellen about marrying Susie.

Feb 1950	15 2p.m.	18 10:15a.m.	18 12:30a.m.	18 1:15a.m.	18 4:20 p.m.	18 7:35 p.m.

AUTHOR NOTES

[Boxed statements are verbatim as they appear on original transcripts including spelling errors]

Feb. 15. Police microphones installed while Dr. Hodel is being questioned by detectives at the DA detectives downtown office at the Hall of Justice. DA investigator Walter Morgan shims locked front door of Hodel residence and sound technicians place two microphones inside the walls in library and master bedroom.

Charles Smith, referred to above, was an abortionist friend of Hodel's and in Sept. 1949, assisted in the abortion of his 14-year-old daughter, Tamar. Smith and a Dr. Francis C. Ballard were arrested by LAPD just days after Dr. Hodel's arrest for incest and both were charged with performing the abortion.

On March 20, 1950, DA investigators Lt. Jemison and Walter Morgan interview Charles Smith's girlfriend, Mildred Bray and discover she witnessed a $1,000 cash payoff from Hodel to Smith. The payoff was made on December 29, 1949, just four days after Hodel's "acquittal" on the child molestation charges. Smith implicated and identified by Tamar is quoted in Lt. Jemison's report as saying:

"Someday I'm going to fix Tamar. I'm going to cut a chunk out of the calf of her leg and fry it and eat it in front of her eyes and then puke it up in front of her face."

On this very first day of recorded conversations we have George Hodel admitting to the murder of Elizabeth Short, payoffs to law enforcement and bragging about his influence in having officers demoted and transferred in connection with his incest trial.

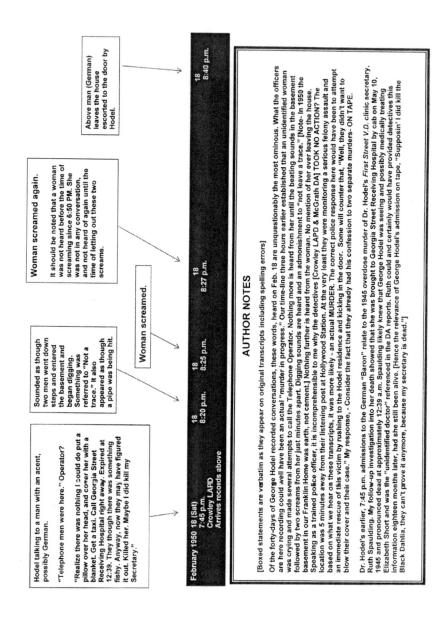

Hodel talking to a man with an accent, possibly German.

"Telephone men were here." Operator?

"Realize there was nothing I could do put a pillow over her head, and cover her with a blanket. Get a taxi. Call Georgia Street Receiving Hospital right away. Expired at 12:39. They though there was something fishy. Anyway, now they may have figured it out. Killed her. Maybe I did kill my Secretary."

Sounded as though two men went down steps and entered the basement and began digging. Something was referred to "Not a trace." It also appeared as though a pipe was being hit.

Woman screamed again.

It should be noted that a woman was not heard before the time of screaming since 6:50 PM. She was not in any conversation, and not heard of again until the time of letting out these two screams.

Woman screamed.

Above man (German) leaves the house escorted to the door by Hodel.

February 1950 18 (Sat)
7:45 p.m.
Crowley LAPD
Arrives records above

18 8:20 p.m.   18 8:25 p.m.   18 8:27 p.m.   18 8:40 p.m.

AUTHOR NOTES

[Boxed statements are verbatim as they appear on original transcripts including spelling errors]

Of the forty-days of George Hodel recorded conversations, these words, heard on Feb. 18 are unquestionably the most ominous. What the officers are here recording could well have been an actual "murder in progress." Our time-line three hours earlier established that an unidentified woman was crying and made several attempts to call the Telephone Operator. Nothing more is heard from her until the beating sounds in the basement followed by two screams from her just minutes apart. Digging sounds are heard and an admonishment to "not leave a trace." [Note- In 1950 the basement in our Franklin Home was earth, not cement.] Nothing further is heard from the woman. No mention of her ever leaving the house. Speaking as a trained police officer, it is incomprehensible to me why the detectives [Crowley LAPD & McGrath DA] TOOK NO ACTION? The location was 5 minutes away from their listening post at Hollywood Station. At the very least they were monitoring a serious felony assault and based on what we hear on these transcripts, it was more likely - an actual MURDER. The correct police response here would have been to attempt an immediate rescue of this victim by rushing to the Hodel residence and kicking in the door. Some will counter that, "Well, they didn't want to blow their cover and their case." My response, - Consider the fact that they already had his confession to two separate murders- ON TAPE.

Dr. Hodel's earlier, 7:45 p.m. admissions to the German "Baron" relate to the 1945 overdose murder of Dr. Hodel's *First Street V.D.* clinic secretary, Ruth Spaulding. My follow-up investigation into her death showed that she was brought to Georgia Street Receiving Hospital by cab on May 10, 1945 and pronounced dead at approximately 12:39 a.m. Spaulding likely knew that George Hodel was seeing and possibly medically treating Elizabeth Short and was the "unidentified doctor" referenced in the DA reports. Ruth could and certainly would have provided detectives this information eighteen months later, had she still been alive. [Hence the relevance of George Hodel's admission on tape, "Supposin' I did kill the Black Dahlia, they can't prove it anymore, because my secretary is dead."]

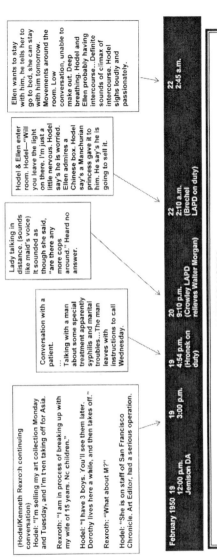

(Hodel/Kenneth Rexroth continuing conversation)

Hodel: "I'm selling my art collection Monday and Tuesday, and I'm then taking off for Asia.

Rexroth: "I am in process of breaking up with my wife of 15 years. No children."

Hodel: "I have 3 boys. You'll see them later. Dorothy lives here a while, and then takes off."

Rexroth: "What about M?"

Hodel: "She is on staff of San Francisco Chronicle. Art Editor, had a serious operation.

Conversation with a patient.
...
Talking with a man about some special treatment apparently syphilis and marital troubles...The man leaves with instructions to call Wednesday.

Lady talking in distance. (sounds like maid's voice) It sounded as though she said, "are there any more cops around." Heard no answer.

Hodel & Ellen enter room. Hodel—"Will you leave the light on there. I'm just a little nervous. Hodel say's he is worried. Ellen admires a Chinese box. Hodel say's a Manchurian princess gave it to him. He say's he is going to sell it.

Ellen wants to stay with him, he tells her to go to bed, she can stay with him tomorrow. Movements around the room. Low conversation, unable to make out. Deep breathing. Hodel and Ellen probably having intercourse...Definite sounds of climax of intercourse. Hodel sighs loudly and passionately.

February 1950 19	19	19	20	22	22
12:00 p.m.	3:00 p.m.	4:54 p.m.	9:10 p.m.	2:10 a.m.	2:45 a.m.
Jemison DA		(Hronek on duty)	(Crowley LAPD relieves Walter Morgan)	(Brechel LAPD on duty)	

AUTHOR NOTES

[Boxed statements are verbatim as they appear on original transcripts including spelling errors]

Kenneth Rexroth was a well-known writer and poet from the San Francisco Bay area. Many consider him to be "the Father of the Beat Generation." He was a friend of both my parents, George and Dorero Hodel as well as other Franklin house guests such as surreal artist Man Ray and his wife, Juliet and writer Henry Miller.

I believe Rexroth's question as to "M" refers to EMILIA, George Hodel's ex-wife, and the mother of my older half-brother, Duncan Hodel. Emilia was then living in San Francisco. Thirty-seven years later, in 1987, Emilia, still living in the S.F. Bay area, would take her own life by ingesting an overdose of barbiturates.

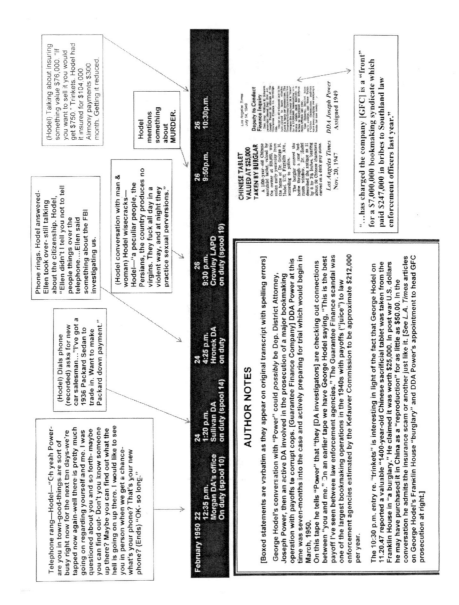

(Hodel) Talking about insuring something value $76,000. "If you want to sell it you would get $750." Trinkets. Hodel had it insured for $104,000. Alimony payments $300 month. Getting it reduced.

Hodel mentions something about MURDER.

Phone rings. Hodel answered- Ellen took over- still talking about the citizenship. Hodel, "Ellen didn't I tell you not to tell people things over the telephone....Ellen said something about the FBI investigating us.

(Hodel conversation with man & woman) Hodel wisecracks— Hodel—"a peculiar people, the Persians, the country produces no virgins. They fuck all day in a violent way, and at night they practice sexual perversions."

(Hodel) Dials phone (recorded) asks for new car salesman... "I've got a 1936 Packard Sedan to trade in. Want to make Packard down payment."

Telephone rang—Hodel—"Oh yeah Power- are you in town-good-things are sort of busy right now for the next ten days-we're tapped now again-well there is pretty much going on regarding yourself and me. I was questioned about you and so forth- maybe you can find out- Don't you know someone up there? Maybe you can find out what the hell is going on up there. I would like to see you in person when we get a chance- what's your phone? That's your new phone? (Ends) "OK- so long."

February 1950	24	24	26	26	26
12:35 p.m. Morgan DA's office On duty (spool 10)	1:20 p.m. Sullivan DA on duty (spool 14)	4:25 p.m. Hronek DA on duty	9:30 p.m. Crowley LAPD on duty (spool 19)	9:50 p.m.	10:30 p.m.

AUTHOR NOTES

[Boxed statements are verbatim as they appear on original transcript with spelling errors]

George Hodel's conversation with "Power" could *possibly* be Dep. District Attorney, Joseph Power, then an active DA involved in the prosecution of a major bookmaking operation with payoffs to corrupt cops. [Guarantee Finance Company] DDA Power at this time was seven-months into the case and actively preparing for trial which would begin in March, 1950.

On this tape he tells "Power" that "they [DA investigators] are checking out connections between "you and me." On an earlier tape we have Hodel saying, "This is the best payoff I've seen between law enforcement agencies." The Guarantee Finance scandal was one of the largest bookmaking operations in the 1940s with payoffs ("juice") to law enforcement agencies estimated by the Kefauver Commission to be approximate $212,000 per year.

The 10:30 p.m. entry re. "trinkets" is interesting in light of the fact that George Hodel on 11.20.47 reported a valuable "1400-year-old Chinese sacrificial tablet was taken from the Franklin House in "a burglary." He claimed it was worth $25,000. In post war U.S. dollars he may have purchased it in China as a "reproduction" for as little as $50.00. In the conversation he admits the insurance scam or another just like it. [See *L.A. Times* articles on George Hodel's Franklin House "burglary" and DDA Power's appointment to head GFC prosecution at right.]

CHINESE TABLET VALUED AT $25,000 TAKEN BY BURGLAR

Los Angeles Times Nov. 20, 1947

Deputy to Conduct Finance Inquiry

Los Angeles Times July 14, 1949

DDA Joseph Power Assigned 1949

"...has charged the company [GFC] is a "front" for a $7,000,000 bookmaking syndicate which paid $247,000 in bribes to Southland law enforcement officers last year."

Hodel- "We'll really have to ride herd on them. 4 young chicks in a strange country."

Man- "Ha- 4 young girls and we two- what a combination."...

Hodel- "I'm the only person who knows where all these things fit into the picture."

Hodel- "You better take a generous supply of penicillin. (Talking to same party)

(Juvenile officers observed a 41 cream 4 door Buick parked in front of Hodel's residence at this time. License #751014 registered to Etoyle E. Bennett. Legal owner, Hollywood Citizen News.)

Hodel- "It wouldn't do any harm to wait another month. There are other type of penicillin who are more apt to get the rash on the second---"

Hodel- "Well anyway she hasn't said she'd committed incest or killed the Black Dahlia. (other man has an accent, talking about this country.)
Man- "She said look what you've put in the paper, I hate you."

Door bell rings. Ellen goes to door. Hodel, "You made headlines today or tomorrow." Man- "Headlines? Hodel- "Like Hitler said. Your a rich man. I can see you beating her up."

... Man (laughing) "Suspicion." Hah. In one place I am a composer of poetry or opera, a hot tempered erratic woman- We've got to get out of here and get some fun for a change."

February 1950 27	27	27	27	27
12:00 a.m.	12:25 a.m. (spool 21)	12:35 a.m.	12:50 a.m.	1:14 a.m.

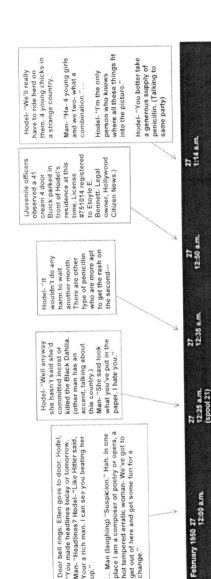

AUTHOR NOTES

[Boxed statements are verbatim as they appear on original transcripts including spelling errors]

The man talking to Hodel is identified as Theodore Kolline, a "composer, poet and painter." As -lodel indicates on the wire, the article did appear in the newspapers later in the day. The vehicle parked outside may have been borrowed and driven by Kolline, but showed registered to the Hollywood Citizen News, one of L.A.'s six newspapers.

On this surveillance tape we hear George Hodel making more references to the Black Dahlia murder and to his committing incest. Most interesting is his reference that, "HE ALONE KNOWS WHERE ALL THESE THINGS FIT INTO THE PICTURE."

See *L.A. Times* article on Composer Kolline dated Feb. 27, on right.

L.A. Times Feb. 27, 1950

Composer Kolline and Protege Feud in Explosive Divorce Suit

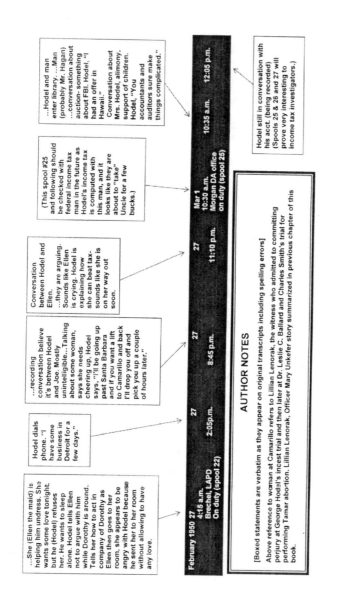

...She (Ellen the maid) is helping him undress. She wants some love tonight but he (Hodel) refuses her. He wants to sleep alone. Hodel tells Ellen not to argue with him while Dorothy is around. Tells her how to act in company of Dorothy as Ellen then goes to her room, she appears to be angry with Hodel because he sent her to her room without allowing her to have any love.

Hodel dials phone. "I have some business in Detroit for a few days."

...recording conversation believe it's between Hodel and Joe. Mostly unintelligible...Talking about some woman, says she needs cheering up. Hodel says, "I'll be going up past Santa Barbara to Camarillo and back and if you want a lift I'll drop you off and pick you up a couple of hours later."

Conversation between Hodel and Ellen. ...they are arguing. Sounds like Ellen is crying. Hodel is explaining how she can beat tax- sounds like she is on her way out soon.

(This spool #25 and following should be checked with federal income tax man in the future as Hodel's income tax is computed with this man, and it looks like they are about to "take" Uncle for a few bucks.)

...Hodel and man enter library....Man (probably Mr. Hagan) ...conversation about auction- something about FBI. Hodel, "I had an offer in Hawaii." Conversation about Mrs. Hodel, alimony, support of children. Hodel, "You accountants and auditors sure make things complicated."

Hodel still in conversation with his acct. (being recorded) (Spools 25 & 26 and 27 will prove very interesting to income tax investigators.)

February 1950 27
4:15 a.m.
Brechel, LAPD
On duty (spool 22)

27
2:05p.m.

27
8:45 p.m.

27
11:10 p.m.

Mar 1
10:30 a.m.
Morgan DA office
on duty (spool 25)

10:35 a.m.

12:05 p.m.

AUTHOR NOTES

[Boxed statements are verbatim as they appear on original transcripts including spelling errors]

Above reference to woman at Camarillo refers to Lillian Lenorak, the witness who admitted to committing perjury at George Hodel's incest trial and then later at Dr. Leslie C. Ballard and Charles Smith's trial for performing Tamar abortion. Lillian Lenorak, Officer Mary Unkefer story summarized in previous chapter of this book.

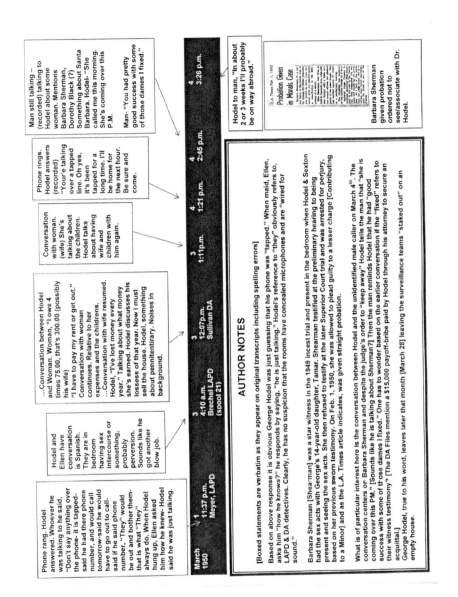

Phone rang. Hodel answered. Whoever he was talking to he said, "Don't say anything over the phone- it is tapped- said he had there phone number, and would call tomorrow-said he would have to go out to call-said if he said phone number, "They" would be out and bother them- that is what "They" always do. When Hodel hung up, Ellen asked him how he knew- Hodel said he was just talking.

Hodel and Ellen have conversation in Spanish. They are in bedroom having sex intercourse or something, probably perversion. Sounds like he got another blow job.

...Conversation between Hodel and Woman. Woman, "I owe 4 times 75.00, that's 300.00 (possibly his wife) "I have to pay my rent or get out." Conversation with woman continues. Relative to her expenses and the childrens. ...Conversation with wife resumed. Hodel, "I've lost money every year." Talking about what money she's earned. Hodel discusses his lossess of that year. Now I must sell the house. Hodel, something about penitentiary. Noises in background.

Conversation with woman. (wife) She's talking about the children. Hodel talks about having wife and children with him again.

Phone rings. Hodel answers (recorded) "You're talking over a tapped line. Oh yes, it's been tapped for a long time. I'll be home for the next hour. Be sure and come.

Man still talking – (recorded) talking to Hodel about some woman. Mentions Barbara Sherman, Dorothy Black (?) Something about Santa Barbara. Hodel- "She called me this morning. She's coming over this P.M."

Man-"You had pretty good success with some of those dames I fixed."

Hodel to man, "In about 2 or 3 weeks I'll probably be on way abroad."

Probation Given in Morals Case

Barbara Sherman given probation ordered not to see/associate with Dr. Hodel.

| March 1950 | 1 11:37 p.m. Meyer, LAPD | 3 4:10 a.m. Brechel LAPD (spool 21) | 3 12:07p.m. Sullivan DA | 3 1:11p.m. | 4 1:21 p.m. | 4 2:45 p.m. | 4 3:26 p.m. |

AUTHOR NOTES

[Boxed statements are verbatim as they appear on original transcripts including spelling errors]

Based on above response it is obvious George Hodel was just guessing that his phone was "tapped." When maid, Ellen, asks him "how he knows?" he responds by saying, "he is just talking." Hodel's reference to "they" obviously refers to, LAPD & DA detectives. Clearly, he has no suspicion that the rooms have concealed microphones and are "wired for sound."

Barbara Sherman [Shea-man] was a star witness in the 1949 incest trial and present in the bedroom when Hodel & Sexton had the sex acts with George's 14-year-old daughter, Tamar. Shearman testified at the preliminary hearing to being present and seeing the sex acts. She then refused to testify at the later Superior Court trial and was arrested for perjury, based on her previous sworn testimony. On Feb. 1, 1950, she was allowed to plead guilty to a lesser charge [Contributing to a Minor] and as the L.A. Times article indicates, was given straight probation.

What is of particular interest here is the conversation between Hodel and the unidentified male caller on March 4th. The conversation centers on Barbara Sherman and despite the judge's order to "keep away" Hodel tells the man that "she is coming over this PM." [Sounds like he is talking about Sherman?] Then the man reminds Hodel that he had "good success with some of those dames I fixed." One has to wonder based on the earlier conversation if the "fixed" refers to their witness testimony? [The DA Files mention a $15,000 payoff-bribe paid by Hodel through his attorney to secure an acquittal.] George Hodel, true to his word, leaves later that month [March 28] leaving the surveillance teams "staked out" on an empty house.

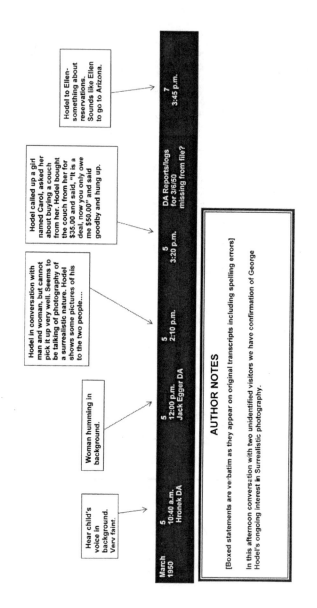

March 1950

| 5 10:40 a.m. Hronek DA | 5 12:00 p.m. Jack Egger DA | 5 2:10 p.m. | 5 3:20 p.m. | DA Reports/logs for 3/6/50 missing from file? | 7 3:45 p.m. |

Hear child's voice in background. Very faint.

Woman humming in background.

Hodel in conversation with man and woman, but cannot pick it up very well. Seems to be talking of photography of a surrealistic nature. Hodel shows some pictures of his to the two people....

Hodel called up a girl named Carol, asked her about buying a couch from her. Hodel bought the couch from her for $35.00 and said, "It is a deal, now you only owe me $50.00" and said goodby and hung up.

Hodel to Ellen- something about reservations. Sounds like Ellen to go to Arizona.

AUTHOR NOTES

[Boxed statements are verbatim as they appear on original transcripts including spelling errors]

In this afternoon conversation with two unidentified visitors we have confirmation of George Hodel's ongoing interest in Surrealistic photography.

132

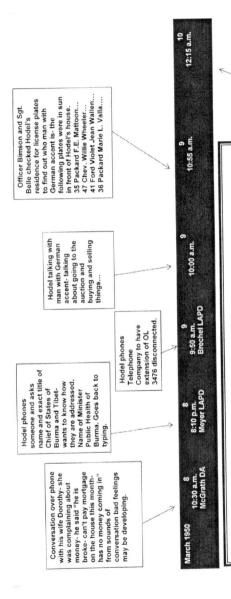

Conversation over phone with his wife Dorothy- she was complaining about money- can't pay mortgage on the house this month- has no money coming in" she said "he is broke- from sounds of conversation bad feelings may be developing.

Hodel phones someone and asks name and exact title of Chief of States of Burma and Tibet- wants to know how they are addressed Name of Minister Public Health of Burma. Goes back to typing.

Hodel phones Telephone Company to have extension of OL 3476 disconnected.

Hodel talking with man with German accent- talking about going to the auction and buying and selling things...

Officer Bimson and Sgt. Belle checked Hodel's residence for license plates to find out who the man with German accent is- the following plates were in sun in front of Hodel's house.
35 Packard F.E. Mattoon....
47 Chev. Willie Wheeler....
41 Ford Violet Jean Wallen...
36 Packard Marie L. Valla.....

One or two men and about same amount of women—talking to Hodel. Hard to understand—something about a place in Mexico not too far from AZ—good roads—something about a Whore House, or sanatarium. One man seems to be a doctor. Talking about she at Camarillo. Hodel- "She was going to shoot me and commit suicide- "Tamara" (way it sounded) Talking about fishing trip to Mexico ...looking at map—mentioned Sonora, Mexico. ...says he will leave - Hodel know about noon tomorrow-Friday about trip.

| March 1950 | 10:30 a.m. McGrath DA | 8:10 p.m. Meyer LAPD | 9:50 a.m. Brechel LAPD | 9 10:00 a.m. | 9 10:55 a.m. | 10 12:15 a.m. |

AUTHOR NOTES

[Boxed statements are verbatim as they appear on original transcripts including spelling errors]

The March 10 "she – Camarillo" entry refers to Lillian Lenorak and is independent corroboration to statements made by witness/roomer. Joe Barrett who came home to the Franklin House in Jan. 1950, to find Lenorak in George Hodel's bedroom holding his loaded rifle and threatening to kill George "for what he had done." Barrett in a 2003 on-camera television interview stated that this referred to the murder of Elizabeth Short. Barrett claims he took the rifle away from Lenorak "and calmed her down." This incident and the fact that Lenorak threatened George Hodel that "she was going to tell the DA that she had committed perjury in both Dr. Hodel and Dr. Ballard's trials" likely was what precipitated the drugging and superficial cutting of her wrists BY DR. HODEL. This staged "attempt suicide" by Hodel as documented in the officer Mary Unkefer/Lenorak Letter, was his way of discrediting Lenorak and getting her admitted to Camarillo hospital for temporary observation for being "emotionally distraught." This March 10 conversation occurred six weeks after officer Unkefer picked up Lenorak from the Franklin House and transported her to Santa Barbara and then on Jan. 30, 1950, wrote her letter to the DA informing them of Dr. Hodel's actions.

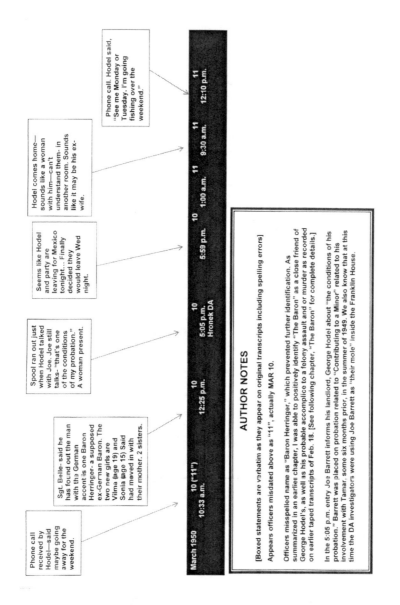

March 1950

10:33 a.m. — Phone call received by Hodel—said maybe going away for the weekend.

10 ("11") — Sgt. Belle- said he has found out the man with the German accent is one Baron Herringer- a supposed ex-German Baron. The two new girls are Vilma (age 19) and Sonia (age 15) Said had moved in with their mother. 2 sisters.

12:25 p.m. — Spool ran out just when Hodel talked with Joe. Joe still talks- "that's one of the conditions of my probation." A woman present.

5:05 p.m. Hronek DA — Seems like Hodel and party are leaving for Mexico tonight... Finally decided they would leave Wed night.

5:59 p.m.

1:00 a.m. — Hodel comes home—sounds like a woman with him—can't understand them- in another room. Sounds like it may be his ex-wife.

9:30 a.m.

12:10 p.m. — Phone call. Hodel said, "See me Monday or Tuesday. I'm going fishing over the weekend."

AUTHOR NOTES

[Boxed statements are verbatim as they appear on original transcripts including spelling errors]

Appears officers misdated above as "11", actually MAR 10.

Officers misspelled name as "Baron Herringer," which prevented further identification. As summarized in an earlier chapter, I was able to positively identify "The Baron" as a close friend of George Hodel's, as well as his probable accomplice to a felony assault and or murder as recorded on earlier taped transcripts of Feb. 18. [See following chapter, "The Baron" for complete details.]

In the 5:05 p.m. entry Joe Barrett informs his landlord, George Hodel about "the conditions of his probation." Barrett was placed on probation related to "Contributing to a Minor" related to his involvement with Tamar some six months prior, in the summer of 1949. We also know that at this time the DA investigators were using Joe Barrett as "their mole" inside the Franklin House.

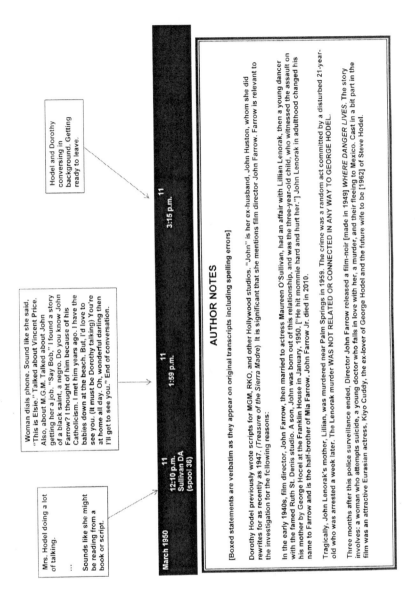

Mrs. Hodel doing a lot of talking.

...

Sounds like she might be reading from a book or script.

Woman dials phone. Sound like she said, "This is Elsie." Talked about Vincent Price. Also, about M.G.M. Talked about John getting her a job. "Say Bob," I found a story of a black saint, a negro. Do you know John Farrow? I thought of him because of his Catholicism. I met him years ago. I have the babies down at the beach. But, I'd love to see you. (It must be Dorothy talking) You're at home all day. Oh, wonderful darling then I'll get to see you." End of conversation.

Hodel and Dorothy conversing in background. Getting ready to leave.

March 1950   11   11   11
12:10 p.m.   1:59 p.m.   3:15 p.m.
Sullivan DA
(spool 36)

AUTHOR NOTES

[Boxed statements are verbatim as they appear on original transcripts including spelling errors]

Dorothy Hodel previously wrote scripts for MGM, RKO, and other Hollywood studios. "John" is her ex-husband, John Huston, whom she did rewrites for as recently as 1947. (*Treasure of the Sierra Madre*) It is significant that she mentions film director John Farrow. Farrow is relevant to the investigation for the following reasons:

In the early 1940s, film director, John Farrow, then married to actress Maureen O'Sullivan, had an affair with Lillian Lenorak, then a young dancer with the famed Ruth St. Denis studio. A son, John, was born out of this relationship, and was the three-year-old child, who witnessed the assault on his mother by George Hocel at the Franklin House in January, 1950. ["He hit mommie hard and hurt her."] John Lenorak in adulthood changed his name to Farrow and is the half-brother of Mia Farrow. John Farrow Jr. died in 2010.

Tragically, John Lenorak's mother, Lillian, was murdered near Palm Springs in 1959. The crime was a random act committed by a disturbed 21-year-old who was arrested a week later. The Lenorak murder WAS NOT RELATED OR CONNECTED IN ANY WAY TO GEORGE HODEL.

Three months after this police surveillance ended, Director John Farrow released a film-noir [made in 1949] *WHERE DANGER LIVES*. The story involves: a woman who attempts suicide, a young doctor who falls in love with her, a murder, and their fleeing to Mexico. Cast in a bit part in the film was an attractive Eurasian actress, Kiyo Cuddy, the ex-lover of George Hodel and the future wife to be [1962] of Steve Hodel.

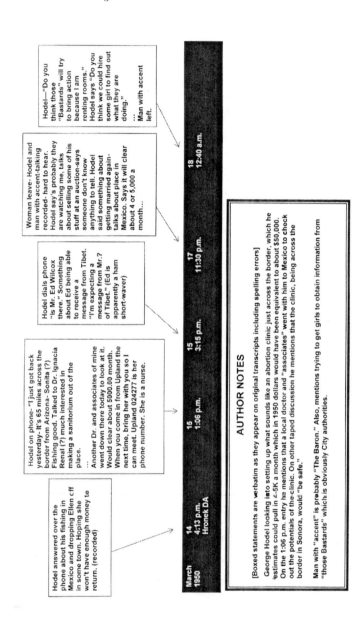

Hodel answered over the phone about his fishing in Mexico and dropping Ellen off in some town. Hoping she won't have enough money to return. (recorded)

Hodel on phone- "I just got back yesterday- It's 65 miles across the border from Arizona- Sonita (?) Fishing good. Talked to Dr. Ignacia Renal (?) much interested in making a sanitorium out of the place.
...
Another Dr. and associates of mine went down there today to look at it. Would clear about 5000.00 month. When you come in from Upland the next time, bring her with you so I can meet. Upland 024277 is her phone number. She is a nurse.

Hodel dials phone "Is Mr. Ed Wilcox there." "Something about Ed being able to receive a message from Tibet. "I'm expecting a message from Mr.? of Tibet." (Ed is apparently a ham short-waver)

Woman leave- Hodel and man with accent-talking recorded- hard to hear. Hodel say's probably they are watching me, talks about selling some of his stuff at an auction-says someone don't know anything to tell. Hodel said something about getting married again- talks about place in Mexico. Says it will clear about 4 or 5,000 a month...

Hodel—"Do you think those "Bastards" will try to bring action because I am renting rooms." Hodel says "Do you think we could hire some girl to find out what they are doing."
...
Man with accent left.

| March 1950 | 14 4:13 p.m. Hronek DA | 15 1:06 p.m. | 15 3:15 p.m. | 17 11:30 p.m. | 18 12:40 a.m. |

AUTHOR NOTES

[Boxed statements are verbatim as they appear on original transcripts including spelling errors]

George Hodel looking into setting up what sounds like an abortion clinic just across the border, which he estimates could pull in 4-5K a month which in 1950 dollars would have been equivalent to about $50,000. On the 1:06 p.m. entry he mentions that a local doctor and "associates" went with him to Mexico to check out the potentials of the clinic. On other taped discussion he mentions that the clinic, being across the border in Sonora, would "be safe."

Man with "accent" is probably "The Baron." Also, mentions trying to get girls to obtain information from "those Bastards" which is obviously City authorities.

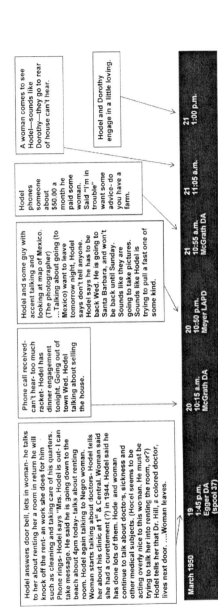

March 1950	19 1:45 p.m. Egger DA (spool 37)	20 10:15 a.m. McGrath DA	20 10:50 p.m. Meyer LAPD	21 10:55 a.m. McGrath DA	21 11:05 a.m.	21 1:00 p.m.

19 1:45 p.m. Egger DA (spool 37):
Hodel answers door bell, lets in woman- he talks to her about renting her a room in return he will knock off the rent- an work she does for him such as cleaning and taking care of his quarters. Phone rings- Hodel says "Mrs. Hodel is out- I can take message. He said he is going down to the beach about 4pm today- talks about renting room. Hodel again talking to Negro woman. Woman starts talking about doctors- Hodel tells her about his clinic at 1st & Central. Woman said she had a curettement (?) in 1944. Hodel said he has done lots of them. Hode and woman continue to talk about docto's, sickness and other medical subjects. (Hode seems to be acting overly nice to this woman. He must be trying to talk her into renting the room, or?) Hodel tells her that Dr. Hill, a colored doctor, lives next door. .....Woman leaves.

20 10:15 a.m. McGrath DA:
Phone call received- can't hear- too much racket- Hodel has dinner engagement tonight. Going out of town Wed. Hodel talking about selling the house.

20 10:50 p.m. Meyer LAPD:
Hodel and some guy with accent talking and looking at map of Mexico. (The photographer) ...Talking about going (to Mexico) want to leave tomorrow night, Hodel says don't tell anyone. Hodel says he has to be back Wed. He is going to Santa Barbara, and won't be back until Sunday. Sounds like they are going to take pictures. Sounds like Hodel is trying to pull a fast one of some kind.

21 11:05 a.m.:
Hodel phones someone about $50.00 a month he paid some woman. Said "I'm in trouble" want some advice- do you have a farm.

21 1:00 p.m.:
A woman comes to see Hodel—sounds like Dorothy—they go to rear of house can't hear.

Hodel and Dorothy engage in a little loving.

AUTHOR NOTES

[Boxed statements are verbatim as they appear on original transcripts including spelling errors]

Here we have Dr. Hodel actually admitting on tape that he has performed many surgical abortions! "I've done lots of them." The term currettement is synonymous with what is known as a "D&C"- Dilation & Curettage. Here is the medical definition:

"A gynecological procedure performed on the female reproductive system that used to be a common method of abortion. The procedure involves dilating the cervix and inserting instruments to clean out the lining of the uterus, which can include an embryo o' fetus, while the woman is under an anesthetic. Curetage is performed with a curette, a metal rod with a handle on one end and a sharp loop on the other."

Dr. Charles Hill, a dentist and our neighbor directly to the west of the Franklin House, was a highly respected member of L.A.'s Black Community and reportedly a "Mover & Shaker" in 1940s local politics. Joe Barrett mentions Dr. Hill owned a bail bonds company and was the one who put up the bail on Barrett's "Contributing" arrest. The following day, after bailing Joe out of jail, Dr. Hill invited him to accompany him to a swank gathering where Joe recalls the mayor, police chief and other City officials were in attendance.

The March 21 1:00 p.m. entry underscores that despite my parent's five-year divorce, they still remain on *intimate* terms.

DA investigator Jack Egger appears on a number of stake-outs throughout the surveillance. Egger after leaving the DA's Office will join Beverly Hills Police Department and promote to Captain of Detectives. He will then become Chief of Security at Warner Brothers Studio. In a strange coincidence, this same Jack Egger in 1946-7 was a young head-usher at *Columbia Broadcasting Studios* in Hollywood, and was familiar with Elizabeth Short on sight as she regularly attended the radio shows. In a later chapter of this book I detail the connections between Egger and Short and his 2003 positive identification of Dr. George Hodel as being the man with her at CBS studios, just days before her murder.

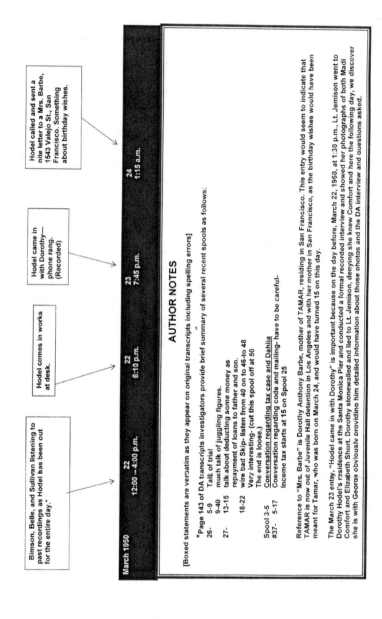

Bimson, Belle, and Sullivan listening to past recordings as Hodel has been out for the entire day.*

Hodel comes in works at desk.

Hodel came in with Dorothy— phone rang. (Recorded)

Hodel called and sent a nite letter to a Mrs. Barbe, 1543 Valejo St., San Francisco. Something about birthday wishes.

March 1950			
22 12:00 –4:00 p.m.	22 6:10 p.m.	23 7:45 p.m.	24 1:15 a.m.

AUTHOR NOTES

[Boxed statements are verbatim as they appear on original transcripts including spelling errors]

*Page 143 of DA transcripts investigators provide brief summary of several recent spools as follows:

26-   5-9   Talk of trial
      9-40   much talk of juggling figures.
27-   13-15   talk about deducting some money as
          repayment of loans to father and son.
    18-22   wire bad Skip- listen from 40 on to 46-to 48
          Very interesting- (cut this spool off at 50
          The end is loose.)

Spool 3-5   Conversation regarding tax case and Dahlia
#37-   5-17   Conversation regarding code and mailing- have to be careful-
Income tax starts at 15 on Spool 25

Reference to "Mrs. Barbe" is Dorothy Anthony Barbe, mother of TAMAR, residing in San Francisco. This entry would seem to indicate that TAMAR is now out of Juvenile Hall detention in Los Angeles and with her mother in San Francisco, as the birthday wishes would have been meant for Tamar, who was born on March 24, and would have turned 15 on this day.

The March 23 entry, "Hodel came in with Dorothy" is important because on the day before, March 22, 1950, at 1:30 p.m., Lt. Jemison went to Dorothy Hodel's residence at the Santa Monica Pier and conducted a formal recorded interview and showed her photographs of both Madi Comfort and Elizabeth Short. Dorothy stonewalled and lied to Lt. Jemison, denying she knew Comfort and here the following day, we discover she is with George obviously providing him detailed information about those photos and the DA interview and questions asked.

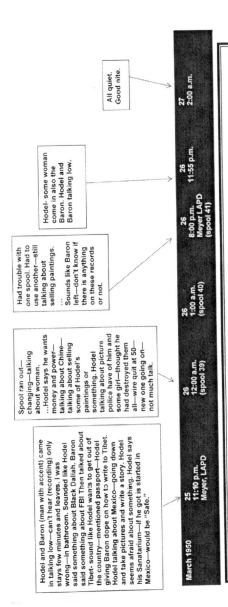

Hodel and Baron (man with accent) came in talking low—can't hear (recording) only stays few minutes and leaves. I was wrong—in bathroom. Sounded like Hodel said something about Black Daliah. Baron said something about FBI Then talked about Tibet- sound like Hodel wants to get out of the country—mentioned passport—Hodel giving Baron dope on how to write to Tibet. Hodel talking about Mexico—going down and take pictures and write a story. Hodel seems afraid about something. Hodel says his Sanatarium—if he got is started in Mexico—would be "Safe."

Spool ran out—changing—talking about woman. ...Hodel says he wants money and power—talking about Chinese—talking about selling some of Hodel's paintings or something. Hodel talking about picture police have of him and some girl—thought he had destroyed them all—wire quit at 50—new one going on—not much talk.

Had trouble with one spool. Had to use another—still talking about selling paintings. ... Sounds like Baron left—don't know if there is anything on these records or not.

Hodel- some woman come in also the Baron. Hodel and Baron talking low.

All quiet. Good nite.

| March 1950 | 25 11:10 p.m. Meyer, LAPD | 26 12:00 a.m. (spool 39) | 26 1:00 a.m. (spool 40) | 26 8:00 p.m. Meyer LAPD (spool 41) | 26 11:55 p.m. | 27 2:00 a.m. |

AUTHOR NOTES

[Boxed statements are verbatim as they appear on original transcripts including spelling errors]

THE DA/LAPD SURVEILLANCE-STAKE-OUT UNEXPECTEDLY ENDS HERE, WITH GEORGE HODEL EITHER BEING TIPPED OFF OR DECIDING ON HIS OWN THAT THINGS ARE TOO HOT.

He splits, literally leaving the DA/LAPD teams with their microphones in the walls of the Franklin House.

On this last night we hear Hodel confiding to his accomplice, "The Baron" of, "wanting to get out of the country", the "FBI", talking about "The Black Dahlia," and "pictures police have of him and a girl" which Hodel says, he "thought he had destroyed."

Just four days earlier, on March 22, 1950 DA Lt. Frank Jemison interviewed Dorothy Hodel at her home on Santa Monica Pier *and informed her that Elizabeth "Black Dahlia" Short had been identified by witnesses as "knowing and being with Dr. Hodel at the Franklin House before the murder."* Lt. Jemison further confronts Dorothy with the fact that he had information that she had stated to Tamar Hodel that George Hodel, a day or two after the crime, came home intoxicated and said, "They will never be able to pin that murder on me." [In his closing typed report, Jemison presents the actual wording as,] "They will never be able to prove I did that murder." In her interview, Dorothy stonewalls Lt. Jemison, denying any knowledge, and lying about not knowing Madi (Mattie) Comfort. [As we now know, George and Dorothy and Madi were lovers in the 1940s] Then on the following day, we discover she meets and provides George with the details of the interview and the fact the police have the photographs.

While it sounds like George Hodel may have initially taken off for Mexico, we cannot be sure, where he went and how long he was absent. New details will be presented in a later chapter providing updated information on this subject.

Chapter 7

"The Baron"

In February 2009, almost fifty-nine years to the day after the "Baron" is first overheard by detectives speaking in conversation with my father on the DA Hodel-Black Dahlia transcripts, *he has been identified.*

Previously, all we—the LAPD and the DA detectives—knew about the mysterious "Baron" was that he had a German accent. And according to the 1950 transcript, his possible last name was HERRINGER.

Over the years, while I came up with several *possibles*, I was never able to actually correctly identify the Baron. None of the later police reports in my possession ever even showed an attempt at trying to learn his identity.

Then on February 9, 2009, I received the following e-mail from Jil Anderson, a genealogist/researcher, who succeeded where the rest of us had failed. Here is her original verbatim e-mail:

Dear Steve,

After having read all of your website, I forgot to mention that I think I may have discovered the identity of "Baron Herringer", not that it will make any difference, but thought you might be interested to know what popped up on a genealogy website. (I have frequently done "random acts of genealogical kindness" for people searching their ancestry; and likewise, people have helped me with discovering my own family tree.)

Maybe you already know about him, but your intriguing statement that no one knew who he was, made me wonder if I could locate him in the genealogical databases. Since he was German, and I know that families wanting to express nobility frequently use the name "von" in their names, I looked him up that way. The fact that he was called "Baron" makes me think

140

that was a nickname, leading people to believe him to be of noble heritage. So I have attached some records of one "Ernst Von Harringa" who emigrated from Germany, via Chungking China, to the United States. He applied for naturalization 5 times and wed an American in 1939. (Actually he had changed his name from Ernst Franz Meyer which was his name in Germany.) He was a writer and an art dealer and married a socialite by the name Alene.

Also in a book about Aleister Crowley, titled *The Unknown God*, there is a mention of "Baron Ernst Von Harringa".

I've attached these documents . . . the extent of my suspicion of who "Baron Herringer" was.

Best, Jil Anderson

I spent the next two months conducting a background investigation and further research on the name provided by JIL, and my findings proved her "suspicions" to be correct.

Baron Ernst von Harringa, aka Ernst Meyer was in fact the same man tape-recorded by law-enforcement and overheard in multiple conversations with Dr. George Hodel at the Franklin house in February and March 1950.

Who was "Baron" Ernst Von Harringa?—A Timeline

Here is what my follow-up research to Jil Anderson's identification has produced so far:

Born Ernst Franz Meyer in Netteln, Germany on March 4, 1899.

Fought as a soldier in WW I, during the Second Reich (Weimar Republic 1919-1933)

Worked as a "banker" in Chungking, China

Meyer sailed from Shanghai, China to San Francisco on the vessel *Taiyo Maru* and entered the US on August 21, 1925

On November 4, 1931, Von Harringa was arrested by LAPD for "attempted extortion." The victim was Dr. H. Clifford Loos and his former wife, Mrs. Anita

Johnson. The charges alleged that "Von Harringa" demanded $5,000.00 from Dr. Loos and Mrs. Johnson under threats of defaming their character in published articles." Baron Harringa was found guilty of the charges, but then, the case was later overturned on appeal.

[Dr. Clifford Loos was the older brother to then popular Hollywood author/screenwriter Anita Loos. Dr. Loos with his partner, Dr. Donald E. Ross, founded the Ross-Loos Medical Group in Los Angeles in 1929.]

Ernst von Harringa, 1931 Extortion Arrest

On December 11, 1932, "The Baron" wrote a lengthy article for the *LA Times*, entitled, "I FOUGHT AMERICANS—But, they healed my hate."

His introduction began, "My first contact with them was on the battlefields, and they were such good sports I decided to become an American citizen myself—which I've just done." [His entire article was a blatant attempt to help him gain citizenship, which was denied.]

On April 2, 1933, "The Baron" wrote a second lengthy article which was also published in the *LA Times* entitled, "I WAS A BANKER IN CHINA." The introduction began, "Far in the interior, near the Tibetan border, I ran into strange customs-forty-course banquets, ninety kinds of currency, bandits who robbed one politely...and business methods, which will make you smile."

Baron von Harringa *Los Angeles Times* articles 1932-1933

He legally changed his name to "Ernst Von Harringa" and on a 1933 "Declaration of Intention" the document lists his physical description as: Male, White, age 34, 5'10", 175, blonde hair, blue eyes, occupation:"Writer"— Residence, 947 Parkview St., Los Angeles, California. Marital Status: Single.

In 1935, Los Angeles artist, Robert McIntosh created a portrait of Ernst Von Harringa entitled, "The German Art Dealer." [At the time I was conducting my background investigation on Baron Harringa, the oil painting was on display at the Trigg Ison Art Gallery in West Hollywood with an asking price of $30,000].

In 1937, Baron von Harringa opened his art gallery in the posh OVIATT BUILDING and received a write-up and opening announcement in the *Los Angeles Times* from then art critic, Arthur Millier, who had this to say about Baron Harringa's gallery:

Los Angeles Times, May 9, 1939

NEW GALLERY

Good clothes and good pictures consort well together. So we have the Oviatt Galleries, just opened by Ernst v. Harringa in the well-known clothier's establishment downtown.

Some excellent pictures by older masters are in this first showing, among them two exceptionally fine "Scenes Galeantes" by Pater of eighteenth century France, a very pure "Madonna," attributed to Luis de Morales, the great sixteenth century Spanish religious painter; a fine anonymous Flemish "Bearing of the Cross," done about 1820; Joseph Highmore's, "Portrait of a Gentleman," better than many an alleged Gainsborough; an exquisite small circular river scene by Herman Saftleven, pupil of Van Goyen, a portrait by Rembrandt's pupil, Levecque, and canvases by Gillis van Tilborch, Charles Le beran, Berne-Bellecour, Charles Hoguet and an anonymous Spanish painter of "St. Francis." The choice of works shown inspires confidence in the future of this enterprise.

The Oviatt Building, 617 South Olive Street, is still standing and is a striking art-deco built in 1928, and remains one of LA's finest architectural structures. The clothier with its clock-tower restaurant was home to Hollywood's rich and famous. The building and Baron Harringa's art gallery was less than one block south of the Biltmore Hotel and just three blocks from Dr. George Hill Hodel's then private medical practice at Seventh and Flower Street.

Here is how the *Art Deco Society* described the OVIATT building for a 2008 lecture and film screening:

Through lecture and film screening, here is the untold story of downtown Los Angeles' first Art Deco jewel: the 1928 Oviatt Building and its opulent penthouse. Virtually a second home to Clark Gable, Errol Flynn and other male stars of Hollywood's Golden Age; the Oviatt Building housed L.A.'s finest haberdashery and catered to filmdom's titans. For eight decades, its glamorous and controversial history has been shrouded in mystery and clouded by misinformation...until now. Full of long-lost archival images and long-forgotten events, this myth-busting documentary spans more than a century and interviews the men and women who shaped the Oviatt Building's turbulent history.

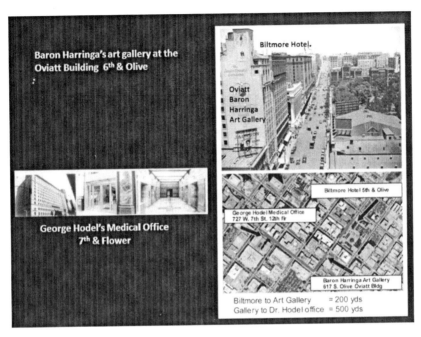

On a 1939 petition for naturalization, Von Harringa provided additional information: a residence address listed as, 946 Arapahoe Street, Los Angeles and occupation as "Art Dealer."

He claimed he was married to Alene von Harringa on January 14, 1939 in Calabasas, California, declaring his wife to be a US citizen with a birth date of May 12, 1912. He listed her residence address as, "3747 ½ W. 27th St., Los Angeles." Additional documents indicated Harringa had previously requested, but was denied, citizenship in 1931.

In November 1952, Harringa reportedly left the US "For a job building dams in India."

Baron Harringa and W.T. Smith—Church of Thelema Connections

In my further search for information on Baron Harringa, I found very little personal information available but did find some important insights in the book mentioned by Jil Anderson in her email, *The Unknown God: W.T. Smith and the Thelemites (Teitan Press, November 2003)* written by Martin P. Starr.

An excerpt from the publisher's description of the book reads:

> The first documentary study of Aleister Crowley's contemporary followers in North America, told through the life of their de facto leader, Wilfred Talbot Smith (1885-1957). ...To promulgate the Crowleyan teachings, in 1934 Smith incorporated his own "Church of Thelema"—known to Los Angeles newspaper readers as the "Purple Cult." The following year he initiated OTO activity in Los Angeles which attracted its own cast of occult characters.

It turns out that Wilfred Talbot Smith and Baron von Harringa, according to author/researcher Martin Starr, were close friends in Los Angeles. Mr. Starr in his book included some brief but quite remarkable insights into Ernst von Harringa and his personality. I quote from the excerpted pages of Starr's book:

The Unknown God, page 322-323:

> In the hiatus, Smith had befriended Baron Ernst von Harringa (b.1899), a naturalized German art dealer and importer who worked as the director of the Oviatt Galleries in Los Angeles. Von Harringa had studied in Count Hermann Keyserling's "School of Wisdom" which had been founded in Darmstadt, Germany in 1920; he also claimed the passing acquaintance of Theodor Reuss. However, he knew nothing of Crowley's work prior to his friendship with Smith. The Baron was a lover of Chinese art and bestowed many prize objects of virtu on Smith and Helen. Calling on his training as a cabinetmaker, he had Smith construct replicas of Asian furniture for sale in his gallery. Helen cheerfully waited on her two "big boys" as they spent long hours drinking tea and sharing their ideas. Given von Harringa's level of understanding, Smith considered him the equivalent of an Exempt Adept; Jane, too, was impressed by his person, thinking him a second Crowley, but changed her mind after she read several analyses of the Baron's horoscope, including one prepared by Phyllis Seckler. Von Harringa was an extreme individualist and he felt that any effort for humanity was a waste, in view of the catastrophe that he believed was just around the corner. ...

Smith felt himself loved and understood by von Harringa, who left California in November 1952 for a job building dams in India and never saw his friend alive again. Helen and Smith kept up a regular correspondence with the Baron, and frequently lamented his absence from their lives. To his intellectual soulmate Smith revealed his thoughts on politics, gender roles and the future of humanity, sometimes all rolled into the same paragraph:

> We are headed for a radical social change; which among other things, will ultimate in the ladies fulfilling the function nature (not man) adapted them to better grace, and less intrusion into spheres of activity they are so unsuited to occupy. Men will find them at hand when they are needed and in the interim enjoy tranquility and peace, or the company of an intellectual, wise, and understanding companion. (Smith to Ernst von Harringa, June 28, 1954, WTS Papers.)

What was the George Hodel—Ernst von Harringa Connection?

With the identification of "The Baron," it seems we have created as many questions as we have found answers, which is frequently the case.

Did George Hodel and Ernst von Harringa's friendship in LA trace back to the Baron's arrival in the mid-twenties? Probably.

Did Ernst Harringa as a high-profile art-dealer know and possibly even represent George Hodel's close friend, artist Fred Sexton? Very likely. At the very least, they must have known each other—perhaps much more?

Was Baron Harringa associated with many or most of the men and women of the LA art world, listed in Mark Nelson and Sarah Hudson Bayliss's book, *Exquisite Corpse: Surrealism and The Black Dahlia Murder* with its extensive listings and map: *Los Angeles 1935-1950, A Web of Connections.*

We have established that Baron Harringa and George Hodel's LA offices were within three blocks of each other, and, in their chosen professions as art dealer and physician, both socialized with the rich and famous, as well as city politicians and men in power.

147

It is obvious that the two men were kindred spirits. Both had a love of art and enjoyed intellectually stimulating conversation. Both shared a burning desire to travel and had been to many of the same locals in China, including Chungking and Shanghai. Both were extremely eccentric, and, from what we know from the bugging tapes, were politically connected and at the very least were involved in payoffs to law enforcement, as well as being accomplices together in the assault or possible murder of a female victim at the Franklin house. "We're just a couple of smart boys. Don't confess ever."

What other crimes had the two men committed? It is likely we will never know. But now, thanks to JIL ANDERSON's efforts, we do know "The Baron's" identity and have gained some fairly good insights into his background.

DA Lt. Jemison's Response

A TAPE RECORDED MURDER?

Within days of recording the February 18, 1950 conversation between George Hodel and "The Baron," Lt. Jemison ordered his men into action.

While we do not know the full extent of what was done, I did find three separate investigative documents in the DA file that relate directly to the February 18 Hodel-Harringa conversations. And that confirmed that detectives definitely suspected a murder may well have occurred.

The first document prepared by DA investigator James McGrath and submitted to his direct supervisor, showed that investigative attempts were immediately initiated to determine if potential witnesses could substantiate any signs of digging and or graves in the Franklin house basement.

As evidenced in the report, apparently a day or two after the February 18 assault, George Hodel called a plumber to the residence to unclog a plugged drain. McGrath located the plumber [Mr. Stokes, an employee of Sonntag Co. 5156 Hollywood Boulevard] and *questioned him as to whether he had seen any evidence of fresh digging or anything unusual in the basement.*

The plumber responded that he had been in the basement, unclogged the drain, but really hadn't looked or paid any attention other than to simply perform his work. While McGrath wrote both of these reports in late March 1950, the investigations obviously occurred in the days following the suspected "foul play." McGrath's surveillance log is dated February 23.

[Note: For those thinking "forensics" in 2002, prior to the publication of BDA, during major renovations of the Franklin house, much of the basement area was cemented over and a home office was constructed. It remains highly doubtful that any trace evidence from sixty years past would still be accessible.]

Detective McGrath's "Elizabeth Short Murder Report" is reproduced below and is a scan of the original:

DA investigator James McGrath follow-up report March 24, 1950

30-1266   James F. McGrath   March 24, 1950

Elizabeth Short   Murder

Unknown

I contacted the H. A. Sonntag Company, 5156 Hollywood Blvd., a plumbing organization, and spoke to Mr. Francis W. Stokes, who is the manager of the firm. This person was questioned as to whether or not he was one of the parties who did plumbing work last week for Dr. George Hodel, 5121 Franklin Avenue, or if he was familiar with the work done. He stated that he was one of the men who entered the basement and opened up a clogged drain. Upon further questioning, he stated that he did not notice any fresh diggings in the basement, or anything of an unusual nature, however, he did assert that at the time he was not looking for any fresh earth. Investigation has revealed that over the last two years this plumbing firm has done quite a bit of work for this subject. Records were checked and it was found that numerous calls were made to the suspect's residence in the past. Either Dr. Hodel or his wife, Dorothy, had signed the work slips but for the following exceptions: on February 4, 1947, a person by the name of L. S. Burgeon signed the work slip; on April 25, 1947, one Floyd C. Hagan signed the work slip; March 25, 1948, it was signed by Mrs. E. M. Walker; on April 20, 1948, a Katherine Dawn signed the slip, and on May 18, 1948, a Connie Coahram, or Cochram, signed the work order. No further information was obtained from this informant. He was requested by the undersigned not to discuss this visit with him, and the purpose of it, with the suspect, Dr. Hodel.

_____
James F. McGrath

The second DA document informs us that in addition to the ongoing electronic bugging of the Franklin house, just four days after the Hodel/Harringa admissions, Lt. Jemison ordered that a physical surveillance be placed on Dr. George Hodel.

Detective James McGrath, partnered with Walter Morgan, took up the surveillance. Here is their original two-page typed report of a vehicle surveillance they conducted on George and Dorothy Hodel on February 23, 1950:

DA Investigators McGrath & Morgan Physical Surveillance Report of Dr. George Hodel 3.27.1950

30-1266   REPORT BY James F. McGrath   DATE March 27,1950

Elizabeth Short   Murder

Unknown

Information regarding Dr. George Hodel, 5121 Franklin Avenue, Hollywood, California.

February 23, 1950, in company with investigator Walter Morgan of this office, I placed the subject under surveillance. The following is a route of his actions of this date:

12:00 noon	I took position of surveillance in vicinity of house; no further action until 3:05 P.M.
3:05 P.M.	A Packard car, bearing license number 3N 2948, arrived at the house. This car was driven by a man whose description is as follows: male Caucasian, 42 to 46 years of age, 5'7", 180 lbs., stocky build, wearing a dark blue hat, gray shirt, dark blue pants. These license plates belong to a 1936 Packard coupe registered to W. G. Holland, 1221½ West 1st Street, Los Angeles; legal owner, John F. Casey, mother's address, 1036 South Figueroa Street, Los Angeles.
3:15 P.M.	Subject came out of his residence, and accompanied by this man, drove this car to the vicinity of Western and Franklin, where they parked the car and both seemed to enter into a general discussion about the car, walking around it and looking it over as if the subject was contemplating buying it. They then left and drove south on Western, where they parked between 6th Street and Wilshire Blvd. on the west side of Western. They remained in the car approximately 15 minutes talking.
3:55 P.M.	They left this location and drove to the corner of 3rd and Union, where subject let the other man out. This other man walked to the Taxi Driver's Social Club, located at 3rd and Union.
4:07 P.M.	Subject drove alone to Hollywood and Sycamore Streets, arriving at 4:30 P.M. Sitting on a bench at this corner was subject's ex-wife,

151

Dorothy Hodel. She got in the car, and
they parked same on Sycamore Street just
north of Hollywood Blvd., where both of
them got out of the car, proceeded to the
rear of the house, and looked at an old
Stutz automobile. They then both entered
the car and drove to Wilshire and La Cienega
Blvd. in Beverly Hills, where subject entered
the Orient Art Galleries.

4:55 P.M.   Subject left the art galleries, entered car
and drove to the Frank Perl's Art Galleries,
arriving at 5:20 P.M. These art galleries
are located on Camden Drive north of Wilshire
in Beverly Hills. Subject and his wife remained in this art gallery until approximately
5:35 P.M., when they both left. With subject
driving, they proceeded in a westerly direction
on Wilshire Blvd. Agents then dropped surveillance, inasmuch as subject was proceeding
to the vicinity of his ex-wife's residence in
Santa Monica, and because of the fact that
this surveillance was instituted because of
information received that subject was contem-
plating getting $1,000.00 on this date, which
we now have reason to believe was from the
sale of paintings at these art galleries.

James F. McGrath

Author prepared diagram showing route and stops of February 23, 1950
surveillance by Investigators McGrath & Morgan

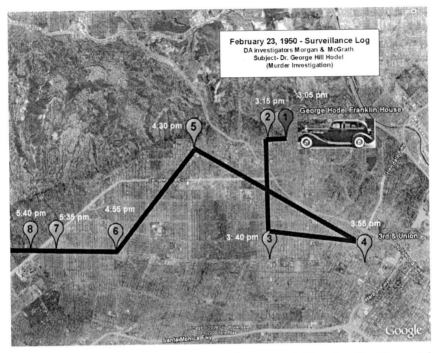

Investigators McGrath and Morgan tail George and Dorothy Hodel to eight
separate destinations

1. 5121 Franklin Avenue, George Hodel's Franklin house residence

2. Western and Franklin Avenue

3. Western and Sixth Street

4. Third Street and Union

5. Hollywood Boulevard and Sycamore Avenue

6. Wilshire and La Cienega Boulevard

7. Wilshire and Camden Drive

8. Wilshire and Beverly Glen [terminated vehicle surveillance at 5:40 p.m.]

The third Hodel-Harringa related document is written in Lt. Jemison's own hand. They are his personal notes and list his "To Do's" relating to George Hodel.

Jemison's notes are dated March 2, 1950 and relate to the need to interview various friends and acquaintances of George Hodel.

Number 4 "To Do" on that list is clearly the result of the Hodel-Harringa conversations and confessions.

Here we see that Lt. Jemison, now obviously convinced that George Hodel killed his personal secretary, Ruth Spaulding, had decided to reopen the original Spaulding death investigation and REINTERVIEW ALL THE WITNESSES.

Lt. Jemison's note to himself reads:

"3/2/50 Interview-

...

4. –all witnesses In re: Ruth's death–Secretary to Hodel."

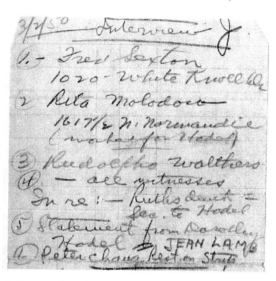

March 2, 1950 handwritten notes of DA Lt. Frank Jemison

A Personal Meeting with Baron von Harringa

In mid-January 2010, I personally met and shook hands with Baron von Harringa.

Baron von Harringa (his given name) is the grandson of Ernst von Harringa. Baron is a handsome young man of just eighteen-years. He too was looking for answers.

We met at one of my favorite breakfast spots, Art's Deli, in Studio City. Both of us were there with the same hope—Baron wanting to learn more about his mysterious grandfather and I wanting to discover additional background on my father's old friend, confidant, and possible *accomplice to murder!*

Our talk lasted nearly two hours, but unfortunately provided little new "hard" information for either of us. Here is what I learned from the grandson:

1. Von Harringa family rumors have it that his grandfather, Ernst von Harringa, aka Ernst Meyer, may have been related to nobility in Germany, but nothing to support the information and no actual names.

2. Ernst von Harringa apparently returned to the US (possibly from India) in the mid-1950s and supposedly died in Los Angeles circa 1960. [I have yet to find a death certificate or obituary as documentation.]

3. He [the grandson] met his grandmother, Alene Valla Von Harringa, several times before she died in 2001 and he had heard that her family (Valla) had owned large land parcels in Orange County in the early days, possibly at the turn of the century.

4. Baron gave me the following photograph of his grandfather, believed taken sometime in the 1940s or possibly early 50s?

Baron Ernst von Harringa circa 1949
[Courtesy of grandson, Baron von Harringa]

Chapter 8

"Back again at George's after two weeks away. ... It is acutely dangerous for the children to be here. There is a growing threat of no control and physical violence..."

Excerpt from Letter No. 6 from Dorothy to John, mailed from Franklin house, 1950

The following highly personal letters were written by my mother, Dorothy Huston Hodel, to her ex-husband, film director John Huston.

The letters span nearly a decade of time, beginning in 1948 and continuing through 1957.

All are highly personal and accurately inform us in real time of the tremendous stresses, both psychological and financial, that our mother was under BEFORE and AFTER our father's arrest for incest.

The letters shine new light into a very dark period of Dorothy's life where we learn that she was attempting to be the sole family breadwinner, as well as a full-time mother, raising three young boys aged 6, 7, and 9.

I am going to let my mother's own words, written in confidence to John, recreate what can only be described as her personal horrors. Her letters capture the very real fear and terror she was experiencing when her ex-husband, our father, George Hodel, was about to harm both her and us!

The first letter to John [April 1948] began a little over a year after the Black Dahlia murder and the tension builds up to and through our father's 1949 LAPD arrest for child molestation and incest, where, according to Mother, he was becoming increasingly unhinged and dangerous. The peak of her personal terror came in the spring and summer of 1950, just after the DA Surveillance of the Franklin house and as George Hodel was preparing to leave the United States.

The source of my discovery of these letters was pure *happenstance*. I came across them while browsing through the John Huston Files at the *Academy of Motion Pictures Arts and Sciences, Margaret Herrick Library in Beverly Hills, California.* Within those files, I found an index labeled, "Dorothy Huston." I requested that file and found it contained these *original letters* written by my mother to John.

Letter No. 1

2313 Bushrod Lane
Los Angeles 24

April 7, 1948.

Dear John,

This letter really should begin: "Stranger, you ask me why I am so sad..." Its precipitating cause is a check I didn't get. I wrote a radio script dealing with a romantic and lovely <u>Russian</u> princess, which was accepted with a perfunctory "Charming" and has remained in the producer's archives since November. When I timidly asked for a check, he recoiled in horror. In view of the Russian Situation and his job, the script can't be produced. <u>No</u> Russian, even one long dead, can be permitted on the air in a glamorous light. And so, so close is the margin on which the babes and I exist, no food, no rent paid, George hasn't given us any alimony for months, and in view of his mental difficulties, I don't want to be unpleasant. I'm really having a tough time, since both the boys and earning a living are a full time job. There aren't enough hours. So many things take time: like listening to a neighbor elucidate Technocracy, so he'll be won over and let Mike ride his pony. Something's always cropping up! We're very happy, and life is good; difficult, but good.

I've got eight radio scripts assigned, but I can't get them out fast enough, or get paid for them fast enough to meet this emergency. Listen...

Two boys in bed with fever and virus x.

Third slightly lacerated from aforementioned pony.

Mother out of hospital after major operation, with us,

Needing medicine and nursing.

No rent paid.

No electric bill paid.

No grocery bill paid.

No bills paid.

No bank balance.

I'll be forty two next week

STRANGER, YOU ASK ME WHY I AM SO SAD.

If you could loan me, and I mean loan, about five hundred dollars (or even five!) I could repay it within six months. This epidemic can't last forever. I finished a script by working all night last night, rushed it by messenger to the producer today, only to discover I can't get paid for it for at least three weeks. Gandhi could have weathered it, but not the boys! I did a washing this morning, cooked, cleaned, took three temperatures, all too high, placed a cool hand of three fevered brows in rapid succession, and ironed until eleven tonight. If this letter sounds flippant or gay, it's only because I'm frightened. I've done everything I could, and it isn't enough

If you're able to help, please do.

Dorothy

Author Notes-

Based on the return address, this letter indicates we are living in a rental several miles north of Sunset Boulevard in Beverly Glen Canyon. The home was called, "ROBBER'S ROOST." Immediately behind the house, there were some high caves set into the mountain. According to legend, these caves were used as a hideout for *Banditos* at the turn of the century. Situated as they were, literally, in our own backyard, we three brothers would climb up and into them to hangout and "make our plans."

George and Dorothy were separated in 1944 and formally divorced in 1945.

In this April 1948 letter, Mother made reference to our father's "mental difficulties," a full eighteen months in advance of his October 1949 arrest for incest and child molestation, *which informs us that they were preexisting and ongoing.*

"Mother" was Dorothy Harvey, our maternal grandmother, who in 1948 would have been in her late sixties.

Letter No. 2

5121 Franklin Ave
Los Angeles 27
October 24, 1949

Dear John,

I'm sending you this because I think it is the kind of story you would like. Please let me know how you like it. It is a pattern that particularly fascinates me: one that Bierce used first, and later Conrad Aiken used in a beautiful tale called "Mr. Arcularis." In your opinion is it too slight for a motion picture?

I'm working at General Service Studios with Rowland Brown.
Call me there if you can – GR 3111- or at home OL 3476.

Dorothy

Author Notes:

While there is no mention about George Hodel in this letter, he had been arrested for incest/child molestation on October 6, just eighteen days prior.

"Bierce" is Ambrose "Bitter" Bierce, one of Mother's longstanding HEROES. [She wrote a screen or radio play about the journalist's mysterious disappearance called, *"Occurrence at an Unknown Bridge."*

As mentioned previously, Mother was having an ongoing affair with film director Rowland Brown. And here we learn that Rowland has hired her to work/write at his office.

Letter No. 3

410 Santa Monica Pier
Santa Monica, Calif.
February 2, 1950

Dear John:

Thank you very much for the needed $$$$. They averted famine and the sheriff. I feel a certain hesitancy about calling you at home and there are two matters to ask you about.

I saw George's attorney yesterday. He thinks it will be about six months before the house and antiques can be sold and a trust fund set up. George has sent out about a hundred letters to find work in outlying parts of the world. My problem is to keep the children alive for the next few months. As I told you I have various scripts out and something may happen at any time. It's the uncertainty!

Could you help to keep the children going until affairs straighten out? $200 a month will do it. I have no claim on your generosity and this is a difficult letter to write. I have lived so close to terror and disaster; and it is impossible to conceal this entirely from the children.

I went to an employment agency down here and got some work—night work at a hotel for a couple of nights. But I can't do that and take care of the children too. The certainty of a sum of money on the first of the month would make it possible to plan and budget and work out a way of life. I'm sure I can repay it soon. But if you feel hesitancy about doing it, and cannot for any reason, please say no.

The second thing whether or not Horizon Pictures is interested in acquiring outside money for making pictures. There are Philippino [sic] business interests (friends of George) who want to put money ($250,000 up to a million) in a motion picture. They don't want any voice in the making of it; they would like a part to be done in the Philippines.

They want an Academy award director; they care less about name actors. John Ford was going to do it, but his recent removal to Republic gives him no time for a year to do anything outside, and they want to act sooner. If this interests you, why don't you call George at Normandy 2-7464.

They've given him full power to act; and he doesn't know anything about pictures. It might be a chance to do something really good – Hardy's Return of the Native? If it's not the sort of thing you care about, maybe you could suggest someone?

Please let me hear from you. I've started work on the cowboy Hamlet. Do you honestly think it might get a production?

Dorothy

Author Notes

We see that this was written on February 2, 1950 from the apartment on Santa Monica Pier. Two weeks later, the DA/LAPD secretly installed the microphones at the Franklin house and began recording George Hodel's conversations. Lt. Jemison will interview Dorothy at this address in March.

The Filipino "money connections" could well be Hortensia Laguda, who, in two years, would become George's wife. Hortensia met my father after responding to a personal advertisement he had placed in the *Saturday Review Literature* magazine requesting to correspond with "an Oriental woman of sensitive tastes." In 1949, Hortensia, who was taking some classes in New York, responded to the ad and followed up with a visit to George at the Franklin house where she met George, Dorothy, and Tamar, and attended several social parties.

Letter No. 4

410 Santa Monica Pier
Santa Monica, Calif
June 13, 1950

Dear John,

I have the impression that you are very busy and it is difficult for you to get away. It might be a short cut to put down a plan:

1. I could start working on a treatment of THE MYSTERIOUS STRANGER.

2. I could submit one-page suggestions for stories. I read enormously and have run across a great deal of material: To do SERENA BLANDISH as a musical. MGM owns the rights. I think it would be better than GENTLEMEN PREFER BLONDES.
    To do a picture like QUARTET: one whose subject matter concerns children. The beautiful mood story of Conrad Aiken's SILENT SNOW...FALLING SNOW together with MY OLD MAN of Hemingway's, and perhaps one other. The Jose Allonada story.

3. I could finish a novel I have 100 page start on. It isn't one you have seen. It is experimental and candor compels me to admit it has more in common with New Directions than with Bessie Smith. Still if you would care to gamble on the royalties....

I'm afraid you were right about George...several jobs were offered and then withdrawn when they found out about the recent trial. He will work out something, but right now I feel as though we were walking a tightrope. Kelvin is ill (aftermath of mumps, he almost had encephalitis) and I don't even have carfare to take him to the doctor's. I literally don't know where the children's next meal is coming from. It takes $250 to cover the monthly necessities. I don't know if you can afford to gamble that much on my accomplishing anything; I imagine your responsibilities are heavy. Please let me know what you want me to do, what would be most useful for your purposes. It is a situation that calls for the Marines!

Why don't you send Pedro down to stay with us for a week or two when school is out?

Dorothy

Letter No. 5—The Telegram

JOHN HUSTON - MGM AUG 4, 1950 9:49 A.M.

YOUR HUNCH ABOUT GEORGE TRUE CAN YOU HELP CHILDREN AND ME GET OUT OF HIS HOUSE TODAY IF POSSIBLE OLYMPIA 3476

DOROTHY

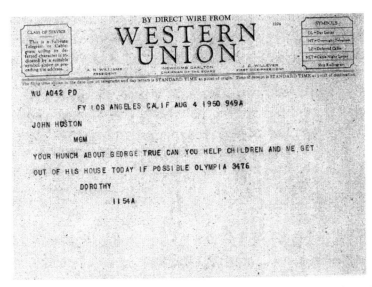

Copy of original Telegram sent by Dorothy from Franklin house to John at MGM on August 4, 1950

Author Notes:

It doesn't get any more ominous sounding than this. We can only guess at John's "hunch about George." Had he heard that George was the Black Dahlia killer? Another murder? Whatever it was, it is clear that Mother was confirming that John was correct and believed that she, and we, her three sons, were in IMMINENT DANGER and must immediately flee the house for our safety. [More information on what John may have known will be presented at the end of this chapter.]

Letter No. 6

5121 Franklin Ave
Los Angeles 27
August 23, 1950

Dear John:

Back at George's again, after two weeks away – nothing to eat, nowhere to go. It is acutely dangerous for the children to be here. There is danger from two sources: George (I won't go into that one! – except to say there is a growing threat of no-control and physical violence;) the second source is from neighborhood hostility towards everyone connected with George's house, which centers on the children because they are the only ones who have contact with the neighbors. I have had to keep them entirely indoors after one woman heaped the most unspeakable abuse on them because they were their father's children! The boys were completely bewildered, because they know nothing of the trial at all. They shouldn't know anything about a world like that.

The children and I went to Palm Springs Sunday. (Steve was looking for a horned toad and a mirage. I was looking for a house, in which to live a less frenzied future – (possibly a mirage, too!) I found one, built in the modern charming desert fashion – 4 bedrms, 2 baths, and large grounds for $85 a month, furnished....by the year. Palm Springs is probably as safe a place to be as any if people start exploding bombs— (Duncan has just been inducted, by the way) and anyhow I love the desert, and it's a fine place for the children...(but there were no horned toads)!...bombs or no bombs, it gives them room to expand and a horizon to see. The schools there are excellent.

I would have to take it right away – this weekend, because rents there start soaring, and they won't hold it longer. They could probably get 200 for it during the season. It would require 170 dollars for 2 mos rent on the year's lease, and something for utility deposits. George will give me 100 on Sept 5, and 200 every month hereafter, he says. He is working at Ross-Loos clinic. If you could (as Mark suggested) put me on your payroll for 100 a month starting Oct (and I will work on Mysterious Stranger) –I think I can just make it.

I have 6 prospects of jobs – mostly television; they can be worked out there with occasional commuting... the Greyhound bus is a block from the house.

So all our future depends on you, and if you can send enough now to get in the house – 200 for that and about 50 more for groceries and moving. And a hundred a month after, which I will do my best to earn.

Darling, I know you have immense responsibilities. I hate piling mine on top of you. But there is no one else I can go to; and the danger to the children is very real. I'll keep my fingers crossed and wait to hear from you.

Dorothy
Olympia 3476

Author's Notes:

A couple of new points are contained in Mother's letter of August 23rd.
The first is that *George Hodel is back in town* and has taken a temporary
job with ROSS-LOOS clinic. Perhaps his presence was necessary for the
sale of the Franklin House. [We know that he will be gone in six to eight
weeks and relocate to the Territory of Hawaii, where he has accepted a
professorship at the *University of Hawaii* and will begin teaching a course
in Abnormal Child Psychology, as well as counseling the criminally insane
in the prisons.]

Secondly, are the comments regarding the neighbors coming down hard on
us three boys for father's actions? While I have no memory of this, I do
recall that my brother, Kelvin and I at about this time, lit an empty
cardboard egg carton on fire and threw it into the next door neighbor's
garage. The garage caught fire requiring the fire department to respond
and put it out. There was minimal damage to the residence structure. In
later years, when I asked Mother why we did that, she responded that we
claimed, "We simply wanted to see the fire trucks roll," which made very
little sense. Based on what was revealed in these letters, I have to believe
our motive was to get even with our neighbors for "the bad things they said
about our father." [I guess I can clear my conscience on this now, since
there is only a three-year statute of limitations for committing arson.]

John must have "come through again with the money" as mother did rent the
house and we moved to Palm Springs that fall. [Actually, Rancho Mirage, where
we lived very close to Rowland Brown and his wife, and their son, Steven.]

Duncan is my older half-brother, born to Emilia and George Hodel in 1928.

Again, Mother made clear references to the threat of physical danger to her
and to us from Father. As we know from earlier chapters, Mother did
suffer physical violence from George. I suspect quite a lot!

While the remaining series of letters have no direct bearing on my
investigation, I am going to include them here due to their historical value and
interest to film buffs, historians, and the general reading public. [I must
confess a second motive, which is to put on display the absolute elegance of my
mother's intellect and her remarkable ability to communicate.]

Letter No. 7

754 Locust St.
Pasadena, California
June 10, 1954

Dear John,

I have a wonderful – although startling suggestion to make. Let's do Ulysses. You've told me you think I have talent, and you'd like me to write something, and I think you mean it sincerely. Who except you and I could do such a picture? I am sure we are the only two people in the world who have ever read it through twice <u>aloud</u>. If it came off it would be the greatest picture ever made. The freshness and vitality of the book and of the language, the panorama of Dublin from dawn through the night; the changes of style in story-telling from girly-girly Gertie on the beach to the drunken dreamlike sequence of the whores—there has never been a picture like it. Ulysses remains for me after countless readings the most exciting and living book ever written.

Please let me try! I should like to begin right away. I am still working in the real estate office, because I can't find a job that pays more. Of course it would be ideal if you could keep me on salary while I wrote the picture. But if that isn't feasible I could work on it nights. George isn't sending me anything, so all I have is my salary, and I do loath the work. I am revoltingly good at it. Please let me know right away!

The boys are getting very grown-up. They are really wonderful. I am trying to model them on you, because you remain the man in the whole world I most admire, probably because you caught me young and made so deep an impression upon my malleable nature! I came upon a photograph of you as a child—do you remember that very beautiful one your mother wrote a verse on? Twice I have carried it to the post office to send to you thinking you would probably like to have it, and then brought it back home because I didn't want to part with it. It should belong to your children, I suppose. Perhaps I can have it copied.

Let me know right away about Ulysses. If you think it is not feasible, I would also like to do Mr. Gilhooley. But Ulysses is all I can think about at the moment!

Love,

Dorothy

Letter No. 8

754 Locust St.
Pasadena, Calif
November 9, 1954

Dear John,

An English poet and bullfighter wrote once a description of our bullfighter, Manolete:

"Andalusian art reach the summit of its expression in the style of the bullfighter Manolete. He was ornate yet severe like Seneca. He was called 'the tower of Cordoba'. He personified opposite extremes at one and the same moment contrasting, in one being the austerity, coldness and hardness of a statue with the softness and warmth of a flower: for while his brain, his muscles and his sword were dedicated to the clear and icy geometry of death, yet with his crimson cape and his scarlet mulete he sculptured to the imagination of the full-blown corollas of magnolias, roses, and camellias."

This sums up; it seems to me, the whole essence of what we should try to do in the picture. Therefore, your suggestion of using the rigid pattern of the bullfight as frame for the story, and keeping it within the confines of the ancient stole of La Maestranza is exactly right. The story is a duel between Life and Death enacted almost as a ritual dance between the superb overflowing vitality of the matador and the cold shadow of Absence, while each augments and enhances the stature and mystery of the other. A towering spiral—Lorca's "spiral of whiteness" in which the two forces contend in a sort of ecstasy. I hope this doesn't sound too high flown or too abstract. I have to think this way! If I get clear sure feeling of the bones of the story, in this case the bullfight, then I get a fine feeling of freedom in describing the flesh on the bones, the whole glorious exhuberance [sic] and sound and smell of life and its great careless profusion thrown into relief by the Shadow.

So now I am trying to translate all this into words and scenes. I confess to stage fright since I want this to be so very good, and it will inevitably fall way short. I hope you will not be disappointed in it. It is good to be working at writing again. The papers here say Ferrer is planning to direct and act in Matador with Aubrey [sic] Hepburn. Does this affect anything? Hope not!

I'm working hard and hope to send you some scenes soon.

Love,

Dorothy

(The children send love and want to know how soon can they see Moby Dick? It is their most favorite story.)

Letter No. 9

754 Locust St.

Pasadena

Jan 10, 1955

Dearest John,

You will never know what your Christmas gift meant to the children. It arrived at the psychological moment on Christmas Eve. It was the only gift they received, except the things I gave them, so it had a special and unexpected magic about it. It set in motion one event....It seems that Kelvin, who is 12, has been harboring a passion for paint. As the messenger left the door, Kelvin was demanding $33.33 immediately! (He waived the 1/3 cent). He made a beeline for the art store 2 blocks away, and came back loaded down with easel and paints. He set up the easel and hasn't stopped painting since. I am sending you his first efforts. His mind is made up. He is merely marking time until I (who in his eyes can accomplish any miracle) make the arrangements to go to Paris. His teachers are a somewhat paint smeared copy of Goya reproductions, and a very smeared copy of Picasso reproductions. I got them the Metropolitan Museum reproductions—have you seen them? –but he ignores all other painters. He is a gifted child, but what direction he will go needs time to see.

He is now acting out the story he told me when he was three: "Blood and brains were going for a walk and they met a skeleton. Blood said, "Can I have a ride on you?" Brain said, "Let me ride on top!" The skeleton said, "All right!" "But it was the WRONG BODY!" –This beautiful little parable, which he has forgotten he told me, is now being demonstrated. Whether painting is his particular skeleton I don't know. I think all one can do is to praise and admire and wait. The paintings are his way of thanking you.

Too bad about MATADOR – but we'll find something better. Paul wishes to talk to me about BRIDGE OF SAN LUIS REY. We've been delayed getting together. First he had flu, and then the children in pitiless succession for the last two weeks. When a germ reaches our house, it ceases to be a sickness and becomes an epidemic! I am enclosing a clipping I found. What about this—as a hot jazz musical? It is your St Louis.

I'd love to have an indication of what you'd like me to do. I'm dying to get started earning this money you are giving me!

All my love and the childrens.
Dorothy

I found the perfect story for you: BRIDGE OVER THE RIVER KWEI. [Sic] Got terribly excited and wrote the publisher about the rights. Found they were already sold to guess who?—Sam Spiegel! Have you a way—guile or force—to get it from him?

[Author Note: Mother's intuition was spot on! Sam Spiegel produced the film and it premiered in Los Angeles in December 1957. It was a huge hit, winning seven Academy Awards (Oscars).]

Letter No. 10

754 Locust
Pasadena

May 7, 1955

Dear John,

I read in the paper yesterday that Bogeaus has signed Barbara Stanwyck to do THE BRIDGE OF SAN LUIS REY and has a cameraman scouting out locations in Lima. So for the second time in the last six months I pulled a page out of the typewriter rolled up a useless bundle of MS and threw it in the deepest drawer of my desk. What rotten luck! – wasted money and wasted time. To interpolate a gentle criticism, that bastard Paul <u>might</u> have checked on ownership. Bogeaus did produce it before.

I feel I still owe you a script for the money you sent me. As you know, it was the desire to write a good script that prompted my letter to you. I'll follow my original hunch and do an original story, probably a book. But it will belong to you. I hate the feeling of all that unearned money. Most of all I want to give a good concrete reason for the completely irrational belief you have always had in my talents! And how important that belief has been to me you will never guess.

I have been thinking about a story of a little boy and his mother, loosely based upon you and your mother and that kind of gay, piratical gallantry she had, and Gram, rooted so solidly in the soil of the country. I saw them, I think, in a way that no one else did; they lived vividly and recreated their lives for me. Their own and that of your great-grandfather, and your grandfather' (you must resemble him a little). I feel a kind of nostalgia for that breed which seems to be dying out; I despise the small cautious people who have taken their place. Their story is one of trains, of constant journeying, of precariousness; of that curious deep-seated love of horses which your mother had – remember the kind of funeral she wanted? It should have the mood of a lazy summer day in a small town, so quiet you can hear the buzzing of flies and the switching of horse's tails, but with a thunderstorm brewing on the edges of the town; never breaking, but just about to. It should be told very simply, with a little of the feeling of Sherwood Anderson, only different. If you come right down to it, it's a story <u>you</u> should write.

Anyhow, thank you for everything, darling. I'm sorry the other things didn't work out. All my love, as always.

Dorothy

Letter No. 11

Courtown House
Kilcock
County Kildare
Ireland

4th June, 1955

Dear Dorothy:

I am ever so sorry, dear, that things turned out the way they did on Matador. However, whatever you read about the *Bridge of San Luis Rey* was inaccurate. The story has not been sold and I think it would be a good idea for you to do a screenplay of it – that is if it is sufficiently attractive to you.

I love the drawings you sent me. The photograph of "The Artist as a Young Man" does everything to explain why you are so proud of him...you might tell him that I am too.

I very much like your idea about the novel, but it would be my suggestion that you do the screenplay first.

I might be paying a fast visit to California during the next few weeks, and when I do I want very much to see you and the boys.

Meanwhile...

All my love,

John

Letter No. 12

1014 Milan St.
South Pasadena
[Nodate]

Dear John,

I am completely at the end of my rope and I don't know what to do—for the first time in my life. I was in the hospital for three days (they suspected cancer, but this I couldn't tell anyone) – The possibilities of that are pretty well eliminated, I think. Steven brought me a letter to the hospital which said we had to be out of our house in three days. That means we should have been out today. I called my employer today and he said since I had used company money ($500) he was going to proceed on embezzlement charges unless it was paid back this week. Of course I left the hospital immediately. Steve gave me the dispossess notice, without notifying my doctor or anything. I seem to fail at everything I attempt. If it were not for the great and generous love of the children, and of you, I would not care to live. But this love obliges me to go on.

I am in such fear about the children I even cabled George asking him if I could send them to him. This is the last thing I want for them, and in any case he will probably politely refuse. What will happen to them? They are so wonderful, and I am so afraid for them. It isn't your problem, but I feel like someone who is drowning. I called Morgan today and explained a little of this, although being in the accountant's office I couldn't say much. If the 500 is returned I can go back to my job (not that I want to) but it is a living. We are homeless, and tomorrow I have called in a second hand man to buy what things we have. I have 25¢ at the moment. I was supposed to be in the hospital for another two weeks, but I have medicines which I think will enable me to go on working. The doctor does not believe there is anything wrong with me except complete physical and nervous exhaustion. It has been a long hard pull for the last twelve years, and I suppose it's finally catching up with me, in my old age. The job plus washing, ironing, cooking and cleaning is hard, but when I'm well I can do it. Don't you think the children are fine? But now, when in some ways they need me the most, I seem to be giving out.

It will only be a few years more that they need me. If only I could be strong just a little longer!

I'm not throwing this problem in your lap. But I would appreciate some advice.

Love,

Dorothy

Author Notes:

I have serious doubts that Mother ever actually sent a cable to our father, requesting sending us to him in the Philippines. Her whole life was about trying to keep the four of us together until we "became of age." It is dramatic and I'm sure John responded by sending the necessary money to help keep mother and children together.

Letter No. 13

JOHN HUSTON
KATEL ITO JAPAN- NOV 14, 1957

DOROTHY HODEL INFORMED ME ONE SON IN HOSPITAL
RENT DUE OTHER OBLIGATIONS PRESSING SHE DESIRES
300 DOLLARS IMMEDIATELY YOU ALREADY ADVANCED HER
LAST NINETY DAYS IN EXCESS OF 1,000 DOLLARS. CABLE
INSTRUCTIONS

MARK

MARK COHEN
9606 SANTA MONICA BLVD.
BEVERLY HILLS CALIFORNIA - NOVEMBER 14, 1957

IS HODEL KID REALLY SICK OR ANOTHER DODGE ACT ACCORDING YOUR OWN JUDGMENT.

REG RDS

JOHN

Author Notes:

These sets of telegrams were the last two "letters" in the Huston File.
Mark Cohen was John's long time agent/business manager. Most of Dorothy's "emergency pleas for money" went through Mark. Here we see Mark relaying an urgent request from Dorothy to John and his reply, with eyes wide open, wanting to know if Mark thinks it is "real" or just another ploy [in his words, "a dodge act"] from Dorothy?

After seeing these letters for the first time, my personal respect for John has gone WAY UP. While he may have been known in filmdom as "A Genius and a Monster" it is clear from these many letters that he continually threw lifesaving dollars our way throughout the decade of the 1950s. Without his aid, it is doubtful that we would have been able to stay together as a family, and for this I would like to offer a most sincere, THANK YOU, JOHN!

It was only two years after this letter that I joined the Navy as soon as I turned 17. [1958]

John Huston—What did he know? When did he know it?

Earlier, I alluded to the fact that I believed that John Huston's "hunch" was that he either knew or strongly suspected that George Hodel was the killer of Elizabeth "Black Dahlia" Short, and possibly other victims.

We have already examined a number of my previously stated reasons why I believe this. Here is a quick review:

1. John and George had been close friends since their teens.
2. Both were geniuses who looked at life and shared a slightly different wiring than most of us mere mortals. Both men listed the Marquis de Sade high on their list of heroes, and were recognized as having "sadistic natures."
3. Both were in competition for and shared the mind, heart, and body of a truly remarkable woman, Dorothy Huston Hodel.

4. John, as a Hollywood A-list filmmaker, knew and associated with screenwriters: Rowland Brown [also a paramour of Dorothy Hodel] Gene Fowler, Steve Fisher, Ben Hecht, as well as being a close personal friend of Peter Viertel, who John hired in 1950 to write the screenplay for what would become one of his greatest films—*African Queen*.

Keeping in mind what we've learned from the newly discovered "Huston Letters" with emphasis on those communications from 1948 to the summer of 1950 when George Hodel left the country, let's now consider some new information.

Peter Viertel—African Queen-*White Hunter Black Heart*
Collier's, June 13, 1953

White Hunter, Black Heart
By PETER VIERTEL

John Wilson had become a violent and ruthless man. Now he was obsessed with a crazy urge to kill—to kill the greatest beast in the jungle—and perhaps destroy himself

Excerpt from Collier's introduction of Viertel's novel:

John Wilson is a man of limitless energy, determination and creative artistry. His reputation as a motion-picture director is tremendous. As a human being, he is unsuccessful—selfish, cynical, loveless and cruel. His projects are destined for great success or doomed to spectacular failure: for him, there is no middle ground, no mediocrity.

White Hunter, Black Heart is the story of the filming of a movie. It is also the story of Wilson's growing compulsion to destroy, at any cost, a creature nobler than himself. It is the story of a great talent gone haywire.

Peter Viertel, the author, worked with John Huston on The African Queen in the Congo in 1951. His novel, of which this story is the final section, will be published soon by Doubleday & Company.

In 1952, screenwriter/author, Peter Viertel wrote an absolutely riveting novel, *White Hunter, Black Heart.* [Doubleday & Co. Garden City, NY, 1953]

Its subtitle read:

A NOVEL OF BIG-GAME HUNTING IN THE BELGIAN CONGO AND ONE MAN'S OBSESSION WITH IT.

A Roman a clef, Viertel simply changed a few names, calling John Huston, John Wilson and himself, "Peter Verrill," he moved forward with a spectacular narrative. Viertel documents his close friendship with John and the events surrounding the 1951 making of the *African Queen*, and gives us a full—and in my opinion—fair view of the real Huston. We see and hear both sides: Huston's shining genius along with his dark-sided views of life, which gained Huston the well-earned reputation of being both, "A Genius and a Monster."

Having had a father of similar character—with tremendous strengths and weaknesses—who was both generous and sadistic in nature, I felt I better understood Viertel's expressed love and disgust for Huston after recently rereading the "novel."

John was a serpent who hypnotized his prey with charm and humor, then struck quickly and sank his fangs deep into his victim's flesh.

In the light of what is now known about George Hodel, a number of quotes attributed by Peter Verrill [Viertel] to John Wilson [Huston] take on a much deeper meaning. As you read the first comments on

Huston's view and attitude on testing "friendship," keep two things in mind. First, George Hodel and John Huston were *friends* since high-school, and second, John's observations are made circa 1950-1951, just after George Hodel was about to be arrested and decided to flee the country. As we now know, George was fleeing from being apprehended for the commission of a cold-blooded, premeditated murder. [Several actually.]

Here are Huston's comments on "Real Friendship."

White Hunter, Black Heart, page 64:

> ...
> "No, it's not. To try and find out who your real friends are is very important.
> "How would you propose to go about doing that, John? Randsome asked.
> "Well, I don't know. It's kind of difficult. I think the perfect test would be to go to your friends and tell them you've just committed a murder, a cold-blooded, premeditated murder, and that you want to escape. There are no extenuating circumstances. All you want is help. The people who'd stick to you and help you escape without asking any questions would, I believe qualify as real friends."

The following comments related to my mother, Dorothy, John's first wife. They were married for seven years. The "I'd done something wrong" refers to Mother walking in and catching him in bed with another woman fairly early on in their marriage.

White Hunter Black Heart, page 214:

> ...
> "I believe in the signs, you know. I've met them too often in my life to doubt them. In everything I've ever done. Work, or women, or gambling. Everything."
> "How do you mean?"
> "Well, when I broke up with my first wife for instance. I knew I'd lost the best dame I was ever likely to meet, and I'd lost her because I'd acted like a horse's ass. And it turned out that way. I'd done something wrong and I had to pay for it, and so every time I fell in love again after that, I knew the disenchantment would ultimately turn up. And it did. Never failed. Because you get one good chance at everything in life, and that's all."

Finally, I believe the following excerpt captures John's true psychology.

It is dangerous, over the edge, and guaranteed to fill one's life with excitement, adventure, and, in all likelihood, misery and disappointment. I make no moral judgment here. Those, like John Huston and George Hodel, make the choice with eyes wide open. Their thinking compels and propels them forward into the Abyss.

The below conversation was between Peter Viertel and John Huston [Peter Verrill and John Wilson]. They were in Africa and far behind schedule on the filming of the *African Queen*. A screenwriter and close friend of Huston's, Peter Viertel was attempting to dissuade Huston from going on an elephant hunt.

White Hunter, Black Heart, page 295-296:

Verrill [Viertel] say's:

> "Well, in order to kill one of them, you're ready to forget the rest of us, and let the whole goddam show go down the drain. It's not a passion this time that's guiding you, that's pulling you away from your responsibility. A passion would be an excuse. This time it's a crime. Because it's a crime to kill an elephant. And in order to commit this crime you're willing to ruin everyone else. If you were running out on the picture because of a woman, or a better offer, or because you'd suddenly gotten bored with the whole thing, I'd go along. But this way, it's even too rough for my taste."
>
> Wilson looked intensely serious for a minute. He drew reflectively on his cigarette. I knew something I had said had made an impression on him. Most of it, I realized, had gone past him into the warm African night, but something had struck him in the strange way it occasionally did, had pierced into his armor-plated process of thought. He was pausing now to give his answer weight. I knew him so well, I thought.
>
> "Kid," he said, after a long pause, "you're wrong. It's not a crime to kill an elephant. It's bigger than that. A crime....what the hell, that isn't much. And that isn't it. It's a sin to kill an elephant, you understand, a sin. As basic as that. The only sin you can buy a license for and then go out and commit. And that's why I want to do it before I do anything else. You understand?"

Thirty years later, Peter Viertel, by then long married to actress Deborah Kerr, wrote another book which I highly recommend,

Dangerous Friends: At Large with Hemingway and Huston in the Fifties. [Nan A. Talese/Doubleday, New York, 1992]

Viertel's recounting of his time shared in the 1950s with both of his "dangerous friends," Huston and Hemingway, gives us a fascinating behind the scenes look into both men's personalities.

I will close this chapter with a short excerpt from a full page letter written by Hemingway to his good friend, Peter Viertel in 1958. [Viertel adapted two of Hemingway's novels for film—*The Sun Also Rises* and *The Old Man and the Sea*.]

In reading Hemingway's letter, it becomes obvious that a bitter Papa has nothing but contempt for Hollywood film-making and its hacks, and he would like to see Viertel, [who he believed has genuine talent] give up his day-job as a screenwriter and throw himself full-time into real writing—novels.

The letter to Viertel was written on May 1, 1958 from *Finca Vigia* [Lookout Farm], Hemingway's home near Havana, Cuba.

> ...Wish to Christ you would write and not do that picture shit. Leave that to swine like Irwin and Hecht....Last winter I re-read all your books. The only one that is worthless is Line of Departure which is much worse than when I read it. But the Africa one [*White Hunter Black Heart*] in spite of carelessness re-reads very damned well.
>
> Go ahead and write your damned book. But don't think you can keep jerking yourself off for pictures and then command any fee at stud...in writing they can't yank you when you lose your stuff. What the hell. You get it back the next day or the next week. What if they knock the shit out of you? You can cut that out and go on when you have your stuff going again.
> Excuse bad letter. Now I have gotten rid of this lousy bitterness about the pictures will write you good and cheerful next time.
> ...

Love from us both,

Papa

["Us both" would include his wife, Mary Hemingway. Three years after writing this letter, Hemingway, back in the United States and being treated for severe depression, committed suicide in Idaho on July 2, 1961.]

Chapter 9

Lt. Frank Jemison

DA Investigator, Lt. Frank B. Jemison

One of the few men in the Black Dahlia investigation who it can be said was actually wearing a white hat was Lt. Frank B. Jemison of the LADA's Bureau of Investigation.

From everything that I have been able to ascertain, he did his job, solved the case, and was just about to make the arrest when the powers that be pulled his plug.

We can speculate all day as to the WHY? The reasons are many and varied.

However, what is not in dispute is *The Order*. Lt. Jemison, in his final closing report, made it crystal clear that he had been removed from the case [later independently confirmed in a 2004 television interview of DA investigator Walter Morgan] and ordered to hand over his investigation, interviews, and all his evidence, which included the wire recordings and transcripts directly to LAPD chief Thad Brown.

As I said in an earlier chapter, Lt. Jemison's saving grace was to copy his original investigation, complete with the *Hodel Black Dahlia File,* and secure it in the DA's vault, where it would remain hidden for the next *fifty-three years* until finally being opened and revealed.

Los Angeles Hall of Justice

210 W. Temple Street, Los Angeles

The above photo taken by the author in 2008 shows the downtown Los Angeles Hall of Justice at the corner of Temple and Broadway Streets. The HoJ built in 1925, has a long, colorful, and macabre history. Most of LA's famous trials were held in this courthouse. The building served as a jail detention facility for prisoners awaiting trial, as well as housing the LA Sheriff's Department, LA County Coroner's Office, and the DA's Office, including Lt. Jemison's office in the Bureau of Investigation.

The HoJ was within easy walking distance of all three of Dr. George Hodel's medical facilities: Health Department, Chinatown, *First Street VD Clinic* at First and Central, and his private medical office at Seventh and Flower Street.

The building has a direct connection and link to our investigation for the following reasons: (1) In the early 1940s, Dr. George Hill Hodel's Health Department office was located inside this building [1938-1942];(2) In 1947, the autopsy on Elizabeth "Black Dahlia" Short was performed in the Coroner's Office in the basement of the

HoJ, and the inquest into her death was held in a courtroom of the building; and (3) In 1949, Dr. George Hodel was arrested and booked into the jail facility here and was later tried in Superior Court on the lower floors of the premise. On February 15, 1950, George Hodel was detained and questioned by Lt. Jemison here, while at the same time, LAPD and DA sound technicians and detectives broke into the Franklin house and installed the microphones.

Dr. Hodel was "free to go" only after Lt. Jemison got the "all clear" call from detectives as they exited the Franklin house, having "wired it for sound."

Charles Manson and the rest of his "Family" were tried and convicted here as was Sirhan Sirhan, Bugsy Siegel, Mickey Cohen, Robert Mitchum, as well as most of LA's historic homme and femme fatales. In addition to Elizabeth Short, this was also the location where the autopsies on Marilyn Monroe and Robert Kennedy were performed.

The building was deemed "unsafe" after the1994 Northridge earthquake and has been vacant for nearly two decades. With such a distinguished history, hopefully, it will be saved from the wrecking ball, updated to current codes and preserved.

Dr. George Hill Hodel's four downtown LA medical office locations: (1) Health Dept. Chinatown;(2) Health Dept., Hall of Justice [1938-1940]; (3) His privately owned, *First Street VD Clinic*; and (4) His private practice at *Roosevelt Bldg.*

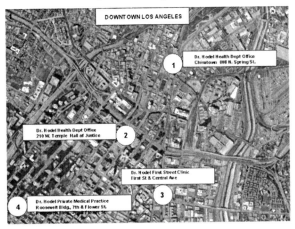

Upper left GHH Chinatown office; upper right /*First Street Clinic* Bottom Dr. Hodel's private practice 12th floor Seventh and Flower

A Family Secret

"The Dahlia murder suspect was a doctor and we know who did it, but we couldn't put him away."

Lt. Frank Jemison
Hall of Justice
Summer, 1951

In mid-October 2006, I was contacted by a close surviving relative of DA investigator, Lt. Frank B. Jemison. For privacy's sake, I will simply use his initials—"J.F." He advised me that he was Jemison's nephew [Jemison's sister's son], a medical doctor, and a retired Air Force colonel. Here in his own words is his description of his Uncle Frank, and one very important meeting he remembers from 1951:

Family background:

Frank was my mother's brother, the only son of a Methodist minister. He seemed a little eccentric to me. Every two years, he and his wife would fly to Detroit, pick up a new Cadillac, and drive through Ohio unannounced to visit his three sisters. If they weren't home—too bad, until two years later. He had not followed his father Dave's advice and entered the ministry and after graduation from Ohio Wesleyan College, he took off for the west coast. I thought he had a Law degree. Family rumor has it that he earned a good bit of money in real estate and as a financial advisor prior to his career as a DA investigator.

I know he was proud of his fortune, which was, at least in 1951, over one million dollars. While there was some family friction with Uncle Frank, he was always described as a person of impeccable personal integrity. I surmise that this integrity plus the fact that he had already made his fortune made him an excellent choice as investigator in the midst of apparent corruption. At his wife's death, the estate was left to Ohio Wesleyan.

The Black Dahlia Murder Case:

When I was 12 years old in the summer of 1951, I accompanied my family to a medical convention in San Francisco and we stopped in LA for three days, my only extended contact with Uncle Frank. At dinner, he asked if my father, a family physician, and I would like to see where he worked. At that time, the Hall of Justice was one of the, if not the, tallest buildings in LA. My father and Uncle

Frank sat in the front seat and I sat in back. As they drove, Dad turned and said, "You know your Uncle Frank was the investigator for the Black Dahlia case." I liked the name but it didn't mean much to me. They explained that it was a famous murder case. I didn't listen too hard to the conversation until they said the body was cut up. Then I was all ears. Uncle Frank described the cuts, etc., and asked Dad what he thought. My father said he thought it had to be the work of a surgeon. Uncle Frank agreed and said that "We know who did it but we didn't have enough to put him away." For some reason, my twelve year old mind couldn't understand that. I wondered why, if they knew who did it they couldn't arrest him. I never thought of that case from that time, but the name "Black Dahlia" remained stuck in my mind. Just thought this might be interesting to you as background information. Really have enjoyed your book!

Sincerely Yours,
J.F. M.D. COL USAF (ret)

Dr. J.F.'s "background information" is much more than "interesting." With what we already know, his family reflections are extremely illuminating, especially because of his certainty as to *when Uncle Frank met with him and made these statements.* It was the summer of 1951!

Let's briefly review Lt. Jemison's investigative chronology:

1. <u>October1949</u>- 1949 Grand Jury appointed Lt. Frank Jemison to take-over the Black Dahlia and other *LA Lone Woman* murder investigations. George Hill Hodel became DA Lt. Jemison's prime Dahlia suspect.

2. <u>February15-March 27, 1950</u>- Jemison established an eighteen-man task force assigned to twenty-four-hour electronic-surveillance of Dr. Hodel's Franklin house.

3. <u>March28, 1950</u>- George Hodel tipped to surveillance, realized he was about to be arrested and fled the residence. DA Lt. Jemison forced to remove surveillance equipment and shut down operation. *Lt. Jemison and law enforcement never again have contact with prime suspect, Dr. George Hill Hodel.*

4. <u>February 1951</u>- Lt. Jemison ordered to "close Dahlia case and turn all investigation and evidence and Hodel surveillance recordings and associate interviews over to LAPD. Complies, "closes" case, and locks away a "second set of investigative files" in the DA vault, where they remain untouched and unexamined until 2003.

5. <u>July 1951</u>- Lt. Jemison brought his vacationing brother-in-law, a medical doctor, and his twelve-year-old nephew, "J.F." [who will follow in his father's footsteps and grew up to become an MD and a US Air Force colonel] to his office at the downtown Los Angeles, Hall of Justice and informed them that "The Dahlia murder suspect was a doctor and we know who did it, but we couldn't put him away."

On August 15, 1967, some seventeen years after solving the Black Dahlia murder and locking his secret away in the DA vault, Frank Jemison died in Beverly Hills, California. He was sixty-eight.

He died a rich man, and in his will provisions were made for some of it to go to his alma mater, Wesleyan College in Ohio. And the rest of his assets, after the death of his wife, Jane, were placed as a trust fund for the Los Angeles District Attorney's Office.

In 1979, the Frank Jemison Award was established from monies specifically bequeathed for the purpose of selecting and acknowledging, "Excellence in Public Service."

The award was to be made each year to two outstanding employees selected from the DA's Office. One of the recipients should be a DA investigator, and the second honoree would be chosen from the DA's support staff. Each winner will receive a $5,000 gift for outstanding service. The Jemison Award has been given annually for the past thirty-two years.

DA Investigator Walter Morgan—The Last Coyote

"I guess there's not too many left in the hills in the city—least near where I live. So whenever I see one, I get this feeling that it might be the last one left out there. You know? The last coyote. And I guess that would bother me if it ever turned out to be true, if I never saw one again."

> Detective Harry Bosch,
> From Michael Connelly's *The Last Coyote*

The following is a revision from of an obituary I wrote about DA investigator Walter Morgan at the time of his death four years ago in 2007.

September 8, 2007
Los Angeles

DA investigator Walter Morgan,
Black Dahlia Murder's Last Coyote *dies* at 92

1915-2007

Walter Morgan, the Los Angeles District Attorney's Bureau of Investigation "old school" detective and the last surviving member of the 1950 Black Dahlia DA Task Force, in the final years before his passing, linked Dr. George Hill Hodel to the 1947 murder.

In a 2004 *CBS 48 Hours* crime-special, Morgan publicly acknowledged bugging the doctor's private residence. He also confirmed the existence of secret surveillance tapes and transcripts, and that the DA's taskforce in 1950 was unexpectedly and summarily shutdown. In a surprisingly candid on-air response, Morgan acknowledged that he and his fellow officers suspected that the shutdown was the result of a payoff and cover-up.

For me, it ended as it began with this morning's call from my half-sister, Tamar Hodel. "Steve, I just heard from my daughter, Fauna. Walter Morgan died this morning."

In my book, *Black Dahlia Avenger: A Genius for Murder*, published in 2003, here is how I originally described my introduction and first meeting with Walter Morgan, then an eighty-seven-year-old retired LA district attorney investigator.

Page 449:

> My INVESTIGATION HAD BEEN COMPLETED for some four months. I was working on the final editing of the manuscript when on April 24, 2002, my phone rang. It was my sister Tamar. "Steven," she said, "I have the most amazing news. Fauna [her eldest daughter] has just spoken with a man named Walter Morgan." (I immediately recognized his name as a district attorney investigator, Lieutenant Jemison's partner from the 1950 investigation, and swallowed hard at hearing his name come from her lips.) "He was a private detective or something back in the 1940s," she said. "He was involved in investigating, guess who: *Dr. George Hodel!* He told Fauna that they put a bug in the Franklin House to listen in on Dad's conversations. Can you call Fauna and find out what this is all about?"
>
> I assured Tamar I would check it out immediately. Contacting Fauna, whom I had not spoken to for ten years, I learned she was working in the San Fernando Valley and had been visited in her place of work by a casual acquaintance, Ethel. In her seventies, Ethel was with her boyfriend whom she introduced as Walter Morgan. Walter shook Fauna's hand and said, "'Hodel?' That's an unusual

name. I once worked a murder case on a Dr. Hodel. Any relation?" Fauna and Walter compared notes, and quickly learned that Morgan's suspect and Fauna's grandfather were one and the same.

Two days later, on April 26, I called Walter Morgan and told him my name was Steven Hodel, the uncle of Fauna Hodel, and the son of Dr. George Hill Hodel, who had died in 1999 at the age of ninety-one. I also informed him that I had retired from LAPD after working most of my career as a homicide detective in Hollywood Division.

Morgan greeted me warmly, in that unspoken bond that exists cop to cop, and proceeded to reminisce about the Hodel story.

Morgan, now eighty-seven, said he had worked for the sheriff's department from 1939 to 1949 on radio car patrol, in vice, burglary, and in other details. Then he left LASD and became a DA investigator in 1949, where he remained until retirement in 1970. He worked homicide on temporary assignment for a few months back in 1950. He was sent over to help out Lieutenant Frank Jemison, who he said "had picked me to be his sidekick."

Walter Morgan remembered well the day they had installed listening devices at the Franklin House, which he authoritatively informed me "was built by Frank Lloyd Wright." (As we know, the true architect was his son, Lloyd Wright.) Morgan continued:

> "We had a good bug man, a guy that could install bugs anywhere and everywhere. He worked in the DA's crime lab. So the chief assigned me to take him over to the house on Franklin, and he was going to install a bug system at the Hodel residence. My chief at the DA's office had me take him over there and we met the LAPD at Dr. Hodel's house. It was during the daytime and nobody was home. I remember there were some ranking LAPD officers outside, and no one could figure out how to get in. I suggested, "Well, have any of you officers tried a card to see if it would open the door?" They laughed, so I pulled out my wallet, and took out some kind of a credit card or whatever card I had, slipped it through, and the front door popped right open! They couldn't believe it. Anyway, our man went in and installed some bugs there. That was our job, to get the bugs installed so we could listen in."

Based on Walter Morgan's confirmations that my father was the Black Dahlia suspect and our Franklin house was bugged and secret tapes obtained, I closed the chapter (written in 2002) by publicly asking the following questions:

BDA page 454:

> Standard operating procedure would have been to make transcripts of these conversations, as well as investigative follow-up reports documenting the findings. **Where are these transcripts? Where are these reports? What do they say?**

A month after publication (May 2003), those questions were answered.

Los Angeles District Attorney Steve Cooley granted me access to the locked and vaulted *Hodel-Black Dahlia Files,* which had remained unexamined for over fifty-years, and, as they say, "the rest is history."

In June 2004, the five-decade old surveillance transcripts and investigative reports, along with photographs and copies of the DA files were released to the public by way of a new chapter, the "AFTERMATH," added to the BDA HarperCollins paperback edition.

DA Lieutenant Walter Morgan—Biography

- 1939- Appointed a deputy with the Los Angeles Sheriff's Department. Highly skilled in firearms, became one of the sheriff's department's "crack shots" after qualifying as a "Distinguished Expert" marksman.

- 1940-1949- LA deputy sheriff for nine years. Assignments included: patrol car, vice, and detective bureau (Burglary Detail).

- 1949- Left the sheriff's department and appointed a detective with the Los Angeles District Attorney's Office, Bureau of Investigation.

- 1950- Selected by Lt. Frank Jemison to assist him in the Grand Jury ordered reinvestigation of the Black Dahlia case.

- February15, 1950- Morgan, ordered by Lt. Jemison to coordinate a meeting between DA crime lab electronics' expert and LAPD detectives for the specific purpose of surreptitiously installing microphones inside the Franklin house residence of Dr. George Hill Hodel. Morgan accompanied by "bug men" and "high ranking LAPD officers" proceeded to 5121 Franklin Avenue and personally "shimmed" the front door of Dr. Hodel's residence. [To prevent him from walking in on them, the "installation" was coordinated and done at the same time George Hodel was being detained for questioning by DA investigators at the Hall of Justice.]

- March 1970- Morgan, retired from the DA's Office.

- April 2002- Interviewed by me related to my Black Dahlia investigation, and, for the first time in fifty-two years, disclosed his connections to the case and confirmed George Hodel as the prime suspect and the "bugging of the Hodel residence."

- May 2004- Agrees to be interviewed on CBS *48 Hours*, stated publicly his involvement in the investigation, acknowledged that he "shimmed the front door of Dr. Hodel's residence, and "electronic experts placed bugs in the walls." Morgan confirmed that he and Lt. Jemison were unexpectedly removed from the case and it was returned back to LAPD for further investigation. In an on-camera statement, Morgan indicated that in 1950, "a cover-up and payoff was suspected."

- September 8, 2007- Walter fell ill and passed away in Los Angeles.

In my several meetings with Walter Morgan since our introduction in 2002, I became acutely aware that he was a man of many moods who held many secrets; most of them from a long time ago.

In his prime, Walter lived and breathed *Chinatown* and *LA Confidential*. He *was* LA Noir—only this gumshoe was no celluloid fiction—*he was the real deal*. As you will read below, he was Philip Marlowe [before Marlowe got fired from the DA's Office for insubordination] and Dirty Harry rolled into one. And in 1944, a couple of street thugs would "make his day."

In the mid-1940s, Walter was close to the power that influenced and ran Los Angeles: gangster Mickey Cohen, Florentine Garden's owner; Mark Hansen and his "Mr. Show Business," M.C. Nils Thor Granlund, better known as-"N.T.G."

In 1945, Walter married the Florentine's lead showgirl, Tanya "Sugar" Geise. Best man at his wedding was no less a luminary, than LA County's top-cop, Sheriff Eugene Biscailuz. Tanya was good friends with Lavonne Cohen, Mickey Cohen's wife, who also attended the wedding. Mickey Cohen was Bugsy Siegel's lieutenant, who, in two short years, would take over as LA's *Numero Uno* gangster after his boss was gunned down in Beverly Hills.

Below I've included just a few press clippings from Walter's Feisty Forties, to give a sense of the man in his time.

In 1944, Walter, then still a deputy sheriff, was parked in a car with his fiancé, Sugar Geise on the Sunset Strip. The couple was approached by two armed robbers:

Excerpt from *LA Times* article on September 30, 1944:

Dead-Shot Deputy Foils Two Asserted Bandits
...

Suddenly one of them (Gallentine) shoved a pistol
through a partly open window, rapped on the glass, and said,
"O.K., give us the dough and the jewels"

Let "Jewels" Go

"I (Morgan) stepped out and said, "O.K., here are your jewels—
and let go eight 'little jewels' from my automatic."

SHARPSHOOTER—Deputy Walter Morgan, sheriff's department champion shot, shows Dancer "Sugar" Geise gun with which he shot two bandit holdup suspects.

Dead-Shot Deputy Foils
Two Asserted Bandits

ARRAIGNED—Manuel Riofrio, left, and Joseph Gallentine, charged with attempting to hold up deputy sheriff and fiancee Sept. 28, shown at their arraignment.

Men Who Picked on Deputy
as 'Soft Touch' Arraigned

Florentine Gardens Showgirl Tanya "Sugar" Geise

Florentine Gardens singer/dance Sugar Geise with mother

Walter Morgan weds Sugar Geise in June 1945
Sheriff Biscailuz "Best Man"

June 8, 1945 Los Angeles Times

Sugar Geise Wed to Deputy Sheriff

Dep. Sheriff Walter Morgan and Tanya (Sugar) Geise, Florentine Gardens night-club singer, whom he once saved from two bandits, yesterday were married in Superior Judge Edward R. Brand's court chambers.

Best man at the double-ring ceremony was Sheriff Biscailuz, with Mrs. Sam Katzman, wife of the R.K.O. producer, acting as matron of honor.

The couple met two years ago while Miss Geise was the star attraction at the Florentine Gardens. Last September, while Morgan was escorting her home, two bandits attempted to hold them up. Morgan leaped from the automobile and wounded both men in a blazing gun battle. Later they were convicted of robbery and sentenced to San Quentin.

"That convinced me I had met the right guy," Sugar declared yesterday after the wedding. She gave her age as 28 and Morgan admitted to being 30.

Other attendants at the wedding were Sugar's father, Harry (Pop) Geise, Lt. John Law, Morgan's immediate superior officer,

and Mrs. Lillian Cohen and Miss Pauline Davis, friends of the bride.

Immediately after the ceremony the couple left for a honeymoon trip which will include San Francisco and Reno.

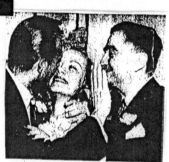

THREE'S A CROWD—Dep. Sheriff Walter Morgan, about to kiss his bride, Tanya (Sugar) Geise, night club singer, following wedding ceremony yesterday, apparently intends to push Sheriff Biscailuz, best man, out of picture.

2004- 48 HOURS BLACK DAHLIA CONFIDENTIAL

CBS investigative reporter, Erin Moriarty, questions Walter Morgan regarding the Black Dahlia case being closed down and turned back to LAPD:

Morgan: The only thing I can think is that some money must have transpired between people.

Moriarty: It sounds like you think it may have been a cover-up of some sort?

Morgan: Well, everybody thought that.

Dr. George Hill Hodel Surveillance Transcripts 40 days~(146 pages)

DA investigator Walter Morgan in 1952
walking across the street from his office at
the Hall of Justice. [Federal Court in background.]

To DA investigators Frank Jemison and Walter Morgan I want to take this opportunity to personally thank both of you for your service to the City of Angels and its people. Thank you for your honesty and integrity. You did what others could not. One of you preserved the truth and the other told it.

May you both –REST IN PEACE!

Chapter 10

Hollywood Roomers—*Tree of Life, 1948*

In 2001, after my relocation to Los Angeles, one of the potential witnesses I made contact with was an ex-roomer [perhaps lodger is more apropos] who had lived for several years at the Franklin house. For privacy's sake, let's call him Chris D. Chris was an artist, who, in 1948-1949, shared the rent in the north-wing studio with his friend and fellow painter, Joe Barrett.

I made phone contact with Chris who was living with his wife in a beach community several hours north of Los Angeles. We agreed to meet next time he came to LA.

Some months later, Chris called. He said he was in town and stopped by with his wife for a visit. We talked about "the old days" for about four hours, but nothing of any real consequence surfaced. Since my investigation at that time was sub rosa, naturally, I made no mention of the "Black Dahlia" or any other suspected criminality. It was obvious that Chris was saddened about my father's passing and his memories of the man were seemingly filled only with fondness and respect. After listening to Chris talk about Dad for a number of hours, my sense was that he considered George his *mentor*.

I had no further contact with Chris for about two years. By then, my book had been published. In 2004, I received a letter informing me that he had read BDA and found it difficult to believe that the George Hodel he knew could have committed such crimes. He remained highly skeptical.

Also enclosed in his letter was the below copy of a photograph of some of the 1948 roomers then living at our home. The photograph was entitled "Tree of Life—Shangri-LA, 1948." Chris identified each individual in the photo by hand writing their name next to their "branch" on the tree.

"Tree of Life-Shangri-LA 1948"

Franklin house tenants from top down:

1. Suzanne D'Albert
2. Gladys Krenek
3. Dorothy Bowman
4. Fuji Walker
5. Tony Walker
6. Chris D
7. George Hodel
8. Ellen Taylor

[1948 tenants: artist Joe Barrett and actress Carol Forman not in photograph.]

I have very few specifics on the various roomers living with us back in the late forties. I do know that Dad did not begin to rent any rooms out until 1948, which was *at least one full year after the Black Dahlia murder.*

I believe that most of the above named tenants were gone either before or soon after George's arrest for incest in October 1949. We know that Joe Barrett is still there in February 1950, and that George was interviewing prospective tenants as late as March 1950. But based on the transcripts, it sounded as if conditions may have prevented any new occupancy.

I am going to provide a very brief and limited sketch of some of the named tenants because I think it is important to understand that George Hodel, in addition to being connected to Hollywood's elite—A-list writers and directors—also had direct "in-house" connections to its working actors and artists, which may well provide us with some future LINKAGE.

Let's start at the top of the "tree" and work our way down.

Suzanne D'Albert

Suzanne D'Albert circa 1949

Suzanne D'Albert was born in France on May 12, 1927 and would have been just twenty-one when she moved into the Franklin house. She was reportedly discovered by Paramount mogul, Hal B. Wallis. Suzanne spoke five languages (French, English, German, Russian, and Spanish.) Her filmography credits her with twenty-seven acting parts in film and television. Tragically, she died from an apparent suicide from an overdose of sleeping pills in Paris in 1971 at the age of forty-three.

In the photo below, we see Suzanne posing with seven other young woman, including Marilyn Monroe and Enrica "Ricky" Soma in a 1949 *Life Magazine* article featuring up-and-coming Hollywood starlets. Monroe, at the time this photo was taken, was in Los Angeles shooting a small part as "Angela" in John Huston's *Asphalt Jungle*. Ricky Soma would marry John Huston that same year and became his fourth wife. Bizarrely, this photo with Suzanne D'Albert appeared in the October 10, 1949 edition of *Life Magazine*, which was George Hodel's forty-second birthday. [He had been arrested for incest just four days prior.]

Life Magazine October 10, 1949

(1) **Marilyn Monroe** (2) Laurette Luez (3) Lois Maxwell
(4) **Suzanne Dalbert** (5) **Ricky Soma** (6) Dolores Gardner
(7) Jane Nigh (8) Cathy Downs

Gladys Nordenstrom-Krenek

Gladys Krenek was born in Mora, Minnesota on May 23, 1924. I have little information on her life. She was an accomplished composer, and, shortly after residing at the Franklin house, married world renowned Austrian composer, Ernst Krenek in 1950.

Dorothy Bowman

At the time Dorothy Bowman was renting a room at the Franklin house, she was twenty-one and already had become a recognized and respected Los Angeles artist. Her works had been shown at galleries throughout the Southland and she most certainly would have been a friend and acquaintance of fellow artist and regular houseguest, Fred Sexton and his wife, Gwain.

Dorothy attended LA's *Chouinard Art Institute* where she met fellow painter, Howard Bradford. The two also studied together at the *Jepson Art School* in Los Angeles. [This is the same school where Fred Sexton was an art instructor and was fired, because according to Joe Barrett, who also attended the school, "He [Sexton] was hitting on all the young girls and half the class left, so Herb Jepson fired him."]

Dorothy Bowman and Howard Bradford relocated to the California coast of Big Sur circa 1950, where they became part of that community and befriended writer Henry Miller, another Franklin house visitor. The two artists eventually married. Both Dorothy and Howard became internationally respected and their paintings and serigraphs can be found in museums throughout the world.

Dorothy Bowman art shows 1950
[Los Angeles Times]

Fuji and Tony Walker

I have no biographical information on Fuji or her son, Tony, but I'm sure, like all the others, there's is a story just waiting to be found and told.

Ellen Taylor

Ellen was the maid. I am not sure exactly when she began working for Dad. Perhaps in mid-to-late 1947. From the photograph, we know she was there in 1948 and remained until the spring of 1950.

We also know from the DA tapes that she was a "full-service maid." Sex with George was, from the sound of the explicit recordings, a part of her regular duties. To quote the eloquence of the detective's log, "Sounds like Ellen just gave George another blow-job." It is also clear from the tapes that she wanted and demanded sex and became very upset when George told her, "No, not tonight."

In BDA, in the chapter, "The Franklin House Revisited," I made mention of an interview I conducted with "Bill Buck" [not his real name] who owned and had been living in the house for thirty years, and whose father, a medical doctor, bought the home from Dad back in 1950.

It's worth retelling here, since I am sure his descriptions coupled with Joe Barrett's separate comments clearly suggested that the person they were describing was Ellen Taylor.

BDA page 263:

> Another strange incident: Buck told me about the appearance of a "bag lady" who came to the door back in the 1970s or early '80s. "She looked quite old," he said, "but with street people it's hard to tell." I spoke with her and she said, 'This house is a place of evil'." He said that normally he would have simply dismissed her, but then she continued to describe the interior of the house. "It was very scary," he said. "She obviously had been inside this place before we owned it. She described in detail to me: the great stone fireplace, and your father's gold bedroom, and the all-red kitchen that your father had painted. No question that she was very familiar with the house when your dad had lived here. She looked at me and said again, 'This is a house of evil.' God knows what connection she had with this place. She left, and I never saw or heard from her again."

> Based on a conversation I had with former tenant Joe Barrett, it is my belief that the person Buck described as a "bag lady" was most probably our former maid, Ellen Taylor, Father's live-in housemaid/girlfriend, who lived at Franklin House from 1945 to 1950. In later years, Joe Barrett had run into Ellen on the street in downtown Los Angeles and discovered that she had been in and out of mental hospitals. Joe Barrett described her as "living on the fringe, delusional, claiming she had had affairs with a number of prominent and locally famous personages." (Knowing what we now know, perhaps Ellen was not as delusional as Barrett thought.)

While we cannot be positive that the "bag lady" was Ellen, all the pieces fit together quite well. The discovery and reading of the DA files established that Mother and we three boys were not at the house during the weeks preceding and after the murder of Elizabeth Short. But now, a new question arises—was Ellen? She was talked to by DA investigators in 1950, but unfortunately, her and many of the other George Hodel acquaintance interviews—while conducted—were not included in the DA papers secured in the vault. And, as we know, LAPD's copies have all "disappeared."

Carol Forman

Carol Forman was also a roomer at the Franklin house; she was just not at home when the *Tree of Life* photo was taken. [Unless she took it.]

Carol was born June 19, 1918 and would have been thirty at the time she was renting a room at the Franklin house. According to her filmography, her first part was in the 1946 RKO film, *From this Day Forward*. That same year, Carol had a bit part as a secretary in the noir-thriller, *Nocturne*, a story written by Rowland Brown, who, in 1946, was involved in an ongoing romance with my mother, Dorothy Hodel.

Carol Forman secretary scene in *Nocturne* (1946)

In 1947, Carol played Sombra in *The Black Widow*, establishing herself as a leading villainess. True to form, in 1948, she starred as Spider Lady, taking on mild mannered reporter, Clark Kent [Kirk Alyn], in Columbia's big screen serialization of *Superman*.

1948 clips of Carol Forman as Spider Lady in *Superman*

As if written for a *Twilight Zone* episode, Carol Forman was selected and appeared on this *January 1947* calendar, which was the same month Elizabeth "Black Dahlia" Short was brutally murdered at George Hodel's Franklin house. Then one year later, the unsuspecting actress rented a room and moved into and resided at *the crime scene.*

Carol, Tim Holt, and my Bro

My younger brother, Kelvin "Kelly" Hodel, was born in October 1942, just eleven months after the birth of my twin, John, and I. He would be Dorothy and George's fourth and final son. Kelly, from an early age, "loved the girls," and believe me—the girls LOVED him. A 1949 Franklin house Kelvin anecdote is appropriate:

At the time Carol was living with us at the Franklin house, she was dating film star Tim Holt. The two actors had worked together in a number of B-Westerns, including the 1947 *Under the Tonto Rim* and again in 1948 on *Brothers in the Saddle*. Tim Holt [who had just received huge critical acclaim for his role as the down-on-his -luck drifter, Bob Curtin in John Huston's *The Treasure of the Sierra Madre*], naturally, came and visited Carol at the house on a regular basis.

Brother Kelly, then aged six or seven had a terrible crush on Carol. And whenever Tim showed up to take her on a date, Kelly would object, informing Holt in no uncertain terms, "She's my girlfriend." Finally, Holt could take it no longer and took Kelly into the center courtyard, *mano-a-mano*, and came up with the following suggestion:

> "Look Kelly. You're too young to be with Carol now. I will date her only until you get old enough. And then you and Carol can get married. And I will get on my horse and ride off. Fair enough?"

Kelly agreed. Holt and Hodel shook hands, and the battle for Carol's heart was ended—without having to fire a shot and find out which of the two was the fastest gun alive.

My brother, Kelly, [left] and I in the courtyard of Franklin house circa 1949

Carole Forman, after appearing in more than twenty-four separate films, then turned her acting skills to television and theatre. She died in Burbank, California in 1997.

The short peek behind the door and into the lives of these five Franklin house tenants gives us a much broader understanding of just how eclectic and far-reaching was George Hodel's—web of connections.

In the 1940s, his hand was either directly ON or at least only one-degree-away from the power and the politics that was Los Angeles. As he told Baron Harringa on the DA tape:

"I'm the only one that knows how all these things fit together."

Edmund Teske

"Bill Buck," the former Sowden/Franklin house owner, who I interviewed in 2001, after telling me about "the bag lady," went on to mention a second visitor.

BDA, pages 263-264:

> Bill Buck also told me that another man who had visited the house on three different occasions over the years was a photographer named Edmund Teske, "a local photographer and sort of a fixture here in old Hollywood. He had a home just down the street on Hollywood Boulevard. He visited here three separate times over the years and told me he was a good friend of both your father and Man Ray."

In 2001, I had never heard of Edmund Teske, and his name meant nothing to me. I ignored the information for about a year until it came up again, this time from former Franklin house tenant, Joe Barrett.

I was visiting Joe in his home in Ventura, California and we were looking at some old photographs that my father had given me, one of which was my favorite. It showed my two brothers and I standing inside the Franklin house courtyard. I had dubbed it, "The Three Musketeers."

I showed this photo to Joe and told him that I suspected it might have been taken by Man Ray.

Joe smiled and said, "No, not Man Ray. It was taken by another photographer friend of George's. His name was Edmund Teske. I know, because I was there when he took it. Teske was a friend of both your dad and Man Ray."

Photos by Edmund Teske circa 1948

"The Three Musketeers" [Left to right: Steven, Michael, Kelvin]

Second photo by Edmund Teske taken from inside the living room [Left to right: Michael, Steven, and Kelvin]
My brothers are now holding the two black cats while I blow bubbles.

This second reference got my attention. In doing some research, I discovered that Edmund Teske, while ever remaining the eccentric, had a remarkable past and deep ties to Hollywood up until his death in 1996.

Here is an excerpt from the J. Paul Getty Museum on a retrospective called, "Spirit into Matter: The Photographs of Edmund Teske that ran from June-September 2004.

Edmund Teske (1911-1996) was one of the most significant artist-photographers active in Los Angeles in recent decades. He approached photography as a highly malleable medium, open to the artist's intervention at several points in the creative process. An inventive darkroom technician, Teske created photographs that expressed his emotional and spiritual concerns. His images reveal the power of memory and dreams to transform our perception and understanding of the visual world.

...

And from a Getty Research biography:

...

In the mid-1940s, Teske relocated to Los Angeles, where he initially worked at Paramount Pictures in the photographic still department. He continued to photograph and began to exhibit his images more frequently. His increasing experimentation led to his use of the solarization technique to reverse highlight and shadow. In 1956 he detoured briefly from photography to appear in the film biography of Vincent van Gogh, *Lust for Life*. After 1960 he frequently returned to older negatives, reinterpreting them through the use of experimental printing techniques.

From the Edmund Teske Archives:

Teske was drawn west by the allure of the motion picture industry and a desire to meet Greta Garbo. He worked in the stills department of Paramount Studios. He lived at the Frank Lloyd Wright residence of Aline Barnsdall on Olive Hill where he met Man Ray and other notable folk. He photographed actors and notable folk throughout his career. To name a few: Joel McCrea, Geraldine Page, Kenneth Anger, John Saxon, Ansel Adams, Jim Whitney, Ramblin' Jack Eliott, Will Geer, Anaiis Nin, Jane Lawrence, and others.

Edmund Teske, friend to Aline Barnsdall, was an artist in residence Here at "Hollyhock House" in Studio B from 1944-1949.

Hollyhock House, 4800 Hollywood Boulevard, Hollywood, California

The Frank Lloyd Wright designed residence known as "Hollyhock House" rests atop a hill at 4800 Hollywood Boulevard in East Hollywood.

It was built for Aline Barnsdall in 1921, who would later donate the home and its surrounding eleven acres to the city of Los Angeles to be preserved as a public art park.

The home is located only *five blocks* from the Franklin house, and, as a child, I have many fond memories of my brothers and I riding our bikes the short distance to play all day in "Barnsdall Park."

"Synchronicity Happens"

Just one week ago, in mid-September 2011, I received a notification of the imminent closing of one of Los Angeles's oldest and most respected downtown restaurants, Clifton's Cafeteria at Seventh and Broadway. The notice also contained an invitation for those interested to meet and have a "last luncheon" before the closing and renovation by the new buyer. Though I didn't know any of the dozen or so persons planning to attend, I decided to go out of respect for the original philanthropist owner, Clifford Clinton, who had done so much for Angelenos in the 1930s and 1940s.

The small group of us met outside at noon, introduced ourselves, then proceeded inside to make our selections from hundreds of cafeteria "choices." Out of homage to the establishment, I went with the blue-plate special, a traditional turkey, mashed potatoes, and gravy, which Clifton's sold during the Depression to the needy for—*one penny!*

The brainchild for the luncheon was Steve Lamb, a residential architect from Altadena, California. Steve and I got to talking and it turned out that he had read my books. He then went on to tell me a most remarkable story that he said he had been relating to his friends for *over thirty years*. After hearing the story, I asked him if he could "write it up" and send it to me. He did, and here is a scan of his letter, which I received on September 28, 2011:

STEVEN S. LAMB

P.O.BOX 333, ALTADENA CA. 91001 ████████████████

28 Sept. 2011

MEETING ED TESKE

Back in the late 1970's I used to volunteer at a Christian ministry to street people in Hollywood called CENTRUM OF HOLLYWOOD. Often I volunteered on our suicide prevention hot line called the Hollywood Lifeline. Before I would do my shift on the lifeline, I would go over to the Sowden house on Franklin and park my Triumph T.R. 3 in front. I'd try to park about half an hour before sunset. As the sun would set the colors and shapes of the textile blocks on the house would seem to change and I would take those wonderful moments of beauty with me as I volunteered.

One cold fall evening in 1978 I was leaning against my Triumph with my deerstalker on lighting my calabash pipe. I was looking east and I saw a tall thin man with a purple coat and a limp walking towards me. He looked like an old wino. The man came up to me and stood very close leaning over me and with a expressive voice said

"DO you like the House?"

"Why yes, Sir, it's a very important and early Lloyd Wrigh.."

"It's an E V I L place! Artist's Philosophers,accountants and politicians we all played and paid there. Women were tortured for sport there. Murders happened there. It's an E V I L place."

He walked down about half a block, spun on his heels and pointed at me like an Old Testament movie prophet and again said

"It's an E V I L place."

I thought he was just some old wino. All the street people said the Sowden house was evil. I assumed it was because the roof and balcony configuration were different, and it was kind of run down in those days, so there had to be a Hollywood legend about it. I figured this guy was just another half crazed old street person and that in any case his facts were all wrong, he was confusing this house with Fatty Arbuckle's house down the street, and whatever happened there, happened in San Francisco, anyway.

About a decade later, I was a member of both the Taliesin Fellows and the Wrightian Association. Those groups were having a combined event at the Pacific Design Center, on photographing Frank Lloyd Wright. We were doing so in part to honor a new book by Pedro Guerro, who had been Frank Lloyd Wright's personal photographer in the late 1930's, 1940's and 1950's.

In the lobby of the Auditorium there was a large U made up of several
tables selling various books, ties, T shirts and photographs related to
Frank Lloyd Wright. I bought a copy of Pedro's book and got it
autographed and looked over the stuff for sale, most of it I had
already.

At the end of the U, as far away from the entry as possible, were a
collection of large sepia toned photographs, each about 16" wide and 24"
long. The Photographs were mounted on brown construction paper and there
were geometric Wrightian designs drawn sometimes at a corner, sometimes
at a side. They were in the new gold ink paint pens that had just come
out and were each signed in gold "Edmund Teske". I thought this was
strange, the signature looked right, but I had assumed Teske to be long
dead, since I had seen no new photographs of his in some twenty years.

As I was looking through the pile of sepia prints of Hollyhock house, a
tall thin man entered the room and was warmly greeted by Paul Bogart,
Eric Lloyd Wright and Pedro Guerrro. This I thought was strange, as I
recognized the man as the wino who told me the Sowden house was a evil
place a decade before.

The tall man walked over to where I was looking through the Sepia
Prints. He stood in front of me, leaned in towards me and said

"Do You like the photographs?"

**"Yes,Sir. I like them very much. They are the most beautiful photographs
of any Frank Lloyd Wright building I have seen, they have captured the
buildings the way Architects see them before they are built."**

(He had, too. His photos were much more evocative of the spirit of the
Architecture within it than any Pedro or anyone else I have ever seen
has done.)

The man smiled at me and held my gaze for a very long time. He had a
pride in his eyes. Incredulous, I asked him-

"Sir, are YOU Edmund Teske?"

"Well I'm Ed Teske, or what's left of him."

He said roaring as he laughed with an open mouth devoid of many teeth.

"Would you like to B U Y a photograph?"

**"Sir, I would very much, but they are $300.00 and I only have $280.00 in
the bank. May I come see you when I have some money and buy one?"**

"Certainly."

He wrote his name and address down for me on a scrap of paper. I still
keep it at the front of my address book, and like a fool, I never did go
back and buy one of Ed Teske's prints. Now they are worth a cool $30,000
or so each…

This apparent chance meeting with Steve, his wife, Jeanette, and a
handful of his friends at Clifton's is another remarkable example of
how the facts and corroborations just keep coming. All I can say is:

SYNCHRONICITY HAPPENS!

Some Teske Afterthoughts

Edmund Teske in scene clip from MGM's *Lust for Life* [1956]

In this scene with Kirk Douglas [Vincent Van Gogh] and Anthony Quinn [Paul Gauguin] Edmund Teske, a fellow artist, is questioning Van Gogh's skill as an artist. Teske was forty-five years-old when the film was released. Quinn won an Oscar for Best Supporting Actor.

For those who would categorize this chance conversation between Steve Lamb and Edmund Teske as nothing more than the ranting's of a "mad artist," a lost and delusional soul whose words were not to be trusted, consider the following—his well-documented biography.

I will pick up his bio *just from 1978 forward.* The conversation in front of the Franklin house occurred when Teske was sixty-six. Here are *some* of the highlights of his life and some remarkable personal accomplishments *following that conversation:*

My biographical source came from: *Edmund Teske: A Chronology* compiled by Michael Hargrave, as found in *Spirit into Matter: the Photographs of Edmund Teske* by Julian Cox, Edmund Teske, J. Paul Getty Museum. What follows is only a partial summary from Mr. Hargrave's chronology:

...

1978 Conducted workshop for the Friends of Photography and Lectures at the Society for Photographic Education National Conference, Pacific Grove, California

1979 Invited and became visiting professor of the Photography Department at California State University, Los Angeles.

1980 Led a workshop at the Victor School, Victor, Colorado.
Guest speaker at Camera vision's Artist's Hot seat series, Los Angeles.

1981 One group show. Photographer or Priest maker, Ferens Art Gallery, Hull, England (followed by several other British venues).

1982 Presented slide lecture at the University of Colorado at Boulder; conducted a one-week workshop at the School of the Art Institute of Chicago.

1983 Taught a photography workshop at Otis Art Institute of Parsons School of Design, Los Angeles.

1986 Gave a workshop and seminar at the Victor School, Victor, Colorado.

1987 One group show, Los Angeles County Museum of Art.

1988 Was the subject of a two-part television film produced by Light-borne Communications, Cincinnati, Ohio.

1989 Lectured at the Santa Monica Public Library on Photographers and their Art.

1990 Teske was shot by an unknown assailant in the doorway of his Hollywood studio on Harvard Boulevard; suffered debilitating injuries to his jaw and the left side of his face.

1991 Participated in a symposium at the J. Paul Getty Museum, The Relevance of History and Theory to the Creative Process, moderated by Weston Naef, with Ralph Gibson, Jo Ann Callis, David Hockney, Gay Block, and Richard Misrach.

1993   One-man exhibition at J. Paul Getty Museum

1995   Gave a talk at UCLA at the Armand Hammer Museum of Art.

1996   Died at his downtown Los Angeles studio on November 22 of a heart attack. Memorial service was held at Hollyhock House on December 14.

These active and very dynamic eighteen years following Teske's *conversation* demonstrate him to be a lecturing professor and world traveler, with all of his faculties completely intact.

With the further understanding that Edmund Teske was clear-headed and of sound mind in 1978, some twenty years before I even began my investigation, let us reexamine his disclosure to Steve Lamb in front of the Hodel Franklin house. [Also, let's keep in mind that Teske was a close friend of both Man Ray and George Hodel, and obviously, a regular visitor to the house, as well as (at least on one occasion) being our "family photographer."]

> "It's an evil place! Artists, philosophers, accountants and politicians *we all played and paid there.* Women were tortured for sport there. Murders happened there. It's an EVIL place."

I have no reason to doubt or question Steve Lamb's specific quoting of Teske's words.

What Teske told Lamb some thirty-three years ago independently supports what the "bag lady" [probably our maid, Ellen Taylor] had said, as well as the words spoken by fellow insiders, Joe Barrett and Lillian Lenorak, and certainly underscore Mattie Comfort's 2003 declaration that, "We all knew George Hodel did it. There was no doubt."

For Teske to disclose these secrets to a complete stranger begs the question: who else did he tell and in what detail? Certainly, he would have shared this knowledge with at least some of his own close personal friends and confidants.

Edmund Teske, July 1996

Screen capture from YouTube video interview in tribute to Global Liberty Exhibition by Jean Ferro. Teske died just four months later in November 1996.

Chapter 11

Urban myth (noun). An often lurid story or anecdote that is based on hearsay and widely circulated as true.

Merriam Webster Dictionary

The Black Dahlia's Three Greatest Urban Myths

Urban Myth No. 1- "A Standalone Murder"

The Black Dahlia murder was a standalone. Her killer never committed a crime before or after her brutal murder.

LA Lone Woman Murders

In March 1947, *LAPD informed the public they believed a number of the recent lone woman murders were committed by the same suspect*, and released a written "11 Points of Similarity" summary to the daily newspapers in support of their belief.

In the below *Los Angeles Examiner* March 14, 1947 article, printed just eight weeks after the Black Dahlia murder, LAPD informed the public that it was their considered opinion that the murders of Elizabeth Short (January 15), Jeanne French (February 10), and Evelyn Winters (March 12) *were all committed by the same suspect* and went on to publicly list their reasons WHY. I quote from the article:

"Dahlia Case Similarities Checked in Fourth Brutal Death Mystery"

...

Checking similarities between the death of Miss Winters and the Short, and French killings, police listed the following:

1) All three girls frequented cocktail bars and sometimes picked up men in them.
2) All three were slugged on the head (although Mrs. French was trampled to death and Miss Short tortured and cut in two).

3) All three were killed elsewhere and taken in cars to the spots where the bodies were found.
4) All three were displayed nude or nearly so.
5) In no case was an attempt made to conceal the body. On the contrary, bodies were left where they were sure to be found.
6) Each had been dragged a short distance.
7) Each killing was a pathological case, apparently motiveless.
8) In each case, the killer appears to have taken care not to be seen in company with the victim.
9) All three women had good family backgrounds.
10) Each was identified by her fingerprints, other evidence of identity having been removed.
11) Miss Short and Miss Winters were last seen in the same Hill Street area.

In January 1947, the press suggested a link to four of the victims. Then by 1950, it was up to seven.

The 1949 Grand Jury issued a scathing report on the unsolved Black Dahlia and new *Lone Woman Murders* and ordered the investigation of these crimes be taken away from LAPD and reinvestigated by the District Attorney's Office.

LAPD and the LA Sheriff's Department were both convinced that many of their 1940s crimes were committed by the same suspect.

Posted below are two separate 1949 front page headlines where *police and press both link a new killing, Mrs. Louise Springer, to the Black*

Dahlia suspect and speculate that perhaps at least NINE of the previously unsolved "Horror Murders" are connected to the same man.

"Mother Kidnaped, Slain; Seek Curly-Haired Man New 'Black Dahlia' Case"

Los Angeles Examiner
June 17, 1949

"Police are not overlooking the possibility that a single slayer committed all [nine] of the Los Angeles "Horror Murders."

Long Beach Press Telegram
June 17, 1949

The *Long Beach Press Telegram* article provided details on the June 16, 1949 slaying of Mrs. Louise Springer and then went on to name the eight previous victims possibly killed by "a single slayer":

1. Elizabeth Short ("Black Dahlia")
2. Mary Tate
3. Evelyn Winters
4. Jeanne French ("Red Lipstick Murder")
5. Rosenda Mondragon ("Silk Stocking Murder")
6. Dorothy Montgomery
7. Laura Trelstad
8. Gladys Kern (Real Estater Murder)
9. Louise Springer

Three months later, in September 1949, LAPD chief of detectives Thad Brown removed any question that LAPD suspected many of the LA murders were connected when he informed the press and the public that they were checking out a sex strangulation murderer, Ray Dempsey Gardner, age twenty-seven, arrested in Ogden, Utah.

In the *Los Angeles Times* piece, "**Alleged Garroter May Be Linked to Killings Here,**" Chief Brown is quoted as saying, "...efforts will be made to trace his activities in the hope of forming a connection with local murders."

The article goes on to specifically name the suspected crime victims as: "...Elizabeth Short, Jeanne French, Louise Springer, Georgette Bauerdorf, as well as other and similar cases.

Los Angeles Times, September 14, 1949

Alleged Garroter May Be Linked to Killings Here

A sex killer who has confessed three garroting murders at Ogden, Utah, was seen as a possible suspect yesterday in Los Angeles' long series of violent sex slayings.

Asst. Police Chief Thad Brown, chief of detectives here, dispatched a written request to the Sheriff at Ogden requesting details of the story told by Ray Dempsey Gardner, 27, in jail there on the sex crimes.

Brown said that accounts from Ogden detailed Gardner's admitted stranging of Shirley Gretzinger, 17, in Ogden last July. He also took police to the body of a second victim, Sue Horn, 39, of Montana, and yesterday said he strangled a cellmate in a North Dakota jail.

Strangling and sex motives have figured in the murders here of Elizabeth Short, Jan. 15, 1947; Mrs. Jeanne T. French, Feb. 10, 1947; Mrs. Louise Springer, June 16, 1949, and Miss Georgette Bauerdorf, Oct. 12, 1944, as well as other and similar cases.

Brown said that if Gardner is unable to account for his movements during the times of any of the unsolved Southland murders, and if his record indicates possibility of his presence here during those times, efforts will be made to trace his activities in the hope of forming a connection with local murders.

The FACT that law enforcement suspected a serial killer from the get-go was eventually covered over by tabloid accounts which created the DAHLIA MYTH. The truth was replaced by pulp fiction magazines and sexploitation novels. Hollywood dream makers and spin doctors have never really cared about facts. Nightmares are the stuff their dreams are made of—and so it went.

By the nineties, even the cops bought into the myths and legends. "A standalone crime, none before, none after." None of the "new breed" had ever read the case files or did any in depth study of the original investigation. They were simply ignorant of what their "old school" predecessors, the original Black Dahlia investigators had suspected all along—many of the 1940s *Lone Woman Murders* were serially connected to the same killer.

Lone Woman Murders—Updates

LA Lone Woman Murders 1943-1949 Category I (definites)

In my original BDA 2003 and in the updated chapters published in the *HarperCollins* revised editions ["Aftermath" chapter, 2004 and

"New Investigation," 2006], I broke the suspected crimes into separate categories: I-"Definites" [strong M.O. and signature linkage] II-Probables, and III-Possibles.

Within the Category I range, I initially listed seven (7) victims, most of whom corresponded with LAPD's suspected list of serial victims. Those original seven were:

1. Ora Murray-1943
2. Georgette Bauerdorf-1944
3. Elizabeth Short-1947
4. Jeanne French-1947
5. Gladys Kern-1948
6. Mimi Boomhower-1949
7. Jean Spangler-1949

Ora Murray- "White Gardenia Murder" Update

Sixty-seven years after the crime was committed, I believe I have found an additional signature-link to the brutal murder of Mrs. Ora Murray, one of the eight "Category I (definites) *LA Lone Woman Murders*, which was originally summarized in my 2003 publication of *Black Dahlia Avenger*.

Below is a brief summary of the crime M.O. (For those wanting a fuller description, I suggest you read BDA Chapter 23, pages 294-306.)

On the evening of *July 26, 1943*, Mrs. Ora Murray, age forty-two, accompanied by her sister, Latona Leinann, went out for a night of drinks and dancing at the *Zenda Ballroom*, located in downtown Los Angeles at Seventh and Figueroa. [The dancehall was located just one block from Dr. Hodel's medical office at Seventh and Flower.]

The victim, married to an Army sergeant stationed in Mississippi, was temporarily visiting her sister in Los Angeles.

At the dancehall the two women met and danced with a man named, "Paul." Ora's sister later described "Paul" as being "tall and thin, very dapper and a very good dancer. He wore a dark double-breasted suit and a dark fedora." Paul claimed he was from San Francisco, "just down to L.A. for a few days." After a number of dances, Paul offered to drive Ora Murray to Hollywood and show her the sights. Mrs. Murray accepted and after first driving the sister home, the couple then continued on to supposedly tour Hollywood.

Some eight-hours later, Ora Murray's partially nude body was found on the grass at the Fox Hill Golf Course in West Los Angeles. She had been severely beaten about the face and body and the cause of death was found to be, "constriction of the larynx by strangulation." *Ora's killer had ceremoniously wrapped her dress around her body like a sarong and then carefully placed a white gardenia under her right shoulder.* Based on this unusual M.O. the press dubbed the crime, *The White Gardenia Murder.* The investigation was handled by LA County Sheriff's Homicide, as it was just outside of the city limits.

"White Gardenia Murder"
July 26, 1943

Body of Beaten Woman Found on Golf Course

Seminude, the mutilated body of Mrs. Ora Murray, 42, was found at dawn yesterday on the grounds of the Fox Hills golf links.

Inspector William Penprase of the Sheriff's office said she apparently had been strangled.

Search was instituted for a man identified only as Paul, who was with her when she was last seen alive at 11 p.m. Monday.

Mrs. Murray, who came here five days ago from Mississippi, met the stranger at a dance hall and later left with him for an automobile ride, according to her sister, Mrs. O. P. Leimann, 1201 Maryland St.

Clothing Torn

[...] of her cloth-[...]

SLAIN — Mrs. Ora Murray, 42, found murdered on Fox Hills golf course.

Ora Murray- 1943 White Gardenia Murder victim

231

A Copycat Crime-Murder as a Fine Art

I enjoy listening to *OTR* (Old Time Radio) programs. In April 2010, I was reviewing an on-line index of the old CBS *Suspense Theatre* dramatizations, and one of the titles caught my eye. It was called, *The White Rose Murders*.

The show was originally broadcast from CBS's then relatively new *Columbia Square Playhouse Studio*, located in Hollywood, at Sunset and Gower. The radio dramatization starred the beautiful twenty-two-year-old actress, **Maureen O'Hara** and was first aired on, *July 6, 1943, just twenty days prior to the commission of the Los Angeles, "White Gardenia Murder" of Ora Murray.*

The radio mystery-play was written by a popular novelist and pulp-fiction writer, **Cornell Woolrich**, who also used the pseudonyms of: William Irish and George Hopley.

During the 1930s and 1940s Woolrich saw more than thirty of his short stories and several of his novels made into films. [Two of the best known being: *The Night has a Thousand Eyes (1948)* directed by John Farrow, and the Alfred Hitchcock classic, *Rear Window (1954,)* which was adapted from Woolrich's original short-story, "*It Had To Be Murder.*"]

Cornell's 1943 radio drama, *The White Rose Murders* told the story of a "homicidal maniac" who frequented the city's downtown dancehalls, where he met, danced with and picked-up lone women. The killer then lured them out into the night where he strangled them to death. As a signature of his kills the madman carefully placed a "white rose" next to the body of each of his victims.

In the vernacular of the day, the police detective described him as "a chain killer" and as the story begins we find the city is gripped in terror as the unidentified suspect has just slain his fourth victim, and is about to kill his fifth.

The motive for the serial-killings was presented as that of a deranged "Avenger," a woman hater, seeking personal revenge on young women for having been rejected by them in his youth.

We recall that George Hodel, in his 1944 Georgette Bauerdorf murder note, informed the public that the reason he killed her was for, "Divine Retribution." And, in his 1947 note, as the "Black Dahlia Avenger" he assured us, "The Dahlia Killing was justified."

The *Suspense Theatre* radio-plays, were hugely popular and always introduced by, "The Man In Black." I am surprised that neither the press nor apparently anyone in law enforcement, made what seems to have been an obvious connection between the radio dramatization and the Ora Murray murder that followed, *just three weeks later.*

Those of you, who have read my sequel, *Most Evil,* will have a fuller understanding of the importance of this newly discovered link to the 1940s. Why? Because, in my father's later serial killings it became an important and recurring theme which he used as part of his murder-signature.

In the crimes of the 1960s he expanded his *Murder as a Fine Art* from just the surrealistic plagiarism of Man Ray's photography, as seen in his Black Dahlia murder, and opened it to a much broader canvas.

In *Most Evil,* we discovered that George Hodel expanded the signature of his killings, his "masterpieces," beyond modern art and ventured into the world of: music, film and literature.

This is why this new discovery, demonstrating another example of his early plagiarism of Cornell Woolrich's short-story, adapted to radio, is so important. It reinforces my theory that this was a signature-act which George Hodel used in 1943, some three-years prior to his imitation of Man Ray's art, recreated as the macabre Black Dahlia murder. *This establishes that George Hodel had already "been there and done that"–four-years earlier.*

Within two weeks of the fictional *White Rose Murders* having been broadcast to the public, I submit, Dr. George Hill Hodel, as "Paul," the dapper businessman from San Francisco, made it REAL by following the original *White Rose Murders* script and sought out and auditioned his own dancehall partner-victim, Ora Murray—*for the part.*

As "Paul" he danced with her, bought her drinks, and then wooed her out of the *Zenda Ballroom* with an invitation to, "See Hollywood for a night-on-the-town." He then drove her to an isolated golf-course, beat and strangled her, and with a final dramatic flair, carefully placed a "white gardenia" next to the dead body.

In *Most Evil* we examined several separate murders which I believe my father "adapted from film," and used in his real life killings. One of these, Richard Connell's, *The Most Dangerous Game,* was famously used by the Zodiac Killer as part of his signature M.O. and was subsequently mentioned in his letter writing campaign to the press and police.

In checking the list of 1940s Suspense Theatre programs. I noted that *The Most Dangerous Game* was also listed as being performed at the same CBS Theatre. It aired in Hollywood on February 1, 1945, and starred Orson Welles as the psychopath, General Zaroff. [In 1969, the serial killer, "Zodiac" costumed himself in the fashion of General Zaroff and terrorized the Bay area, informing the public that in committing his murders he was playing, "The Most Dangerous Game."

How many more of these fictional stories from literature and film might George Hodel have *adapted and abridged into his real life murders? So far we have documented four: Charlie Chan at Treasure Island, The Most Dangerous Game, The Gold Bug, and now, The White Rose Murders. I am aware of a fifth film, which will be discussed in detail in an upcoming chapter of this book. I expect more will be found.*

Since my last publication in 2006, based on new investigative findings, I am adding two more victims to that Category I list. One victim, Louise Springer, I am upgrading from a Category II "probable" to a definite, based on new information.

The second victim came onto my radar screen in 2009. Her name is Lillian Dominguez and she was slain in October 1947.

Here is a brief summary on both of the new Category I crimes.

Louise Springer-June 13, 1949

"The Black Dahlia and the Louise Springer murders might be linked. Both crimes could have been committed by the same man."

Detective Harry Hansen LAPD Homicide
Los Angeles Times, June 1949

Detective Harry Hansen reviewing Dahlia Files

At approximately 9:15 p.m., on the evening of June 13, 1949, Laurence Springer drove his new Studebaker convertible to pickup his wife. Louise Springer met him in the parking-lot on Crenshaw Boulevard, near Santa Barbara, where she worked as a beautician. As she entered the car, Louise noticed that she had left her eyeglasses inside the beauty parlor. Her husband offered to get them for her and also purchased a newspaper and cigarettes at an adjacent drugstore. He was gone less than ten minutes. Upon his return, both his car and his wife, Louise, were gone.

The husband immediately contacted LAPD which referred him to University Division Police Station, where the desk officer advised Mr. Springer, "They could not take a formal Missing Person Report for 24-hours." The husband attempted to convince the officers that his wife would not simply drive away, and that she had to have been the victim of a kidnapping or foul play. Sadly, his pleas fell upon deaf ears. Frustrated and angry, the husband returned to his Hollywood home to be with their three-year-old son, and could only hope his wife would call.

Three days later, Laurence Springer's suspicions were confirmed. Louise Springer's body was found in the backseat of their car, which the suspect, by circumstance, had been forced to park on a quiet residential street, just an hour after the abduction and murder. Here is the investigative chronology and findings:

June 13, 1949- 9:15 p.m.

The victim, Louise Springer, a twenty-eight-year-old female, was kidnapped [abducted in her own car] while sitting and waiting for her husband to return from a short errand.

Within a forty-five-minute time period, the suspect [s] abducted her from the location, strangled her with a pre-cut clothesline rope that he brought with him, and then sexually assaulted her [sodomy] using a fourteen-inch long tree-limb.
The suspect then placed her body in the rear seat of her car and covered it with a beautician's tarp, which was in the vehicle and which Louise used in her work.

The kidnap location was on South Crenshaw Boulevard, just north of Santa Barbara Avenue [now renamed Martin Luther King

Boulevard] and was just 500 yards southwest of where Elizabeth "Black Dahlia" Short's body parts were found in the vacant lot at 3815 South Norton Avenue some two years prior.

Springer – Short crimes 500 yards apart

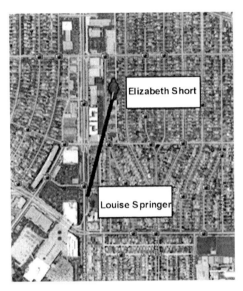

June 13, 1949 - 10:30 p.m.

Four neighborhood witnesses looking out their window, observed Springer's vehicle, a 1949 Studebaker convertible being driven eastbound on Thirty-Eighth Street, and saw the car suddenly swerved to the south curb and quickly parked in front of 126 W. Thirty-Eighth Street.

Then they saw the driver turn off the headlights and slump down behind the steering wheel.

Seconds later, an LAPD uniformed patrol car, with its emergency lights blinking, pulled over a teenage driver for a traffic violation. As the witnesses watched from their residence, the man in the Studebaker sat motionless while the officers exited their patrol car and wrote a ticket to the teenager, who was standing just a few yards away.

The officers, after citing the teen, then reentered their patrol car and drove off.

The witnesses continued looking out their window and saw the man reach toward the backseat, as if to adjust something. At that point, they stopped their observations.

Due to the darkness, the only description they could provide was "A white male with curly hair."

These actions occurred just forty-five minutes after the abduction. But because the witnesses were unaware that any crime had been committed, nothing was reported for three days.

On June 16, a separate neighbor became suspicious of the abandoned Studebaker and called the police.

Officers checking the license plate number determined that it was the missing Springer vehicle and responded to find the victim strangled to death under a tarp in the backseat. A neighborhood check by homicide detectives for witnesses resulted in the four witnesses coming forward to describe what they had seen on the night of June 13th.

The below map shows the probable route taken from the abduction to where the vehicle was parked at 126 W. Thirty-Eighth Street. Driving distance was 4.0 miles.

126 W. 38TH St. - 4 miles [10 minutes] from abduction location

Louise Springer Murder Headlines June 17, 1949

Los Angeles Examiner—June 18, 1949

"Police Missed Mad Killer, in Auto with Slain Victim, Parked Near Squad Car."

The *Examiner* printed a diagram showing the relative positions of the police, the traffic offender, and the murder suspect on 38th Street.

Los Angeles Examiner, June 18, 1949

Los Angeles Examiner of June 17, read:

...

Body Violated

"And with a 14-inch length of finger-thick tree branch, ripped from some small tree, the killer had violated her body in such manner as to stamp this crime at once and indelibly in the same category as the killing of Elizabeth Short, "the *Black Dahlia*."

LAPD Criminalist Ray Pinker called in a botanist expert on the Louise Springer investigation who examined and identified the tree branch as coming from a "Bottlebrush tree."

The below photo shows a bottlebrush tree which is indigenous to all neighborhoods of Los Angeles and the actual tree branch used by suspect in the sexual assault. [Cropped by author from the original Louise Springer coroner's photograph.]

Top: Bottle Brush Tree. Bottom: photo is the actual tree branch used by suspect in the sexual assault.

This October, 1949 Booking photo of George Hodel showing his "Black, curly hair" was taken just three months after the Louise Springer murder.

Photo showing "Springer Murder Car"
Article reads, "The discovery has touched off the wildest man hunt since the slaying of the Black Dahlia."

241

The autopsy was performed by Drs. Newbarr and Cefalu, the same two assigned to perform the Elizabeth Short autopsy two years prior. Their examination revealed that Louise Springer suffered multiple blows to the head that would have likely rendered her unconscious. After which she was strangled with a white clothesline cord, which the suspect brought with him.

Autopsy photo [cropped] showing clothesline ligature

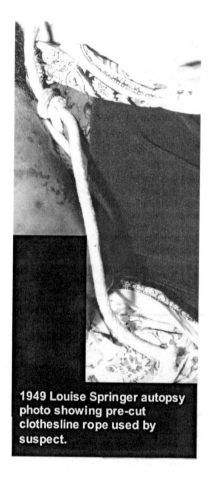

1949 Louise Springer autopsy photo showing pre-cut clothesline rope used by suspect.

Some additional investigative findings:

- Police suspected that killer may have known the victim prior. Possible jealous ex-boyfriend? Detective Hansen and partner traveled to San Francisco for a full week investigation into the victim's background. Newspapers of the day hinted at a "possible romantic affair." No hard evidence believed found.

- Prior to the murder, a male called Laurence Springer's work telephone (six times) over six days, and kept hanging up. Also, called Springer's home residence.

- Though LAPD continued to suspect that the Springer and Elizabeth Short and other lone woman crimes could have been connected, Louise Springer's sadistic killer, like the others, was never identified.

- 1949 Grand Jury demanded a reinvestigation of the Elizabeth Short and other unsolved murders as is evidenced by the below 1949 headline, which adds Louise Springer's photo to the long list of unsolved murders and read:

"L.A. POLICE BAFFLED BY NINTH WEIRD MURDER IN 29 MONTHS"

Long Beach Post-Telegram
June 17, 1949

Lillian Dominguez—An Overlooked 1947 *Lone Woman Murder*

Based on my examination and review of the known facts surrounding the stabbing-murder of Santa Monica victim, Lillian Dominguez, age fifteen, which occurred in October 1947, I am now adding her name to the list of Category I, Los Angeles *Lone Woman Murders*, that I believe were committed by my father, Dr. George Hill Hodel.

On the night of October 2, 1947, Lillian Dominguez, a fifteen-year-old student at John Adams Junior High was walking home from a school dance with her sister, Angie, and their friend, Andrea Marquez.

As the three girls approached the intersection of Seventeenth Street and Michigan Avenue in Santa Monica, a man approached them in the darkness and walked by them. Seconds later, Lillian told her sister, "That man touched me." She took a few steps and yelled out, "I can't see." Lillian staggered against the fence, collapsed, and died.

An autopsy established that Lillian had been stabbed in the heart with a long, thin bladed "stiletto-type knife" or possibly an icepick. The half-inch wide blade penetrated three and a half inches **directly into** the heart. No real accurate description of her attacker was believed obtained other than the teenager's initial description of him being "a man."

Santa Monica detectives had very little to go on. The suspect description was almost nonexistent and it was a completely motiveless crime. Lillian had no boyfriends and there was no trouble at the dance, which had been held at Garfield Elementary School.

LA Times October 7, 1947, victim's sister, Angie Dominguez and friend Andrea Marquez:

AT INQUEST—Angie Dominguez, 17, left, sister of girl stabbed to death, and Andrea Marquez, 17, friend, testify at inquest for victim, where open verdict was returned.

The Murder Weapon

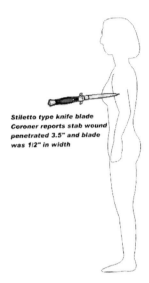

Stiletto type knife blade
Coroner reports stab wound
penetrated 3.5" and blade
was 1/2" in width

Stiletto-type knife or icepick used

Based on the limited information as reported in the 1947 newspaper article, I sent an e-mail inquiry to my friend and fellow writer, Dr. Doug Lyle M.D., a forensic expert, as well as a heart specialist. Here is an excerpt from that e-mail:

May 9, 2010

Hi Doug:

...

In reviewing a press article on the stabbing/murder the info from the coroner's office printed in the paper reads:

"Dr. Frederick Newbarr, county autopsy surgeon, reported after performing an autopsy that the stab wound in the girl's left breast is 3 3/4" inches deep and a half inch wide and that it penetrated only the heart muscle, not the heart itself.

Death, he said, apparently was caused by internal bleeding. Severance of nerves could have numbed pain and caused the blindness of which the girl complained, Dr. Newbarr said."

1)   Forgive my anatomical ignorance, but what is the distinction/difference between "the heart and the heart muscle?" What are they saying here?

2)   Any thought on the blindness. Would that be unusual or common with the facts as stated?

Thanks,

Steve

And, here is Dr. Lyle's reply:

Howdy:

This shows you how far behind they were 70 years ago. The heart muscle is the main part of the heart and the part that would be stabbed in such an injury as this. Severing of nerves—of which there are no major ones in that area—would NOT cause blindness. Either she had some other injury or the blindness could be the hysterical type. Some people under extreme stress go blind—it is all psychiatric—and is called hysterical blindness. Or in this case she could have been in shock or her blood pressure could have suddenly dropped from the heart injury and if so the low blood pressure could cause blurred and then dim vision just before losing consciousness and dying. I'd suspect this latter is what happened since she died almost immediately after her visual complaints.

Doug

Avenger Note

On the evening of October 9, 1947, exactly one-week after the stabbing, Lillian's killer left a handwritten note under the door of a *Los Angeles* furniture store.

The note, written in pencil on the back of a business card of a "Mexican restaurant" read:

"I killed that Santa Monica girl. I will kill others."

While neither the furniture store nor the Mexican restaurant locations were identified by police, the information and threat from the killer was published in the *Santa Monica Evening Outlook* on October 10, 1947, which was George Hodel's fortieth birthday.

We do know that the furniture store was outside the city of Santa Monica and in Los Angeles. We recalled in some of the other *Lone Woman* murders, that George Hodel left or mailed the Kern and Short notes just blocks away from his downtown medical office. Was either the furniture company or the Mexican restaurant also near his medical offices?

Dominguez "Avenger" Signature

In my 2009 sequel, *Avenger, Zodiac, and the Further Serial Murders of Dr. George Hill Hodel* [Dutton], I explored the possible connections of George Hodel to three 1946 Chicago "Lipstick Murders." In that book, I also examined the 1966 knife slaying of a Riverside student; the "Jigsaw Murder" in Manila, where my father was living at the time and where police suspected the killer was a trained surgeon; and finally, I explored and presented compelling evidence potentially linking my father to the 1968-1969 Bay Area murders committed by the suspect calling himself, "Zodiac."

In this review, I am only going to present one specific and highly unusual aspect of the killer's M.O.–that being his "promise to kill more victims." That act combined with the fact that we are dealing with a serial killer is so unique that I believe it qualifies as a part of his actual SIGNATURE.

Let's examine the below photograph which is a reproduction of the separate notes left by the killer [s] in: Chicago, Los Angeles, Riverside, and the San Francisco Bay Area.

The Notes

The Los Angeles Dominguez Note, "I killed that Santa Monica girl. I will kill others." was discovered post-publication to my 2009 sequel, *Most Evil* and is here presented only as a "reproduction" of what the killer wrote as law enforcement never released a sample of the actual 1947 handwriting. The Chicago, Riverside, and San Francisco notes are all actual copies of the killer's original handwriting.

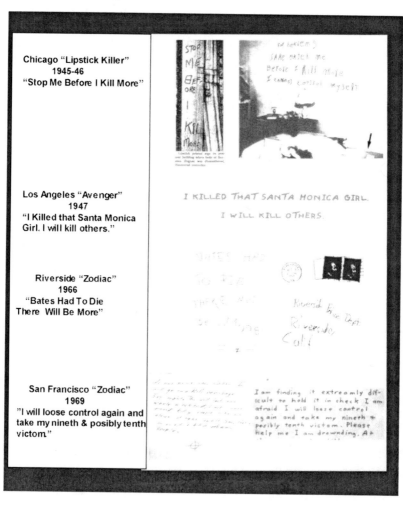

Chicago "Lipstick Killer"
1945-46
"Stop Me Before I Kill More"

Los Angeles "Avenger"
1947
"I Killed that Santa Monica Girl. I will kill others."

Riverside "Zodiac"
1966
"Bates Had To Die There Will Be More"

San Francisco "Zodiac"
1969
"I will loose control again and take my nineth & posibly tenth victom."

Chicago, 1946–(written in lipstick)

"For heavens sake catch me before I kill more. I cannot control myself.

"Stop Me Before I Kill More."

Los Angeles,1947

"I killed that Santa Monica girl. I will kill others."

Riverside, 1966

"Bates Had To Die. There Will Be More."

Z

San Francisco, 1969-

...

"I am afraid I will loose control again and take my nineth &possibly tenth victom. Please help me I am drownding."

In *Most Evil*, one of my most important signature links was the fact that the killer in Chicago, Riverside and the San Francisco Bay Area was an "urban terrorist," and left notes in each of those cities, threatening to "KILL MORE." If this was an accurate assessment then [playing Devil's Advocate] why had he excluded this important signature in his many LA crimes in the 1940s?

He had threatened the citizenry before and after, so why would he choose to exclude them in his hometown of Los Angeles?

Until now, we had no answer. And the absence of a Los Angeles "urban terrorist threat" weakened my hypothesis. However, with this recent discovery of the Dominguez Note, we now have an answer. Fact is, HE DIDN"T EXCLUDE LA. The threat was always there, it was just overlooked. I didn't make the connection until discovering the note in my recent review of the facts surrounding the Dominguez Cold Case which read:

"I Killed That Santa Monica Girl. I Will Kill Others."

The Location

In the below diagram, we see that the Lillian Dominguez murder is just two miles away from another 1947 *Lone Woman* murder—Mrs. Jeanne French.

According to Head Deputy District Attorney, Steve Kay, the French crime was committed by Dr. George Hill Hodel, and based on the evidence presented, had George Hodel still been alive and the witnesses available, *he would have prosecuted the case, as a companion filing to the Elizabeth Short, "Black Dahlia" murder.*

Two miles between 1947 Dominguez and French motiveless murders

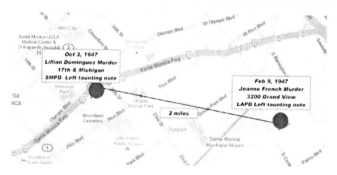

An Avenger Motive?

In the 1966 Riverside Cheri Jo Bates murder, the victim was a teenager, who had just graduated from high school.

Riverside PD investigated the possibility that her killer was a high school classmate. They followed this lead based on a literal interpretation of a second typed note mailed in by her killer on the six-month anniversary of the Bates crime. [George Hodel mailed in both, a lengthy handwritten and a typed letter in two of his 1940s LA crimes: Georgette Bauerdorf [typed] and Gladys Kern [handwritten].]

In that lengthy Bates typewritten note taunting the police and press, he referred to his next victim and speculated on who it might be:

... "a babysitter, or MAYBE SHE WILL BE THE SHAPELY BLUE-EYED BROWNETT THAT SAID NO WHEN I ASKED HER FOR A DATE IN HIGH SCHOOL..."

San Francisco PD in 1971 connected the Riverside Bates murder to their Northern California, Zodiac crimes.

Six of their seven victims were either teenagers in high-school, or recently graduated. All these victims were parked in "lover's lane" type locations. This too reinforced the possibility of a serial killer, an avenger, exacting revenge for being rejected in his high-school days by some young "shapely blue-eyed brownett." [I hypothesize that George Hodel, the "super nerd," could well have been rejected numerous times by girls both in high-school and in college, since he was one of the few fifteen-year-olds at Cal Tech. He would very likely have been rejected by many college classmates because of his youth.]

The apparent totally unmotivated and cold-bloodedness of the 1947 attack and murder of high school student Lillian Dominguez fits in quite well with what we know about these later crimes against high-schoolers, as well as ZODIAC's stated need for revenge for being rejected by a teen sweetheart.

Based on the "hit and run" nature of the Dominguez crime and absence of any real physical evidence or witnesses, I doubt that the crime is now solvable.

It would be interesting to see the original note and compare it to George Hodel's known handwriting. Also, I am curious as to where the Mexican restaurant and the furniture company were located?

But regardless, I do think this crime plays an important role in providing the missing piece to a much larger puzzle, and based on its unique signatures, location, along with what is known about George Hodel's later crimes, I do believe it should be considered and included as a 1940s Category I, *Lone Woman murder.*

LONE WOMEN MURDER MAP [revised 2011]

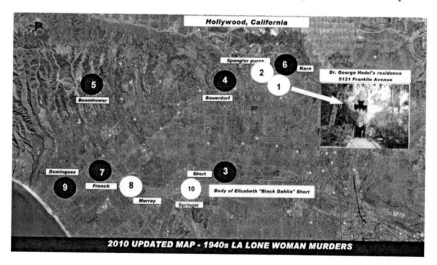

In this updated victim map, I have added both the 1947 Lillian Dominguez murder [9] and the Louise Springer murder [10].

There are now a total of *nine* Category I victims. All of the crimes occurred within a one-half- to nine-mile distance from the Franklin house.

The black circles are 1940s victims where a letter or note was left or mailed in by the "Avenger." This is an exceptionally rare signature act and we find that in *six of the nine* local Los Angeles murders, he taunted police with such a note or letter. [Short, Bauerdorf, Boomhower, Kern, French, and Dominguez]

A *serial killer* sending taunting notes to the police in the 1940s was so rare that preceding the "Black Dahlia Avenger," police would have to have gone back in time some six decades to London's "Jack the Ripper" [1888] to find a similar signature.

The authorship of most of the Avenger notes has been independently identified by a court certified questioned document expert as having been written by Dr. George Hodel. To date, no certified expert has offered an opinion that the handwriting IS NOT GEORGE HODEL'S. [In the past seven-years, two separate television documentaries have claimed that "an expert contradicted my expert."]

In fact, he did not; he simply stated that in examining the few samples he was provided, he was unable to offer an opinion either way. He told the producers, *"His findings were inconclusive. He was unable to rule Dr. Hodel in or out as to having authored the notes."* I will provide further details related to the handwriting evidence in a later chapter.

Elizabeth Short and Gladys Kern letters mailed from same downtown mailbox

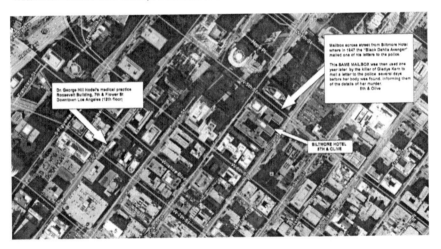

Killer uses *same downtown mail box* to post both his Elizabeth Short (Jan.1947) and Gladys Kern (Feb.1948) handwritten notes to police. *The mailbox he used was across the street from the Biltmore Hotel and just 300 yards from Dr. George Hodel's private medical practice.*

1950 DA Files Reveal Investigators Believed Crimes Linked

Documents discovered by me in LADA, Lt. Frank Jemison's 1950 investigative files, show that his detectives were actively investigating the following *Lone Woman* murders:

Elizabeth Short, Jeanne French, Jean Spangler, Gladys Kern, Ruth Spaulding [George Hodel's secretary], and the February18, 1950 "Jane Doe" suspected felony assault and or possible murder heard being committed on-tape in the basement of Dr. Hodel's Franklin house.

By the Numbers

As I pointed out in my original 2003 investigation, if one takes the position that none of these 1940s crimes were connected, **then statistically, at least half of the *Lone Woman* murders should have been solved.** How many were? NONE.

As is now obvious, the fact is these murders were not committed by eleven different sadistic sexual psychopaths all operating within the same locales and tripping over each other's bodies. No! The reason none were cleared was because *all were committed by the same suspect.*

Despite the fact that sixty-years ago, law enforcement did not really think in terms of "serial killings," LAPD [with a lot of help from the press] still managed to go public with their belief that many or most of these crimes were committed by the same suspect.

With the June 13, 1949 murder of Louise Springer, police once again confirmed, as they had from the very beginning, their suspicions that many if not all of the crimes WERE CONNECTED.

"Police are not overlooking the possibility that a single slayer committed all [nine] of the Los Angeles "Horror Murders."

Long Beach Press Telegram
June 17, 1949

254

Long Beach Press Telegram, June 17, 1949

The newspaper article goes on to name the nine victims *they suspect are related as:*

1. Elizabeth Short
2. Mary Tate
3. Evelyn Winters
4. Jeanne French
5. Rosenda Mondragon
6. Dorothy Montgomery
7. Laura Trelstad
8. Gladys Kern
9. Louise Springer

[*All of these names* are included in my original investigation; however, some are listed by me as Category II and III.]

Chapter 12

Urban Myth No. 2- "The Missing Week"

On the evening of January 9, 1947, Elizabeth Short, the Black Dahlia, walked out of the Olive Street entrance of the Biltmore Hotel, turned right, and was last seen walking south on the sidewalk. She was never seen again, until her nude, bisected body was found six days later, on January 15, posed on the vacant lot.

One of my biggest investigatory revelations came to me late in the year 2000, when I was just completing my first full year on the case. I had spent four full months chronicling the KNOWN facts and had amassed 150 different witness interviews covering the time period from 1943-1999.

After sorting them by date, time, and location, in looking at the limited time frame of January 9-14, 1947, it became obvious *that there never was a missing week.* All of the original witness interviews from that time period, which law enforcement had collected independent of each other, supported the same truth—there was NO MISSING WEEK.

Apparently, no one before me, including post-1960s LAPD detectives had taken the time to take a look at this. [Partly understandable on LAPD's part as it was extremely time-intensive research, which required many months to compile.] But there it was!

Only now in recent years, have I come to understand why modern day authors, theorists, and even LAPD have no desire to underscore the obvious. Why?

In LAPD's case, it proves that their official public position, which has been in place for decades—is simply not true. If confirmed, it exposes the department to open criticism of being either inept or ignorant and misinformed as to the true facts.

No conspiracy here—the truth is simply that no modern day LAPD detective is familiar with the facts of the case, nor have they been since the 1950s.

In the 1970s, when LAPD Robbery Homicide detectives John St. John ["Jigsaw John"] and his partner Kirk Mellecker were assigned as the official custodians of the case, they were at least honest enough to admit, they "didn't have the time to fully review the facts of the long cold case due to active case demands."

By the 1990s, when detective Brian Carr inherited the forty-year-old case, there was no longer even any pretense at familiarity with the facts. Carr was quick to name himself a "gatekeeper" and advised the public in his opinion "the case will never be solved and he would pass it on when he retired."

By 2007, Detective Carr, confronted with constant questions from the press related to my investigative findings, was forced to give an on-camera interview where he simply stated, "I don't have time to prove or disprove Hodel's investigation." Carr, true to his word, "passed the case on" when he retired from LAPD in May 2009.

LAPD Wanted Information Bulletin contributed to "Missing Week" Myth

At first glance, without reading the information, the official *LAPD Wanted Information Bulletin* would appear to confirm a missing week between January 9-15, 1947.

However, closer examination proves that it does just the opposite. The bulletin is actually a REQUEST FOR INFORMATION.

It was prepared and circulated just four days after the identification of the body as being that of Elizabeth Short and is exactly what it purports itself to be: a WANTED INFORMATION BULLETIN.

The bulletin was originally printed and distributed to uniform patrol officers and detectives at all roll-calls, and instructed officers to attempt to locate witnesses that may have seen her. I quote verbatim from the Bulletin:

> **"Make inquiries at local hotels, motels, apartment houses, cocktail bars and lounges, night clubs to ascertain whereabouts of victim between dates mentioned."**

On January 21, just five days into the investigation, LAPD officers did as requested and began distributing the bulletin and asking questions if anyone had seen the victim between the dates of January 9 to 15?

Their actions resulted in twelve (12) *verified reliable sightings* of the victim. Elizabeth Short was seen on every day of the week from January 9 through January 14. Half of these witnesses PERSONALLY KNEW HER and could not have been mistaken.

Here are THE FACTS.

All of the witnesses listed below made official reports directly to the LAPD. They are fresh accounts from January, 1947.

They were published in the various Los Angeles newspapers in the days and weeks immediately following the discovery of the body. [See BDA Chapter 18, pages 232-238 and page 527 for a detailed narrative of each of these 1947 witnesses statements and where and when they were documented.]

Witnesses Chronological Sightings During Elizabeth Short's "Missing Week"

(Name in **bold/italic** indicates witness **personally acquainted** with Elizabeth Short)

WITNESS	DATE	LOCATION
Mr. Studholme Biltmore Hotel employee	Jan. 9 (Thur) 7-10 p.m.	Biltmore Hotel 5th & Olive St. (Olive Street entrance) Downtown L. A.
"John Doe #1" (LAPD withheld name)	Jan. 10 (Fri) evening	7200 Sunset Blvd. Hollywood (street) Hollywood
Miss Iris Menuay ***(Former roommate/friend)***	Jan. 10 (Fri) 8:30 p.m.	1842 N. Cherokee Ave Chancellor Hotel (lobby) Hollywood
Christina Salisbury ***(Restaurant owner/friend.*** ***Employed victim in Florida)***	Jan. 10 (Fri) 10:00 p.m.	7290 Sunset Blvd. Tabu Club, Hollywood (street) Hollywood
Buddy La Gore ***(Bartender, knew victim as a*** ***"regular")***	Jan. 10 (Fri) 11:30 p.m.	6818 Hollywood Blvd. Four Star Bar & Grill (bar) Hollywood
"John Doe #2" (Hotel service. station attendant LAPD withheld name)	Jan. 11 (Sat) 2:30 a.m.	9641 Sunset Bl. Beverly Hills Hotel (gas station) Beverly Hills
Mr. Paul Simone ***(Maintenance man Chancellor*** ***Hotel)***	Jan. 11 (Sat) daytime unstated hour	1842 N. Cherokee Ave Chancellor Hotel (rear and front) Hollywood
Mr. I. A. Jorgenson (Cab driver)	Jan. 11 (Sat) afternoon unstated hour	112 W. 5th St. Rosslyn Hotel (Entered cab at front of hotel) Downtown L. A.
Mr/Mrs William Johnson (Hotel owners/on-site managers)	Jan. 12 (Sun) 11:30 a.m.	Hotel 300 E. Washington Bl. (Hotel lobby/registration desk) Downtown L. A.
Mr. C. G. Williams ***(Bartender, knew victim as a*** ***"regular")***	Jan. 12 (Sun) 3:00 p.m.	634 S. Main St. Dugout Cafe (bar) Downtown L. A.
Mr. John Jiroudek ***(Jockey/friend, knew victim from*** ***Camp Cooke military base)***	Jan. 13 (Mon) unstated hour	Hollywood & Highland (Street) Hollywood
Officer Meryl McBride (LAPD uniformed police officer, two contacts half hour apart)	Jan. 14 (Tues) 3:30 -4 p.m.	6th & Main St. Bus Depot(street/bar) Downtown L. A.

DIAGRAM OF LOCATIONS

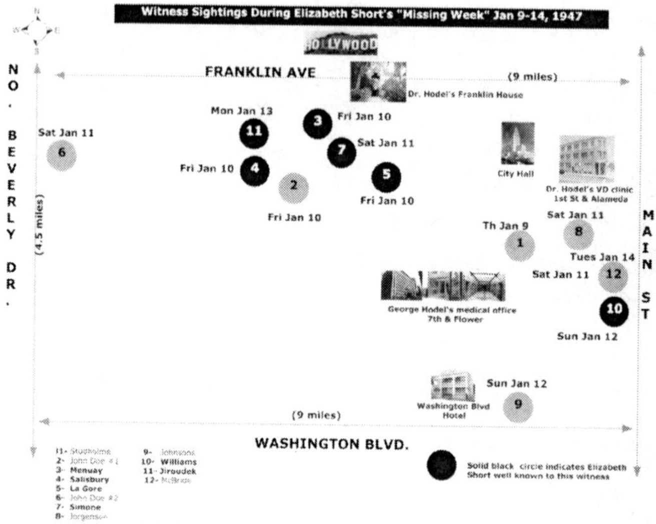

Witness Sightings During Elizabeth Short's "Missing Week" Jan 9-14, 1947

Above diagram shows the 4 x 9 mile perimeter between Hollywood and downtown Los Angeles, within which boundaries Elizabeth Short was seen on *twelve separate occasions* during the five days (January 10—January 14) prior to the discovery of her body on January 15, 1947. *Incredibly, six of these twelve witnesses were personally acquainted with the victim, so their positive identifications are not in question.* (Solid black circles signify those witnesses.)

Also included in the diagram are: Dr. George Hodel's 1947 private residence, the Franklin house at 5121 Franklin Avenue, his privately owned downtown VD clinic at First and Alameda Street, and his private medical practice, at Seventh and Flower Street, just three blocks from the Biltmore Hotel [1].

Sightings of Elizabeth Short by location and day of the week during the five-day period:

<u>Downtown Los Angeles</u>—five independent sightings

1. Thursday, January 9
2. Saturday, January 11
3. Sunday, January 12
4. Sunday, January 12
5. Tuesday, January 14

Though each witness report to the police was *individual and separate* from the other reports, nevertheless, *all separate downtown sightings of Elizabeth Short were within a one-mile radius of each other on four separate days of the week.*

Hollywood—six independent sightings

1. Friday, January 10
2. Friday, January 10
3. Friday, January 10
4. Friday, January 10
5. Saturday, January 11
6. Monday, January 13

Though each witness report to the police was *individual and separate* from the other reports, nevertheless, *all Hollywood sightings of Elizabeth Short were within a four-block radius of each other on three separate days of the week.*

Beverly Hills—one sighting

1. Saturday, January 11

This sighting was close in time to the four January 10 Hollywood sightings as it occurred just a few hours after midnight. This location is approximately four [4] miles west of the earlier Hollywood sightings, and was immediately west of the Sunset Strip, just inside the Beverly Hills city limits.

Los Angeles Herald-Express
Feb 7, 1947

'Dahlia' Seen in 'Lost Week'

The "lost week" of the "Black Dahlia" prior to her murder was narrowed by two days today with a report that placed her in the city on Jan. 11, four days before her body was found.

A service station attendant ... handles the gasoline pumps at the Beverly Hills Hotel "positively" identified the slain beauty, Elizabeth Short, as one of the occupants of a car that drove up for gas between 2:30 and 3 a. m. on that date.

The attendant said the "Dahlia" was accompanied by another woman and a man, and that she seemed "very upset and frightened."

The man driving the car, a 1942 tan Chrysler coupe, was described as about 30 years old, 6

(Continued on Page 10, Column 2)

LAPD Capt. Jack Donahoe was convinced that the January 11, 1947 witness sighting at the Beverly Hills Hotel gas-station was accurate and kept the "John Doe No. 2" witness' name confidential. Here is the report from the February 7, 1947, *Herald Express* article on that sighting:

The "lost week" of the "Black Dahlia" prior to her murder was narrowed by two days today with a report that placed her in the city on Jan 11, four days before her body was found.

A service station attendant who handles the gasoline pumps at the Beverly Hills Hotel "positively" identified the slain beauty, Elizabeth Short, as one of the occupants of a car that drove up for gas between 2:30 and 3 a.m. on that date.

The attendant said the "Dahlia" was accompanied by another woman and a man, and that she seemed "very upset and frightened." The man driving the car, a 1942 Chrysler coupe, was described as about 30 years old, 6 feet 1 inch tall and weighed about 190 pounds. The other woman was dressed in dark clothing, the attendant said.

Capt. Jack Donahoe ordered an immediate check on the car and its occupants.

...

During her so called, "Missing Week" [it was actually only a five-day period], Elizabeth Short was seen in Hollywood on six separate occasions by six different witnesses. *Five of the witnesses KNEW her personally and could not have been mistaken.* [The sixth may have also known her, but his name was withheld by police and released publicly only as "John Doe."] All of these Hollywood contacts were within a four square block area occurring on three separate days of the week. [January10, 11, and 13.]

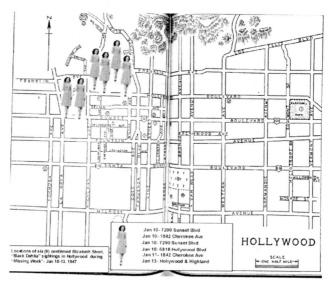

Jan 10 - 7200 Sunset Blvd
Jan 10 - 1842 Cherokee Ave
Jan 10 - 7290 Sunset Blvd
Jan 10 - 6818 Hollywood Blvd
Jan 11 - 1842 Cherokee Ave
Jan 13 - Hollywood & Highland

Locations of six (6) confirmed Elizabeth Short, "Black Dahlia" sightings in Hollywood during "Missing Week" - Jan 10-13, 1947

HOLLYWOOD

SCALE
ONE HALF MILE

Chapter 13

Urban Myth No. 3- "Black Dahlia Murder Never Solved"

Since 1947, hundreds of suspects were questioned by LAPD detectives, but the killer of the Black Dahlia was never identified. The case was never solved.

LAPD, LASD, DA Bureau of Investigation officers past and present agree:

"CASE SOLVED"

Despite the nearly sixty-year chasm that divides the investigation past and present, we now have statements from the four highest-ranking police officers *confirming that the Black Dahlia case was solved. These four detectives were directly involved in the original Dahlia investigation and privy to its secrets.* These officers represented all three law enforcement agencies in Los Angeles: The city [LAPD], the county (LASD) and the Los Angeles District Attorney, the prosecutor for both city and county. Their statements are all the more remarkable in that they were made in absolute confidence, *yet each independently substantiates the others,* though each is derived from a separate person, place, and time. That's *corroboration!* None of these command officer's statements were ever intended to be made public. Each was a personal communication, which remained private and confidential decades after their respective deaths. All four indict the same man, "a Hollywood physician, living on Franklin Avenue, involved in abortions." They kept his name secret for over five decades.

Now, thanks to the 2003 access and release of the secret DA FILES, we now know his name and address as revealed in those original reports.

Though never arrested, the Black Dahlia murder, according to top commanders from all three Los Angeles law enforcement agencies agree, "The case was solved."

Out of the past- The Black Dahlia's top brass:

LAPD chief of detectives Thad Brown circa 1950

"The Black Dahlia case was solved. He was a doctor who lived on Franklin Avenue in Hollywood." [Statement made in the 1960s to his close personal friend, actor Jack Webb. *Dragnet's*, "Sgt. Joe Friday".]

LAPD chief of police William H. Parker circa 1950

"We identified the Black Dahlia suspect. He was a doctor."
[Statement made to his personal physician circa 1964.]

LA Sheriff's captain of detectives J. Gordon Bowers 1947

"The Black Dahlia case was solved, but it will never come out. It was some doctor they [LAPD] all knew in Hollywood involved in abortions." [Statement made by LASD Undersheriff James Downey to his chief of detectives J. Gordon Bowers circa 1961. Statement made in the presence of Downey's driver, Deputy Tom Vetter, who would later be promoted to LASD Commander.]

DA Lt. Frank B. Jemison

"We know who the Black Dahlia killer was. He was a doctor, but we didn't have enough to put him away." [Statement made to Jemison's visiting nephew and his physician brother-in-law at the LA Hall of Justice in the summer of 1951. Jemison's nephew grew up and became a medical doctor.]

Out of the present- The DA's Office, LAPD, and LASD:

Steve Kay, LA County Head Deputy DA [ret.]

2006

"Steve Hodel has taken this way beyond the pictures. It no longer depends on the pictures." [Statement in *Los Angeles Times Magazine*, November 21, 2004.]

"I have no doubt in my mind that George Hodel murdered Elizabeth Short...If the witnesses were alive today, I believe if I took that case in front of a jury, that I would convict him." [Rue 13, French television documentary, *The Truth about the Black Dahlia*, November 6, 2006.]

LAPD deputy chief James McMurray [ret.]
Chief of Detectives

"The hardcover book was pretty compelling. Then when all the transcripts and stuff came out from the D.A.'s Office that took it over the top for me. That would have been enough for me to bring a case against Dr. Hodel." [*LA Times*, November 21, 2004.]

"I have told my detectives, unless that can find some major holes in Hodel's investigation—to go ahead and clear the Black Dahlia murder." [November 2004]

LASD commander Thomas Vetter [ret.]
Lt. Col. USMC [ret.}

"In 1962, I was a detective and was the driver for Undersheriff James Downey who was the sheriff department's number two man. One day, he was going to lunch with his good friend, Gordy Bowers, chief of detectives. Somehow, the Black Dahlia murder came up in the conversation. I heard Jimmy say, 'Oh, that had been solved, but it will never come out. It was some doctor they [LAPD] all knew out in Hollywood.' In my own professional opinion, Hodel has put the pieces together and solved the case." [Television interview, October 2004]

LAPD deputy chief of detectives James McMurray and
Chief William Bratton honor author at LAPD Author's Night function-
2004

1947- Then Capt. Gordon Bowers "Working the Black Dahlia Case"

Los Angeles Times 1947

MURDER CLUES SOUGHT—Inspector Norris Stensland and Capt. Gordon Bowers of sheriff's department search canyon culvert near Malibu for possible Short murder clues.

Canyon Combed in Short Killing

Sheriff's officers yesterday searched an area in Las Tunas Canyon, near Malibu, for possible clues to the murder of Elizabeth Short after a blood-drenched man's shirt, bow tie, and a rusty, blood-caked razor blade were found inside a culvert.

Inspector Norris Stensland and Capt. Gordon Bowers, of the Sheriff's office, explored the possibility that the "Black Dahlia" was slain and her body severed in the culvert, but a search by them and four deputy sheriffs turned up nothing to bolster the theory.

Stensland said nothing definite yet linked the bloody clothes and razor blade with the Short murder. But, he added, the culvert quite possibly could be the scene of the butchery.

The clothes and razor blade were being scrutinized under microscopes to determine if the dried blood is the same type as Miss Short's.

Los Angeles Sheriff's Department Commander Thomas M. Vetter

I originally met sheriff's commander Tom Vetter in 2003 at a book signing in Orange County. At that time, he was wearing a different hat and was Lt. Col. Vetter, U.S.M.C., active president of the First Marine Division. [July 2003-August 2005]

I would later discover that Tom was one of LASD's most respected command officers with forty years of distinguished service to law enforcement. His reputation as a leader in both the sheriff's department and the US Marine Corps are twenty-four carat gold.

In September 2004, Commander Vetter was interviewed by a television producer in connection with his knowledge of events that occurred back in 1962, which related to the Black Dahlia investigation. But due to time restraints, the interview never aired.

Historically, this is a truly amazing interview which documents the then [1962] young sheriff detectives' first person exchange with his Chinatown drinking buddy detectives and as driver for Undersheriff James Downey, LASD's number two command officer. As Downey's driver, he was privy to a conversation wherein he learned that "the Dahlia Case was solved."

Vetter's first person account leaves no doubt that many "old-timers" on both the LAPD and LASD KNEW who the Dahlia killer was, that there was a 'cover-up,' and the reasons why he was not pursued.

As a young sheriff in the detective bureau, Tom Vetter WAS THERE. Listen to his words as he takes the interviewing television producer back in time to a backroom bar at *Little Joe's Restaurant* in the heart of Chinatown. The bar was one of the favorite "watering holes" for old-school cops and sheriffs to meet, drink, and exchange scuttlebutt.

Thank you Tom Vetter! A heartfelt thank you for your years of dedicated service to Angelenos and for your outstanding leadership as an officer and a gentleman!

The Interview:

Commander Tom Vetter (ret.)
Los Angeles Sheriff's Department
Lieutenant Colonel, USMCR (ret.)
President, First Marine Division, July 2003-August 2005
Interviewed–September 2, 2004
Los Angeles, California
(Tape transcription)

QUESTION:
Tell me a bit about yourself—how you started in the sheriff's department, and what you did there.

TOM VETTER:

I started off on the City of Bell Police Department. I was there about a year and a half. And—started there in January of '57, and—then I went on the Los Angeles County Sheriff's Department—graduated from the Academy and worked prisoner transportation, and Norwalk Station, and Lakewood Station, and—Firestone Station in the Night Detective Corps.

I went on the Academy staff as a Drill Instructor—because of my teaching ability and Marine Corps background. I spent three years there training new cadets. Then I was transferred to Detective Headquarters, and—from there I was selected to work—as an aid to Under sheriff Jimmy Downey.

I worked Headquarters Detective Division, and—I commanded the Arson and Bomb Squad, working antiterrorist investigations. Got promoted to captain, and—went to the Labor Relations Detail—commanded that. Then I commanded the San Dimas and Walnut Sheriff Station—a regional command. I was promoted to commander. I worked at our Headquarters of the Sheriff's Department, and also commanded the Training Bureau later on.

I was a field commander. Also, within patrol with the Sheriff's Department, was assigned as the night duty commander. So, I had nearly forty years law enforcement and serving the people of Los Angeles County.

QUESTION:

That's quite a resume—Tom, tell me—tell me about the Black Dahlia murder. It was a big deal back then, right?

TOM VETTER:

That was a great big deal—of course, it happened in the late '40s, but— carrying right on into the '50s and '60s, and so on. It's been a big deal, because it's been unsolved and of great notoriety, and it was always of interest—to everyone.

QUESTION:

You were how old at the time? Do you remember it at all?

TOM VETTER:
In 1947—I was twelve years old.

QUESTION:
Do you remember hearing anything about it?

TOM VETTER:
No, not at all. I was raised in Missouri and—I don't remember it being in the papers back there then.

QUESTION:
Big story here, but maybe not so much there.

TOM VETTER:
Right.

QUESTION:
But, surely when you moved out here and—joined law enforcement here, it's always been—tell me if I'm wrong, but I—I believe it's always been one of those—one of those big cases—that cops talk about.

TOM VETTER:
It's always been on the front burner. You always hear everybody talking about it. It was always a big deal case, and you—you'd—hear it being discussed every now and then by the detectives and—talking about it. It was of great interest to them.

QUESTION:
Why did they—was there ever any as to why the thing was—with all of the manpower that was put on it—why it was never—never solved? Did you ever hear that kind of scuttlebutt?

TOM VETTER:
Yeah, I have. Just—that scuttlebutt was going around and—it'd come out in the scuttlebutt that they had really solved the case, and they knew who did it. However, he was a doctor out in Hollywood, and—fairly prominent. And—back in those days that—some of the police officials, or District Attorney officials—City officials—would take their girlfriends there for abortions. And he was doing abortions, and he had a lot of information on various people, and they—they were afraid of it.

QUESTION:

You're saying this was the scuttlebutt in the Sheriff's Department when?

TOM VETTER:

All through the '60s—usually after work we'd go down to Chinatown and—have a taste or two while we were waiting for rush hour traffic to clear. And, the Sheriff's detectives and LAPD detectives and that—we'd meet down there. We became good friends and we'd talk about various cases.

QUESTION:

Well, run this down for me again. So, there you are in Chinatown. It's—it's the early '60s—you're all having a drink after work, and what's the scuttlebutt about the Black Dahlia case?

TOM VETTER:

Well, it came up occasionally, not often, but it came up occasionally. And, usually around the time of the anniversary of her death or murder. That's when they'd start talking about it, and the scuttlebutt was going around that it was known who did it, but they were afraid of it.

QUESTION:

Why?

TOM VETTER:

He was a prominent doctor in Hollywood. He hung around public officials, and—the police officers and this and that. And, the rumor was that many of them went to him to have abortions performed on their girlfriends, or whatever. And—they were afraid he had the—the goods on them.

QUESTION:

You heard this in scuttlebutt—off-hour scuttlebutt in the early '60s?

TOM VETTER:

Yes.

QUESTION:

From the way you tell it, the sense was—as you say, he had the goods on people? It that—am I correct?

TOM VETTER:

Right. He did according to them. They were afraid of him, because they had taken—girlfriends to him to get abortions performed, and—he knew them and he had the goods on them.

QUESTION:

Was a name ever connected to this person?

TOM VETTER:

Never. I never heard a name.

QUESTION:

But it was fairly common knowledge that—that this was the story? Am I correct?

TOM VETTER:

That's true. It was fairly common knowledge that it was a doctor in Hollywood.

QUESTION:

And, in 1962, you heard a very specific conversation about this, right?

TOM VETTER:

I did.

QUESTION:

Tell me the circumstances.

TOM VETTER:

I was a detective then in 1962 and I was driving Undersheriff Jimmy Downy and—he was going to lunch with then chief of detectives—Gordy Bowers, and they were good friends. As we were driving along—somehow the Black Dahlia murder case came up in their conversation.

And, I heard Jimmy say that "Oh, that had been solved, but it will never come out. Because, it was some doctor that they all knew out in Hollywood."

QUESTION:

Any name attached?

TOM VETTER:

No name.

QUESTION:

Did he go into any more detail about it?

TOM VETTER:

No, he didn't. He really didn't.

QUESTION:

Did that surprise you? Or, did that fit in with what you had heard before to that point?

TOM VETTER:

It surprised me somewhat, yes, because at—such a high level—the under sheriff is the number two man in the Los Angeles County Sheriff's Department, and he's privy to anything going on in the area. I knew that he knew—Chief Thad Brown, the chief of detectives for the Los Angeles Police Department then. It surprised me that—he would say that.

QUESTION:

Would you presume that—he got the information from Thad Brown?

TOM VETTER:

No, I wouldn't presume that, no. But, certainly he had to hear it from someone.

QUESTION:

Set the stage for me if you will a bit about the climate back then in the late '40s in—you know, in terms of—law enforcement and how clean or dirty it was, or compromised it was? What was going on during that period?

TOM VETTER:

Of course, I wasn't active in law enforcement at that time, but—talking to a lot of my friends that I worked with in the Sheriff's Department and policemen that I met, it was a whole different atmosphere and—the Department, perhaps both departments, the Sheriff's Department and Los Angeles Police Department—had a graft problem. And—they were not an honest department at that time.

And I say—perhaps unethical, to say the least—in many ways. It was a different atmosphere. Politics was very big and everything in those days. I think you could get things done or covered up, or whatever—with a payoff.

...

QUESTION:

In all those years—clearly there are unsolved cases, and then there are big unsolved cases. Where—where does the Black Dahlia fit in all of that?

TOM VETTER:

Probably one of the biggest, if not the biggest. I've heard about the Black Dahlia murder case ever since I came on and after I retired. And, I read in the paper where Steve Hodel was going to speak at—one of the local book stores. And—it's always been a fascinating case for me as a professional law enforcement officer. I felt I really wanted to go up and meet him. I did and I listened to his talk, and—afterwards, I went up and talked to him a while. And—I thought, 'This guy is really on to something. He really knows what he's doing and talking about.'

QUESTION:

It had the ring of truth to you from what you knew about~ what you'd been hearing back in the '60s?

TOM VETTER:

Yes, it did. It was all fitting in—all these little pieces. It's almost like a jigsaw puzzle, and it started fitting in, and from a professional standpoint. And looking at it from the outside, I could see where it was falling in place.

QUESTION:

Once again just about the climate back then in law enforcement in the '40s that you—that you were talking about.

TOM VETTER:

The Sheriff's Department and especially the Police Department in Los Angeles—did not have a good reputation then for honesty, integrity, ethics. They had some great problems then. They were known for payoffs and graft, and what have you. And—and the atmosphere was bad. Probably stayed that way until about the early '50s when Chief William

Parker came in and he really reformed the Department and cleaned it up then.

QUESTION:

Do you think—as you know, Steve has written that—that he believes that a command decision was made—that for whatever reason we're going take a pass on this. We're going to let the guy get out of the country, or, you know, kind of sweep it under the rug. Do you believe that? Is that in keeping with what you know about—about Parker?

TOM VETTER:

Not really. I just don't think Chief Parker would do something like that. He was a man of integrity and honesty, ethics—just top man. However, it might be in keeping with some of the—people at lower ranks below him.

QUESTION:

And, the conversations that you've described for us would certainly indicate that something like that did happen?

TOM VETTER:

We could assume that.

QUESTION:

That there was a suspect. They knew who he was, and for whatever reasons, they either couldn't touch him or didn't want to touch him.

TOM VETTER:

I would think they probably did not want to.

QUESTION:

Because?

TOM VETTER:

Because of his political connections, it would appear. And, his personal—personal knowledge of them. You know, really back in those days, abortion was of course, a crime, and certainly if somebody got caught performing abortions, or having one done, or what have you, they were in great trouble. People would go after them. The law would go after them.

QUESTION:

Do you think this case—has been solved?

TOM VETTER:

I think so. From my own professional viewpoint. I think Steve Hodel did an outstanding job in putting the pieces together. I think it's been solved.

QUESTION:

And, when you read his book, it—tell me if I'm wrong, but it would seem that it had—again, the ring of truth about it based on what you knew and had heard forty years ago.

TOM VETTER:

Exactly, because just some of the pieces—what I'd heard were small pieces. But, when you put them all together, it's bringing the whole big picture together of the Black Dahlia murder. I think Steve solved it.

I wouldn't be surprised if that doctor kept a diary of some type or note, and—certainly he knew who these politicians and officials were in government. And—I think they were really afraid of him. I would have to think that many of them were married, and had these girlfriends or mistresses on the side.

...

QUESTION:

Tell me once more...what would you hear? What sorts of things would you hear—the scuttlebutt?

TOM VETTER:

They'd just start talking about her murder, and—how she'd been murdered—how they found her—how she'd been carved up. And, because of the cuttings on her—if you will, and dismemberment, it had to be done by some medical person, probably a medical doctor. And, they'd discuss that. A lot of guessing on everybody's part as to what happened.

QUESTION:

But educated guesses, apparently, right?

TOM VETTER:

Educated guesses—I was a pretty young detective during those years in—in the '60s and—these other—these other men down there—other detectives had many years' experience. So, it was interesting to listen to them and just gain knowledge from their expertise.

These guys had worked the Homicide Detail and places like that and he had—great experience, so—

QUESTION:

And once again, just putting a—putting a cap on it.... Did he ever mention—use the term "covered up," "covered over" or you know, because of the doctor's influence or power. Do you know if they ever used those terms?

TOM VETTER:

Yeah, it was a cover-up. Just the scuttlebutt going around that—they had found who had murdered—they had discovered who had murdered her, and it was really a cover up. Somebody had covered it up.

QUESTION:

Because?

TOM VETTER:

Because they were afraid that the doctor had the goods on too many people in high places—police official and city officials—politicians and that—regarding abortions.

QUESTION:

Abortions involving what?

TOM VETTER:

Abortions involving their girlfriends—their mistresses. Many of them were married at the time, and—they just felt the doctor had a lot of goods on them and perhaps he kept a diary or notes, or something.

QUESTION:

Now, as you say, you're a young cop—a young—sheriff's deputy at this—at this point—kind of learning the ropes. Were you shocked at this?

TOM VETTER:

Yeah, a little bit. You hear things, and you know, you experience things as these cases unfold, and you go through your career, but—it was a little bit shocking. I had to adjust my thinking back to the 1945s and what type of—atmosphere pervaded the Police Department then, and the Sheriff's Department.

END OF INTERVIEW

Chapter 14

"A Doctor Did It"

"The fact that the killer was a physician, skilled in surgery, very much limited the suspect pool."

Stephen Kay,
LA County, Head Deputy District Attorney

One of the rare points that *all of the professionals* involved in the Dahlia investigation, past and present law enforcement officers, district attorney investigators, coroner's experts, and FBI were in full agreement from the get-go was that *the Black Dahlia's killer was a physician skilled in surgery.*

Elizabeth Short Autopsy

On January 16, 1947, the day after the body was found, Dr. Frederic Newbarr, then chief autopsy surgeon for the County of Los Angeles performed an autopsy on the victim. His findings determined that the cause of death was, "hemorrhage and shock from a concussion of the brain and lacerations of her face." It was Dr. Newbarr's further opinion that "the trauma to the head and face were the result of multiple blows using a blunt instrument."

Later sources provided the following additional information:

1) As earlier described, the body had been neatly and cleanly bisected in half.
2) A sharp, thin bladed instrument, consistent with a scalpel, had been used to perform the bisection.
3) The incision was performed through the abdomen, and then through the intervertebral disk between the second and third lumbar vertebra.

In 1947-1948, LAPD criminalist Ray Pinker and criminalist Lemoyne Snyder M.D. J.D., two of the most respected forensic experts of that day, after thorough study of the autopsy photographs and enlargements of tissue samples, concluded the killer had to have had advanced knowledge of anatomy and a high degree of surgical skill. [Ray Pinker had personally attended the original January 16, 1947 Elizabeth Short autopsy. And the Black Dahlia investigation was one of the first to use LAPD's newly acquired high tech equipment to obtain high resolution color photographs documenting the trauma.]

Popular crime and mystery writer of the time, Craig Rice, would later publish a book, *45 Murderers: a collection of true crime stories,* [Simon and Schuster, New York, 1952] with one entire chapter devoted to "The *Black Dahlia.*" I quote relevant excerpts from that chapter:

> Everyone now knows that the body of Elizabeth Short was cut in two, severed at the waist, but what everybody does not know is the fact that the job was done with great precision, and with every evidence of professional skill.
>
> This fact had been noted by police criminologist, Captain Ray Pinker from the start; and his deductions were verified some time later in a joint study he made with Dr. Lemoyne Snyder, of the Michigan State Police Crime Laboratories, and a member of the editorial advisory board of *True Police Cases.*
>
> Going over the detailed photographs of the body, taken at the morgue, the two experts noted the clean knife marks made by the sharp instrument used in bisecting the body. They noted that not a single organ of the body was severed. They studied enlargements of some of the tissues, and came to the conclusion that the job showed extraordinary knowledge of human anatomy.

Dr. Lemoyne Snyder was both a medical doctor and lawyer and literally "wrote the book" on homicide investigation. His book was my bible during my early training at the LAPD Police Academy, and an important reference guide during my eighteen years working Hollywood Homicide.

LAPD criminalist Ray Pinker is legendary. A highly skilled scientist, he basically single-handedly brought LAPD into the twentieth century regarding criminal investigation of crime scenes.

Ray was considered an expert witness in almost every field of forensics. He did it all—polygraph, chemistry, ballistics, trajectories, etc. You name it, he did it. [In the "it's a small world category," Ray Pinker was good friends with my uncle, Charles Eugene Harvey (my mother's brother) who was a scientist, and, in the 1940s, was considered one of the leading world experts in the then brand new field of SPECTROSCOPY. Uncle Gene worked on the MANHATTAN PROJECT at Los Alamos, New Mexico, and, after the war, became a college professor, taught spectroscopy, and wrote three separate text books on the subject.]

LAPD criminalist Ray Pinker, 1947, examining Black Dahlia "tip" Letter

CBS television program, *48-Hours,* in their October 2004, hour-long documentary, *Black Dahlia Confidential,* sought out their own expert to reexamine the photographs and provide an independent opinion.

They went to the top and consulted with Dr. Mark Wallack, chief of surgery at St. Vincent Hospital in New York.

CBS producers had Dr. Wallack review all the Dahlia related photographs and then asked him for his professional opinion as to whether a doctor had performed the bisection? His on-air answer:

"You don't get this kind of training where you can invade a human body unless you've had some sort of medical training. Yes, in my opinion, a doctor did it."

Dr. Mark Wallack,
Chief of Surgery, St. Vincent Hospital, New York
On-air interview for *CBS 48 Hours, Black Dahlia Confidential*
October, 2004

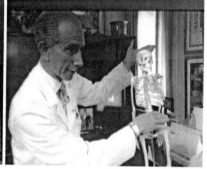

Dr. Mark Wallack, informs CBS's Erin Moriarty, in the 2006 airing of *Black Dahlia Confidential* that in his expert opinion, the bisection on Elizabeth Short's body was performed by a trained physician.

Here is a partial review of another expert's opinion, also from 2004, which was totally unsolicited. Surgeon, Dr. Michael Keller's opinion was included in an updated chapter of BDA. At that time, he had been practicing and instructing in surgery for over twenty-years.

...

The photos of the scene and the morgue which I looked at appear to show a very clean procedure. Surgeons make bold clean incisions thru each layer of tissue with the correct amount of pressure to divide only the tissues they are attending to. The uninitiated—laypersons—usually underestimate the amount of pressure it takes just to divide skin, let alone an intervertebral disc. Their procedures often result in cuts that are serrated at the ends from going over the tissue repeatedly. We derogatorily call these "Staging Laparotomies—going thru the skin in stages." Additionally, amateurs often skive the incisions. Their cuts go thru skin at an angle to the horizontal plane so that one edge is "feathered" and the other appears peeled.

The killer here [Black Dahlia] was educated enough not to attempt going thru the bones of the lumbar spine. He was savvy enough to locate and divide at the disc space. An amateur would probably have left hack marks on the vertebral bodies as he "casted about" for the interspace.

Also, the willful performance of a hysterectomy which at that time [1947] would have been done through a lower vertical midline as the photos appear to show. That was a medical decision.

The Trauma- Crime Scene and Autopsy Photographs

As you, my readers, know from the inception of my investigation, now in its twelfth-year, I have always been reluctant to present photographs depicting the sadistic trauma inflicted on Elizabeth Short and some of the other victims.

However, over the years in updated chapters, I have included some crime-scene and autopsy photographs to establish and support a point of evidence.

In this investigation, YOU are the jury, and I find myself again placed in the role of the prosecutor's investigator, who has the responsibility of preparing and making ready the exhibits and evidence to be submitted in court.

Your need to know and view these important photographic exhibits, which in this case helps establish the absolute fact that A SKILLED SURGEON INFLICTED THE TRAUMA, demand that I include them here.

As documented in the 2004 *HarperCollins* revised "Aftermath" chapter of BDA in 2003, I was contacted by Judy May, the granddaughter of Dahlia detective Harry Hansen. Judy informed me that she was in possession of her grandfather's original photographs and provided me with an original full set of both the Black Dahlia crime scene and autopsy photographs. Several of these have never been previously published.

Exhibit No. 1- The Hemicorpectomy

In the below diagram [Exhibit 1] the arrows show us the location where the bisection was performed, which was done by incising between the second and third lumbar discs, the only location where a body can be divided without having to "saw through bone."

Exhibit No. 1

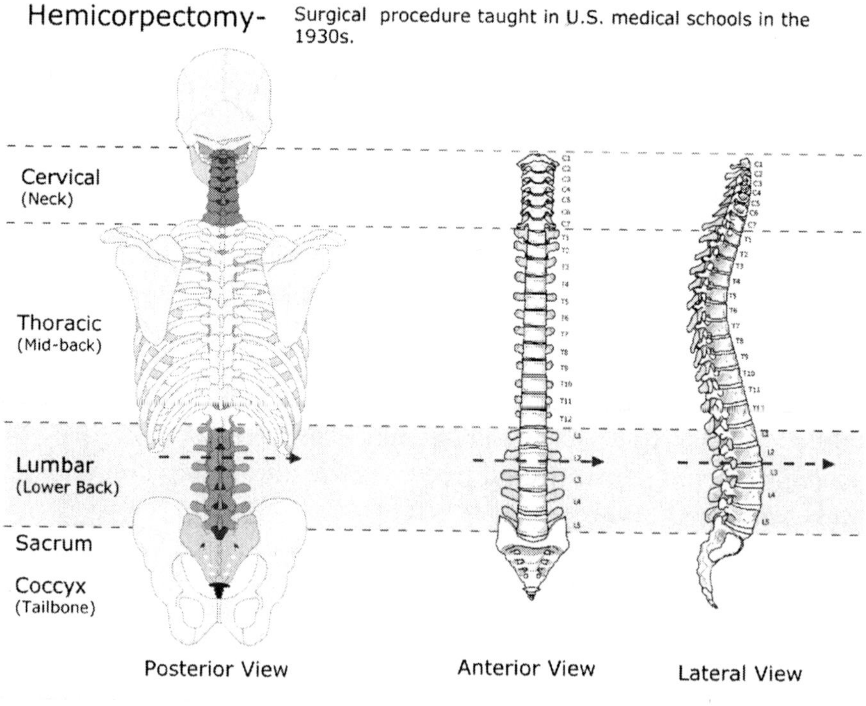

Hemicorpectomy- Surgical procedure taught in U.S. medical schools in the 1930s.

Cervical (Neck)

Thoracic (Mid-back)

Lumbar (Lower Back)

Sacrum

Coccyx (Tailbone)

Posterior View   Anterior View   Lateral View

Exhibit No. 2- Bisected upper torso at crime-scene

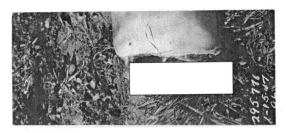

Exhibit No. 3- Bisected body at Coroner's Office

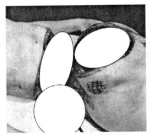

Exhibit No. 4 Coroner's Office

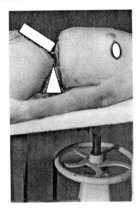

Exhibit No. 2 documents how responding officers observed the perfectly bisected body at the crime scene. Even to the untrained eye, it was obvious that this was done in the detective's words, "with medical finesse."

Exhibit No. 3 shows the two halves removed from the crime scene and placed together on the gurney at the coroner's office made ready for the autopsy. The crisscross incisions seen on the right hip and enlarged in the photo were clearly inflicted using a thin bladed knife, most probably a surgeon's scalpel.

Exhibit No. 4 shows the body part as viewed from the left side. Here, we see another expertly performed scalpel incision where the surgeon has removed a small oval section of skin immediately to the right of the victim's left breast.

Exhibit No. 5 – Coroner's Office

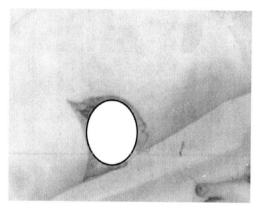

Exhibit No. 5 is a view of the large section of skin [weight approx. one pound] which was excised from the left thigh and placed inside the victim's vagina. Again, it appears a scalpel was used and we see another example of what appears to be a carefully cut out "geometric shape."

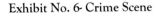

Exhibit No. 6 Crime Scene

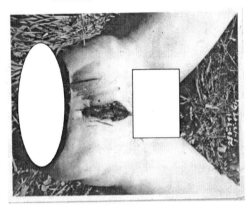

Exhibit No. 6 shows the "hysterectomy incision" as seen by officers at the vacant lot, 3815 S. Norton Avenue. Chief of surgery, Dr. Mark Wallack described this in his on-air television as:

> "The willful performance of a hysterectomy which at that time [1947] would have been done through a lower vertical midline as the photos appear to show. That was a medical decision."

Exhibit No. 7 Crime scene comparison to Coroner's Office

As seen at crime scene prior to removal for autopsy

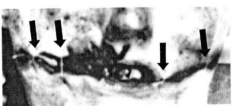

Arrows mark coroner's sutures used to close mouth

Exhibit No. 7 establishes two important pieces of information. First, the top photograph was taken at the crime scene and clearly shows that the mouth wound was NOT A SLASHING, but rather, like all the other trauma, was an exceptionally skillful and carefully rounded incision, as if the surgeon was carving a smile into the face of the victim. The killer also made five distinct vertical incisions extending upward from the top lip.

The urban-myth has it that Elizabeth's mouth was "slashed from ear to ear." NOT SO, and this photograph proves it. Like all myths it was born from individuals seeing the above coroner's photograph and believing that was the madman's butchery. Actually, what they are seeing is the work performed by the medical examiner. Note the black arrows I have inserted which show the four sutures that were put in place and used to stitch together the mouth for closing *after the autopsy was completed.*

Exhibit No. 8 shown below are the cigarette burns marks on Elizabeth Short's back which both the LAPD and the DA's reports claim DID NOT EXIST. That would have forever remained A LIE had Harry Hansen's granddaughter, Judy May, not given me the full set of coroner's photographs to share with the public.

Lt. Jemison wrote in his October 1949 report to the Grand Jury on two separate pages as follows:

> Page 7- ...There were no cigarette burns and no tattoo marks on the body.
> Page 13-...It was found that there were no cigarette burns or other burns on her body as he had maintained.

Lt. Jemison was either (1) deliberately lying to the 1949 Grand Jury or (2) deliberately lied to by the LAPD who wanted to keep the burn marks secret.

It is one thing to verbally lie about facts in a criminal investigation, which is done fairly frequently in order to maintain secrets, but to put it in writing as part of your formal presentation to a seated grand jury is a whole different matter.

For that reason, it is my belief that LAPD deliberately kept DA investigator, Lt. Jemison in the dark about this particular aspect, which they had kept secret from EVERYBODY for the three-years prior to his being assigned by the grand jury to reinvestigate THEIR handling of the case.

Exhibit No. 8 Cigarette burn marks [8 or 9] to victim's back

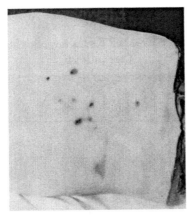

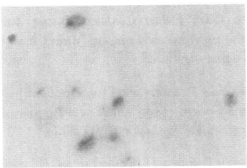

An independent review of the above photographs by nationally respected forensic expert and cardiologist, Dr. D.P. Lyle, M.D. provided the following opinion:

> ...The lesions on the mid-back appear to be traumatic in nature. They appear to be cigarette burns, which are partially healed. They could be only hours old but are more likely 1 to 3 days old, since they seem to display some degree of healing in the central portion of each.

Dr. George Hill Hodel—A skilled surgeon

Over the years, a few critics have tried to suggest that Dr. Hodel had no training in surgery and was just a VD specialist and an "Administrator."

A&E Cold Case Files TV Host Bill Kurtis interviewing LAPD Det. Brian Carr in 2006

LAPD detective, Brian Carr, prior to his retirement, informed Bill Kurtis on *A&E Black Dahlia Confidential* that due to heavy case demands over the previous six-years, he "didn't have time to prove or disprove Hodel's investigation."

In an earlier *Court TV* interview, Detective Carr [now retired], when questioned about George Hodel's skill as a surgeon, replied, "He was not a skilled surgeon. He worked at a VD clinic."

To set the record straight, I decided to see if I could document my father's background, skill, and experience *as a surgeon.*

First, I contacted my father's medical school, University of California at San Francisco, and they provided me with his official transcripts and an "ANNOUNCEMENT FOR 1932-33," which listed all of the required curriculum and course hours.

Unlike today's medical training where "specialization rules," medical students in the 1930s underwent very heavy course training in the field of SURGERY. All students were required to accomplish 744 *hours in surgery.*

In their four years of medical school, twenty-three percent [23%] of their entire medical training was devoted to SURGERY. This does not include their fifth year of internship, which would require much more "hands on training."

Here are George Hodel's specific surgery courses, as listed in his personal transcripts, taken by my father during his four-years at UCSF. His totals actually exceed the required number of hours:

1)	Surgery 101	48 hours
2)	Surgery 102	64 hours
3)	Surgery 103	280 hours
4)	Surgery 104	16 hours
5)	Surgery 105	214 hours
6)	Surgery 106	64 hours
7)	Surgery 107	32 hours
8)	Surgery 108	32 hours
9)	Orthopedic Surgery 101	6 hours

George Hodel's Surgery total hours   **766 hours**

His UCSF transcripts further show that during his four-years, he attended and personally performed:

"53 separate surgical operations and 12 autopsies"

His fifth year was his internship at San Francisco General Hospital, where he practiced and performed emergency surgery on a daily/weekly basis for a full year.

This photograph was taken by George Hodel in 1935 and shows students receiving surgical instruction in the operating theater at UCSF School of Medicine. These photos, along with others taken by my father, were part of a large mural on display for decades in the campus medical-building.

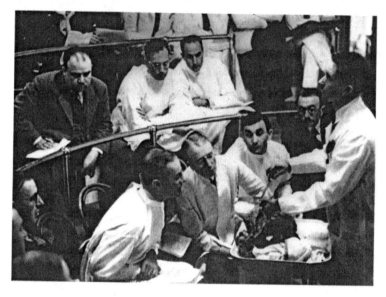

George Hodel's classmates and physician instructors identified above as: [front row left to right] Drs. Glaven Rusk, Edwin Bruck, Leroy Briggs, Herbert Moffit, Salvatore Lucia, and Guido Milani; [back row, left to right] Urriola Goiota, Clayton Mote, and Walter Port. The lecturer was identified as Dr. Jesse I. Carr.

Note from my father to me, circa 1994 that accompanied
copy of his 1935 UCSF photograph

From Dr. George Hill Hodel

Dear Steve:

This is one of quite a few
photos which I took at University
of California Hospital in San
Francisco, when I was a senior
medical student, in 1935. This
one and a few others were enlarged
and put up as murals in the medical
school building (which has now been
rebuilt so that these no longer
exist).

This one shows our professors
and mentors in the front rows (now
all gone, of course), some of whom
were world-famous medical leaders.
My classmates (now also almost all
gone) are in the rows behind them.

DAD

After graduating and receiving his M.D. in 1936, George Hodel's
first medical assignment was that of "camp surgeon" at a logging camp
in New Mexico. He then went on to attend and treat patients on the
Navajo and Hopi Indian reservations in Arizona and New Mexico.

George Hodel's employment application showing he was the Conservation
Corp. "camp surgeon" in New Mexico from 1936-1937

12. Give a brief résumé of your activities from time of graduation to the present time, including a statement of all positions which you have held, giving inclusive dates.

                                                                         2—17636

    Intern, San Francisco County Hospital, 1935-36.
    Camp Surgeon, CCC, New Mexico, Dec. 1936 - June 1937.
    District Health Officer, Second Health District of New Mexico
       (County of McKinley and County of San Juan; headquarters,
       Gallup, New Mexico); Chief, McKinley County Venereal Disease
       Clinic; July 1937 - April 1938 (while health officer was on
       leave).
    Social Hygiene Physician, Los Angeles County Health Department,
       in charge of venereal disease clinics at Santa Monica, Whittier,
       Compton, and East Los Angeles; May 1938 - Fakxxx January 1941.
    Chief, Division of Social Hygiene, Los Angeles County Health
       Department, January 1941 to present.

1941-1949 Documents listing George Hodel's occupation as a "Physician & Surgeon."

Section of author's <u>1941</u> birth certificate listing father's occupation as, "Physician & Surgeon."

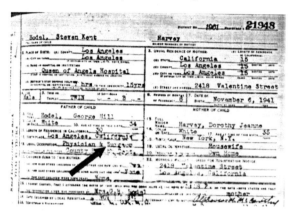

George Hodel's <u>1942</u> commission as "P.A. Surgeon" [equivalent rank of military lieutenant] in US Public Health Service. Appointment signed by President Franklin D. Roosevelt on May 18, 1942.

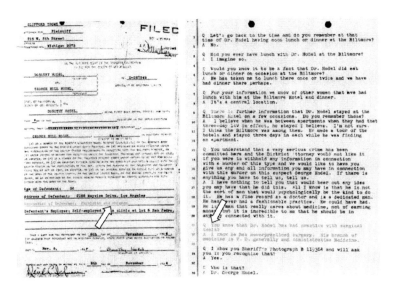

Document above on left is Dorothy Hodel's 1944 "Affidavit for Divorce" listing husband's occupation as "Physician and Surgeon." On the right is Dorothy Hodel's 1950 DA transcript of interview where she stonewalls Lt. Jemison's question regarding her ex-husband, George Hodel, "using surgical tools?" While knowing full well he was a highly skilled physician and surgeon, she outright lied, claiming he has "never practiced surgery, his branch of medicine is VD and Administrative Medicine."

Note that Dorothy Hodel's Divorce Affidavit was dated and signed by Mother UNDER PENALTY OF PERJURY on November 9, 1944. This was six months BEFORE my father fell under LAPD suspicion for the murder of his secretary, Ruth Spaulding, from an overdose of barbiturates (1945), *and some two years before the surgical murder of Elizabeth Short.*

In her signed affidavit, *Dorothy Hodel vs. George Hill Hodel*, near the bottom she states the following:

"OCCUPATION OF DEFENDANT: PHYSICIAN AND SURGEON."

Finally, on page 133 of the DA surveillance tapes, we have George Hodel talking to an unidentified woman and admitting to performing curettage (D&C–Dilation and Curettage) "lots of them" at his downtown *First Street Clinic* at First Street and Central. This was a surgical procedure, and the 1940s "curettement" was a medical term used and synonymous with performing ABORTIONS.

DA Hodel Electronic surveillance transcript page133
George Hodel informs woman he has done abortions, "lots of them."

HODEL FILE - ~~114~~ / 3 2

1:45P	Hodel answers door bell, lets in woman - he talks to her about renting her a room in return he will knock off the rent - at work she does for him such as cleaning and taking care of his quarters. Negro woman has her minor daughter with her.
1:50P	Phone rings - Hodel says "Mrs Hodel is out - I can take message. He said he is going down to the beack about 4 PM today - talks about renting room.
2:00P	Hodel again talking to negro woman. Hodel asks her daughter where she goes to school - the girl says-a catholic school.
2:10P	Colored woman and child leaving. woman is going to think it over - about renting room. Woman then starts talking about Doctor's-Hodel tells her about his clinic at 1st and Central Woman said she had a curettemet (curettement ?) in 1944. Hodel said he has done lots of them. Hodel and woman continue to talk about doctors, sickness, and other medical subjects. (Hodel seems to be acting overly nice to this woma He must be trying to talk her into renting the room, or ?) Hodel tells her that Dr. Hill, a colored Doctor, lives next door.
2:30P	Woman leaves
2:50P	Phone rings 2 times, must have been answered in another room Hodel moving about desk.
3:15P	Hodel leaves room - all quiet.
3:45P	All quiet.
SPOOL 38 4:00P	Hronek, L.A.'s office, on duty.

Chapter 15

...Bosch had an idea what was coming. The fixer was here now.
The investigation was about to go through the spin cycle where decisions
and public pronouncements would be made based on what best served the
department, not the truth.

From Angels Flight by Michael Connelly

DAHLIAGATE—A Cover-up? Why?

Over the years, I have been repeatedly asked by readers about "Dahliagate." They ask if I truly believe that there was an organized conspiracy to allow George Hodel to go free.

An important question and a fair one.

My short answer is YES, I do believe that there was an LAPD "cover-up" and the 2003 access to the DA "Hodel-Black Dahlia Files" granted me by DA Steve Cooley, has in my opinion—gone a long way to help prove it.

To fully answer the question, we need to ask another. Was there a logical reason *why* LAPD would do something so inconceivable?

Absolutely, but the answer cannot be found by looking at today's LAPD, which is a very different department from what it was in 1950.

Let's briefly go back to that time—the spring of 1950. The previous year, 1949, was packed full of dynamite sticks, any one of which could have blown the lid off—its police department and its politicos. *Here are just a few of the active fires that surrounded and were burning out of control near city hall:*

- Gangster Mickey Cohen had been recently shot on Sunset Boulevard, and was threatening to testify about police corruption, extortions, and payoffs.

- Crime was rampant—murders of lone women and gangland mobsters went unsolved.

- The Brenda Allen Vice scandal with payoffs to LAPD officers was in the headlines.

- Four LAPD officers were indicted for corruption, including LAPD chief of police, Clemence "Cowboy" HORRALL, and his assistant chief, Joe Reed. [Both resigned-retired]

- The grand jury had ordered LAPD's Black Dahlia investigation taken away from LAPD detectives and turned over to the DA detectives for reinvestigation.

- LAPD Sgt. Charles Stoker, in addition to informing the grand jury about the Brenda Allen payoffs to LAPD command, was also secretly testifying regarding his knowledge of a protected abortion ring involving Los Angeles medical doctors and chiropractors run by LAPD detectives in the Homicide Detail. [By the summer of 1950, ten abortionists would be indicted and arrested on related charges.]

- Dr. George Hodel's top criminal attorney, Jerry Giesler, had just beat a slam-dunk prosecution put together by the LAPD charging Hodel with child molestation and sexual intercourse with his own fourteen-year-old daughter. With three adult witnesses present who participated in the sex acts and the victim's testimony, along with pornography recovered from the residence, the case was considered air tight. But the jury acquitted. [Documents found in the 2003 DA file allege that a $15,000 payoff may have gone to someone in the DA's office to help obtain the acquittal.]

- February 15–March 27, 1950, DA investigator, Lt. Frank Jemison, had Dr. George Hodel's Franklin Avenue residence bugged and he is placed under both audio and physical

301

surveillance and is the prime-suspect in the Black Dahlia murder. Dr. Hodel makes damning statements and admissions about the Dahlia murder as well as other crimes. "Supposin' I did kill the Black Dahlia. They couldn't prove it now. They can't talk to my secretary anymore because she's dead." "This is the best payoff I've seen between Law Enforcement Agencies." In addition, during this surveillance stakeout, conversations were overheard *that strongly suggest an actual murder may have occurred, while police officers listened in!* [In the actual transcripts of February 18, 1950, officers document the following: a woman was heard crying, then heard to dial the telephone operator, then screams were heard, then the sound of blows being made with a pipe, more screaming, then silence. Sounds of digging were heard in the basement and George Hodel said to a second male [later identified as Baron Ernst Harringa], something about "not a trace." Incredibly, though detectives were listening in and were only five minutes away—they took no action! *[If arrested, George Hodel's public admission to this crime, while law enforcement listened in and did nothing, would have, by itself, been enough to end the careers of both DA and LAPD top brass.* At the time, George Hodel fled the country. LAPD's William Parker was just three months away from being appointed the department's new chief.]

- On March 27, 1950, with Lt. Jemison's team of eighteen detectives still maintaining a twenty-four-hour audio surveillance on Dr. Hodel, he slipped away. George Hodel left the country and was GONE. After this date, he was never again seen or talked to by any law enforcement agency. [In 2004, today's LAPD detectives retracted earlier claims that "they cleared Dr. Hodel," admitting that it was the DA's office that had been directly involved with the Hodel surveillance, and a check of LAPD files resulted in no information on Dr. Hodel other than "a one-page memo mentioning his name related to some work done at his residence." The hundreds of pages of investigation and transcripts, as well as the hundreds of hours of tape recordings—all turned over by DA investigator, Lt. Jemison to Thad Brown—were nowhere to be found in LAPD files. All of it just—disappeared.

- In 1950, at the time the electronic surveillance was ongoing at the Hodel residence, LAPD deputy chiefs William Parker [Internal Affairs] and Thad Brown [Chief of Detectives] were involved in a power struggle, both wanting to become LAPD's next chief of police. Thad Brown had the majority of Police Commission votes (three to two) and had been given the nod to become chief in July 1950. Just weeks before the formal vote, one of the police commissioners, Mrs. Curtis Albro, became ill and died unexpectedly. This tipped the scales back to even—and the commission was now divided—two votes for Parker, two votes for Brown.

It is critical to our understanding that we take all of these historically documented events into account.

At that very moment in time (the spring and summer of 1950), surrounded by multiple scandals all threatening to take down the current administration, a new fuse was lit, which, if it became public, would certainly have been a death blow to the administration.

Just when Chiefs Parker and Brown were about to take over and totally reform and professionalize a previously corrupt LAPD, the shit hits the fan—BIG TIME.

Here is a likely scenario of what I believe happened:

A late night top secret staff meeting of LAPD and DA brass took place in a backroom at Deputy Chief Parker's newly established Internal Affairs Division.

I'm guessing the date was sometime in early April 1950. Likely present were: (1) Interim LAPD Chief William Worton, (2) Deputy

Chief William H. Parker, head of Internal Affairs Division, along with several of his investigators, (3) Chief of Detectives Thad Brown, (4) Lt. Frank B. Jemison, LADA's Bureau of Investigation, and probably his commanding officer, DA Bureau Chief H. Leo Stanley.

The briefing likely began with Lt. Jemison informing all present of just exactly what they had on Dr. George Hill Hodel as the prime Black Dahlia suspect. Lt. Jemison informing those present of Hodel's connections to Elizabeth Short, along with his taped admissions as to killing her, as well as overdosing his secretary, Ruth Spaulding in 1945. Lt. Jemison likely concluded his part of the briefing with the fact that just as his men were about to arrest Dr. Hodel, he split and his best information was that Dr. Hodel was out of the country, and, based on taped conversations, had likely fled to either Mexico or Asia—possibly Tibet.

Lt. Jemison would have gone on to inform all present that in addition to those crimes, a murder of an unidentified woman may have occurred during the electronic surveillance of the Franklin house and was possibly "caught on tape." He would have had the brass' full attention as he described the dramatic February 18, 1950 incident with the woman whom Dr. Hodel questioned about what she knew of the different things (connected to his criminality), and, according to the monitoring detectives, "wrote down her answers." Jemison could have even "played the tape" as he read the detectives' log notes reporting the later screaming sounds and blows being struck, digging sounds in the basement, and then Hodel stating to a male, "not to leave a trace" then finally—nothing but silence.

As Chiefs Worton, Parker, and Brown sat in shocked disbelief, LAPD Internal Affairs detectives would have likely continued the briefing with their own separate investigative findings.

This likely included their discovery that Dr. Hodel was *known and friendly* with two LAPD detectives connected to either the Homicide or the Gangster Squad Details. That there may or may not have existed a relationship between Hodel and the two detectives in regards to a protected abortion ring where the detectives were receiving payoffs from doctors in exchange for not arresting them.

These same two detectives, two years earlier, in 1947, directly assigned to or on loan and assisting in the Black Dahlia investigation, either knowingly or unwittingly misdirected the investigation after discovering that Dr. Hodel and Elizabeth Short were connected as boyfriend and girlfriend.

As a result of these detectives' 1947 actions, Hodel was given "a clean bill of health." And now, some three years later, the facts indicate that in addition to admitting to police payoffs and two murders, he could well be responsible for additional *Lone Woman Murders* all occurring between 1947-1950.

Further, the IAD investigation was ongoing, and the facts may reveal that the two detectives were simply trying to protect Hodel from becoming involved as a suspect, as they initially assumed his only involvement was that he was intimate with the victim prior to her murder and nothing more. In other words, there may have possibly been nothing more sinister than initial poor judgment on the part of the LAPD detectives, which may well have resulted in some terrible consequences.

In closing, Lt. Jemison would have advised the commanders that current intelligence information suggested then that Dr. Hodel had left the country and may never be located. And if located, he may never be able to be extradited back to the US.

Further, if he was located, arrested, and returned, Hodel would probably disclose all that he knew regarding police payoffs. [Statements recorded during the surveillance had Hodel saying, "This is the best payoff between law enforcement agencies I have ever seen. Only I know how all the pieces fit together."]

If arrested, Dr. Hodel would further inform and make public all that he knew of the protected abortion ring, as well as his personal relationship to city and county officials in connection with his VD clinic. He could very well confess to and identify the female victim of the murder that occurred during the February 1950, DA/LAPD stakeout on his Franklin residence.

So now, we have the WHY. It satisfies both sense and reason. In one word—SURVIVAL.

Chiefs Worton, Parker, and Brown had no other options. This was a MANAGEMENT DECISION. The powers that be reasoned that: (1) it was highly doubtful that George Hodel could ever be located and brought back;(2) if he was located and extradited, there were no guarantees he would be convicted [and he had just beat a major felony beef for incest and presumably would have Attorney Jerry Giesler defending him again]; and (3) if he was prosecuted, he could and likely would take down and destroy everything and everybody with him. This would have included politicians, police authorities, gangsters, doctors, lawyers, and entertainers—literally, the entire heart and core of LA's power structure.

The city coffers would be emptied from the civilian lawsuits that would follow as a result of the detective's obstructions of justice, which resulted in many more murders.

Both Parker and Brown would be forced to resign, like their predecessors. If forced to retire, they would become powerless to "move forward to clean up and reform the department."

It would take decades for the LAPD's reputation to recover from the scandal.

NO! Attempting to locate and arrest Dr. Hodel was simply not an option. It would be better to sanitize the files, remove anything and everything that connected George Hodel to the crimes, and then seal the remaining files off. Lock them up forever.

And that is what was done. The Hodel friendly detectives were Thad Brown's men, and the buck stopped with him. The decision was made. Parker would be the next chief of police while Brown would remain chief of detectives. Those involved would quietly retire from the department or be transferred out of harm's way. And each officer who was present swore to take this horrible secret to their grave.

Parker and Brown were not criminals but rather Machiavellian princes who reasoned that desperate times demanded desperate actions. They fully justified their actions as being the only available choice. They reasoned that these actions were done for "a Higher Good"; for the *good* of the *department*, for the *good* of the *city*. And naturally, for the *good* of themselves.

We also have to keep in mind that George Hodel had extensive and long-standing connections with corrupt Los Angeles city officials.

His close friendships and quid pro quos within the LAPD and the DA's Office led all the way back to 1925 when he was just a young crime reporter riding with LAPD's vice and homicide detectives. Those same detectives, his former friends and "partners," were now the top brass and running the department.

I have additional information at hand that will, in time, give much stronger support to the fact that George Hodel had the city, especially its then DA and LAPD leaders, by the short hairs. With the information I possess, which will be explained and expanded on in detail in a future book, he literally was holding a gun to their heads, and the administration HAD NO CHOICE BUT TO COMPLY. HE HAD MADE HIMSELF UNTOUCHABLE.

The Missing Evidence and Hodel Files
PowerPoint Lecture, Pompidou Centre, Paris France
June 1, 2006

Pompidou Centre
Paris, France
Author PowerPoint
presentation
1 June 2006

Author giving PowerPoint Talk, Paris 2006

In 2004, my book was translated and published in France as, *L' Affaire du Dahlia Noir*, and became a national bestseller in that country. That same year, I was invited to Paris by my publisher, Seuil, and did a number of press, radio, and television interviews.

Two years later, in June 2006, I was invited back to Paris to speak at the Pompidou Centre.

My talk included an hour PowerPoint presentation followed by a second hour of audience participation—Q & A. A number of subjects were explored and the entire talk was videotaped.

One of the questions asked dealt with the subject of the LAPD. The questioner wanted to know what exactly they had done as follow-up in the three years since my investigation was made public.

Here is my unedited verbatim transcribed response to her question on the evening of June 1, 2006. Though a bit redundant to what has just been discussed, I will include it since I believe it does add some further insights as to how it all "played out."

Q: Has the Los Angeles Police Department responded to your Black Dahlia investigation?

SH: Yes, and that response has been, NO RESPONSE. It has been very frustrating.

Because, frankly speaking, I was an honored detective highly respected. And I thought the first thing that would happen...this was going to be a slam dunk case.

You've got DNA. They've got the envelopes. They've got the saliva where he licked the stamps. All of that. You do the DNA. It will be a slam dunk match and there were also some proof sheet papers, if you remember from the reading. Very unique, that I felt we would make to the notes that were mailed in.

So, I never thought that there would be any kind of closing down. So, initially LAPD took the stance of, "This is an active case, we are not going to publicly talk about it."
Then, the press are the ones we really have to thank for forcing the door open to get inside the vault of the DA's office. Now, I don't know if this is clear or not, but the DA is a completely different entity, agency than the LAPD.

So, in fact, what we discovered when we got there was that it was a different set of books. I came to the suspicion, as you know in the book, that maybe they [LAPD] had sanitized it. Maybe they had removed everything from the LAPD files?

In fact, once the LAPD was backed up against the wall and had to "fess up" as we say, they said, they admitted, "Everything is gone." They don't know when it vanished? All the evidence, all the potential DNA—the hair follicles, the envelopes. Everything connected to the case, the most famous case LAPD has ever had, has vanished.

Now, they said, their excuse was, "Well, it's a long time ago, these things happen and sometimes evidence gets lost." I would agree with that. As a supervisor in homicide, I saw detectives dispose of evidence that shouldn't have been. It happens. So, I'll give them that. Maybe, although there were very few that had access to these files.

But, the bigger question is: everything that linked George Hodel to the crime from the LAPD files as missing. All of the fourteen interviews. His interview. All of the Tamar interviews. Everything that connected him. Now, these were not evidence that was disposed of...these were in a file, in a central file. Somebody had to take those and remove them. So that to me is really...and I'm not saying that it was today's LAPD. It wasn't done in modern times. This was done back then.

And the reasons for the...the reasons they did this, I take three chapters to try and explain them. I don't think we have time tonight to go into all of that. But, what it really comes down to is a management decision on the part of LAPD. I'll try. I'll just say it briefly here, as I read it.

LAPD had just overcome a major scandal about eight years before, where sixty-eight officers were fired; twenty-five high-ranking officers.

Chief Parker, who was the department's most famous chief of police, was just trying to turn the department around and be progressive and get rid of all the corruption.

And, I think what happened, in about 1950, was that a couple of....I'm not saying that Parker was involved in criminality, or Chief Brown was, but what happened I think was that a couple of detectives, Internal Affairs perhaps, came to them and said, "Look, we've got a problem. A couple of our gangster squad detectives turned away a possible suspect who was dating Elizabeth Short. A guy by the name of George Hodel. He's a doctor. As a result of that, it looks like maybe in the last couple of years, maybe he killed two or three more victims. He's now split. He's out of the country. We're not sure where he is. What do we do?"

So, I think that Parker and Thad Brown, chief of detectives looked at each other and said, "Well, let's see. We could reveal this and if we do we're out of power. The city's coffers will be emptied by the lawsuits that come from it. And LAPD's reputation will never recover. We could do that. He's out of the country. We probably can never bring him back. We may not be able to locate him. Probably have problems with prosecution. If he does come back, he's going to lay out a lot of information on a lot of different people.

"Maybe its best from a management standpoint that we just seal this off and leave it go at that." And, I think that's what happened. I think they said, "For a higher good, they needed to be a couple of Machiavellian princes, perhaps....for the higher good. And, we have evidence to support that.

We know that Thad Brown, came out with a statement to Jack Webb, who was the actor that played *Dragnet.* They had a conversation and he, Thad Brown, told Jack Webb, "Well, you know the Black Dahlia case was solved. It was a doctor that lived on Franklin Avenue in Hollywood."

Now, it may have been another that lived in Hollywood on Franklin, but I don't think so. [Laughter] So, that's a very damning statement. We have the second highest ranking officer on the Sheriff's Department, a commander, actually a deputy chief and the under sheriff who said that, "It was a doctor in Hollywood, the case was solved."

We have lots of different after the fact indications that they knew who it was, and this was an inner secret that was kept a secret. Nobody in today's LAPD knew about it. That's why when they searched the files to see and there was nothing there [about George Hodel], they felt fine in giving him a clean bill of health.

Next question?

"Parker on Police"

In 1963, as young idealistic rookie cops, my partners and I really believed we were Chief Parker's "Thin Blue Line." At police academy graduation, he looked us in the eye, shook our hand, and told us that was so. Life for me back then was literally and philosophically, "black and white."

Today, decades later, I realize that neither life nor people were ever that simple. Most of us are a combination of the two—black and white—which makes for lots of gray.

Today, with a much fuller historical perspective and understanding, I realize that my early hero, Chief Parker was both a white and a black knight.

In May 1949, LAPD Vice Sergeant Charles Stoker was called to his second secret meeting with then Inspector William H. Parker, commander of the newly formed LAPD Internal Affairs Division.

For me, the most riveting section of Sgt. Stoker's 1951 *Thicker' N Thieves* expose on police corruption was the *Parker-Stoker conversations* as documented by him at the time they actually occurred.

For those who remain skeptical that Chief Parker would or could ever have been party to any kind of "cover-up," especially one that allowed a known, identified murder suspect to remain free, I answer—listen to Chief Parker's own words.

These Parker/Stoker conversations occurred in May 1949, less than one year before the George Hodel bugging tapes, which I allege became a separate—Dahliagate.

Sgt. Charles Stoker wrote this account just a few months after it occurred, and then published the full expose in 1951.

Thicker'N Thieves, Chapter 14, Grand Jury Preview page 161-162:

I appeared before the Criminal Complaints Committee on May 5, 1949, and answered each of its questions, truthfully and to the best of my ability. I told of the Brenda Allen investigations and explained in great detail exactly how they had occurred.

I was warned to say nothing regarding the fact that I had been before the grand jury.

...

About a week after my appearance before the committee, I received a telephone call from Inspector William Parker. He asked me to meet him at the same place where we had met on the occasion when he had wanted me to put Officer Jimmy Parslow of Hollywood vice in the middle. I kept the date, and Parker gave me a preliminary build-up to the effect that he and I were of the same faith, and that it was directly due to his hard work that the Catholic boys on the Los Angeles police department were getting an even break. He reminded me that we were both veterans of World War II.

After these pleasantries, Parker asked what I knew about the Brenda Allen investigation in Hollywood. When I related the story as I had told it to the grand jury, he indicated that it was as he had suspected, since he knew positively that there were two sources of corruption in the police administration.

According to Parker, one source was controlled by Chief of Police Clemence B. Horrall. Aligned with him as a lieutenant was Sergeant Guy Rudolph, his confidential aide. He then related this story concerning Rudolph, which I have never verified.

For years, while Bowron was in office, Rudolph had controlled the vice pay-offs in Los Angeles, and when Horrall held the chief's job, Rudolph was under his wing. At one time, Rudolph had kicked a colored prostitute to death on Central Avenue; and during the investigation of that incident, he and his partner had gone to a local downtown hotel where they engaged in a drunken brawl with two women. Then, while Rudolph was out of the room buying a bottle of whiskey, one of the prostitutes had been killed.

He asked me if I had heard the story. When I replied that I hadn't, Parker told me that he could prove what he had related to me. He added that Rudolph also controlled the lottery and numbers rackets operated by Chinese and Negroes, and that he had a Chinese as a partner, and maintained a business office on San Pedro Street.

According to Parker, Horrall's other lieutenant was a Captain Tucker, who was commander of the metropolitan squad, which numbers over one hundred men. He said that the metropolitan squad furnished Los Angeles police officers to act as strike-breakers in studios for so much a head. The taxpayers paid the policemen's salaries, while Horrall and Tucker collected the revenue, Parker declared.

Parker explained that this money was split with members of the city council, and that Tucker maintained a metropolitan vice division, whose only duty was to see that Chinese, gamblers and prostitutes were kept in line.

...

Parker went on to say that the other sources of corruption within the police department directly were controlled by Assistant Chief of Police Joe Reed. He explained that Joe Reed's chief aide was Lieutenant Rudy Wellpott, head of the powerful administrative vice squad, who in turn had as his assistant, Sergeant Elmer V. Jackson. Parker related that Jackson had been exempted from military duty with the police department's help and had stayed out of the war. The department's main source of revenue during this period was the "shaking down" of bar owners on Main and East Fifth Streets to allow B-Girls, a polite name for prostitutes, who are proscribed by law, to operate.

This activity constituted a million dollar source of revenue, according to Parker; and although the average cost of a liquor license was in the vicinity of five hundred dollars, a license in those areas sold for not less than ten thousand dollars during the war.

Parker said that Nate Bass, a bar owner, was middle man between the police and bar owners.

...

What ever became of this information, including the LAPD IAD investigative files that in Parker's words, "he could prove that the officers murdered the two downtown prostitutes"?

Obviously, nothing. None of the allegations of police graft, abuse of power, and even police officer murders, ever came to light. No officers were charged with the murders. They were simply *covered up*. The murder investigation on the two victims was simply, "filed and forgotten"—two more "unsolved" to add to the stack.

Any arrest of corrupt LAPD officers in 1950, especially officers who could name names and identify their "partners in crime," would have resulted in too much scandal at a critical time of transition and reformation.

The involved officers retired and the department "moved forward" to deal with new problems and new challenges. Sound familiar?

William H. Parker

LAPD Chief of Police from 1950-1966

Chief Parker on Police Investigations and *"The Law of Double Effect"*

Earlier in this chapter, I indicated that it was my belief that Chiefs Parker and Brown, reasoned that their actions relating to not pursuing and arresting George Hodel, "... were done for 'a Higher Good'; for the *good* of the *department*, for the *good* of the *city*, and naturally, for the *good* of themselves."

In short, their decision was not a legal one, but rather –a moral call based on what they believed was best for the future of the department and the city.

315

I originally included those thoughts in BDA in 2003. I was expressing *my opinion* based on what I knew about the investigation and my limited knowledge of Thad Brown and Bill Parker, both of whom, as I have indicated, were my personal LAPD heroes from my 1963 academy days—forward.

Never in my wildest dreams did I expect to find confirmation and corroboration coming from *the man* himself! But I did and here it is— IN HIS OWN WORDS.

Three days ago, on September 5, 2011, I found and ordered a rare book. It was one I knew existed, but had never read. It is, **Parker on Police,** written by William H. Parker and published in 1957. [Charles C. Thomas, Springfield, Illinois, 1957]

I knew it contained his thinking on police administration, which has never particularly interested me. But I felt I should have it in my library, at least for historical reference. I received the copy today.

I began scanning the book and came to a chapter which DID INTEREST ME. It is entitled, *Surveillance by Wiretap or Dictograph: Threat or Protection?*

I'll set the scene and cut directly to the chase.

It is February 1954. Bill Parker has been LAPD's police chief for three and a half years. He is testifying before the Appropriations Committee, House of Representatives in Washington, DC.

Chief Parker is arguing in support of the need for law enforcement to be able to wiretap [listen in on telephone and telegraph lines] and eavesdrop by dictograph [use of a hidden microphone and recording device, as was done in the Franklin house.]

After making various legal arguments [Parker was a licensed attorney] on why he felt that it was absolutely essential to allow law enforcement to continue their efforts to fight crime by using wiretaps and dictograph recordings, he then gave the committee his "closing arguments." Here is his verbatim testimony to the committee as recorded in his book, *Parker on Police*, pages 111-112:

> ...
>
> In a consideration of the morality of wiretap and dictograph, we may apply the principle of ethics entitled, "The Law of Double Effect." This law posits that when an action produces two effects, one good, and one bad, as long as the good effect is intended, and as long as the means are either morally good or morally neutral, *the act may be morally justified.* Thus, when this nation was faced with the ethics of warfare in the use of the atom bomb, it was obviously morally justified according to this principle. ... In the case of the wiretap or dictograph the identical rationale *may* be applicable.
>
> We would not attempt to justify a wiretap or dictograph if the ends sought were extortion, blackmail, or like evil. If these techniques are used they must, of necessity, be rigidly controlled. But if the end is the protection of the commonwealth, then the evil effect (eavesdropping upon the conversations of the innocent) is not intended, and the action may be morally justified.
>
> ...
>
> We are not arguing that the end justifies the means; on the contrary, we argue that the means are neutral—as is any mechanical technique, and that the use of these means is justified by moral as well as by statute law. Behind all statute law stands moral law. If an action is morally defensible, then, too, it is legally defensible. It is my opinion that the use of the wiretap and dictograph do not violate a moral precept, and that, therefore, the statute law should echo this viewpoint.
>
> Far from being a *threat* to our freedoms, the use of modern technological devices by the police service may well be its most powerful weapon in combating our internal enemies, and a vital necessity in the protection of our nation's security, harmony and internal well-being.

To my mind, Parker's words here leave no doubt as to where he stood. This was a man of religion and passion who would follow HIS moral compass whichever direction it pointed. Be that to the heights of *heaven* or to the depths of *hell.*

A Conspiracy of Silence

It is now, November, 2011. This week's headlines are just beginning to uncover what has overnight become one this year's biggest news stories—*The Jerry Sandusky-Joe Paterno, Penn State Sex Scandal.*

Former Penn State defensive coordinator, Jerry Sandusky, has just been arrested and charged with *sexually molesting eight young boys over the past fifteen year period.*

This week, PSU's president, Graham Spanier, and his legendary head coach, Joe Paterno, have both been fired from the university as a result of failing to report and take necessary action after being notified of Sandusky's criminality *more than nine years ago.*

A reading of the 2011 "Finding of Fact" transcript as summarized by the Pennsylvania Grand Jury reveals that Coach Sandusky allegedly committed serial child molestations including oral copulation and sodomy on minor boys. The offenses have apparently been ongoing for more than a decade.

The transcripts further describe a 1998 child molestation incident that was investigated by Penn State University Police, which included detectives, eavesdropping on a conversation held between one victim's mother and Sandusky. In May 1998, detectives with the mother's permission, listened in on two separate conversations and overheard Sandusky admit to the crimes committed against her then eight-year-old son wherein he stated to the mother, "I understand I was wrong. I wish I could get forgiveness. I know I won't get it from you. I wish I were dead."

The case was submitted to the then Centre County District Attorney's Office who advised there would be no charges filed and the investigating detective was ordered to "close the case" by the director of the campus police.

318

While this story is just beginning to unfold, early indications are that had the information been aggressively acted upon when first reported in 1998 or in the subsequent offenses in 2002, both of which should have resulted in Sandusky's arrest; *it would have prevented six or more young boys from becoming his later victims of sexual assault.*

As more information is forthcoming we will very likely discover that the motivations, the WHY of the Penn State Sex Scandal cover-up, will turn out to be for the same reasons they always are—a conspiracy of silence to protect the powerful and their institutions.

Now that the facts have become public, those men in power who failed to disclose and report known criminal activity will likely try to justify their actions and attempt to rationalize their cover-up and silence by saying they wanted to try and protect the University and the Team from becoming embroiled in a major scandal that would expose the university to costly civil lawsuits.

Their twisted view of morality is that iconic institutions like Penn State and national heroes, like Head Coach Joe Paterno, are to be protected at all costs; even if that means that a known identified serial-pedophile was allowed to remain free to continue his sexual abuse and rape of children for more than a decade.

Sound familiar?

In the case of Los Angeles' 1947 Dahliagate, another conspiracy-of-silence, let's take a moment to assess the consequences that resulted from police and politicians deliberately shutting down of the Black Dahlia investigation.

What was the result of their backroom decision to not pursue and arrest Dr. George Hill Hodel, once authorities had eavesdropped and recorded his confession and positively identified him as a serial killer, in the spring of 1950?

If my investigation is correct as presented in my sequel, MOST EVIL, coupled with the fact *that we know serial killers do not simply STOP committing crimes*, then the resultant effects of law enforcement allowing George Hodel, a known, identified serial killer, to remain free with no further attempts to apprehend him—were devastating.

The Consequences?

Just as in the case now unfolding against coach Sandusky, George Hodel did not stop his predatory serial crimes after fleeing the country in 1950. The likely results:

Manila, Philippines, 1967, "Black Dahlia copycat murder" of victim Lucila Lalu, who was abducted, bound with rope; slain and according to the Manila coroner, "her body was then bisected by a skilled surgeon." After the dissection, her killer posed the body parts on a vacant lot, just three miles distant from Dr. Hodel's then residence/office on Manila Bay. The case, a copycat Black Dahlia murder was dubbed by police and press as, "The Jigsaw Murder," and forty-four years later, it remains one of Manila's most horrific unsolved crimes.

How many other Manila and Asia related crimes occurred throughout the decades will never be known. However with George Hodel home-based in the Philippines with offices in Tokyo, Hong Kong and travelling throughout Asia, Europe and the United States for forty-years, the final body count could easily be several dozen more.

If I am correct that my father replaced his "Black Dahlia Avenger" sobriquet of the 1940s with "Zodiac" in the 1960s, and *resumed his letter writing, city-terrorizing campaign*, promising, "There will be more," then we must add, at minimum, another eight known victims to the count. They would include:

1966, Riverside victim, Cheri Jo Bates

San Francisco Bay Area victims:

1968, Betty Jensen and David Faraday

1969 Darlene Ferrin and Michael Mageau (Mageau survived the attack)

1969 Cecelia Shepard and Bryan Hartnell (Hartnell survived the attack)

1969, San Francisco victim Paul Stine

Chapter 16

Grandfather Harvey

In physical appearance, I favor my mother's side of the family. The Harvey's (UK) and the Boyles (Cork County, Ireland) from whom I also inherited my thirsty Irish genes.

From my boyhood, I remember my grandfather, Charles Eugene Harvey as a bear of a man, with snow white hair and a big smile, but that's about all.

Mostly, I remember my mother's stories about him. Her father was born in Pittsburgh, PA. He was one of six brothers, four of whom worked in the coal mines. Mother would frequently tell us three sons the story of how, at the turn of the century, these six burly brothers would walk into a bar-room, all order "sarsaparillas" [a nonalcoholic precursor to "Root Beer"], and look around the room just daring anyone to make a snide remark or snicker. Tough coalminers all.

Mother was born in 1906 in New York's Central Park West. Three-years later, the family moved west to Los Angeles. Grandfather got a job with the *Los Angeles Examiner* newspaper as a linotype operator.

Grandfather Harvey's second career began after his divorce from Grandmother when he started teaching printing at Hollywood High School in the 1920s.

Hollywood High claims over 500 "celebrity students" including a couple well known to our own investigation. To name just a few from their alma mater:

Vincent Bugliosi, Carol Burnett, Lon Chaney Jr., Judy Garland, Laurence Fishburne, Carole Lombard, Ricky Nelson, Sarah Jessica Parker, Jason Robards, Alexis Smith, Lana Turner, and Fay Wray. Both DDA head prosecutor Stephen Kay and my half-sister, Tamar Hodel also attended Hollywood High.

1928 Hollywood High School Year Book—Men Faculty

First Row: Henry, Sarno, Cruse, Harvey, Snyder, Fretter, Garrison, Gray, Winchester.
Second Row: Evans, Black, Myrick, Abbott, Williams, C. S. Williams, Thorpe, Hamilton.
Third Row: Wescott, Booth, Foley, McLeod, Burleigh, Lyons, C. G. Smith, Thompson.
Fourth Row: Blair, McCausland, Staples, Johnson, De Shazo, McAfee, Hanks, Wright.

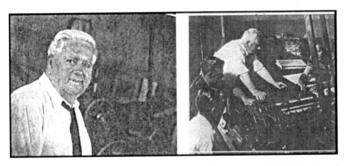

Photos of printing instructor, Charles Harvey in 1939 Yearbook

"Those who study printing with Mr. Harvey are given a chance to print programs, papers, and the *Crimson and White* for Hollywood."

"Mr. Harvey, printing instructor collects rare books and fine printing. In his collection he has a page from an original Gutenberg Bible."

Hollywood High Year Book 1939

After twenty years of teaching at the high-school at age sixty-two, Grandfather washed his hands of the printer's ink, and, in semi-retirement, donned the uniform of a doorman complete with gold buttons and epaulets at one of Hollywood's fancy hotels.

Mother had a tremendous love for her father. She spoke proudly of the chess-playing atheist who was a voracious reader, a liberal, a thinker, and a scholar. She affectionately described him as a lover of people and life.

My favorite anecdote about Grandfather was the story Mother told us as children. It was when Grandfather Harvey was working as a doorman in Hollywood.

As the story goes, while working at the hotel, Grandfather met a woman who was staying as a long-term guest. Each day, he would be there to open the door for her as she came and went. The woman was a writer, and being kindred spirits—naturally, they soon became friends. A greet, a nod, a smile, and some small talk.

One day, the woman checked out of the hotel and returned to the East.

During her stay at the hotel, she had written a play. In November 1944, it premiered on Broadway. It was a smash hit and ran for nearly five years. It won the Pulitzer Prize for Drama in 1945. The name of the playwright? Mary Chase. Her play? *Harvey*.

Based on her brief friendship and affection for Grandfather, the friendly hotel doorman, she honored him by naming her *pooka*, the invisible six feet six inches rabbit, after him!

It would be nice to end my story about Grandfather Harvey here on this high note. However, like most twists and turns in my ongoing investigation, it seems there is always something more...

A Death in the Family

"I fear this means that there is some mischief afoot."

Sherlock Holmes in, *The Valley of Fear* by Sir Arthur Conan Doyle

In the past ten years, I had never done any research into my grandfather's life. There was no real reason to as nothing ever surfaced to suggest he had any role to play in any part of my investigation.

I knew practically nothing about his life, other than the few stories told by my mother. I didn't know when he was born nor could I recall when he died, other than having a vague impression. It was sometime in the 1950s. In the spring of 2010, I decided to order his death certificate, as a first step, to see what family information it might contain such as: his birth date, relatives etc. Here's what I discovered:

Copy of Death Certificate of Charles Eugene Harvey

The facts surrounding my grandfather's death appeared clear and simple.

Apparently, on a cold winter morning in December 1949, he suffered a heart attack at his residence, The Vine Manor Hotel, 1814 N. Vine Street in Hollywood.

From there, he was rushed to a nearby medical facility where he died two hours later. His attending physician arrived and indicated he had last seen his patient some two weeks prior on December 9. The doctor noted a ten-year medical history of "arteriosclerotic heart disease." Obviously, the death was from "natural causes" and the doctor, when filling out the death certificate, checked off "no autopsy to be performed." My grandfather's body was cremated three days later without further ceremony. End of story. Well, not quite.

When I first saw my grandfather's death certificate, my eyes were instantly drawn to the distinctive hand-printed block lettering entered by the doctor in the cause of death section. I believed I recognized the handwriting. From there, my eyes flashed to the bottom signature line for confirmation—"G. Hill Hodel, M.D."

So, from the death certificate, we learn that not only was George Hodel claiming to be Charles Harvey's "attending physician" and was at the medical facility soon after Grandfather's initial heart attack, but he also instantly took charge of the body and ordered, "no autopsy to be conducted," insuring cremation without any examination or lab tests.

Bottom portion of Grandfather Harvey's death certificate

My next surprise was when I read the actual date of death—*December 23, 1949.* A date thoroughly familiar to me from my own investigation. Why?

Because *that is the very day* that Dr. George Hill Hodel *was acquitted by a jury of felony child molestation and incest,* charges that, for those who knew him and had followed the trial were convinced, would be sending him to prison for a very long time.

326

Even my father believed he would be convicted. In a conversation with house roomer Joe Barrett, just days before the verdict, Dad reflected on prison life, saying to Joe, "It won't be so bad. I'll be able to read and perhaps work in the hospital."

LA TIMES December 24, 1949

Acquittal Won by Doctor on Morals Case

Dr. George Hill Hodel, 38-year-old physician, yesterday was acquitted of morals charges involving his 14-year-old daughter Tamar. (12.23.49)

A jury of eight women and four men returned the verdict of not guilty in the court of Superior Judge Thomas L. Ambrose after three and a half hours of deliberation.

The doctor was charged with two separate morals offenses against his daughter and the trial was featured by hotly contested points between the prosecutor, Dep Dist. Atty. William L. Ritzi, and the defense attorney, Robert A. Neeb Jr.

After the jury announced its decision freeing the physician, Dr. Hodel remained in the courtroom to shake the hands of several jurors as they left.

Some will say that these set of facts are nothing more than "coincidence." That could be the case, but I seriously doubt it. The timing, along with my father's actions in the weeks that followed, is just too revealing.

Consider this:

1) According to both my grandmother and mother, Charles Harvey hated George Hodel. He hated my father because of how Dad physically and psychologically abused his daughter, Dorothy. That being the case, *he certainly would not have allowed George to be his personal physician.*

2) Mother knew the truth of father's crimes, and, most probably, had related them to the man she loved most—her father. Grandfather knew some if not all of the details and very likely was aware that Elizabeth Short had been to the Franklin house and had dated George. He would also have known that Tamar had obtained an abortion and that witnesses perjured themselves.

Despite the jury's "not guilty" verdict *that very morning*, Charles Harvey was still a danger and threat to George. Perhaps hearing the unjust verdict just hours earlier, Grandfather became enraged and threatened to go to the police with what he knew.

3) As we know, George Hodel had a history, a track record of silencing those who threatened his freedom. How? By drugging them! There was Ruth Spaulding's 1945 death investigation, which LAPD was convinced was a forced overdose by Dr. Hodel but couldn't prove it. Again, the probable motive was to silence her from revealing what SHE KNEW.

Then in mid-January 1950, *just three weeks after Grandfather Harvey's death,* came George Hodel's staged "attempted suicide" of Lillian Lenorak. Again, with the same motive, he drugged her unconscious and set her up to discredit her and keep her silent from speaking out and confessing her perjury. We know from his own admission to Officer Linkefer that he "gave her a sedative injection and she won't wake up for hours."

I'm also convinced that Elizabeth Short and others were drugged before he killed them.

Just weeks before grandfather's death, there was also the mysterious circumstances of actress Jean Spangler's late night disappearance. She was last seen in public in Hollywood at a restaurant, arguing with a man fitting George Hodel's description *the very day after he bailed out of custody on his arrest for incest.* This was in October 1949, just one week before George Hodel was formally arraigned on felony charges that could send him to prison for decades. Did Jean also make the fatal mistake of threatening to reveal what she knew or suspected about him to the police?

Recall my half-brother Duncan's words, "... I remember one of the girl's Dad was dating back then was a drop-dead gorgeous actress by the name of Jean."

But back to Grandfather Harvey. How easy would it have been for George to have given him a "hot shot" say, a large dose of an amphetamine, which, with his bad heart, would have readily induced a "cerebral hemorrhage," coma, and death?

This was followed-up by George's claims that Grandfather was his patient. And, within hours of the death, his filling out the death certificate as "by natural causes—no autopsy." It was followed by the cremation of the remains three days later. George, as usual, was in complete control.

The really "perfect crimes" are those that are never detected. This could well be such a case.

ALL MY LOVE AND REST IN PEACE - GRANDFATHER

Chapter 17

Captain Jack Donahoe—A Print Shop Connection

On Saturday, January 24, 1947, the below cut-and-paste note was sent to the *Los Angeles Examiner*, along with a package containing Elizabeth Short's personal effects—her birth certificate, social security card, personal papers, address book with seventy-five names in it, and six personal photographs of the victim which showed her in the company of various ex-boyfriends.

This first note and the victim's personal property were sent by the killer a day after making a taunting phone call and speaking with the *Los Angeles Examiner's* city editor, James Richardson.

In closing his brief conversation with the city editor, the killer told Richardson:

> I'll tell you what I'll do. I'll send you some of the things she had with her when she, shall we say disappeared? "See how far you can get with them. And now I must say goodbye. You may be trying to trace this call.

The package with Elizabeth Short's personal effects and the note arrived a day later with the killer promising, "Letter to follow."

"Here is Dahlia's belongings. Letter to Follow"

Avenger posted this note to *Examiner* in a mailbox located just three blocks from George Hodel's downtown medical office

On Monday, January 26, 1947, the second promise "Letter to Follow," a postcard addressed to the *LA Examiner*, was received. It, like the first message, was mailed just a few blocks from Dr. Hodel's private medical practice.

George Hill Hodel's undisguised handwriting on a postcard promising to "turn himself in" in two days.

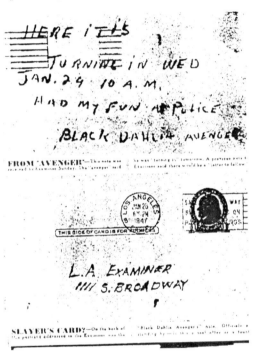

Capt. Jack Donahoe, commander of LAPD's Homicide Unit informed the public:

> "We believe this postcard is from the killer and is legitimate and is the 'letter to follow.' The fact that the postcard was printed rather than lettered with words cut out of newspapers also supports the theory that the killer intends to turn himself into the police, and no longer needs to take pains to conceal his identity."

Captain Jack Donahoe,
LAPD Homicide Division

LAPD's Scientific Investigation Division analyzed the note and writing and determined that it was written using a *ballpoint pen with blue ink*. [In 1947, ballpoint pens had only been on the market for one-year and were both rare and expensive. They were selling for approximately $12.50, the equivalent of about $125.00 in today's dollars, and due to their expense were primarily used and possessed by lawyers, physicians, business executives, and military officers.]

Capt. Donahoe responded with a public message directed to the killer, which was printed in all of the LA dailies, informing the "Avenger":

> "If you want to surrender as indicated by the postcard now in our hands, I will meet you at any public location at any time or at the homicide detail office in the City Hall. Communicate immediately by telephoning MI 5211 extension 2521, or by mail."

The Black Dahlia Avenger taunted police with several more notes, one of which demonstrated his journalistic skill in writing headlines. Some detectives voiced their suspicions that it may have been written by reporters hoping to keep the story alive. [What no one suspected was the bizarre truth of it—that the killer had actually been a journalist! George Hodel, as we know, was a crime reporter covering the police beat and had written his own headlines in the 1920s for one of LA's largest newspapers, *The LA Record*.]:

"Dahlia Killer Cracking, Wants Terms"

In another cut and paste the following day, he wrote:

"I Will Give Up In Dahlia Killing If I get 10 Years Don't try to find me

On the morning of January 29, Capt. Donahoe, confident that the killer would actually turn himself in, positioned his detectives at all the local police stations. But by evening, it became obvious that the suspect was a "no show."

The following morning, January 30, the Avenger's message addressed to Capt. Donahoe was received in the mail:

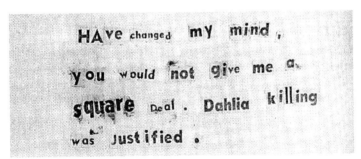

Have changed my mind.
You would not give me a SQUARE deal.
Dahlia killing was justified.

Proof Sheet Paper

> "At least one of the notes sent in by the Dahlia killer in that case, used proof-sheet-paper, of a type commonly found in printing shops."
>
> Captain Jack Donahoe
> LAPD Homicide Division

Capt. Donahoe also made public a second important link in hopes of capturing the Avenger. He was confident that the killer either worked for or was connected in some way to a printing company.

Why?

Because at least one of the posted notes sent in was placed on a unique *proof sheet paper*, commonly used in print shops.

Proof sheet paper was a lower grade of paper stock used in print shops to proof copy before it went to press on a higher grade of paper, thus saving money.

As detailed in BDA, one of LAPD's first really viable suspects in the Black Dahlia murder was, Otto Parzyjegla, a tall, thin, thirty-six-year-old linotype operator who worked at a Los Angeles printing company.

Parzyjegla had been arrested in February 1947 for the vicious murder of his employer, Swedish newspaper publisher, Alfred Haij, whom he had bludgeoned to death and then "hacked the torso into six pieces and then crammed them into three boxes at the rear of the print shop."

Donahoe declared Parzyjegla to be, "the hottest suspect yet in the 'Black Dahlia' killing."

On February 19, 1947, a formal "live show up" of Otto Parzyjegla was conducted by LAPD detectives at Wilshire police station. In attendance were six women victims of attempted attacks, as well as additional witnesses from both the Elizabeth Short "Black Dahlia" and Jeanne French "Red Lipstick" murders. After viewing the line-up, all of the witnesses *eliminated* Parzyjegla, informing detectives that he was not the man they had seen as witnesses in the Dahlia, Jeanne French, and other related crimes.

In connection with the Parzyjegla investigation, Capt. Donahoe informed the press, "at least one of the notes sent in by the Dahlia killer in that case, used proof-sheet-paper, of a type commonly found in printing shops."

LAPD chief criminalist Ray Pinker made the comparison of the Dahlia proof sheet paper to the proof sheet paper found at Parzyjegla's printing shop. But they did not match and were found to be of different stocks.

George Hill Hodel- Printing Press and Proof-Sheet Papers

"Among the anonymous notes sent police in the 'Black Dahlia' case," said Donahoe, "there was one which was obviously prepared in a print shop. At the time we discounted its importance. Now, however, it may take on new significance."

Captain Jack Donahoe LAPD Homicide
Los Angeles Times, February 17, 1947

**Los Angeles Times
February 17, 1947**

Publisher Slain, Body Mutilated;
Police Report Employee Confession

• • •

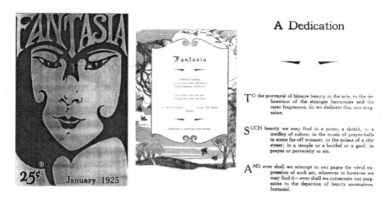

uereu noay.

Other Questioning Due

Capt. Jack Donahoe of the homicide detail said that Parzyjegla will be questioned about the recent mutilation murders of Mrs. Jeanne T. French, former nurse, and Elizabeth Short, the "Black Dahlia."

"Among the anonymous notes sent police in the 'Black Dahlia' case," said Donahoe, "there was one which was obviously prepared in a print shop. At the time we discounted its importance. Now, however, it may take on new significance."

Two radio patrolmen, B. H. Brown and A. J. Drobatz, made the arrest and obtained a confession in a brief two hours after other officers uncovered the crime as they sought the p...

George Hodel, owned and operated his own home printing press, both before and after the 1947 murder of Elizabeth "Black Dahlia" Short.

George first used his printing press in 1925 to publish his own avant-garde magazine, *Fantasia*, from his father's home at 6512 Monterey Road in South Pasadena.

A Dedication

TO the portrayal of bizarre beauty in the arts, to the delineation of the strange harmonies and the rarer fragrances, do we dedicate this, our magazine.

SUCH beauty we may find in a poem, a sketch, or a medley of colors; in the music of prayer-bells in some far-off minaret, or the noises of a city street; in a temple or a brothel or a gaol; in prayer or perversity or sin.

AND ever shall we attempt in our pages the vivid expression of such art, wherever or however we may find it—ever shall we consecrate our magazine to the depiction of beauty anomalous, fantasia!

In 1925, as editor-in-chief and publisher, he informed us that his magazine was dedicated:

To the portrayal of bizarre beauty in the arts, to the delineation of the stranger harmonies and the rarer fragrances do we dedicate this our magazine.

...

Such beauty we may find in ....the noises of a city street; in a temple or a brothel or a gaol: in prayer or perversity or sin.

1920s vintage small printing press *similar* in size to that used by George Hodel

From 1946 through 1949, the small printing press was operational in the basement of our Hollywood Franklin house where father printed advertising materials and product labels for his "Five Dynasty Tea" business.

My brothers, Michael and Kelvin, and I were the "work force," for *China International Exports,* 5121 Franklin Avenue, happily earning our nickels and dimes for the weekend cowboy double-features at the Hitching Post theatre by packing Dad's fancy Five Dynasty Lapsang Souchong Tea into one pound tins and then sticking on the freshly printed labels, preparing them for distribution and sale to many of Los Angeles's top department stores and restaurants.

Below, we see actual samples of George Hodel's original home printed labels and brochures promoting *Five Dynasty Tea.* Also, shown is a list of George Hodel's eighty-four separate "Accredited Retail Distributors" throughout California, which included many of the top department stores and restaurants. Local LA distributors included: All four Brown Derby restaurants [Wilshire, Vine Street, Los Feliz and Bronson Avenue], Bullocks, Don the Beachcomber's, Jurgensen's Market, Hollywood Farmer's Market, Perino's Restaurant, and the Jonathan Club.

George Hodel used his home printing press to print these labels and brochures circa 1947 and 1948

In 1948, George Hodel advertised his *Five Dynasty Tea* in many of the top magazines including: *Vogue, The New Yorker, and House Beautiful.* Seen below [top right] is original product label for *Five Dynasty Lapsang Souchong Tea* printed by George Hodel on his home printing press which my brothers and I placed on cylindrical tins for distribution to stores and restaurants.

During my research, I happened upon an article written and printed in the *Los Angeles Times* on October 1, 1949, just four days before my father would be arrested by LAPD on the incest and child molestation charges.

I am including it here because it demonstrates his skill and ability as a marketing genius, almost fifteen years before he would enter the field and develop INRA-Asia, which became Asia's most respected market research firm.

I strongly suspect he actually wrote the following article. If not, he certainly edited it for the writer, giving his special spin, transforming what was probably a rather ordinary, albeit smoky-tasting tea into something rare and exotic, *creating his own legend* to turn it into a "must have" product.

Here is the original *LA Times* article as it appeared just days before his arrest:

Los Angeles Times
October 1, 1947

Farmer's
Market
Today
...with Neill (Mrs.) Beek

HOW GOOD can tea be, and how do you rate as a tea taster?

Before answering those two questions, please consider the following:

The interesting study of tea, and its history, establishes that in one small district of Fukien Province, there has long been grown à tea–(Lapsang Souchong)–so superb that its use for centuries was confined to the Emperors of China, and those close to the emperors.

This noble tea–this royal tea–was for the high and mighty. Its history is ancient.

With the final fall of the Manchu Dynasty, J.P. Morgan the elder, a tea fancier, sent agents to China to acquire a supply of the tea–and in 1912 J.P. Morgan succeeded in making arrangement for the entire, and limited, output of the tea to be assigned to him.

At Christmastime he would send small chests of the tea to his friends. It became known informally, as "Morgan's Tea."

Upon J.P. Sr.'s death, the House of Morgan continued the custom. High and mighty Americans continued to receive Morgan's Tea at Christmastime, for awhile. But the custom was dropped in the late 30's, and oddly enough it was dropped while a final shipment of the rarest of all Lapsang Souchongs was in shipment. The final shipment was put in storage in San Francisco.

A certain Doctor Hodel, of Los Angeles, a tea fancier, heard of the tea, managed to sample it, and was so elated over its quality that he bought the entire supply. Hodel packaged it, and began marketing it by mail through small advertisements in the luxury magazines. Meanwhile he took steps to obtain the supplies of the tea previously absorbed by the House of Morgan. Then—Pearl Harbor!

It is only recently that Dr. Hodel has again been able to obtain the tea, which he is now marketing under the name *Five Dynasty Tea.*

A rather nice name. There were four Chinese dynasties wherein tea held sway. The fifth tea dynasty is made up of you and me and all the other poor people who can afford expensive tea.

The tea is sold in only a few places; Marshall Field, Bloomingdale's, B. Altman, City of Paris, Bullock's Pasadena, and Balzer's. Oh yes—and at one more place— the Farmer's Market. (Could you imagine B. Altman advertising that the Farmers Market also carries this tea?)

It is R.B. Curl's fancy groceries stall that has it in the Farmers Market.

The 120-cup tin sells for $3.75—and a tin of 25 tea bags is $2.00. That's expensive.

If you will taste this tea you will learn how good tea can be. For a mere 25c we've arranged for you to taste *Fifth Dynasty Tea.* We have a 3-bag sampler at 25c—and a leaflet gives the instructions for its preparation.

There is not enough Five Dynasty Tea in the world for it to become widely known. We shall not advertise it again. You may not care for Five Dynasty—but if you use tea, you should sample this brand. The Farmers Market is at 3rd and Fairfax.

Shortly after his October 1949 arrest, and while on trial for incest, Dr. George Hodel used his home printing press to prepare the below sales brochure, advertising the Franklin house as a "SHANGRI-LA" putting his home on the market with an asking price of $44,500, indicating that its 1949 market appraisal was $60,000.

[The Sowden/Franklin home just closed escrow in July 2011 showing a sale price of 3.85 million.]

Proof Sheet Papers and Blue Ink

During the late 1940s, reams of this unique "proof sheet paper" were stored in the basement of the Franklin house. The proof sheet paper was frequently used by my brothers and I to make our childhood drawings. My father kept several of my original drawings [I was then seven-years-old], and after saving them for over forty-five-year's, returned them to me, circa 1995, after his permanent relocation to San Francisco.

In 2001, after two-years of full time investigation, I came to realize that these original *proof sheet papers* could well be important forensic evidence, potentially linking directly the stock proof sheet papers mailed in by the Dahlia killer to these original papers now in my possession. I was confident that a spectrographic comparison of the size, texture, and fiber content could establish and link them as coming from the same unusual stock.

In my 2003 post-publication briefing to LAPD "brass," this was one of the first forensic comparisons I suggested be made. Both I and the senior staff officers were unaware at that time that "all the Dahlia evidence, including all the original Avenger mailings had disappeared from the locked evidence room."

Below are copies of my original child drawings drawn on *proof sheet paper* from the basement of the Franklin house stock. All the handwriting on the "Chinese Chicken, Apr.1949" was *written by my father **using a ballpoint pen with blue ink.***

Father asked me what the drawing represented and then handwrote my response using **his ballpoint pen with blue ink**. It reads:

Steven Apr 1940 7-5 [my age in years and months]
"Chinese Chicken" (Mountains, Sun)
"Biggest chicken in China—they've been looking for him a thousand years."

Dad returned all of the below drawings to me, circa 1995. All were drawn by me using proof-sheet-paper from the Franklin house basement, which also served as the Five Dynasty Tea packing and "printing office."

In these five drawings returned to me by my father, three contain my father's handwriting and two show my mother's handwriting. The additional four drawings read:

[Top left] "Joe lying Down- Steven 7-6" [Handwriting of Dorothy Hodel. "Joe" would have been our then tenant/roomer, artist Joe Barrett. My age-"7-6" would convert to April 1949.]

[Top right] "King on the Throne" Steven [Handwriting of Dorothy Hodel]

[Middle left] "Little Me Steven" – Steven Self-Portrait 7.7 [Handwriting of George Hodel. 7.7 would convert to May 1949]

[Middle right] "Chinese Chicken- Steven 7-3" [Handwriting of George Hodel. 7.3 would convert to January 1949]

[Bottom center] "Chinese Chicken" - Detailed previously

In February 1947, Homicide commander, Capt. Jack Donahoe, was in charge and control of the Black Dahlia investigation. During that time period, he made a number of important public statements related to the investigation. They included:

1. Elizabeth Short was most likely slain in a bathtub at a private residence.

2. The Elizabeth Short and Jeanne French murders were committed by the same man.

3. The killer wrote his "Turning myself in..." message using a ballpoint with blue ink.

4. The fact that it was the only undisguised note led detectives to believe the suspect was actually going to give himself up to police.

5. The killer was likely connected with a printing company as some of the notes were "obviously prepared in a print shop."

6. Wrote a letter to be published in all the newspapers, offering to "meet the killer anytime, anywhere."

Shortly after making these statements, Capt. Donahoe was transferred from Homicide and placed in charge of the Robbery Detail.

Why the unexpected change in command? Were there ulterior motives in his transfer, or was it because the brass simply felt Donahoe was both "grandstanding," as well as releasing vital confidential information that could put the investigation in jeopardy? [Incidentally, I would agree. In my opinion, none of the above details should have been made public.]

That said, the information that Capt. Donahoe released in both the Elizabeth Short and Jeanne French murders, did ultimately result in helping to link Dr. George Hill Hodel to both of those crimes.

Chapter 18

Handwriting Update

As part of my original investigation, readers are aware that I hired a court certified questioned document examiner, Ms. Hannah McFarland, to examine many of the 1947 Black Dahlia Avenger notes, as well as the lipstick handwriting on the body of Mrs. Jeanne French in the Red Lipstick Murder.

The results of her findings were that, in her expert opinion, it was "highly probable" that Dr. George Hill Hodel wrote at least four of the Avenger notes, as well as the writing on the body of Jeanne French. [A finding of "highly probable" is the highest finding an expert can provide as to authorship without having the original documents in their possession. It is equivalent to the forensic term of being "virtually certain."]

In subsequent examinations of additional *Lone Woman Murder* handwritings, it was also her expert opinion that it was "highly probable" that George Hodel also wrote the printing found on the purse of murder victim Mimi Boomhower who was kidnapped in August 1949.

In a later examination and comparison of the murder note on victim, Gladys Kern, QDE McFarland found that it was "probable" that the note mailed to the police was written by George Hill Hodel. This finding is one degree below the other opinions and is defined as, "The evidence found in the handwriting points rather strongly toward the questioned and the known writings having been written by the same individual; however, it falls short of the "virtually certain" degree of confidence. [*Journal of Forensic Sciences*, Letter to the Editor, March 1991.]

In a previous chapter, I made mention of the August 2006 *CBS* hour-show *Black Dahlia Confidential* in which that network consulted with their own experts to reinvestigate several aspects of my investigation.

I noted that their medical expert, Dr. Mark Wallack, chief of surgery at New York's St. Vincent Hospital after reviewing the killer's skill at bisection stated, "In my opinion, a doctor did it."

On that same program, CBS also consulted an independent questioned document expert, Mr. John Osborn, and hired him to review and compare some of my father's known handwriting samples to the notes written and mailed in by the *Black Dahlia Avenger*.

He gave his opinion, and, as a result, some viewers and a few of my most vocal critics claimed that Mr. Osborn contradicted my expert, claiming "George Hodel did not write the Avenger notes."

John Osborn gave no such finding. Here is his verbatim, expert opinion, as stated on the program:

"There is simply not enough evidence to prove one way or the other whether his father is the writer, or is not the writer."

When asked by the network to conduct his comparison, QDE Osborn was likely provided with only a very limited number of known samples of Dr. Hodel's handwriting. Perhaps as few as only two or three documents. As is usually the case with television, he was likely only given a short time span to review and provide his analysis and results to the network.

Based on those factors, his examination was **INCONCLUSIVE.**

Due to the limited amount of comparative questioned documents provided him for analysis, Mr. Osborn arrived at the only correct finding possible—Insufficient Evidence, Inconclusive.

Whereas, my QDE, Ms. Hannah McFarland, was provided several dozen [approximately twenty-four] separate known documents written by Dr. George Hill Hodel and studied and reviewed them over a six-month period before rendering her expert opinion that George Hodel wrote at least four of the Avenger notes, as well as the Red Lipstick message on the body of Jeanne French. [It is unknown if QDE Osborn reviewed that separate handwriting, as no mention was made of it in his on-air interview.]

Mr. Osborn did discuss a difference in handwriting styles between Dr. Hodel and the Black Dahlia Avenger, specifically pointing to the Avenger's printed block letter "N."

He showed comparative samples of both writings and demonstrated that Dr. Hodel's letter "N," in his words, was "more classic in style, whereas the Avenger's writing was much narrower."

QDE John Osborn on CBS's *48 Hours- Black Dahlia Confidential*, August 2006

Here is a sample of the difference is the two writings of the letter "N" as pointed out by Mr. Osborn:

"Avenger letter-N"   Dr. George Hodel letter-N

George Hodel [top] Black Dahlia Avenger; Disguised HW [bottom]

Below are additional samples of George Hodel's known handwriting that were not shown, and apparently not seen or used in Osborn's comparison. [Although these exact same samples were available and printed in my book.]

Note in these samples how my father writes the letter "N," as compared to the Avenger's letter "N." Though known to be written by George Hodel, it is quite dissimilar to his "Classic N," as described by Osborn and quite similar to the Avenger's style of writing the letter "N." I am confident that *had their expert seen these George Hodel handwriting documents,* it would have altered or at least modified his opinion regarding George Hodel's handwriting of the letter "N."

"Avenger letter-N"   Dr. George Hodel letter-N

1 & 2-   George Hodel known handwriting
3-   Black Dahlia Avenger handwriting

351

George Hill Hodel Handwriting

Those of you that have read *BDA* and *Most Evil* know that I am not a huge fan of handwriting analysis. That is not to say that I totally discredit it—I DO NOT. It has its place and can be a very effective tool in the investigative process—just as *long as the QDE (Questioned Document Examiner) findings are not elevated to an absolute.*

For me, handwriting analysis remains an inexact half science. Why?

Because of its subjectivity. HW is like the polygraph. A useful investigative tool, but cannot and should not be relied on by itself. Two different QDE's of equal stature will and often do provide "expert testimony" that a specific questioned document "WAS" and "WAS NOT" written by a specific individual. Who to believe? Flip a coin. That's not science. The same is true with polygraph examiners' testimony. Examiner #1 say's, "He's lying." Examiner #2, "No, he's telling the truth and was not at the crime-scene."

The same can be said of psychiatric experts. The prosecutor's doctors testified, "He's sane. He knew right from wrong when he stabbed her." The defense psychiatrist countered, "Psychotic and insane during the commission of the crime."

Because of this inherent subjectivity, one must use great caution when considering the results of any single QDE's findings. (That includes my own expert's opinions and reports as presented in *BDA* and *Most Evil*.)

With that disclaimer, let me add that as far as handwriting is concerned, I believe that in both its psychology and technical writing aspects, one cannot ignore the fact that each of us, in our handwriting, regularly and unconsciously display some *unique* "characteristics" in both our cursive and printed writings.

Consider these somewhat akin to the "points" in a fingerprint. The more unique points one finds in a HW sample, the stronger the case becomes that he or she is "probably" the writer. (But unlike fingerprints where a "make" or positive can be scientifically verified to a certainty, HW cannot.)

Bottom Line: In my opinion, HW analysis and findings should be considered as a piece of the overall puzzle and circumstantially relevant, but the "expert findings" should never be overweighed to the point where they become the major consideration in determining an individual's guilt or innocence, especially when the HW is deliberately DISGUISED.

Handwriting is such a large part of both the AVENGER and ZODIAC INVESTIGATIONS that it demands major consideration. In the 1947 Avenger communications, we have about a dozen letters, and twenty years later, Zodiac's separate mailings include two dozen— over 4000 words! [That is approximately ten times the amount of words written in Abraham Lincoln's "Gettysburg Address."]

At the end of this chapter, I will provide twenty-five separate "known" samples of my father's handwriting, which include both letters and numbers. They span a seventy-three-year period from 1925 to 1998. I offer them for your individual consideration and analysis.

1948 AVENGER Kern Letter–1966 ZODIAC-Bates Poem—Some Comparisons

Gladys Kern was one of the Los Angeles *Lone Woman Murder* victims. She was a real estate agent, who, in 1948, was stabbed multiple times in the back with a long-bladed knife. The suspect, posing as a prospective house buyer, met her at her office and requested that she take him to view a vacant Hollywood residence that was up for sale. Witnesses observed two men leaving the residence, but no description was made public on the second suspect.

The Hollywood murder occurred in the Los Feliz district of Hollywood, less than two miles from the Franklin house. The victim's office was just one mile from George Hodel's residence.

1948 witness composite drawing of the Gladys Kern killer

1948 composite drawing of Kern murder suspect [center]
Since no moustache was included in original drawing I have
airbrushed out my father's from the two photographs

KERN MURDER SUSPE

George Hodel circa 1946   Kern Murder Suspect 1948   George Hodel 1952

Body found inside the vacant residence two days after the murder

Woman Slain in Hollywood Mystery; Police Seek Anonymous Note Writer

Real Estate Broker Stabbed While Showing House

Mrs. Gladys Kern, 42, real estate saleswoman of 8200 Ray St., was found stabbed to death with a hunting knife yesterday on the kitchen floor of a $25,000 hillside home at 4217 Cromwell Ave., in the swank Los Feliz district.

She was killed and robbed, police believe. Their major clue was a mysterious tip-off note apparently mailed at Fifth and Olive Sts. only a short time after the slaying Saturday afternoon. The note identified the killer by a name police had been unable to trace up to late last night.

Similar Attack

Apprised of an almost identical attack on an unnamed Redondo Beach real estate woman Saturday afternoon, Feb. 7, homicide detectives last night sped to the beach city to check details of that assault. The victim had been attacked and robbed while showing a vacant house to a man with black, wavy hair. He, too, used a long knife to threaten her, forcing her to disrobe and locking her in the bathroom.

Although Redondo police last night refused to discuss the incident, their report issued at the time of the attack contained a description similar in many ways to that of the accused killer in today's tip-off note.

Mrs. Kern, mother of two grown children, took a prospective buyer to inspect the house Saturday afternoon, after obtaining the key from John H. Gregg, real estate man, at 1 p.m. She never returned from the inspection trip.

MURDER SCENE—New hillside house at 4217 Cromwell Ave., where body of Mrs. Gladys Kern, real-estate broker, was found stabbed to death. She disappeared on Saturday.

Immediately following the murder, her killer mailed a long rambling hand printed letter to the police from a downtown mailbox, located at Fifth and Olive, just three blocks from George Hodel's medical office. *The mailbox was the same one used by the Black Dahlia Avenger in 1947.* The police received the killer's letter *before* the victim's body was discovered at the vacant residence some two days later.

Los Angeles 1948, Gladys Kern Letter—Her Killer's Handwriting

de aquaindance of man three weeks ago while in Griffith Park he
... a good sport we got friendly Friday night askeame if I
...d to make about $300. He said he wanted to buy a home for his to bui...
was a racketeer and no real estater would do business
him he suggested I buy a home for him in my name
...e would go with person to look at property to make sure he
and I went to ...

ash... he ... to ... ect pro... ... alter looking at hose
...ove me to pick him up and he followe in his car they went
use alone to inspect and I waited outside alter while
...up to investigate, there I found her lying on floor, him tiying to
...ing off fingers he pulled gun on me. and told me he
knocked her out he knew I carried money so he took my
with all my. money tied my hands with my belt let me
own on sink and attached belt to faucet. alter he left t
...ree and tried to revive her when I turned her over, I was
...ed with blood pulled knife out then suddenly I came to I washed my
...and knife then I looked in her bag Im her home bhone and
...ess then left and ran out while outside I found he put small
t book in my coat pockets and threw it eway. also in my pocket

...? Pontiac Sedan very dark number plates look Live 46 plates but with
... ...t 5Jt-13 Jet black curly hairt wears blue at ... garbar...he
... m...he was alfigther and looks it I won't rest till I find him
every plac we went to gether I know that man is my only alibi and
... I feel really guilty

Riverside, Cheri Jo Bates Notes—1966

In 1966, in what the San Francisco Police Department now believes was a likely Zodiac connected murder, Riverside college student Cheri Jo Bates was brutally attacked in the dark of night, after she exited the library on the Riverside Community College campus.

It was a savage attack, and, as in the Gladys Kern murder, the cause of death was due to multiple stab wounds to the body.

As he had in the 1947 Black Dahlia Avenger crimes, the suspect, subsequent to the crime, called and taunted both police and press by telephone, and later mailed in multiple handwritten letters, promising "There will be more."

The investigation revealed that the suspect was likely "lying in wait" and wrote the below sadistic "poem" on a library desktop while waiting for the victim to exit the library. The message was discovered only after the attack.

On April 30, 1967, which was the sixth month "anniversary" of his killing, he mailed in more sadistic notes, both to the Riverside police and to the victim's father. One was a lengthy typewritten letter, and the second, scribbled in his distinctive block printing, read: "Bates had to die. There will be more—signed, "Z."

1966 Bates Desktop Poem

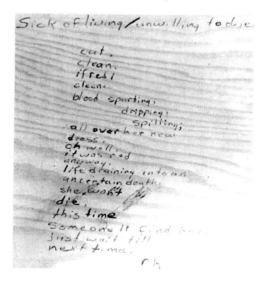

Bates killer's typed and hand printed letters mailed April 30, 1967

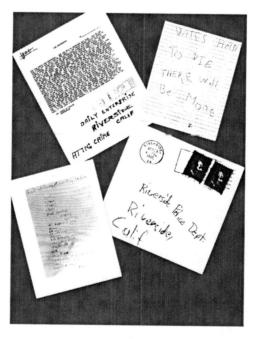

ZODIAC LINKED TO RIVERSIDE SLAYING

In the below exhibit I have taken each letter of the alphabet and created a side-by-side comparison of the 1948 Los Angeles Kern killer's HW to the 1966 Riverside Bates/Zodiac's HW. Keeping in mind that the two author's HW was separated by twenty years, what is the likelihood that so many of the letters would be *identical?* I count twenty-one (21)—what is your count?

SAME AUTHOR?

1948 Avenger - 1966 Zodiac HW letter comparisons

Lower case letter comparisons of 1948 Kern letter to 1966 Bates poem

In the below exhibit I am comparing not just letters, but the HW of the complete words found in both the Kern and Bates writings. The Kern words are found inside the boxes with a line connecting them to their Bates counterparts. Note the highly distinctive and uncommon use of the word "TILL" in both letters. The Kern killer proclaims, "I won't rest *till* I find him." The Bates killer warns, "Just wait *till* next time."

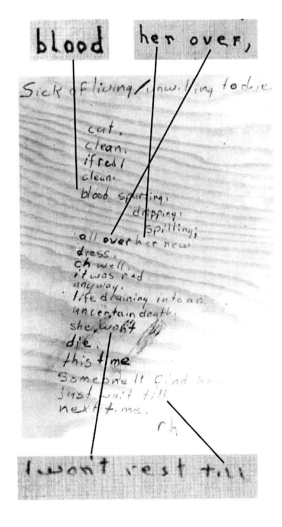

In reviewing the Kern/Bates writings a few years back, I noticed what to me is one of the most distinctive HW "anomalies" yet discovered. Take a look at the unusual letter "h" written by the suspect in the 1948 Kern letter. It is found in the word—"attached" and only appears ONCE in the entire letter.

Now compare it to the letter "h" written by Zodiac in the words: "hell-hole" and "Chronicle" in his 1974 "Red Phantom" letter.

Unusual letter "h" in Avenger-Kern Note compared to Zodiac "h" in Red Phantom letter

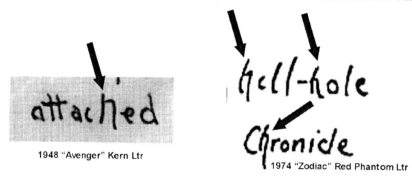

1948 "Avenger" Kern Ltr

1974 "Zodiac" Red Phantom Ltr

Some additional KERN Letter idiosyncrasies:

Note the writing variations on the letter "M" within the same sentence.

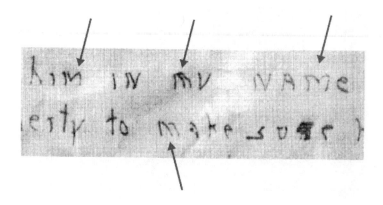

362

Note the stylistic writing variations of the letter "a" [tail up then tail down] and in the letter "n" [upper and lower case [aNd vs. and] all within the same sentence.

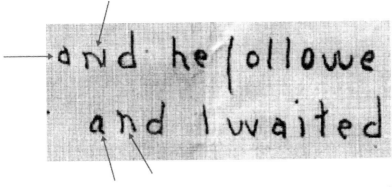

More samples of the writer's fluidity as we see a switch in the same sentence from "aNd" to "And" deviating from the previous use of—"and." Most notably, in the below sentence, he has written a backward or "mirrored" letter r. My guess is that *this was not intentional* on his part, but just "came out" as he wrote it—simply an unconscious writing anomaly.

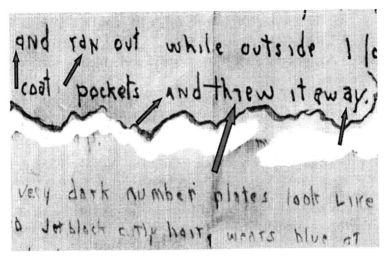

Below we see the killer changing his style of writing the letter "R" from upper case to lower—again within the same sentence and *within a word.*

Are these unusual writing characteristics exhibited in the 1948 Kern letter indicative of someone with high intelligence, who is simply "wired differently" than most of us?

Obviously, we cannot say, but in closing this chapter, let me offer some observations originally made in 2002 by questioned document expert Hannah McFarland.

After positively identifying George Hodel's handwriting as being the same as the "Black Dahlia Avenger" and providing her expert opinion that "it was highly probable that he authored at least four of the 1947 "Black Dahlia Avenger" notes," QDE McFarland went on to describe one of my father's unique and highly unusual HW characteristics.

I quote from *BDA I*, my chapter on "Handwriting Analysis" pages 289-290:

... In the sample below, I have enlarged my name, "STEVEN." During her character analysis of the known writing, Ms. McFarland noted a handwriting phenomenon so exceptionally rare that in her examination of documents over many years she had never come across it. This rarity related to the manner in which the three letters "TEV" in "STEVEN" were written. As Ms. McFarland explained:

It appears that all three letters were highly connected. The T bar connects directly to the top of the E. Most people lift the pen at this point to complete the E. But instead, the printer keeps going in order to form the V, and then goes back to complete the E.

She advised me that to find two connected letters was not particularly rare, but three connected was unheard of, and would indicate the type of exceptionally high intelligence and forethought that might be found in a master chess champion such as a Boris Spassky or a Bobby Fischer. Confirmation of her observation was possible because I possessed the original drawing and was therefore able to verify the three unbroken letters. Thus, in this particular instance, because we were able to view the original document, her analysis of the three connected letters was "positive" instead of highly probable.

Section of George Hodel's handwriting from April 1949

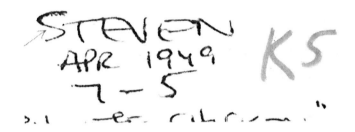

Above is the sample K-5, with an enlargement of the name "STEVEN" demonstrating the printed "TEV" connected and unbroken.

I suspect that some of these other Kern HW "characteristics" we have seen and noted above would fall into a similar classification or category—HW authored by a mind that works quickly and functions somewhat "out of the norm."

The final exhibit compares what also may be an unconscious handwriting "habit" or characteristic. Note that the Bates killer has used a *slashmark* [arrow] to divide two separate thoughts at the heading of his "poem": "Sick of living/unwilling to die." Likewise, George

Hodel at the heading of his conference notes for June Hodel has also used a slashmark to divide his thoughts: "Notes/Qs [Questions].

Coincidence or Characteristic?

Bates Killer Desk Poem Heading   **George Hodel Conference Notes Heading**

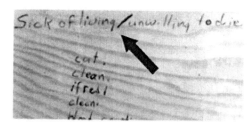

As promised, for those interested in pursuing additional HW comparisons, I have here provided an additional five [5] exhibits which contain a total of twenty-five [25] separate samples of George Hodel's handwriting, spanning some seventy-three years. As can be seen, he nearly always wrote using block printing. Most of his correspondence to me was typewritten. I am in possession of only *one instant sample* of his lower case cursives. [V]

Handwriting samples of George Hill Hodel 1925-1997

I

Respectfully,

II

STEVEN
APR 1949
7-5
" CHINESE CHICKEN "
(MOUNTAINS, SUN)
"BIGGEST CHICKEN IN
CHINA - THEY'VE BEEN
LOOKING FOR HIM A
THOUSAND YEARS)

G H H
Post Office Box 818
Manila, Philippines

A-4820

EXPRESS
MAIL

VIA AIR MAIL
REGISTERED

DOROTHY BARBE
545 O'FARRELL ST.
APT. 111
SAN FRANCISCO, CALIF. 94102
U.S.A.

1949	1952	1952	1952
7-5 1949	317	3, 1952	7‡ 602

1961		1973	
1961,		3-733	261-0088

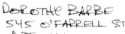
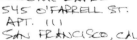
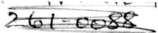

1974	1998
1974	4

III

IMPORTANT

The person to whom ~~this passport~~ is issued
must sign his ~~name on page~~ three immediately
on its receipt. The passport is NOT VALID
unless it has been signed.

The bearer should also fill in blanks below as
indicated.

c/o DR. G. HODEL

Bearer's address in the United States

UNIVERSITY OF HAWAII
HONOLULU 14, HAWAII

317 FLORIDA ST.

Bearer's foreign address

MANILA PHILIPPINES

IN CASE OF DEATH OR ACCIDENT NOTIFY

DR. GEORGE HILL HODEL

Name of person to be notified

317 FLORIDA ST.

Exact address

MANILA, PHILIPPINES

Should you desire to obtain a new passport
after this passport shall have definitely expired,
this passport should be presented with your
application for a new passport.

FOR DORERO
WITH LOVE!

George Hodel

XMAS 1981

CHINESE
CHICKEN
STOVEN
7-3

	18a. STREET ADDRESS (IF RURAL GIVE LOCATION)	18b. CITY OR TOWN	18c. COUNTY	18d. STATE
	1814 North Vine Street	Los Angeles	Los Angeles	California

19-I THIS DOES NOT MEAN THE MODE OF DYING SUCH AS HEART FAILURE, ASTHENIA, ETC. IT MEANS THE DISEASE, INJURY OR COMPLICATIONS WHICH CAUSES DEATH

19-I DISEASE OR CONDITION DIRECTLY LEADING TO DEATH

ARTERIOSCLEROTIC HEART DISEASE 10 YRS

ANTECEDENT CAUSES

19-Ia DUE TO

ANGINA PECTORIS 5 YRS

19-Ib DUE TO

CEREBRAL HEMORRHAGE 2 HRS

19-II CONDITIONS CONTRIBUTING TO THE DEATH BUT NOT RELATED TO THE DISEASE OR CONDITION CAUSING DEATH

19-II OTHER SIGNIFICANT CONDITIONS

HEMIPLEGIA 2 YRS

21. AUTOPSY ☐ YES ☒ NO

20a. DATE OF OPERATION — 20b. MAJOR FINDINGS OF OPERATION —

22a. ACCIDENT SUICIDE HOMICIDE

22b. PLACE OF INJURY — 22c. LOCATION CITY OR TOWN COUNTY STATE

22b. TIME MONTH DAY YEAR HOUR — 22d. INJURY OCCURRED ☐ WHILE AT WORK ☐ NOT WHILE AT WORK — 22e. HOW DID INJURY OCCUR?

23a. CORONER'S CERTIFY — GHH-HW
23b. PHYSICIAN'S CERTIFY 1941 12/10 49
23c. SIGNATURE George Hodel, M.D. 5121 FRANKLIN AVE, L.A. 27 12/24/49

25. SIGNATURE OF EMBALMER ... LICENSE NUMBER 2964

24a. ☐ BURIAL ☒ CREMATION REMOVAL — 24b. DATE Dec.28/49 — 24c. CEMETERY OR CREMATORY Forest Lawn Crematory

26. SIGNATURE OF FUNERAL DIRECTOR FOREST LAWN MEMORIAL-PARK ASS'N, INC. GLENDALE, CALIFORNIA

27. DATE RECEIVED BY LOCAL REGISTRAR DEC 27 1949 — 28. SIGNATURE OF LOCAL REGISTRAR

DEPARTMENT OF PUBLIC HEALTH

IV

V

[Rare sample of George Hodel cursive HW]

o join these
with them   and continue
mate their flight

Chapter 19

George Hodel—Angel City Abortion Ring Link

Just when I thought it was finally okay to file away the *LADA Black Dahlia-Hodel Surveillance Files*—to quote an outdated and overused term—*"The plot thickens."*

In a recent rereading of some of the transcribed pages, I noted the mention of a name that seemed familiar, but I couldn't place—"Dr. E.W. DeLong."

The reference to Dr. DeLong is found in DA investigator Walter Morgan's entry for February 20, 1950, at 4:15 p.m., just three days after the stakeout began.

Detective Morgan, seated at his listening post in the basement of Hollywood Police Station makes the following recorded entry in his log:

> 5:45 P   Telephone rang – answered by Hodel – conversation about
> crime prevention; Delinquent accounts; Dr. E.W. DeLong's
> October 1948 account; Blood and spinal fluids; employment of
> Collector; Hodel's stock ownership in a company – maid entered
> conversation about time; Hodel stated that it was six o'clock, that he
> had to leave at seven, that he would be back at twelve- began to type.

DA Hodel File- February 20, 1950 entry re. Dr. E.W. DeLong

```
HODEL FILE - XX
SPOOL #7
Spool
File
              4:25P        Spool #7
              4:30P        Typewriter noise.
              4:35P        Unintelligible conversation with maid.
              4:48P        Telephone rang - was answered by Hodel - short conversation
                           about price of tea.
              4:56P        Began typing.
      0-1     5:05P        Conversation with maid - Typing.
      1-3.5   5:08P            "         "     "      "
      3.5-5   5:14P            "         "     "      "
      5-6     5:16P            "         "     "      "
      6-8     5:18P            "         "     "      "
      8-11    5:28P        Telephone rang - answered by Hodel - conversation about
                           "Units".
      11-27.5 5:45P        Telephone rang - answered by Hodel - conversation about
                           crime prevention; Delinquent accounts; Dr. E.W. DeLong's
                           October 1948 account; Blood and spinal fluids; employment
                           of Collector; Hodel's stock ownership in a company -
                           maid entered conversation about time; Hodel stated that it
                           was six o'clock, that he had to leave at seven, that he
                           would be back at twelve - begins to type.
      27.5-   6:13P        Noise like writing on paper.
      28.5
      28.5-   6:18P        Hodel asked maid to close door.
      29.5
```

This log entry documents a link between Dr. George Hodel and Beverly Hills physician, Dr. E.W. DeLong.

It mentioned a business connection between the two physicians and that George Hodel was going to pursue a collection of funds owed to him by Dr. DeLong for work performed, apparently related to some laboratory testing. [George Hodel, in addition to his VD clinic and private practice, also owned and supervised his own private serology laboratory in downtown LA.]

What makes this highly relevant to our ongoing investigation is the revelation that Dr. E.W. DeLong was a longtime friend and the personal attending physician to Dr. L.C. Audrain.

More than that, Dr. Delong personally responded to Dr. Audrain's Hollywood Hills home where he pronounced him dead on May 20, 1949 at 3:00 a.m.

Below is a copy of Dr. Audrain's death certificate in which Dr. DeLong listed the cause of death as due to natural causes—"Heart Disease"—and ordered that no autopsy be performed. Forrest Lawn Cemetery picked up the body, and, apparently, that was the end of the story. Natural death—no questions asked. Sound familiar?

Dr. L.C. Audrain Death Certificate May 20, 1949
prepared and signed by Dr. E.W. DeLong

Well, at least not publicly. However, for those IN THE KNOW, I'm sure there were many whispered questions in City Hall, in the DA's Office, and at LAPD's Homicide Division. I'm confident that the late night lamps were burning bright in all three buildings. Here's why:

Who was Dr. Leslie Carl Audrain?

Dr. L.C. Audrain first appeared on the Los Angeles radar screen in June 1921 when the following article was printed in the *Los Angeles Times:*

LURED BY SOUTHLAND

Dr. L.C. Audrain, who as head of the entertainment committee received THE MEMBERS OF THE LOCAL Chamber of Commerce at Mazatlan during their excursion to Mexico, is coming to Los Angeles to live. Mrs. Audrain arrived in this city a few days ago to settle in her home at the Murray Apartments, 1026 Orange Street.

While at Mazatlan a number of Los Angeles Chamber of Commerce members, including President Weaver, were entertained at the home of Dr. Audrain. There the only hospital between San Diego and the Panama Canal is located. Wound soldiers and sailors were received there during the war.

Mr. and Mrs. Audrain will make their home in the United States after a nine-year sojourn on the west coast of Mexico.

Dr. Audrain after relocating from Mexico became a prominent Los Angeles OB-GYN physician and surgeon, and the personal physician to famed evangelist Aimee Semple McPherson, up until her death in 1944.

Records show that his wife; Mathilde Audrain was a nurse who assisted him at his office in the Professional Building, located at 1052 W. Sixth Street.

Dr. Leslie C. Audrain was named by LAPD Sgt. Charles Stoker in a secret 1949 grand jury testimony, *as being the head of an Abortion Ring of Los Angeles MD's all of whom paid "protection money" to LAPD detectives, which kept them immune from being arrested.* [MD's and chiropractors who were performing abortions and who were not making police payoffs to LAPD were arrested and given stiff prison sentences.]

LAPD Sgt. Charles Stoker

"Stoker is the real informer in this case. Brenda Allen is just peanuts compared to what he has given us. He should be under guard. If he continues to name names and situations like he did today, he will be found dead on the curb within five days."

Harry A. Lawson,
1949 Grand Jury Foreman
Los Angeles Times, July 8, 1949

Those of you, who have read *Black Dahlia Avenger*, will recognize Sgt. Charles Stoker's name. I devoted Chapter 25, *"Sergeant Stoker, LAPD's Gangster Squad, and the Abortion Ring,"* and two following chapters in an attempt to provide a historical perspective on his critical involvement and impact in Los Angeles during two of Los Angeles's most dynamic and politically volatile years—1948-1950.

LAPD Vice Sgt. Charles Stoker, circa 1949, assigned to Vice and Uniform Patrol

Thicker'n Thieves originally published in 1951 and republished in 2011

Sgt. Stoker's real-time expose, *Thicker N' Thieves*, published in 1951, documented the police and political corruption of those years. And in his book, he pulled no punches and provided us with real names, dates, and locations.

Up until 2011, it had been virtually impossible to find a copy of his book. The 1951 out-of-print edition was so scarce that it was selling on-line for $300-$500.

In April of 2011, I wrote a short forward to a new, republished edition, which is now available to all as a low cost paperback or downloadable e-book. [*Thicker'n Thieves*, by Charles Stoker, *Thoughtprint Press, 2011, Los Angeles*]

In *Thicker'n Thieves*, Sgt. Stoker documented the historical events that changed Los Angeles and the LAPD and narrated them as they actually unfolded in real time during the years 1948-1950.

Stoker laid out how the police cabal operated, and, in his chapter, "Angel City Abortion Ring," provided critical information and answers to many of my early questions.

His book gives us some real insights into the man and reveals that he was an honest cop, trying to do the right thing. However, being somewhat politically naive, Stoker was unaware of how dangerous it was to try and buck the established system of corruption in the "City of Angles," which had been in place for more than a quarter century.

Sgt. Charles Stoker testified in secret before the 1949 grand jury hearings, revealing graft and corruption and naming names twenty-years before his New York counterpart Frank Serpico. But unlike Serpico, Stoker never received fame or recognition, and he died relatively young, a broken and forgotten man.

Los Angeles Times headlines July 8, 1949

Los Angeles Times July 8, 1949

Grand Jury Chief Fears for Life of Stoker After He Testifies Again

Foreman Lawson Calls Him
'Real Informer in Case'

"Stoker is the real informer in this case. Brenda Allen is just peanuts compared to what he has given us. He should be under guard. If he continues to name names and situations like he did today he will be found dead on the curb within five days."

Harry A. Lawson
1949 Grand Jury Foreman

Sgt. Stoker related headlines 1948-1949

Twenty Years Before SERPICO There Was STOKER

Stoker's testimony opened up a Pandora's Box for LA politicos and LAPD. He blew the lid off most of the major corruption scandals of 1949, which included: Mickey Cohen's wire taps; and Brenda Allen's prostitution ring, and her payoffs to LA vice cops and their superiors.

Earlier in the year, in a sworn testimony, Stoker confirmed Hollywood Vice Squad's intimidations and extortions of bar owners who would not "pay to play," along with the systematic brutality and false arrests of their customers on trumped up charges of "drunk" or "lewd conduct."

As a result of the secret hearings and testimony from Stoker and others, the 1949 grand jury ordered a reinvestigation of the many unsolved *Lone Woman Murders* of the day, *and ordered that the Black Dahlia Murder investigation be taken away from LAPD and reinvestigated by the DA's Office.* [This was an unheard of action coming from a seated grand jury, which to my knowledge had never occurred prior to or after 1949. LAPD command was in a rolling boil over the grand jury's labeling of them as inept and corrupt.]

In 1949, as a result of Stoker's testimony, LAPD, in an effort to "circle the wagons," arrested him on a trumped up "burglary" charge. Their "star witness" was his vice partner, policewoman Audre Davis, whom they approached with an offer that she couldn't refuse. "Testify that you saw Stoker break into an office building, and we will give you immunity. Refuse and you're fired." They knew that the bogus case was a "humbug" and a loser, but, at the very least, it would throw mud on Stoker's bright shiny badge.

Sgt. Charles Stoker was defended by prominent LA attorney, S.S. (Sammy) Hahn, *who ironically also represented my mother, Dorothy Hodel in her 1944 divorce from George Hodel.*

Hahn, as expected, won an acquittal on the trumped up "Burglary" charge against Stoker and later helped establish that his LAPD female partner, Audre Davis, who was the prosecution's star witness, had committed perjury.

Attorney S.S. Hahn was the other go-to attorney in Los Angeles from the 1920s through the1950s. Hahn and his counterpart, Jerry "Get Me" Giesler, pretty much cornered the market on defending high-profile crimes and divorces in LA.

Many of you will recognize Hahn's name from the recent 2008 film, *Changeling*, directed by Clint Eastwood. Geoff Pierson plays Hahn as the "pro bono" attorney, representing the distraught mother, Mrs. Christine Collins (Angelina Jolie), who testified and took down corrupt LAPD Capt. J.J. Jones and LAPD Chief James E. Davis.

As a side note, Attorney Hahn was found dead at the bottom of his swimming pool in 1957. The *LA Times*, in reporting the "mysterious death," quoted detectives as finding "a gash to the forehead and that heavy cement blocks had been tied around his neck which were holding him down at the bottom of the pool." No note was found. The *Times* article also quoted investigating detective Jim Wahlke as saying, "From all indications, it appears to be a suicide, but..."

"Atty. Hahn Dies in Swimming Pool Mystery," *LA Times*, June 26, 1957

BLOCKS AROUND NECK—Building blocks tied with rope were around neck of Atty. S. S. Hahn when he was found drowned in swimming pool. Here Dep. F. L. Smongesky, left, and Sgt. Jim Wahlke, of Sheriff's homicide squad, examine them.

Hahn, like George Hodel, was a Los Angeles taproot. His connections reached deep underground and spanned four decades of LA politics and power.

The third leg of the legal stool in Los Angeles was Mickey Cohen's lawyer, Samuel "Mouthpiece to the Mob" Rummel, who was gunned down in front of his Hollywood Hills home in 1950.

His murder was never solved. Preliminary investigation revealed that Rummel had met with LA Sheriff's Capt. Al Guasti the previous night, just hours before the shooting at his home. Though never actually tied to the shooting, Guasti was shortly thereafter indicted on major corruption charges.

As far as Sammy Hahn's "suicide," what can I say? 1950s business as usual in the "City of the Fallen Angels."

Dr. Audrain, Dr. DeLong, and Dr. Hodel—Connecting the Dots

In *BDA*, I stated early on that I believed that my father, Dr. George Hodel, was a participant in, or, at the very least, had full knowledge of the operations of Dr. Audrain's MD abortion ring, as referenced in Sgt. Stoker's expose.

That was further confirmed post-publication with the revelations from the *DA Hodel-Black Dahlia Files* connecting known abortionist Charles Smith with Beverly Hills Dr. Francis Ballard, performing the abortion on my half-sister, Tamar.

Also found in the DA files was the documented interview with Smith's girlfriend, Mildred Bray Colby, who witnessed the early morning $1,000 cash payoff [$10,000 in today's dollars] from George Hodel to Charles Smith, made at the Franklin house on December 29, 1949. This cash payment was made just five days after George Hodel's acquittal on the Tamar incest/molestation charges.

Next, we had my father's statements in the DA transcripts confirming he performed abortions at his VD clinic, "Lots of them."

Add to that George's separate taped statements to Baron Herringer [Harringa] where he tells him, "I'm the only one who knows how everything fits together. This is the best payoff between law enforcement agencies I have ever seen."

And now, what does this latest discovery tell us?

1) Sgt. Charles Stoker, in conjunction with State Medical Board investigators, utilized a female undercover officer, whom he sent to Dr. Audrain's medical office where Audrain's nurse [not named, but probably his wife, Mathilde who was known to work there] confirmed her worst fears, and told her that "she's pregnant" and scheduled her for an abortion. [According to state investigators and Sgt. Stoker, the sting arrest was blown due to the fact that law enforcement officers warned the performing doctor of the pending "sting operation." And when the undercover officer showed up for her appointment, they found the office locked and closed, and the doctor "on vacation."]

2) **On May 5, 1949**, Sgt. Stoker, under subpoena to a grand jury hearing, testified to all that he knew about LAPD police corruption, vice payoffs to Madame Brenda Allen, secret wire taps at Mickey Cohen's home involving payoffs to cops, abortion ring payoffs, and *most likely named Dr. Audrain as the head of the protected abortion ring.*

3) **On May 20, 1949**, just two-weeks following Sgt. Stoker's testimony, Dr. E.W. DeLong, a close personal friend of Dr. L.C. Audrain, responded to Audrain's home, and pronounced him dead due to natural causes—"heart disease"—and insured that no autopsy or toxicological tests would be performed; the body was removed to a private mortuary for burial.

4) Prior to Dr. Audrain's death, a chiropractor, Dr. Eric Kirk, who was named and figured prominently in Stoker's book, was arrested and was serving prison time for performing abortions. Dr. Kirk was under grand jury subpoena and was going to testify and name names of many of the doctors involved in Audrain's abortion ring.

As a result of his filing a formal affidavit, Dr. Kirk was brought to LA from prison in September 1949, four months after Audrain's death. His wife received death threats if her husband testified against LAPD homicide detectives, and it was unknown if he actually followed through with his promise to identify and name the corrupt cops.

5) Dr. E.W. DeLong was doing business with and was obviously acquainted with Dr. George Hodel, which put him in close association to two known abortionists [Hodel and Audrain]. Working in Beverly Hills, he most certainly would have known George Hodel's abortionists of choice for Tamar's September 1949 abortion—Dr. Francis Ballard and his "assistant," Charles Smith.

Doctors Hodel and Audrain both lived in Hollywood and resided just three miles apart. Doctors DeLong, Ballard, Audrain, and Hodel all lived and worked within six miles of each other.

Did Dr. Audrain in fact die of natural causes and the timing of his death was just "coincidental"? Or, was it a suicide? Murder? We will never know the truth of it now. But, with this latest direct tie-in in the transcripts, there is certainly much cause for reflection.

At the time of his death, Dr. Audrain was seventy-three. If it was his wife, who had falsely confirmed the policewoman's "pregnancy" and made the abortion appointment from their 1052 W. Sixth Street medical practice, then she was at risk and would have most certainly been arrested with him for conspiring to commit an abortion.

Dr. Audrain was facing a major scandal, disgrace, and almost certain imprisonment. Those in power, his fellow abortion ring doctors, MD's all, and the cops receiving protection money would have all wanted him out of the way.

Dr. Audrain's potential grand jury indictment and pending arrest was a huge threat to every corrupt cop and official involved. Fortunately for all of them, his unexpected death, be it "heart attack" or suicide, allowed for their problem, at least as related to Audrain, to just disappear.

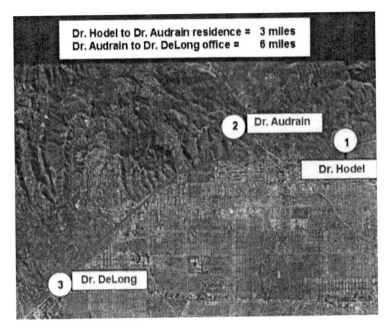

Dr. Hodel to Dr. Audrain residence = 3 miles
Dr. Audrain to Dr. DeLong office = 6 miles

Grand Jury Indicts Ten in LA—Arrests Confirm Los Angeles-San Francisco State-wide Abortion Ring

In April 1950, *just two days after George Hodel fled the country,* the seated 1950 grand jury indicted ten doctors and nurses involved in what the *LA Times* described as, "An alleged illegal surgical operations syndicate, then plunged headlong into investigation of reported protection payoffs to law enforcement officers."

The article went on to indicate that a Dr. Eric Kirk, currently serving time in prison for performing abortions [and a major player in Sgt. Stoker's expose of the LA abortion ring] would be called as a witness and promised to "tell all." [This would be additional testimony on these new arrests as he had already testified before the 1949 grand jury in September 1949.]

Los Angeles Times, April 2, 1950

Illegal Operation Ring Broken With Six Arrests

Police Credit Discovery of State-Wide Organization to San Francisco Informer

A State-wide ring specializing in illegal operations on an assembly line basis was broken up yesterday. Los Angeles and San resident, was flown to the Los Angeles medical building by Dr. Schroeder and an illegal operation was performed there. In

Los Angeles Times, April 27, 1950

Jury Indicts 10 in Surgery Ring Inquiry

The county grand jury yesterday returned criminal conspiracy indictments against 10 persons in an alleged illegal surgical operations syndicate, then plunged headlong into investigation of reported protection pay-offs to law enforcement officers.

As the first step in the pay-off investigation, the grand jury requested a court order allowing three chiropractors now serving prison terms to return here to testify before the panel next Wednesday.

Chiropractors to Talk

Foreman Carey S. Hill identified the three as Samuel Collins, William H. Malone and Eric H. Kirk, all serving terms of from two to five years following illegal operation convictions.

They have indicated a desire to "tell all" concerning bribery payments, it was reported. The court order was requested of Judge Stanley N. Barnes, presiding jurist of the Superior Court criminal division.

Among the indicted persons, charged with *conspiracy* to perform illegal operations, were

Turn to Page 2, Column 6

In the updated version of BDA (HarperCollins July 2006), I included the information related to what DA investigator, Lt. Jemison referred to as, "Hodel's friend, abortionist Charles Smith." That information revealed that Smith, in March 1950, was actively being investigated by law enforcement as being involved in the San Francisco/Los Angeles abortion ring.

On March 20, less than a month from the grand jury indictments in LA, Lt. Frank Jemison, while interviewing Charles Smith's ex-girlfriend, Mildred Bray Colby, said to her:

"Did you know that he [Smith] has been operating girls from San Francisco for abortions?"

Colby responded, "No, But, I wouldn't put it past him."

During this same interview by Lt. Jemison, in reference to my half-sister, Tamar Hodel and Smith's abortion arrest in October 1949 with Beverly Hills Dr. Francis Ballard, Miss Colby told Lt. Jemison:

"Smith said that someday he was going to fix Tamar. He was going to cut a chunk out of the calf of her leg and fry it and eat it in front of her eyes and then puke it in front of her face."

March 14, 1950, Telegram from San Francisco DA Edmund G. "Pat" Brown to Los Angeles DA's Office showing they are cooperating in "Charles Smith, abortionist friend of Hodel" investigation.

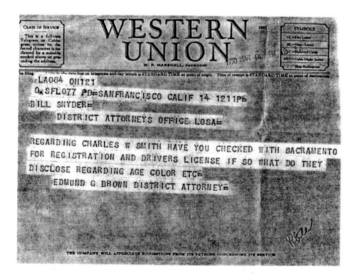

Three weeks prior to this telegram being sent from DA Brown in San Francisco to Lt. Jemison in Los Angeles, Lillian Lenorak appeared at Dr. Leslie Ballard and Charles Smith's trial and perjured herself, claiming that while she was present at Dr. Ballard's with Tamar, " he examined her, but no abortion occurred."

As a result of Lenorak's testimony, the judge dismissed the charges in January 1950. Lenorak later recanted her testimony, admitting she lied to protect Dr. Hodel, Dr. Ballard, and Charles Smith. [The immediate cause of her lying, as we know from the officer Unkefer's letter, was direct threats from George Hodel to harm both her and her son, John, and to have her placed in a mental institution.]

LAPD Capt. Edwin Jokisch (ret.)

"His [Steve Hodel's] father was involved in this 1949 incest case and was apparently guilty as you could be."

LAPD Capt. Edwin Jokisch (ret.)

One of the original detectives involved in the April 1950 San Francisco/Los Angeles abortion ring investigation and arrests was LAPD Sgt. Edwin Jokisch.

In the late 1940s, Detective Jokisch and his partner, Lloyd Burton, were both assigned to the LAPD Homicide Abortion Squad. That was the unit that would have normally handled the investigation into my half-sister Tamar's abortion. [In my original 2003 summary, I incorrectly attributed this detail to being under the direct supervision of the then existent, Gangster Squad. They were not. It was actually assigned to the Homicide Unit. My confusion came because during that time [1947-1949] many of the Gangster Squad detectives were loaned to and working homicide, primarily on the Black Dahlia investigation.]

To this day, I have not been able to determine whether it was Sgt. Jokisch and his partner who made the 1949 abortion arrest of Dr. Ballard and Charles Smith, or if it was other officers assigned to their unit. If it was Jokisch, then in preparing the case for prosecution, he would or should have had direct follow-up contact with: George Hodel, who procured Dr. Ballard to perform the abortion; Tamar Hodel, who received it; and Lillian Lenorak, who was present and witnessed it. [Jokisch's silence on this potential connection in recent years would seem to indicate that it was other detectives on the

Homicide Abortion Squad who investigated and made the Dr. Ballard/Charles Smith arrests.]

Jokisch's career with LAPD spanned thirty-two years, from 1940 to 1972. He was promoted and retired as a police captain and passed away on August 3, 2011 at age-ninety-six.

Capt. Jokisch, upon the original publication of my book in 2003, became one of the most vocal critics of my investigation. It was his belief that I was personally attacking him, as well as Chiefs William Parker, Thad Brown, and his good friend, Capt. Jack Donahoe.

Ed was mistaken, and I told him so. *I had no knowledge that he was connected to the 1948-1950 investigation as a detective assigned to the Homicide Abortion Detail until a year after publication of my book, when he contacted and informed me of his assignment to that unit during those years.*

As it turned out, much to my surprise, Jokisch informed me that he was the real-life, "Bill Ball" and his abortion squad partner, Det. Lloyd Burton was the same "Joe Small" named in Stoker's 1950 expose, *Thicker'N Thieves*. [In my original 2003 publication, I speculated that "Bill Ball" may have been LAPD Lt. Bill Burns, who at the time was head of the Gangster Squad, and who I mistakenly believed was supervising the Abortion Team.]

This admission from Jokisch means that it was his partner, Lloyd Burton, aka "Joe Small," who it was alleged in the *Thicker'N Thieves* chapter, "*Angel City Abortion Ring*" by several witnesses to be, "on the take and receiving payoffs for protecting doctors." In an interview just a few years prior to his death, Jokisch revealed *that he had never actually read Stoker's book,* with its detailed allegation of police corruption in which Stoker provides specific names, dates, and locations.

Ed Jokisch's 2004 admission of being "Bill Ball" to me also informed me that it was Jokisch, along with his partner, Det. Lloyd Burton, who had made the arrest of Dr. Eric H. Kirk just two days prior to Sgt. Stoker and undercover policewoman Audre Davis coming into contact with Dr. Kirk in an attempted abortion sting operation. [For full details see *BDA I*, Chapter 25, "*Sergeant Stoker, LAPD's Gangster Squad, and the Abortion Ring.*"]

I quote from page 346 of that chapter:

On September 17, 1949, an article appeared in the *Los Angeles Mirror* over the headline, "*Wife of L.A. Abortionist in Hiding.*" The story carried a picture of Dr. Eric H. Kirk, captioned: "He'll testify." The article said that Kirk's wife, Mrs. Marion Kirk, "a key witness in a huge abortion-payoff probe, was in hiding after it was learned that she received numerous telephone threats to "keep her mouth shut."

Interestingly, in the totally unrelated April, 1950 LA/San Francisco Abortion Ring arrests by state-wide authorities including, Det. Jokisch, when the case came to trial in 1950, a defendant-witness also received multiple threatening phone calls.

However, this time the threats were specific. I quote from the *LA Times*, September 30, 1950:

PHONE THREATS IN OPERATION TRIAL REPORTED

Telephone threats to "lay off" yesterday were featured in the trial of three persons on charges of criminal conspiracy and illegal medical operations

Henry J. Glynn, 55-year old hospital manager and one of three defendants on trial, reported to Superior Judge Thomas I., Ambrose that he had been the object of threatening phone calls since the beginning of the trial last week. [SKH Note- Judge Ambrose was the presiding judge on Dr. Hodel's three week incest trial.] Officer's Name
Glynn said he received a call last Monday evening from a mysterious person who told him he had "*better lay off Jokisch and his pals.*" [Emphasis mine]

Det. Lt. Ed Jokisch, a police officer, was one of the arresting officers in the case and currently is investigative advisor to Dep. Dist. Attys. Adolph Alexander and Albert K. Lucas.

... Hint Dropped
In early questioning of prospective jurors, Atty A.N. Chelenden, representing Oswald P. Gallardo, an osteopath and one of the defendants, hinted that a part of his defense may be allegations of official corruption and possible graft.

The third defendant, Miss Frieda Zipse, 32, a nurse, was present in the chambers hearing but made no statement.

On two separate occasions, circa 2004 and 2006, retired LAPD Capt. Jokisch, then in his early nineties attended several of my public talks, and, at the second one, in rather heated words, informed me, "Well, maybe you did solve the Black Dahlia murder, but you had NO RIGHT to speak against the fine reputations of Chief Parker, Thad Brown, and Jack Donahoe. Capt. Jack Donahoe was one of my closest personal friends."

Circa 2009, Capt. Jokisch, at age ninety-four, conducted a personal tape-recorded interview with a copy-editor, Larry Harnisch, also one of my most vocal critics, who, for the past fifteen years, has been promising to publish a book claiming that, "Dr. Walter Bayley was the probable Black Dahlia killer."

In a *KFI* "Crime Hunters" radio interview, when queried by the host, Eric Leonard, about Dr. Bayley's possible motive for the killing, Harnisch responded that the Black Dahlia murder "was rage driven." He then made an on-air speculation that Dr. Bayley may have killed Elizabeth Short because of a "sustained rage over the death of his son," who, he informed the interviewer, "was killed in a traffic accident in the 1920s" some twenty-five years prior to the murder.

After Jokisch's death in 2011, Harnisch posted his taped interview on the Internet.

In it, Jokisch reflected on the memories of his time with the LAPD, vented some of his anger about the publication of my book to a sympathetic ear [Harnisch], and then surprisingly, he had this to say in relation to George Hodel's 1949 arrest for incest:

"His [Steve Hodel's] *father was involved in this 1949 incest case and was apparently guilty as you could be.* [Emphasis mine.] But he was found not guilty. But he had the best mouthpiece you could have in those days. He had Jerry Giesler and his partner."

Los Angeles Times, 1957

LOOT RECOVERED

Det. Lt. Ed Jokisch, left, and chief of detectives Thad Brown check portion of
the $88,000 worth of furs and jewelry recovered after arrest of suspects in
robbery of Lauritz Melchior home.

Chapter 20

Mrs. Betty Bersinger—"Witness Number 1"

Had there been an arrest and trial in the Elizabeth Short "Black Dahlia Murder," the very first witness to be called and to testify for the prosecution would have been, Mrs. Betty Bersinger.

I had the privilege of meeting and interviewing Betty in the summer of 2008, some sixty-one years after that fateful morning of January 15, 1947, when as a Liemert Park resident walking her three-year-old daughter to the store, she chanced upon the victim's body lying in the vacant lot.

My interview lasted just under an hour. Betty was eighty-eight years old, exceptionally gracious, and her memory of the event remained sharp and clear. The facts, as is always the case, varied somewhat from those publicly reported by the press, which invariably distorts and revises them to fit what they think their readers want to hear.

This meeting with Betty was very much like my in-person interview with LAPD police officer Myrl McBride, the last witness to see Elizabeth Short alive.

It was special, like stepping into a time-machine and being whisked back to 1947, as if I was one of the original detectives, taking her statement for the first time.

Here is Betty's story just as she tells it. No reporter's deadline to meet, no spin, just the facts, exactly as they occurred—in her own words.

The Interview

"Well, I got up in the morning. I had a daughter, Anne, and Anne was about four then. I put her in her little Taylor Tot, that's what they called those things we tote the kids around in. It was a little stroller thing. And I started to walk down to Liemert Park, to the business area, and to take a pair of shoes that my husband needed to be resoled.

1940s Taylor Tot Stroller

Type of "Taylor Tot" stroller that Betty Bersinger used to take her daughter, Anne, to the shoe store.

It was early in the morning. I don't know, I assume it was about eight. Somewhere in there. I was walking by.... There's a vacant lot. I was living on South Norton. I started walking down Norton and came to the vacant lot that hadn't been developed yet. They had the sidewalks in and the streets but the lot was kind of overgrown with weeds.

I was just making my way through the clutter down Norton and I happened to look over to my side and I saw this.... It looked like a mannequin. That was the impression I had, "Oh, it's a mannequin." It was so white. It didn't register. I had never seen a dead body before anyhow. "Oh, a mannequin." It was divided in the middle, it was in two parts. I said, "Oh, dear, that's kind of strange looking." I thought, *"Well, maybe that will scare the kids as they are coming to school."* Because the kids would be riding their bikes. I thought, *"I'd better call and tell somebody to come out and clear that away."* So, that was my thought. I wasn't thinking about anything other than an old ordinary dumped mannequin.

Black Dahlia crime scene, January 15, 1947

"Mannequin-like" body as it appeared to witness Betty Bersinger

So, I kept going down on Norton to the first house I reached. I don't recall....
Anyway it was the second house that I went to, where a woman came to the
door. I said, "Could I use your telephone? I just want to call the police and let
them know that there is some junk up here that ought to be removed."

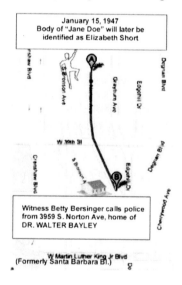

This map shows route taken by Mrs. Betty Bersinger from vacant lot south to
private residence of DR. WALTER BAYLEY, where the doctor's wife allowed
her to use the phone to notify police.

No, I didn't know it was a body. I had no idea it was a body. I thought it was a mannequin because it was so white.

So, I called the police, and Sgt. Somebody answered. And I told him my story, and he said, "Where are you calling from?" So, I looked down and gave him the number of the house where I was calling from.

Then I went on my way and went on down to Liemert Park and got the shoes into the shoe repair place. I took my time coming back. And on my way back, I think I walked up Crenshaw. Yes, that was the next block over.

And...I saw all these people around the area where I had seen the mannequin. I just thought must be something going on. I didn't know what it was. I didn't really think much about it. I went on home and it was time for my daughter's lunch and taking a nap. I didn't pay much attention; this was all before television you know. The only news we had was the papers. If there was anything really exciting, some little newsboy would be running down the street, yelling, "Extra, Extra."

So, I continued with my life. I don't think I even hardly mentioned it to anybody because it wasn't that important to me. It just wasn't that significant. And then I saw in the paper what really was going on. It was a body. And I said, "Oh, my goodness." After that, I didn't pay any more attention. My daughter was having a lot of trouble with breathing and asthma and colds, so I was busy taking her to get help to different doctors and getting her treatment. So, my life was really filled up with her health conditions.

I think I may have called my mother-in-law who lived down on Buckingham Road up. I told her that there was a lot of activity going on; that they found a dead body here. I don't remember when I called her? That day, or maybe a few days later. There wasn't a lot of news coming out, like you get it today—every five minutes.

So, I kind of forgot about it. Then, sometime later, my husband—he worked downtown in Westlake—was going to lunch with some of his friends, and he happened to look at the newspaper stand and there was this headline, "Police looking for finder of Black Dahlia body." Then he called me up and said, "Hey, we had better go down and see the police because I think they're looking for you." I said, "Oh, my God."

As soon as my husband came home, we went down to the police. So that is what happened.

They took my picture at the station and kind of interrogated my husband. (Laugh)

On Norton Avenue, the block I lived in had houses, and then they stopped. Then I think it was one or two vacant lots, I don't remember. Then there was a street, then more houses. A woman was at the house I made the call from.

The police only asked me what number I was calling from, not my name. And I gave them the phone number that was listed on the dial. Yes, it was several houses down [south] from Thirty-Ninth street.

No, I didn't think it was human, just a mannequin. My fear was that it might frighten the kids, because they might think it was human.

I know they made some movie where they said a man was taking his son down the street, and I said, "Well, that's not right." I think that was a television movie. I don't pay any attention to it, I know that they take liberties with the facts and do what they want.

You can take my picture. But first, let me brush my hair.

END OF INTERVIEW....

Mrs. Betty Bersinger seen "reenacting" phone call to police for reporters at University Police Station on January 23, 1947. She made the original call on January 15, 1947, from home of neighbor, DR. WALTER BAYLEY, at 3959 S. Norton Avenue, just a short distance south of Thirty-Ninth Street.

Betty Bersinger, 2008 interview with author

Dr. Walter A. Bayley

Dr. Walter A. Bayley circa 1919 wearing his WW I uniform

Dr. Walter Bayley was a former chief of staff at USC Medical Center [General Hospital] and in the mid-1940s his private medical practice was located in the Professional Building, 1052 W. Sixth Street.

According to LAPD Sgt. Charles Stoker, as summarized in his expose, *Thicker'N Thieves*, this was the *same building* where Dr. Audrain, head of the protected LA abortion ring also had his practice and where Audrain's nurse/secretary [probably his wife] had scheduled an abortion with Stoker's undercover policewoman partner. Dr. Audrain was subsequently warned of the "sting" and pending raid. And when Sgt. Stoker and his partner arrived at the scheduled appointment to make the arrest, Dr. Audrain was a "no show" and his "office remained closed and locked for a week."

While there is no hard evidence that Dr. Walter Bayley was performing abortions, there is a *suggestion that he may have been.* Clearly working in the same office building as Dr. Audrain and both doctors having long established LA practices, they certainly would have known each other and have been well acquainted for decades.

That said, Dr. Bayley's name has never appeared in any official law enforcement report connected with either the Black Dahlia or any other criminal investigation that I have had access to and reviewed. Other than the 1999 reference from the one amateur Black Dahlia theorist, his name remains completely *off the radar screen.*

According to newspaper accounts in 1948, immediately after Dr. Bayley's death at age sixty-seven, civil litigation ensued over his estate. Mrs. Bayley, in formal court papers, alleged that her husband was being blackmailed by his female associate, one Dr. Alexandra von Partyka.

It was established that Dr. Partyka, in December 1947, had gone to the VA Hospital where Dr. Bayley's had been hospitalized for over a month and was literally on his deathbed. [Bayley died on January 3, 1948.] And just weeks before his death Bayley had signed papers agreeing that she should receive *half of his estate.*

Mrs. Ruth Bayley alleged, through her attorney, that Dr. Partyka obtained her husband's signature under duress as his medical partner had threatened to expose him by revealing certain medical practice secrets. Here is an excerpt from the *Los Angeles Times* article of January 19, 1948:

> Dr. Partyka represented that *she had obtained certain secrets concerning his [Dr. Bayley's] medical practice and would expose and ruin him* [emphasis mine] if he returned to his wife, from whom he had separated a year before his death.

... Dr. Bayley lived in constant fear that Dr. Partyka would "disgrace him in his declining years" and accordingly consented to execution of the document.

Clearly, "secrets concerning his medical practice" would suggest at least the possibility that he was either a member of the abortion ring, or perhaps simply performing abortions on his own to earn extra money.

In 1949, Dr. Eric Kirk, the *Angel City abortion ring* whistle-blower agreed to testify before the grand jury as to his knowledge of chiropractors and others involved in the abortion ring, as well as naming law enforcement officers, but said that he would not identify MD's. As he so succinctly put it to the press, "I'm not going to name other doctors. I'm no stool pigeon. If all the doctors who perform abortions in Los Angeles were cleaned out, there wouldn't be many doctors left."

Obviously, despite the risk of going to prison, performing abortions remained a very common and profitable practice. And if a doctor could join a police protected ring, and pay a little "insurance-juice" to avoid being arrested—it was well worth it.

Los Angeles Times, January 19, 1948

THREATS OF DISGRACE ALLEGED IN WILL SUIT

Charges that the late Dr. Walter A. Bayley, physician, executed his will under intimidation of a young woman colleague, Dr. Alexandra Partyka, are made in a contest filed in Superior Court by his widow, Mrs. Ruth A. Bayley.

Threats Alleged

Dr. Bayley, 67, died last Jan. 3, leaving a will dated last Dec. 22 under which he disinherited his wife and left the major part of his estate to Dr. Partyka.

Mrs. Bayley, who lives at 3959 S. Norton Ave., contends that while associated with Dr. Bayley in the practice of medicine Dr. Partyka represented that she had obtained certain secrets concerning his medical practice and would expose and ruin him if he returned to his wife, from whom he had separated a year before his death.

The widow further asserts that Dr. Bayley lived in con-

stant fear that Dr. Partyka would "disgrace him in his declining years" and accordingly consented to execution of the document.

Dr. Partyka, the widow also charges, obtained an undue influence over Dr. Bayley through "unnatural flattery and feminine wiles" and induced him to accompany her on extended trips.

Dr. Bayley's will gave his office equipment and library and half of the remainder of his estate to Dr. Partyka. It divided the other half among a sister, a brother, a sister-in-law and an adopted daughter. No estimate of the value of the estate was given except that it will exceed $5000.

*Los Angeles Times
Jan 19, 1948*

Dr. Partyka threatens to reveal Dr. Bayley's "medical practice secrets."

LAPD Sgt. Finis A. Brown—The Lead Dahlia Detective

When asked the question, "What detective was originally in charge of the Black Dahlia Murder?" Most cops and newspaper reporters back then and today would say, "Sgt. Harry Hansen." Wrong answer! Another myth!

The real lead-detective was Sgt. Finis A. Brown, brother of chief of detectives, Thad Brown.

By all accounts Finis did most of the leg work and pretty much all of the thinking in the first three-years of hardcore Dahlia investigation.

Black Dahlia victim, Elizabeth Short, and lead-detective, Finis Brown shared the same birthday—
July 29

In December 1949, the grand jury subpoenaed a number of LAPD detectives to testify as to the original investigation.

Lead Black Dahlia detective, Finis Brown, was called, as was Lt. William Burns, formerly in charge of LAPD's Gangster Squad who had "assisted" in the Dahlia investigation by loaning his men to Homicide Division to "help work the case."

Unfortunately, the Gangster Squad detectives, who were for the most part untrained and inexperienced in homicide investigations, had made a mess of things and had a tendency to jump on their horses and ride off in all directions.

With the help and encouragement of the LAPD's "department psychiatrist," Dr. J. Paul DeRiver, the Gangster Squad was persuaded to pursue the doctor's red-herring suspect, one Leslie Dillon, who [much to his later regret] had originally contacted Dr. DeRiver from Florida by mail, "with some thoughts on the case."

In January 1949, two years after the murder, Dr. DeRiver and a couple of detectives from LAPD's Gangster Squad lured Dillon to California "to meet and discuss his theories," where—after holding him "incognito" at various hotels for three days—they arrested him as Elizabeth Short's killer.

The Leslie Dillon affair made headlines after the "three-day-detainee" was able to drop a note out of his downtown LA hotel window which gave his location and pleaded for someone to contact famed criminal defense attorney Jerry Giesler to come and rescue him.

Dillon was released several days after his arrest. But the Gangster Squad and Dr. DeRiver remained convinced that he was the actual Black Dahlia killer, and, for the rest of 1949, kept on trying to "build a case."

In October of 1949, at the request of Lt. Jemison, Sgt. Finis Brown conducted a follow-up to San Francisco and was able to establish and verify Leslie Dillon's alibi that he was in that city in the days preceding and following the murder of Elizabeth Short.

The entire affair was a huge embarrassment to LAPD Homicide and both Lt. Burns and Dr. DeRiver were both called on the carpet. Burns had been reassigned and transferred from the Gangster Squad in 1949 and Dr. DeRiver, six-months after the Dillon affair, left his position as "LAPD department psychiatrist."

Los Angeles Times, December, 9, 1949

Grand Jury Hears Two on Black Dahlia

Two police officers yesterday were called as witnesses in the county grand jury's investigation into the Black Dahlia slaying of 22-year-old Elizabeth Short.

The officers are Det. Lieut. Finas Brown of the Police Department homicide detail, who has handled investigation of the crime since the victim's nude, severed body was found in a vacant lot Feb. 15, 1947; and Lieut. William Burns, former head of the special antigangster detail operating from the office of the Chief of Police.

Testimony of the two officers was believed to include a summary of Police Department activities in the investigation. It was further indicated that the grand jury's inquiry is drawing to a close.

My review of the DA files included Sgt. Finis Brown's testimony before the 1949 grand jury. The transcript covered various aspects of his then three-year-old investigation; however, what I found most revealing were several questions asked of him by the grand jury foreman, Mr. Harry Lawson. These were made in the presence of Deputy District Attorney Arthur Veitch and Lt. Frank Jemison.

Here is the verbatim excerpt:

Testimony of LAPD Sgt. Finis Brown
Date: December 6, 1949
Questioned by: DDA Arthur L. Veitch and GJ

Present: 1949 grand jury members and DA investigator Lt. Frank B. Jemison

(Excerpt from page 30 of 1949 Secret Grand Jury Transcript):

Grand Jury Foreman, Mr. Harry Lawson asks Sgt. Brown
Q: Do you care to express an opinion to this Jury as to who you think killed Elizabeth Short?

Sgt. Finis Brown:

A: I can't express an opinion. I don't know. I can this:
That there is over 100 pages of names cut out of this address book;
also, it is known that she was in care of some doctor.
We don't know who that doctor is yet. We have never been able
to find out. We do know this; that on two or three occasions
a doctor identifying himself as a doctor, but refusing to give
his name called the Hollywood Station and gave some information
of where the information—some information might be picked up
on her around Hollywood Boulevard.

Scan of excerpt from *original transcript* found in DA Dahlia Files

```
3      Do you care to express an opinion to this Jury as to who
    you think killed Elizabeth Short?
4      I can't express an opinion. I don't know.  I can this:
    that there is over 100 pages of names cut out of this address
5   book; also, it is known that she was in care of some doctor.
    We don't know who that doctor is yet.  We have never been able
6   to find out.  We do know this:  that on two or three occasions
    a doctor identifying himself as a doctor, but refusing to give
7   his name called the Hollywood Station and gave some information
    of where the information--some information might be picked up
8   on her around Hollywood Boulevard.
```

Keep in mind that this statement was made just a week after Lt. Jemison's report was submitted to this same grand jury informing them that a list of over two hundred possible suspects had now been reduced down to *just five named individuals, only one of whom was a trained physician and skilled surgeon. His name—George Hill Hodel, MD.*

In the following grand jury transcript, we will find that Sgt. Brown was questioned by the jurors as to his opinion of whether the bisection

was done by a doctor? Here is the verbatim Q&A from page15b.
Answers are coming from Sgt. Finis Brown.

Q: You have handled many murder cases, had you not, Sgt., you have seen
     bodies that have been dissected and bisected and so forth?

A: And otherwise mutilated, yes.

Q: Mr. VEITCH: Is this kind of cutting that occurred at all unusual?

A: Yes, it is unusual in this sense, that the point at which the body was
     bisected is, according to eminent medical men, the easiest point in the
     spinal column to sever.

Q: And he hit the spot exactly.

A: He hit it exactly.

Q: And he made clean cuts?

A: That, in my estimation, I'm still only quoting my opinion, my own pet
     theory, that wasn't an accident, I've seen many horrible mutilation
     cases, many of them, and if any of you ladies and gentlemen ever seen a
     case like that, and would see the pictures of this Elizabeth Short case,
     you could detect the difference immediately.

Q: GRAND JUROR: Could a student, that had three months training
     studying to be an embalmer, three weeks, could that have been possible
     that he could have had the knowledge to dissect?

A: My opinion would be only a layman's, I'm not a medical man, I rather
     think that question should be answered by a doctor, my own personal
     opinion is that a person whom you have just described, would not be
     capable of doing it.

Q: Following up your thought, you say as an individual, had you thought
     very much about that medical side of it, have you elaborated in your
     own mind where that party could be, who it could possibly be?

A: Well, this we know, the body had been thoroughly bled, and the body
     had been washed, common sense tells us that it couldn't be done in an
     automobile, couldn't be done on a bed.

Q: Had you discussed your pet theory as you call it, with any medical expert?

A: Yes, I have discussed at length with Dr. Newbarr, the County Autopsy Surgeon.

Q: And I suppose he concurs in your opinion as to the ability of one?

A: Well, he said himself, his remark, "There's a fine piece of surgery." And he said further that couldn't be done in any 15 minutes, half hour or an hour.

Scan of page 15b of Sgt. Brown's testimony to 1949 Grand Jury

```
1   A  Yes, I did.
2   Q  You have handled many murder cases, had you not, Sgt., you
       have seen bodies that have been disected and bisected and so
3      forth?
    A  And otherwise mutilated, yes.
4
    Q  MR. VEITCH:  Is this kind of cutting that occurred at all
5      unusual?
    A  Yes, it is unusual in this sense, that the point at which
6      the body was bisected is, according to eminent medical men,
       the easiest point in the spinal column to sever.
7
    Q  And he hit the spot exactly?
8   A  He hit it exactly.
9   Q  And he made clean cuts?
    A  That, in my estimation, I'm still only quoting my opinion,
10     my own pet theory, that wasn't an accident, I've seen many
       horrible mutilation cases, many of them, and if any of you ladies
11     and gentlemen ever seen a case like that, and would see the
       pictures of this Elizabeth Short case, you could detect the
12     difference immediately.
13  Q  GRAND JUROR:  Could a student, that had three months
       training studying to be an embalmer, three weeks, could that
14     have been possible that he could have had the knowledge to disect?
    A  My opinion would be only a layman's, I'm not a medical man,
15     I rather think that question should be answered by a doctor, my
       own personal opinion is that a person whom you have just
16     described, would not be capable of doing it.
17  Q  Following up your thought, you say as an indivdual, had you
       thought very much about that medical side of it, have you
18     elaborated in your own mind where that party could be, who it
       could possibly be?
19  A  Well, this we know, the body had been thoroughly bled, and
       the body had been washed, common sense tells us that it couldn't
20     be done in an automobile, couldn't be done on a bed.
21  Q  Had you discussed your pet thoery, as youcall it, with any
22     medical expert?
    A  Yes, I have discussed at length with Dr. Newbarr, the Canty
23     Autopsy Surgeon.
    Q  And I suppose he concurs in your opinion as to the ability of
24     one?
    A  Well, he said himself, his remark, "There's a fine piece
25     of surgry."  And he said further that couldn't be done in any
       15 minute, half hour or an hour.
26
                           -15b-
```

"There's a fine piece of surgery. That couldn't be done in any 15 minutes, half hour or an hour."

Dr. Frederick Newbarr
Chief Autopsy Surgeon
L.A. County Coroner's Office

[Statement refers to the bisection of Elizabeth Short's body and was made directly to Sgt. Finis Brown]

That is one hell of a quote!

Dr. Frederick Newbarr performed the January 16, 1947 autopsy on Elizabeth Short. He was the chief autopsy surgeon for Los Angeles County Coroner's Office and had been in charge of the office for decades.

Dr. Newbarr was the "top-dog" and had performed nearly all of LA County's high profile autopsies. For Dr. Newbarr to make that statement to Sgt. Finis Brown, the lead detective—CARRIED TREMENDOUS WEIGHT AND AUTHORITY.

As stated elsewhere, though, both Jemison and Finis Brown were seemingly unaware of the identity of Elizabeth Short's "unidentified downtown doctor." With the information they had, they certainly had to consider and suspect that he was or could have been Dr. George Hill Hodel.

The surveillance and bugging of George Hodel's residence, which resulted in his recorded confessions and admissions to payoffs to police, performing abortions, and the murders of Elizabeth Short and Ruth Spaulding, occurred just six weeks after Finis Brown's testimony which focused on a "Hollywood doctor."

Finally, there can be no doubt that Sgt. Finis A. Brown, as the lead detective in the initial Black Dahlia investigation and brother to Thad Brown, LAPD's top detective and the man who said, "We solved the Black Dahlia murder. He was a doctor, living on Franklin Avenue in Hollywood" ALSO HAD TO KNOW AND TOOK THE SECRET WITH HIM TO HIS GRAVE.

After retirement, Finis Brown moved to West, Texas, where he died in 1990 at the age of eighty-four.

Finis A. Brown 1906-1990

R.I.P.

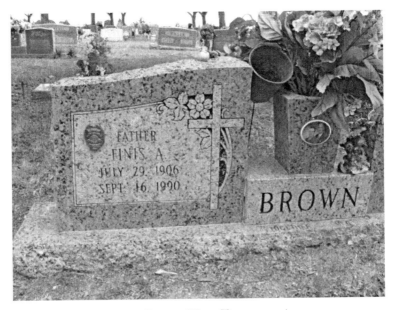

Finis A. Brown, West, Texas gravesite
[Photo courtesy of true-crime author, Ron Franscell]

Chapter 21

People begin to see that something more goes to the composition of a fine murder than two blockheads to kill and be killed—a knife—a purse—and a dark lane. Design, gentlemen, grouping, light and shade, poetry, sentiment, are now deemed indispensable to attempts of this nature...

Like Aeschylus or Milton in poetry, like Michael Angelo in painting, he has carried his art to a point of colossal sublimity; and, as Mr. Wordsworth observes, has in a manner "created the taste by which he is to be enjoyed." To sketch the history of the art, and to examine its principles critically, now remains as a duty for the connoisseur...."

The Society of Connoisseurs in Murder
From Thomas De Quincey's—*Murder Considered as One of the Fine Arts* (1842)

Dr. George Hill Hodel– A Surrealist Serial Killer-

With the publication of my sequel, *Most Evil: Avenger, Zodiac and the Further Serial Murders of Dr. George Hill Hodel,* the weight of evidence that surrealism was the primary motivator of and *signature* to my father's three decades long killing spree is, I believe, established beyond any doubt.

Understanding how his many crimes are linked to this most *unique signature* is the key to understanding both the man and his madness.

We have come a long way in exploring the surreal linkage since my early ruminations written in 2002, where I first explored the possibilities in *BDA* in the chapter, "*The Final Connections: Man Ray Thoughtprints.*"

In that chapter, I explored the various links both in the posing of Elizabeth Short's body in imitation of his surrealist friend, Man Ray's two famous works: *The Minotaur and Les Amoureux, (The Lovers Lips).*

On pages 241-242, I wrote:

> The killer had to make her death extraordinary both in planning and execution. In his role as a surreal artist, he determined that his work would be a masterpiece of the macabre, a crime so shocking and horrible it would endure, be immortalized through the annals of crime lore. As avenger, he would use her body as his canvas, and his surgeon's scalpel as his paintbrush
>
> ...
>
> George Hodel, through the homage he consciously paid to Man Ray, was provocatively revealing himself to be the murderer of Elizabeth Short. Her body, and the way she was posed, was Dr. George signature—both artistic and psychological—on his own surreal masterpiece, in which he juxtaposed the unexpected in a "still death" tribute to his master, *using human body parts!*
>
> The premeditated and deliberate use of those two photographs—one symbolizing my father and Elizabeth as the lovers in Les Amoureux, and another my father as the avenger, the Minotaur himself, the bull-headed beast consuming and destroying the young maiden, Elizabeth, in sacrifice—is my father's grisly message of his and Man Ray's shared vision of violent sexual fantasy. Given George Hodel's megalomaniacal ego, it was also a dash of one-upmanship.

I went on to enumerate the additional surreal connections to his crime.

The comparison of a 1945 Man Ray photograph, *Juliet in Silk Stocking,* showing his wife wearing a stocking mask to that of the Black Dahlia Avenger's mailing to the press of a photo of the teenager Armand Robles, where my father drew an identical stocking mask over his face in imitation of Man Ray's photograph.

I continued by explaining and publishing a painting George Hodel had commissioned by a Manila artist, Fernando Modesto, which was an erotic imitation of the same Man Ray, *Lovers Lips* painting, but in George Hodel's version the lips appear to be dripping blood and overhead are seen three male phalluses, a vagina and spermatozoa. This my father hand delivered to Juliet Man Ray in Paris in the late 1980s. [His good friend, Man Ray had died there a decade earlier, in 1976.]

There was more. Man Ray's 1946 photograph of George Hodel posed holding a statue of the Tibetan deity, Yamantaka, in which the god is in the "yab-yum" position, having sexual intercourse with his consort as dad looks on in what appears to be a sort of worshipful reverence.

I closed the chapter with a reference to the importance of the *dream state* to all surrealists and show a 1929 group photograph of many of the major surrealists in Paris, including Andre Breton, Rene Magritte, Max Ernst, and Salvador Dali and many others, all posing with eyes closed, affirming their support and preference for the subjective dream state in defiance of the conscious and rational.

Here is what Andre Breton had to say about it in his original 1924 Surrealist Manifesto:

The mind of the man who dreams is fully satisfied by what happens to him.

The agonizing question of possibility is no longer pertinent. Kill; fly faster, love to your heart's content. And if you should die, are you not certain of reawaking among the dead? Let yourself be carried along, vents will not tolerate your interference. You are nameless. The ease of everything is priceless...

I believe in the future resolution of these two states, dream and reality, which are seemingly so contradictory, into a kind of absolute reality, a *surreality*, if one may so speak.

In *BDA*, I listed several different instances of how the importance of dreams reconnected to my father:

First, there was the description of George Hodel in the 1925 *Los Angeles Evening Herald* article, "*The Clouded Past of a Poet*," by Ted Le Berthon in which he gives this description:

...

George drowned himself at times in an ocean of deep dreams. Only part of him seemed present.
He would muse standing before one in a black, flowered dressing gown lined with scarlet silk, oblivious to one's presence.

Suddenly, though, his eyes would flare up like signal lights and he would say, "The formless fastidiousness of perfumes in a seventeenth century boudoir is comparable to my mind in the presence of twilight."

...

Then, there are the posed photographs taken in 1946 at the Franklin house where, on two separate occasions, George photographed his subjects with "eyes closed."

In 2006, I identified the one photograph whom we now know was his friend, Marya Marco. The second, the nude may or may not be Elizabeth Short, and she may or may not be dead, but, regardless, she [like Marya] is posed with eyes closed as if "in dream."

Thirdly, are the "dream" references made by George Hodel at the time of his October 1949 arrest for incest and child molestation, which were published in the newspapers where he told the officers:

"We were delving into the mystery of love and the universe.
These acts of which I am accused are unclear, like a dream.
I can't figure out if someone is hypnotizing me or I am hypnotizing someone.
If I am really here, then these things must have happened."

Finally, is Father's "Parable of the Sparrows" letter written to me in 1980, with its mystical questioning:

...

But are there only three of us? The birds, the glass, and we? Or is there a fourth? Who is standing behind our glass, invisible to us, incommunicable to us, gravely watching our brave attacks against the walls we cannot see? Is there a fifth presence, watching all the others? And a sixth, and others, hidden in mysteries beyond our dreams?

L'inconnue de la Seine

It wasn't until the spring of 2006, just prior to making my trip to Paris to speak at the Pompidou Centre that I learned of *L'inconnue de la Seine*.

A woman who had read *L'Affaire du Dahlia Noir,* the excellent French translation of *BDA* by Robert Pepin, contacted me by e-mail and provided me details on the story.

I say story, but it really was much more than that. *L'inconnue* had become a mystery and legend throughout Europe, far outstripping that of our own—*Black Dahlia.*

The body of the L'inconnue, an attractive young woman, was found floating in the Seine sometime near the close of the nineteenth century. The date was uncertain; some believe it was around 1880. Apparently, there were no signs of major trauma. So, while murder could not be ruled out, most suggested she was a suicide.

As was the custom of that time, in hopes that she might be identified, her body was laid out for public display at the Paris Morgue, which was then located behind Notre Dame.

The open-air morgue, apparently, was like a bizarre bazaar, a public marketplace where hundreds of the curious came daily to view the dead.

The young woman remained unidentified, and a death mask—a plaster casting—was reportedly made of her face, which was then sold to the public.

By the 1920s, this mask of *L'inconnue de la Seine,* which many claimed had an enigmatic Mona Lisa smile, found its way inside the home and onto the hearth of many Europeans. It was especially popular in France and Germany.

From there, L'inconnue found her way into literature, with many books and stories, some major best-sellers, each claiming to offer forth the secret of just how she met her fate.

One of the most famous of those works was *Aurelien,* written by novelist, Louis Aragon, first published in 1944. Aragon collaborated with Man Ray, who at the time was living in Hollywood with his wife,

Juliet. And both were regularly socializing with George and Dorothy Hodel.

Louis Aragon, like Man Ray, was a fellow Dadaist and in 1924 had been a founding member of surrealism, along with Andre Breton and Philippe Soupault.

Man Ray created eight photographs of the *L'inconnue de la Seine* for Aragon's 1944 novel. A grateful Louis Aragon had this to say about Man Ray's contribution:

"But in truth it is Man Ray who wrote the novel, playing in black and white with the mask of the *Inconnue de la Seine.*"

That George Hodel in his youth knew about this story and the legend, we can be certain. He would have been one of the many Bohemians cum surrealists who adopted and owned the legend in the 1920s and 1930s. It would not surprise me if he even owned his own mask.

In the 1940s, Dad would have discussed and explored the legend of the *L'inconnue de la Seine* with Man Ray, Juliet, and their friends, even as Man prepared his photographs for publication for the Aragon novel.

But I suspect there was more to it than parlor conversation. Based on my father's photographs in his personal album, all taken by him during that time period, I believe his was an OBSESSION with *L'inconnue de la Seine*. Perhaps, a longstanding one that reached all the way back to his Bohemian and surrealist teens.

In the photographs below found in George Hodel's album of "loved ones," we see four different women. Each taken at a different time in the 1940s. Each woman he has posed with head tilted forward and looking down with eyes closed.

Compare these to the original photograph of *L'inconnue de la Seine*. I believe this was no "coincidence" but was a conscious, intentional posing by George Hodel in imitation of her original death mask.

In some twisted, psychopathological way, Dad connected to her story. The when of it is not so important. It could have been early in his teens or as late as 1944, with the legend first introduced to him by way of his friend, Man Ray, who was then actively working, researching, and photographing the L'inconnue for inclusion in Aragon's novel.

This information also provides us with additional dramatic circumstantial evidence and gives more weight to the theory, examined in an earlier chapter, that the nude photograph, believed to be of Elizabeth Short, could well be a "trophy death mask." George Hodel's own *L'inconnue de la Maison Franklin*.

The below photograph of the Inconnue casting was taken by portrait photographer, Albert Rudomine in Paris in 1927. Rudomine, like my grandmother, was from Kiev, Russia, and, also like my grandparents, fled to Paris at the turn of the century. Rudomine, became a prominent portrait photographer [a number of his works now hang in the Getty museum] and he could well have known my grandparents who lived in Paris and were close friends with the Russian count and sculptor, Paul Troubetzkoy and his family.

L'inconnue de la Seine photo of death mask by Albert Rudomine, 1927

La Vierge inconnue par Albert Rudomine (d'après le masque mortuaire de l'inconnue de la Seine), 1927.

George Hodel photographs – An obsession with *L'inconnue de la Seine?*

1   2   3   4

Four women posed a la L'inconnue and photographed by George Hodel.

1. Unknown woman, possibly Elizabeth Short, taken at Franklin house, circa 1946
2. Marya Marco, taken at Franklin house, circa 1946
3. Kiyo, George Hodel's former mistress and author's future wife, taken circa 1944
4. Unknown woman, believed to be Filipina, taken unknown date and location, possibly early fifties

Exquisite Corpse

In September, 2006, literally on the eve of my television appearance on *CNN's Anderson Cooper 360*, while I was making many of the surrealist connections between the Black Dahlia murder and my father, as well as publicly eliminating the one photograph in his album as not being Elizabeth Short, a new book was published. Combining the genres of true crime and art history, it added new information in support of my original surrealism chapter in BDA, as well as offering additional thoughts as to why "the murder may have been directly linked to surrealist art and ideas."

The book, *Exquisite Corpse: Surrealism and the Black Dahlia Murder* (Bulfinch Press, 2006, New York) was co-written by Mark Nelson and Sarah Hudson Bayliss, two New York writers and art-researchers.

The book's "Web of Connections" is an invaluable aid in helping map out many of George Hodel's links to the art world and fellow surrealist's then living in 1940s Los Angeles.

It also attempts to examine the core question of what were the surrealist's relationships to the Black Dahlia murder. Who knew *what* and *when* did they know it?

Did Man Ray and his close circle of friends, in the days and weeks immediately following the crime, learn that their kindred spirit, and wannabe Dadaist, George Hodel was the prime suspect in her murder?

Did these men with their connections to LA's "inner circle," which included A-list screenwriter, Gene Fowler, acquire their own set of Black Dahlia crime scene photographs?

In his book, *Reporters: Memoirs of a Young Newspaperman*, [*preface written by Ben Hecht*] Will Fowler, son of Gene Fowler, described his 1947 involvement in the Black Dahlia investigation, as a then young crime reporter for the *Los Angeles Examiner* .

416

In his chapter on the Black Dahlia, Fowler described how he and his staff photographer, Felix Paegel, were the first to arrive at the vacant lot. He claimed that with their radio tuned to the police frequency, they had heard the call broadcast and being just a short distance away, "were the first to arrive." Fowler goes on to detail how he examined the body, as his "partner," Felix Paegel, took photographs of the body using his "Speed Graphic."

From pages 74-75 of Will Fowler's book, "Reporters":

...

While I was kneeling next to the body, Paegel took a picture documenting that absolutely no one was in the immediate area. His two principal photos showed the body alone in the barren field, and the second of me stooping beside the body. Before it was published on the front page, it was necessary for an *Examiner* artist to airbrush a large blanket covering all but the upper arms and lower legs. He also removed the deep slashes on either side of her face.

After Paegel photographed the body, Fowler described how the first two LAPD patrol officers arrived at the scene and seeing the two men standing adjacent to the corpse immediately drew down on them with their service revolvers. Fowler identified himself as a press reporter and continued his narrative. Page 75:

They [officers] gave me permission to leave the scene and I ran for a public phone. I stuck a nickel in the slot and dialed the desk, and when he heard me say, "cut in half," Richardson [Los Angeles Examiner's City Editor] told me to get the hell in with the negatives.

The city room was already buzzing about the story as Paegel disappeared into the photo lab to develop the negatives. When he emerged, he was carrying a large dripping wet 11x14 print of the body. Several people gathered around to get a first look.

Based on my follow-up investigation and review of police reports I have found that there is much in Will Fowler's book that is simply NOT TRUE.

417

His chapter on the Black Dahlia is filled with inaccuracies, self-aggrandizement and hyperbole. But, none of that has to do with the point I am making here.

What IS TRUE and factual is: Will Fowler, was at the crime scene and did have his press photographer, Felix Paegel obtain overall original photographs depicting the location and condition of the body. Copies of these photographs were in his possession and also easily accessible to numerous other *Los Angeles Examiner* employees.

Will's father, Gene Fowler and his close circle of friends, which included Ben Hecht, Rowland Brown [Dorothy Hodel's then lover] Steve Fisher, and many more would have seen and very likely obtained copies of these pictures. They were simply too hot, not to handle.

Were copies of these Dahlia crime scene photos given to Man Ray and did he pass them on to his closest friend, Marcel Duchamp, who would use them as the inspiration for his final secret twenty-year art project, *Etant Donnes?*

While no definitive answer to these many questions is found, *Exquisite Corpse* enumerated a myriad of opportunities both direct and "one-degree-of-separations" between my father and the surrealist community that, in the end, it becomes difficult for me to believe these associates did not or could not have known, or, at the very least, strongly suspected George Hodel's involvement in the murder.

The chapter, *"William Copley: Surrealist Confidant"* introduced us to the birth of the friendship between William Copley and Man Ray that began in Los Angeles in 1946.

Copley, a wealthy art collector, opened his own gallery in Los Angeles, dedicated exclusively to surrealism. He befriended and displayed many of the movements major artists' works, including: Man Ray, Max Ernst, Rene Magritte, and Yves Tanguy.

According to *Exquisite Corpse*, while Copley's LA art gallery was not a financial success, his friendship with Man Ray was. In 1951 Copley along with his girlfriend, Gloria de Herrera, relocated from Los Angeles to Paris with Man Ray and his wife, Juliet

Corroborating the Who?

Looking at *Exquisite Corpse* with an investigator's eye, it is my belief that the most singularly important and circumstantially compelling contribution was the book's inclusion of a 1961 painting by William Copley entitled:

Il est minuit Dr. _____. [It is Midnight Dr. ____.]

"It is Midnight Dr. _____."
Oil on canvas by William Copley, 1961
[permission to use painting courtesy of Billy Copley]

419

Exquisite Corpse, page 144:

That same year, as Man Ray was nearing completion of Self Portrait, Copley created a significant artwork. Like many of his other paintings, Il est minuit Dr. _____. (It Is Midnight Dr. _____), 1961, portrays a nude woman and a fully clothed man. The male figure appears at the upper left holding a medical bag. The woman reclines near the bottom of the canvas like an odalisque. It is a classical pose, reminiscent of Ariadne and so many other nudes in art history. She has closed eyes, a hint of a smile, and one hand resting on her forehead. Above her is an array of instruments, including a scalpel and two saws. It suggests that Copley, distanced from the crime scene by fourteen years and thousands of miles, had not forgotten it.

This painting, created some fourteen years after the Black Dahlia murder supports the suggestion that William Copley (and, by extension Man Ray and Marcel Duchamp) may have suspected Hodel of the crime.)

Further, keeping in mind that surrealists loved to conceal secret messages and cryptograms in their works—"riddles, wrapped in mysteries, inside enigmas," let's take a closer look at Copley's painting.

[Note: The following observations are not offered as "proofs." *They are theoretical and speculative* and were sent to me in the past few years, as e-mails, from several of my readers. I believe they may have merit and for that reason present them here for your consideration.]

Back to the William Copley painting:

To the immediate right of the doctor there are five oversized surgical tools each placed in a vertical position. Below them is a sixth instrument laid out horizontally.

In a 2009 e-mail from "D.M." he suggested the possibility that the oversized vertical surgeon's tools might conceal and actually spell out the name—H O D E L.

[Compare to original William Copley painting shown previously]

To be clear, this additional "letter decryption" was not something presented or suggested in the Nelson/Bayliss book, but rather came from, "D.M." as summarized in a website blog I wrote on September 27, 2009, "*A Letter from Dada & Moma - A Surrealist Word Game?*" [Note: In addition to the vertical letters, spelling out the doctor's name—HODEL, others have speculated that Copley *may have* used the horizontal tool to spell out the doctor/killer's profession as —"M.D."]

Art is totally subjective. As to whether these hidden letters exist or not, I'll leave it to you, the reader to make your own call. I'm open to the *possibility*, but would need to see further corroboration and confirmation, perhaps in the form of a "lost letter" or Copley family document.

Man Ray Letters Hidden in Plain Sight for Seventy-Years

Interestingly, and somewhat on-point, I came across an article from *the Smithsonian Magazine* written by, Abby Callard, entitled, *Man Ray's Signature Work.* (November, 2009)

The article details photographer, Ellen Carey's discovery of Man Ray's secret writing, *hidden for over seventy-years* which she found in one of his early photographs. Man Ray unbeknownst to anyone had concealed the letters in plain sight by reversing and disguising his signature and incorporating it as abstract lines in the photograph. Here are some significant excerpts from the Smithsonian article referencing Ellen Carey's decryption:

> Artist Man Ray mischievously scribbled his name in a famous photograph, but it took decades for the gesture to be discovered.
>
> ...
>
> In 1935, the avant-garde photographer Man Ray opened his shutter, sat down in front of his camera and used a penlight to create a series of swirls and loops. ... As a self-portrait—titled *Space Writings*—it seemed fairly abstract.
>
> ...
>
> But now Ellen Carey, a photographer whose working method is similar to Man Ray's, has discovered something that has been hidden in plain sight in *Space Writings* for the past 74 years: the artist's signature, signed with the penlight amid the swirls and loops.
>
> ...
>
> It might have taken seven decades and a like-minded photographer to see the disguised signature, but the evidence is clear. "Oh, it's definitely there," Carey says. "It's saying, 'Hello, how come no one noticed for 70 years? I think [Man Ray] would be chuckling right now. Finally, somebody figured him out."

Did William Copley, close personal friend to Man Ray, follow his mentor's lead and for the past fifty-years disguise and conceal his own secret letters and words as his own riddle wrapped in a real life mystery?

Corroborating the Where?

"From the nature of the cuts the girl was probably in a semi-recumbent position in a bathtub."

Chief Autopsy Surgeon, Dr. Frederick Newbarr, January 1947
[Public statement to the LA Press on his Elizabeth "Black Dahlia" Short autopsy findings]

In *Chapter 5, Scene of the Crime*, we examined in-depth the evidence pointing to and linking the Sowden/Franklin House as being the probable crime scene.

In that review I also theorized that the most logical location for George Hodel to perform his "operation" was in the tub/shower in the master bathroom. [That the crime occurred in a bathtub was independently supported by the very public knowledge, printed in most of the Los Angeles newspapers, on January 22, 1947, quoting both LAPD Captain Jack Donahoe and Coroner Newbarr, "that the bisection probably was done in a bathtub."]

In a just received [November 1, 2011] e-mail question from, Jess Mayeux, one of my readers, in referencing the background squares in the Copley painting, asks:

"Could the grid represent the tiles in the master bathroom of the Sowden House?"

George Hodel's Franklin house, tiled master bathroom as it would have appeared in 1947. As detailed in Chapter Five, this is the probable location of bisection.

William Copley, artist, art-dealer, patron and close friend of Man Ray, and living in Los Angeles from 1946-1951, would very likely have known and socialized with Dr. George Hodel and attended talks and parties at the Franklin house.

Additionally, Copley probably knew and shared acquaintances with many of George Hodel's other friends, including the doctor's 1950 caught-on-tape-accomplice, Baron Ernst Harringa. Copley and Harringa must have been acquainted considering the fact they both owned and operated two of Los Angeles' upscale art galleries, located within just a few miles of each other.

In the title of his 1961 oil-painting Copley has reminded the doctor [regardless of whether he suspects it is Dr. Hodel or another] that, "It is midnight," the witching hour, a time for demons and devils to be about their work. By laying out the surgeon's tools Copley suggested exactly what that work would be—an "operation." With the surgeon standing adjacent to the body, he next introduced us to "the patient/victim." She is young, attractive and is either unconscious or dead and is lying supine on what appears to be a tiled floor. She is carefully posed, with her right arm bent at the elbow

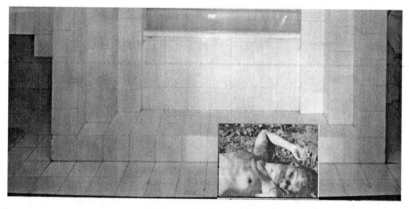

Post-operative upper torso of Elizabeth Short [airbrushed] as actually posed by killer in vacant lot. Compare this to Copley's reclining nude [victim] on *what appear to be* bathroom tiles.

So many questions:

In his singular 1961 art work, *It is Midnight Dr. _____.*, has William Copley represented Los Angeles' most infamous crime- 1947 Black Dahlia Murder?

In that painting did he reveal he had suspicions of the WHO—Dr. George Hill Hodel, and the WHERE—the Franklin house bathroom?

Had William Copley seen the crime-scene photos? Was he privy to the inner-circle's rumors and the not so secret knowledge, shared by Lillian Lenorak, Madi Comfort, Joe Barrett and many others? Was he part of the, "We all knew that he had done it. There was no doubt."

At *the very least* we can be confident that William Copley, living and working in Los Angeles in 1949, and friend and patron to Man Ray, would certainly have known that Dr. George Hodel, was on trial for incest and in December, 1949, had been *publicly accused*, by his own daughter, of having committed the Black Dahlia murder.

"My father is the murderer of the Black Dahlia. My father is going to kill me, and all the rest of the members of this household, because he has a lust for blood. He is insane."

Tamar Hodel, December 17, 1949 [as reported in court testimony and headlined in below daily newspapers]

Girl's Story Is 'Fantasy,' Court Hears

The 14-year-old daughter o prominent Hollywood physici "plotted his downfall" with f tastic stories, including one th he killed Elizabeth (Black Da la) Short, his attorney, Robe A. Neeb Jr., sought to prove day.

Neeb hammered at the "fa tasies" of blonde Tamar Hod in her crossexamination at th morals trial of Dr. George H Hodel, 38.

Sex Charges

Hodel is being tried on charge of improper relations with th girl at their home, 5121 Frankli Ave., in July.

Hodel, who has denied th charges, will seek to show tha

Girl accused of trying to pin Dahlia murder on dad

Tamar, loquacious 14-year-old daughter of Hollywood physician George H. Hodel, today stood interentially accused of trying to pin the unsavory Black Dahlia murder on her father.

This odd turn punctuated the trial of Dr. Hodel by a jury in Superior Judge Thomas L. Ambrose's court on a charge of in-

lested by the girl against her father.

Atty. Robert A. Neeb Jr., in the second day of a blistering cross-examination, suddenly demanded of the young witness if she remembered a conversation with one Joe Barrett a roommate the Hodel home.

Neeb wanted to know if Tamar said to Barrett:

"This house has secret passages. My father is the murderer of the Black Dahlia. My father is going to kill me and all the rest of the members of this household because he has a lust for blood. He is insane."

On the morning of December 17, 1949, in Los Angeles, two separate articles [seen above] "hit the streets." Published in the *Los Angeles Daily News* and the *Los Angeles Mirror,* both accounts reported that Dr. George Hodel had been accused by his fourteen-year-old, daughter, Tamar, of having committed the Black Dahlia murder. What was not made public was the fact that Tamar, who at the time was being held in protective-custody at Juvenile Hall, *had been informed by the very police detectives who were transporting her to-and-from court, that her father "was the prime suspect in the Dahlia murder."*

Henry Miller and George Hodel

We know that Man Ray and Henry Miller, the novelist/painter/surrealist were good friends. That the two of them, along with Beat Generation poet/author Kenneth Rexroth hung out from time to time at Miller's home in Big Sur.

During the 1940s, the three were also friends with George Hodel and visited him at the Franklin house where all could intellectualize and share a free and open discussion, without having to fear any restraints from the bourgeois.

In later years, my mother talked of Henry Miller being a family acquaintance and of having visited him on numerous occasions at his home in the beautiful coastal community of Big Sur in central California.

Though I was aware of Henry Miller's "Tropics" books, banned in the US until the 1960s, I had never previously read any of his writings, and only knew him through his reputation as being highly unconventional, and that many considered his erotic writings both amoral and obscene.

I have no intention here of attempting to make any moral judgment on Mr. Miller's writings, either pro or con. My intent is to examine, as we have with Man Ray, what *influence* Miller may have had on my father's thinking during that period?

A few years back, I discovered a Henry Miller book entitled, *The World of Sex*. The book's front page read, "Printed by J.H.N. for friends of Henry Miller. 1000 copies printed. New York, 1940"

In reading the below passages, I would have to say that HENRY MILLER and GEORGE HODEL obviously shared a *kindredness of thought* as it relates to sex, incest, and their own unconventional sense of morality.

From what MILLER revealed in his privately published book, it is easy for me to imagine the two men sharing a lively discussion at the Franklin house.

Here are some selected excerpts from Henry Miller's *World of Sex*:

page 12

But what is normal and healthy for the vast majority leads us nowhere in seeking a clue to the rules of behavior which govern men of genius. The man of genius, wittingly or unwittingly, through his work and by his example seems to struggle to establish the truth that every man is a law unto himself and that the only way to liberation is through the recognition and the realization that he is a unique being.

page 52

Sex is only one of millions of ways of expressing oneself. The important thing is the expression, not what is expressed. If it would help men to liberate themselves I would recommend them to have intercourse with animals or to fuck in public or to commit incest, for example. There is nothing in itself which is wrong or evil, not even murder. It is the fear of doing wrong, the fear of committing murder, the fear of acting, or expressing oneself, which is wrong.

page77

In fact, it is our dream life which affords a slight cue to the nature of that life which is in store for us. In our dream life we live indiscriminately in past and future. It is the potential, indestructible man who comes to life in the dream. For his being there is no longer a censorship; taboos, laws, conventions, customs are annihilated. In the realm of sex it is the only true freedom he ever knows. He moves toward the object of his desire unimpeded by time, space, physical obstacles or moral considerations. He may sleep with his mother as naturally and easily as with another woman. He may take an animal in the field and satisfy his desires without the slightest revolt. He may fuck his own daughter and find it extremely pleasurable. In the waking world, crippled and shackled by all kinds of fetters, everything is wrong or evil except that which has been prescribed by fear. The real, inner being knows that these things are not wrong, not evil: when he can close his eyes he gives himself up to all these practices and pursuits which are prohibited. In his dreams he follows out his true desires. These desires are not only valid and legitimate but must be realized; if they are thwarted or frustrated the world becomes ugly and death-like.

page 79

A certain amount of killing, plundering, raping, and so on, inevitably occurs whenever there is a burst of freedom. Some kind of crude justice has to be dealt out when the scales are tipped and seek to return to balance. Some specimens of the human race ought, out of decency, kindness and reverence for those to come, be wiped out. Some bastards *should* be buggered and thrown over the fence for the wolves and hyaenas to finish off. Some females *ought* to be raped to death and left lying on the spot for all to see. Some mean, miserly cowards and traitors to the race *ought* to be stripped of all they possess and sent naked into the hills.

A man's prick and a woman's cunt will not need to have a name and address tied to it.

page 83-84

Now and then in the evenings, I pass a show window where a manikin is being dressed. The manikin is standing there nude and the window-dresser is just in the act of putting his arms around the figure to move her an inch to the left or right. Every time this happens I have the same reaction—I feel that the manikin is more alive than the man who is dressing her. Why it is I don't know, but the manikin always seems *sexually* alive. The window-trimmer, on the other hand, is just an indescribable bundle of animate flesh wrapped in meaningless clothes. His movements are utterly senseless. He is going to take the live sexual manikin and make her seductive to the passer-by by putting clothes around her and making her look like the people in the street. He makes the sexual thing dead, just as the undertaker, is ticking up a corpse, makes death look inviting. On every side I see people tampering with the natural order of things, trying to galvanize the inanimate into the semblance of life or else rigidifying the live thing into some death-like pose. Dead or alive, whatever is bare, stark, nude, frightens the shit out of them. A wax cunt in a show window can terrify them even more than a live cunt, so it seems. Even turkeys have to be dressed after the slaughter.

It is one thing to sit around drinking Bordeaux with your fellow *outsiders* and see which one can cast himself in the role of chief nihilist using his pen or paintbrush. But it is quite another to actually step outside the world of words and pictures and TAKE ACTION.

That was the danger and difference between a Man Ray or Henry Miller and Dr. George Hill Hodel.

His friends talked a good game about how there was no difference between the waking and the dream state, but when the wine wore off, they went home to their comfortable beds in the objective real world.

George Hodel DID NOT. He drank the Kool-Aid and BELIEVED.

He heard the words preached by his surrealist gurus like Andre Breton, Man Ray, and Henry Miller, and took them to heart and to action!

George made Breton's words, "Kill, fly faster, love to your heart's content"—REAL.

George made Man Ray's, *Lover's Lips* bleed and the *Minotaur* come to life in the savage torture-sacrifice of a young woman, a surgical murder made REAL.

George read Henry Miller's instructions, "to commit incest," and slept with his teenage daughter. And more, through the decade of the forties committed horrendous acts with woman, "raped to death and left lying on the spot"—all made REAL.

This was the method of his madness. This is what made George Hodel so dangerous and his surrealist signature crimes—so unique.

SPELLBOUND

In Alfred Hitchcock's 1945 classic psychological thriller, *Spellbound*, the original movie poster shows Gregory Peck [John Ballantyne] embracing Ingrid Bergman [Dr. Constance Petersen] as he holds an open straight edged razor in his right hand. The tag line reads:

"Will he kiss me or kill me?"

The story centers on a young amnesiac's search to find who he is and whether or not he has committed a murder. On a parallel track is the romance, which has him, falling in love with his Freudian therapist. Pursued by the police, the two lovers flee to New York City where they seek out the aid of Dr. Constance Peterson's old school professor, Dr. Brulov [Michael Chekov] to help them with a little dream analysis, hoping to find some answers of the *who* and *why*.

Next, we are presented with what many consider the film's signature moment, a surreal "dream sequence" designed and choreographed by Salvador Dali.

Dali's images unfold before us on-screen as Peck describes in detail the sum and substance of his dream to the professor and Constance:

I seemed to be in a gambling house, but there weren't any walls, just a lot of curtains with eyes painted on them. A man was walking around with a large pair of scissors cutting all the drapes in half. Then a girl came in with hardly anything on and started walking around the gambling room kissing everybody. She came to my table first. I'm afraid she looked a little like Constance.

I was sitting there playing cards with a man who had a beard. I was dealing to him. I dealt him a 7 of clubs. He said, 'That makes 21 - I win.' When he turned up his cards, they were blank. Just then the proprietor came in and accused him of cheating. The proprietor yelled, 'This is my place, and if I catch you cheating again, I'll fix you.

There's a lot more to it. Then I saw the man. He was the man with the beard leaning over the slope of a high building. I yelled at him to watch out. Then he went over—slowly—with his feet in the air. And then I saw the proprietor again—the man in the mask. He was hiding behind a tall chimney, and he had a small wheel in his hand.

I saw him drop the wheel on the roof. Suddenly I was running and then I heard something beating over my head. It was a great pair of wings. The wings chased me and almost caught up with me and I came to the bottom of the hill.

Spellbound dream sequence clip "curtains with eyes"

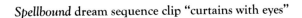

"Man with large pair of scissors cutting the drapes"

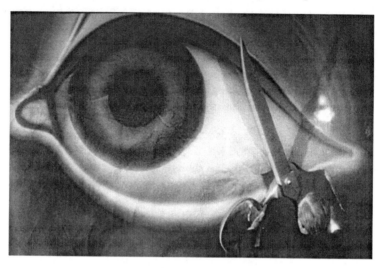

Spellbound dream sequence clip "the man in the mask holding a small wheel"

Spellbound 1945

Spellbound was one of my father's favorite films, and it is easy to understand why.

Not only was Dr. George Hill Hodel captivated by all things Dali and surreal, but add to the mix the fact that he himself was just beginning to flirt with hypnosis and dream analysis and would, within six-years, relocate to Hawaii, where he would hang out his own shingle as a Freudian psychiatrist and begin counseling to the territorial prison population's criminally insane. Psychopath to the psychopaths—perfect!

It is my conviction that the dream sequence in *Spellbound* made such a powerful impression on my father that he could not resist including a reference to it and an homage to Dali as he had done with Man Ray.

I am now persuaded that DALI, like MAN RAY, was also recognized with a wink and a nod in my father's Black Dahlia murder, which was committed just one year after the film's release.

Consider the following:

Man Ray's *Juliet in Stocking Mask* was created in Hollywood in 1945, at the same time they were filming *Spellbound.*

We have examined in-depth the homage paid to Man Ray by George Hodel in imitation of his two works: The *Lovers Lips* and the *Minotaure*, as well as the many other surrealist links.

There can be little doubt that Dali met with Man Ray at his Vine Street apartment when he visited Hollywood in 1945. Though by then, Man Ray had lived in Hollywood for five years, the two had previously been long acquainted as fellow surrealists in Paris. That these two masks by the two surrealists were created within months of each other, I believe, is *not coincidence.*

I linked the *Juliet Stocking Mask* to Man Ray in my previous investigation, and now believe that it was a co-homage to Dali and the "masked man" in his dream-sequence.

Dali Spellbound mask 1945 - Man Ray Juliet mask 1945- Black Dahlia
Avenger mask 1947

Ben Hecht-

"I know the name of the killer and the psychology of his deed."
There is only one form of hatred that can equal in violence the
symbolizing rage of the lunatic—and what that hatred is I will leave unsaid."

> Ben Hecht
> *Los Angeles Herald-Express*
> Sat, Feb 1, 1947

By 1945, Ben Hecht had become Hollywood's highest paid
screenwriter.

He was hired by Hitchcock to write the screenplay for *Spellbound*,
and Dali was to work with Hecht in incorporating the surreal dream
sequence into the film.

George Hodel admired Hecht's writing and as a young
editor/publisher of his own surreal magazine, *Fantasia*, had written a
review in 1925 of one of Hecht's early books, *The Kingdom of Evil*.
Here's an excerpt from Hodel's review:

> ...Macabre forms, more dank and putrescently phantasmal than any of Hecht's
> former imagining, grope blindly and crazedly in the poisonous fog out of which
> loom the rotting fancies that people his 'Kingdom of Evil.'"...

> With almost animate pigments has Hecht painted this monstrous dream of
> Mallare's, and with delicate and meticulous craftsmanship has he fashioned its
> cadaverous and perverse beauty.

> George Hill Hodel
> *Fantasia Magazine*, August 1925

A short time later, the reference from his fellow Bohemians of George Hodel's admiration for Hecht's writings, was published in the *Evening Herald* article, "*The Clouded Past of a Poet*":

> "It's not George's gloom, his preference for Huysmanns, De Gourmont, Poe, Baudelaire, Verlaine, and *Hecht* [emphasis mine] that pains us..."

Prior to writing *Spellbound*, Ben Hecht had worked with Dorothy Huston Hodel's ex-husband, John Huston, as screenwriter to the director/writer on both *Wuthering Heights* and *Maltese Falcon*. He also worked as a writer with Dorothy's then lover, director/writer Rowland Brown on two of his films, *Quick Millions* and *Angels with Dirty Faces*.

There can be little doubt that Hecht not only personally knew George Hodel and very likely frequented and socialized with the same "inner circle" of Hollywood A-list writers, including Huston, Brown, Steve Fisher, Gene Fowler, and others, but that it was George Hodel that he was referring to when, two weeks after the Black Dahlia murder, he wrote in the *Herald-Express* that:

"I know the name of the killer and the psychology of his deed."

Hecht, like his friend and fellow screenwriter, Steve Fisher, knew that the police had the killer's name and was sure they would soon be making an arrest that would surprise and shock all of Los Angeles. Or, as Fisher put it in his separate article for the *Evening Herald Express*, "a lot of people who know him, and do not now suspect he has anything to do with the case, are going to be surprised and terrified."

I believe there is more. The likelihood of a second possible link to both George Hodel and his homage to *Spellbound*, is another murder and another mailing that would come—*two decades later!*

In my sequel, *Most Evil, Avenger, Zodiac and the Further Murders of Dr. George Hill Hodel*, published in 2009, I present what I believe to be compelling evidence linking my father to additional crimes.

Crimes committed in Chicago, Los Angeles, and Manila, Philippines, as well as the possibility that two decades after terrorizing Los Angeles as the "Avenger," he reinvented himself in the San Francisco Bay area and gave himself the name "Zodiac"!

I believe I have made a strong circumstantial case supporting these further series of crimes and will let the evidence speak for itself as presented in that separate investigation.

Unlike, *BDA*, I am not going as far as to claim I have proven he was the killer in those crimes, but suggest that he needs to go to the top of the list of suspects and law enforcement needs to pursue and obtain *confirmed Zodiac DNA* and then rule George Hodel IN or OUT.

In *Most Evil*, I offered evidence that the suspect continued his "Avenger" theme of *murder as a fine art*, not only in the method of his killings but also in his mailings wherein he made references to music, art, literature, and more on point—to specific vintage motion pictures.

I argued that Zodiac was a cinephile who stole both characters and actions from several classic films, plagiarizing and incorporating them into his Zodiac crime signature and M.O.

In *Most Evil*, I named two films: *The Most Dangerous Game* [1932] and *Charlie Chan at Treasure Island* [1939], and went on in separate chapters to detail the evidence and linkage to each movie.

Based on what has been presented in this chapter, I am going to offer the possibility that my father, if he was Zodiac, appears to have hidden a clue to a third classic film in his San Francisco taunts to the press. That being his old favorite—*Spellbound*.

Below is a copy of the Halloween taunt card that Zodiac sent to crime-reporter, Paul Avery at the *San Francisco Chronicle* newspaper in 1970.

On the front, the card refers to Zodiac as being reporter Avery's "Secret Pal" and promises to offer a clue to his identity. On the back,

Zodiac has hand printed the different methods he has or will kill his victims, writing:

"By Fire, By Gun, By Knife, By Rope"

and that they will become his,

"Slaves in Paradice"

Law enforcement, noting the strange way Zodiac wrote the message, theorized that the "clue" he was sending may be the fact that the letters, as written, formed the letter "H" which they suggested could be a monogram clue to the killer's name.

Front and back of Zodiac's 1970 Halloween card sent to *San Francisco Chronicle*

Letter "H"?

But it is the inside of this Halloween card that is on point in our current examination.

Interior of 1970 Halloween Card

In addition to writing his signatory circle and cross, Zodiac included a strange symbol at the bottom of the card, as well as drawing a set of thirteen eyes with a threatening message to the *Chronicle* reporter Avery, reading, "peek-a-boo, you are doomed!"

Keeping in mind that George Hodel had a perfect photographic memory, compare Dali's hand drawn eyes from the dream sequence in *Spellbound* to the eyes drawn by Zodiac.

Dali Dream sequence
in "Spellbound"

1970 Zodiac Halloween card mailed to *San Francisco Chronicle*

Dali eyes [top] compared to Zodiac's hand drawn eyes [bottom] enlarged—another enigmatic clue?

George Hodel as the 1947 "Avenger" very likely paid homage to both Man Ray and Dali in his 1947 mailings to the press. Did he repeat his "M.O." two decades later as Zodiac?

Chapter 22

TOUCH DNA

"The family of JonBenet Ramsey has been formally cleared of any role in the 6-year-old's 1996 murder, a Colorado prosecutor announced Wednesday, citing newly discovered DNA evidence."

USA *Today*
April 16, 2009

The 2009 USA *Today* article went on to state:

> Boulder, Colorado—District Attorney Mary Lacy said in a statement on Wednesday that DNA evidence recovered from the child's clothing [pajamas] pointed to an "unexplained third party." Lacy apologized to the family for the suspicions that made their lives "an ongoing living hell."

> ... The new evidence, described as "irrefutable" in clearing the Ramseys, would be checked against other profiles in the national DNA database managed by the FBI.

The new physical evidence was obtained by technicians from *Bode Technology*, in Lorton, Virginia. *Bode* is considered to be one of the top forensic laboratories in the United States and is frequently the lab of choice used by the FBI, and law enforcement agencies across the nation.

The relatively new procedure used by *Bode Labs* in extracting the suspect's DNA in the Ramsey investigation is called, "Touch DNA."

Touch DNA is the collection of skin cells which have been transferred from an individual's skin to the surface of items it has come in contact with, such as the grip of a gun, luggage, a car's steering wheel, a victim's clothing, or a ligature used in the commission of a crime.

The collection of the skin cells can be accomplished in various methods, such as swabbing, cutting, tape-lift, and scraping.

In the past several years, this method of collecting evidence has resulted in a number of successful murder prosecutions, as well as aiding in establishing the actual innocence of a number of wrongfully convicted individuals.

A Search for George Hill Hodel's DNA

In April 2009, I contacted *Bode Laboratories*. And after exchanging telephone calls, letters, and e-mails with Dr. Angela Williamson, Director of Forensic Casework, we decided on what we hoped would be the best course of action to attempt to isolate and obtain my father's DNA.

I carefully packaged and forwarded to the Virginia based lab a number of my father's personal effects, some of which had been in my possession for over forty-years. They included a pair of his *Bally* dress shoes, size 10e, as well as four separate letters written by him over the past decades—all of which contained stamps and envelopes which could potentially yield his DNA.

By July 2010, over a year had elapsed, and three of the four items, including the shoes, had proved negative for paternal DNA.

We were down to the last item, a letter my father had mailed to me in 1971 from Manila, Philippines.

BINGO!

Success came on this very last evidentiary item—the envelope contained his full genetic DNA profile!

441

George Hill Hodel Letter mailed from Manila in 1971

George Hill Hodel's DNA profile remains in my possession and upon request will be made available to any legitimate law enforcement agency in furtherance of their cold case investigations.

Locus	CCA0972-0134-E04a1
D8S1179	
D21S11	
D7S820	
CSF1PO	
D3S1358	
TH01	George Hodel full
D13S317	DNA profile obtained
D16S539	in 2010 and on file
D2S1338	and available for
D19S433	comparison.
vWA	
TPOX	
D18S51	
Amelogenin	
D5S818	
FGA	

George Hodel 1949 Booking DNA full profile now available

For those who have not read my sequel to *BDA*, *Most Evil: Avenger, Zodiac, and the Further Serial Murders of Dr. George Hill Hodel,* I will here provide only the briefest of summaries.

I will do this so that you may understand that the discussion that follows related to potentially connecting George Hodel's newly obtained DNA to other crimes in other cities is not simply arbitrary, but rather is based on compelling circumstantial evidence as provided in that book.

Los Angeles DA Files—Elizabeth Short—The Chicago Lipstick Murders

In my further review of the Los Angeles DA files, I discovered documents which showed that in July 1946, while my father was stationed with UNRRA in China, *Elizabeth Short traveled to Chicago, Illinois and began her own personal investigation into three exceptionally high-profile crimes known as Chicago's "Lipstick Murders."*

The three crime victims, Josephine Ross, Frances Brown, and Suzanne Degnan had been national headlines in 1945 and 1946.

The third Lipstick victim, gained the most notoriety as it involved the horrific kidnap-strangulation murder and surgical bisection of a six-year-old girl, little Suzanne Degnan. Her sadist killer, after kidnapping the sleeping child from her bedroom, carried her to a basement just a few blocks from her home, where, after strangling her, performed a highly skilled surgical operation known as a "hemicorpectomy" and divided the body by cutting through the second and third lumbar vertebrae. [The exact same operation performed on Elizabeth Short one-year later.] The suspect then carried the body parts to six separate catch basins in and near that north-side neighborhood, and then wrote a message in lipstick on a post in front of the "murder room" which read:

"Stop Me Before I Kill More."

Lipstick printed sign on post near building where body of Suzanne Degnan was dismembered, discovered yesterday.

Chicago's 1945 Frances Brown Lipstick Murder

Written on apartment wall in lipstick less than one month prior to the Degnan murder:

"For heaven's sake catch me Before I Kill more. I cannot control myself"

The DA files document that Elizabeth Short spent three weeks in Chicago and slept with four separate Chicago newspaper reporters, apparently, attempting to gain some "inside information" on the three separate Lipstick Murder investigations. She also informed the newsmen that "she knew a Chicago detective that was working the Degnan case."

The DA files also contained information indicating that the Dahlia suspect could possibly have been an "Unknown Chicago Police Officer." Why?

The information was based on the fact that Elizabeth Short attended the Jack Carson radio show at the CBS studio in Hollywood in early January 1947, just days prior to her being slain.

The chief usher, Jack Egger, identified her as standing in line with an older "dapper male in his 30s" who identified himself to Egger as a "Chicago Police Officer," showing Egger a police badge. Egger allowed both Short and the man to jump the line and enter the studio for the show. Egger was familiar with Short as she regularly attended the shows, but this was the first time he ever recalled her being accompanied by a male.

Jack Egger went on to become a DA investigator, then joined the Beverly Hills Police Department, and rose to command that department's Detective Bureau. After retirement, he became chief of security for Warner Brothers Studio in Burbank.

As detailed in my sequel, I discovered that Jack was still employed with Warner Brother's studio as their chief investigator, and I met with him in 2004.

After reviewing and verifying the facts as detailed by him in his original 1950 DA interview, I then showed Chief Egger a photograph of Dr. George Hill Hodel, circa 1950, *which he positively identified as the person he saw with Elizabeth Short at the CBS studio and the same individual who had shown him a Chicago Police Officer's badge.*

I am also in possession of original Los Angeles Sheriff's Department investigative reports that show that LASD, in 1946, was *actively investigating* the possibility that their 1944 Hollywood *Lone Woman Murder* of oil-heiress Georgette Bauerdorf may have been connected to the later 1945 Chicago Lipstick Murders. Those reports indicate that LASD requested prints and additional information to ascertain if the crimes were linked.

Photo identification by Warner Brother's Studio, Chief Jack Egger

Dr. George Hodel   Elizabeth Short

What's in a Name?—Another Black Dahlia Avenger Taunt

In an earlier chapter, I described how I "reenacted" by driving myself on what I believed was my father's probable original route from the Franklin house to the vacant lot on South Norton Avenue.

On arrival, I spent only four minutes at the vacant lot, just as the original witness had described it when he saw the black sedan pull up and stop on January 15, 1947.

I then resumed my drive home; again taking what I believed was my father's probable route. Driving north, I stopped halfway between the lot and the Franklin house and simulated placing Elizabeth Short's purse and shoes on top of a restaurant trash can in the 1100 block of South Crenshaw Boulevard—just where the witness had described seeing them. And then I went back home to Franklin and Normandie.

Some "theorists" and a few "profilers" have indicated that they suspected there was "a specific reason why the Dahlia killer selected the Liemert Park neighborhood." Maybe the killer "had some connection to the neighborhood."

In my sequel, *Most Evil*, I presented what I believe was the actual reason why he selected that specific location. Again, we will examine the WHY?

It was not because it "connects him to the neighborhood" but rather just the reverse—the placement of the body connects HER, Elizabeth Short, to HIS NEIGHBORHOOD—HIS OTHER CRIMES.

Another one of his diabolical, "Catch me if you can"—CLEWS. Another of the Avenger's highly egotistical TAUNTS, which in the end—as "signatures"—when pieced together, have become his own undoing, and led us directly to his IDENTITY.

Here is the explanation in brief.

The most direct route and the one I drove on January 16, 2011, and the one I believe was driven by my father, was: South on Normandie Avenue to Santa Barbara [now renamed Martin Luther King Jr. Boulevard], right turn on MLK for approximately two miles. He then turned right on a residential street and drove north a few blocks to the vacant lot where he stopped, carefully posed the body parts and was gone in just four minutes.

The name of the street he selected and turned right on? **DEGNAN.**

The very same name as that of his third Chicago LIPSTICK MURDER VICTIM.

Suzanne Degnan, was the name of the child who, just one year earlier, had been slain and a hemicorpectomy performed on her by a skilled surgeon/killer. Just as he had done with Elizabeth Short, he divided the little Degnan girl's body *between the second and third lumbar vertebrae.* The dissected body parts were then posed in a residential neighborhood with a taunting message written in lipstick, which was left near the body, promising, "There will be more."

I believe that Elizabeth Short had somehow made the connection of George Hodel, her "former suitor" and sometime boyfriend, to the Chicago Lipstick murders, and had gone to Chicago to investigate them while she knew he was away in China. The DA reports informed us that she did just that and was in Chicago investigating the crimes in June and July 1946.

I suspect that at some later time, Elizabeth naively disclosed to George Hodel that she knew or suspected his crimes. This may have caused his unexpected return to Los Angeles. She then fled in fear to San Diego and he pursued her, and, once found, she discovered that by disclosing her suspicions to George, she had in effect *signed her own death warrant.*

His choosing and posing of her body on the street whose crime she was about to reveal was his own sardonic and macabre "poetry" to go along with the surrealist homage—to add to his theme *murder as a fine art.*

Norton vs. Degnan

The simple fact is that *George Hodel believed he had posed the body* on DEGNAN and likely didn't discover HIS MISTAKE until reading the afternoon "Extra" edition in the newspaper, which informed readers that the location was: "Thirty-Ninth and Norton."

448

What happened?

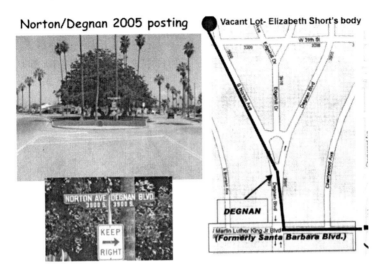

Norton/Degnan 2005 posting

Vacant Lot- Elizabeth Short's body

The above photo exhibit gives us the answer. *The fact is that the one street has two names–Degnan and Norton.* The arrow points to the exact location where the street magically changes its name from Degnan and becomes Norton.

Driving west on Santa Barbara Boulevard [MLK Jr.], George Hodel turned right on DEGNAN, the street he had previously selected. He drove north on Degnan looking for just the right spot. He came to the division and bore left, thinking he was still on Degnan. He simply zigged when he should have zagged. It was a 50-50 coin toss and he lost.

The above photographs show how the streets are currently marked, not how they appeared in 1947. Back then, there was no raised island or "one way sign" just the simple choice. Bear right and remain on Degnan. Bear left and Degnan becomes Norton.

In later years, it had become so confusing that the city had to try and clarify it by adding the "KEEP RIGHT" sign for Degnan and putting in the one-way divider. Even today's Goggle maps, to try and help lessen the confusion, have the street split marked with an arrow.

Keep in mind that in his youth, George Hodel was a Los Angeles cab driver, and, with his perfect photographic memory, could take you to any street in the city. He knew them all.

I previously described this unique act of George Hodel by connecting his victims to a street name as one of his "criminal signatures." It was, and this example *is just one of many*. The additional "signatures" can be found detailed and summarized in the sequel, *Most Evil: Avenger, Zodiac, and the Further Serial Murders of Dr. George Hill Hodel.* [Dutton, 2009, New York.]

Probable round-trip driving route from George Hodel's residence.

1- **Dr. Hodel's Franklin house, 5121 Franklin Avenue**
2- **Vacant lot, 3815 S. Norton (aka Degnan)**
3- **Elizabeth Short's purse and shoes left at 1136 S. Crenshaw Boulevard [Halfway between body and Franklin house]**

LA *Lone Woman Murders*—New Touch DNA procedure potentially opens door to solving many of the 1940s and 1960s serial killings

In addition to the Black Dahlia murder, as has been noted in *BDA* and reviewed again in earlier chapters of this book from 1943-1949, a number of other *Lone Woman Murders* occurred all in a tight geographical area between Hollywood and downtown Los Angeles.

As discussed in previous chapters, LAPD's original on-scene detectives were convinced that many of these unsolved murders were committed by the same suspect and released a summary to the press, listing "11 Points of Similarity," as well as in multiple press releases connected with the additional *Lone Woman Murders* that occurred in 1948 and 1949.

In six of those crimes, the suspect left a taunting note, just as he had in the Elizabeth Short murder. This act, by and of itself, is so unusual a crime signature so as to raise the suspicion of linkage to the other murders.

With the recent obtaining of Dr. George Hill Hodel's DNA profile, along with the newly develop technique of "Touch DNA," which provides a process where the suspect's skin cells can be collected off a victims clothing, or even from a ligature used to tie or strangle the victim, the prospect of solving many of these additional LAPD and LASD murders becomes a very real possibility.

All that is required is THE ATTEMPT.

It would require minimal investigative manpower, a single two-person team to coordinate and oversee the collection of potential evidence for testing to the known unsolved cold cases for the presence of suspect DNA. Those findings could then be entered into state and federal CODIS [Combined DNA Index System] for inclusion or exclusion to the known George Hodel sample, as well as providing an automatic comparison to all DNA samples already in the data banks. The DNA collected by investigators from the various *Lone Woman Murders* cold cases could then also be compared not only to potential suspects but to other existent crime scene DNA already in the data banks for linkage to other unsolved crimes.

The names of some of the 1940s cold cases that remain unsolved and were actively investigated and suspected of possibly being connected and could–*if tested*–potentially yield suspect DNA are:

(Listed chronologically by investigating agency)

LAPD

Miss Elizabeth Short, January 15, 1947

[It is unclear if the victim's purse, known to be handled by the suspect remains in evidence. Retired detective Brian Carr claimed all the physical evidence, letters, etc., had "disappeared" but did not specifically mention the victim's purse.]

Mrs. Jeanne French, February 10, 1947

Miss Evelyn Winters, March 11, 1947

Miss Rosenda Mondragon, July 8, 1947

Mrs. Gladys Kern, February 14, 1948

Mrs. Louise Springer, June 13, 1949

LASD

Mrs. Ora Murray, July 27, 1943

Miss Georgette Bauerdorf, October 12, 1944

Mrs. Gertrude Evelyn Landon, July 10, 1946

Mrs. Dorothy Montgomery, May 2, 1947

Miss Geneva Ellroy, June 22, 1958

Miss Bobbie Long, January 22, 1959

Long Beach PD

Laura Trelstad, May 11, 1947

San Diego PD

Miss Marian Newton, July 17, 1947

Based on my investigation of the publicly known facts of these 1940s *Lone Woman Murders*, it is my belief that the best chance of obtaining positive DNA would most likely come from LAPD's LOUISE SPRINGER murder.

However, all of the above listed crimes are *excellent potential sources* for obtaining "Touch DNA" due to the suspect's extensive use of ligatures and or the unusually rough ripping and tearing of the victim's clothing. Several included a man's handkerchief left at the crime-scene.

Cold cases in the 1940s and 1960s crimes summarized in my sequel, *Most Evil* that could also potentially yield suspect DNA—*if tested*—include:

Chicago

Miss Josephine Ross, June 5, 1945

Miss Frances Brown, December 10, 1945

Miss Suzanne Degnan, January 6, 1946

All three of the Chicago "Lipstick Murders" would offer a high probability of yielding "Touch DNA."

In addition, Chicago PD hand-carried and booked into evidence at the FBI Laboratory, a hair follicle found on Suzanne Degnan's body, which they insisted "had to belong to her killer." Additionally, Chicago PD detectives informed the press that victim Josephine Ross "was clutching in her hand some black hair follicles belonging to the suspect which may help us in identifying him."

Does the hair follicle evidence in both the Ross and Degnan crimes still exist? Can DNA be obtained?

1945 CHICAGO "LIPSTICK KILLER" UPDATE

Attempted rape victim/witness confirmed the Lipstick Killer description as:

"Tall, thin, with black hair used clothesline rope to bind her."

In a recent review of 1945 newspaper articles related to Chicago's "Lipstick Killer," specifically the June 5, 1945 murder of victim, Josephine Alice Ross, I discovered an interesting and hitherto unknown witness/victim account, long buried and forgotten which should have had an important bearing on the later investigation. This is a new discovery, post-publication of *Most Evil*. Therefore, this was not discussed in that sequel.

This new information revealed that *just a few hours prior* to the brutal Lipstick Killer murder of Miss Josephine Ross, another victim, Mrs. Eileen Huffman, age thirty-four was accosted in her apartment house basement by a suspect who was armed with a handgun.

Described as "tall and thin with black hair, "he tied the victim's hands with clothesline and attempted to rape her, but fled when she screamed out.

Shortly after this assault, just a few hours later, and only five blocks away, the first "Lipstick Killer" victim, Josephine Ross was attacked and murdered in her home. [See below diagram for victim locations.]

In the later, December 1945 murder of victim Frances Brown, the same killer would use both a gun and a knife on his victim, stabbing her through the neck and shooting her twice.

Obviously, Chicago detectives made the connection between the Huffman and Ross crimes, and, according to the article, delayed the murder inquest so that they could proceed with their search for a "tall, dark-haired man, wearing a light colored sweater; he was seen leaving the Ross apartment building," and closely fit the description provided by Mrs. Eileen Huffman.

"Tall, black-haired suspect" committed the Huffman and Ross crimes on June 5, 1945, just two hours and five blocks apart

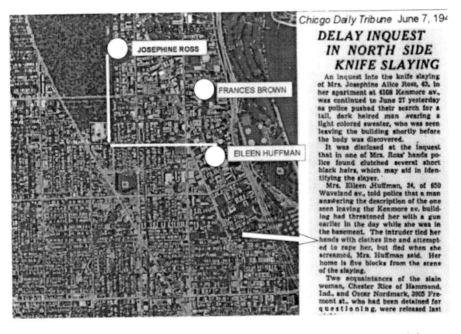

Chicago Daily Tribune June 7, 194

DELAY INQUEST IN NORTH SIDE KNIFE SLAYING

An inquest into the knife slaying of Mrs. Josephine Alice Ross, 43, in her apartment at 4108 Kenmore av., was continued to June 27 yesterday as police pushed their search for a tall, dark haired man wearing a light colored sweater, who was seen leaving the building shortly before the body was discovered.

It was disclosed at the inquest that in one of Mrs. Ross' hands police found clutched several short black hairs, which may aid in identifying the slayer.

Mrs. Eileen Huffman, 34, of 650 Waveland av., told police that a man answering the description of the one seen leaving the Kenmore av. building had threatened her with a gun earlier in the day while she was in the basement. The intruder tied her hands with clothes line and attempted to rape her, but fled when she screamed, Mrs. Huffman said. Her home is five blocks from the scene of the slaying.

Two acquaintances of the slain woman, Chester Rice of Hammond, Ind., and Oscar Nordmark, 3905 Fremont st., who had been detained for questioning, were released last

Can DNA from the FBI Evidence Lab link George Hodel to Chicago Lipstick Murders?

Does the FBI laboratory still have the hair follicle DNA evidence on the 1946 Degnan "Lipstick Murder" investigation?

FBI Receipt No. PC-16339-AO Q21 dated 1/8/46

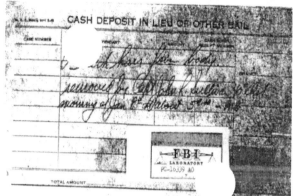

Original Jan 8, 1947 receipt from FBI on hair follicle booked in evidence

Additional Potential Sources for Touch DNA

Riverside PD

Miss Cheri Jo Bates, October 30, 1966

[Hair follicles also found in victim's hand which reportedly have been tested. Do they contain a full DNA profile? Are they available for comparison?]

Manila PD, Manila, Philippines

Miss Lucila Lalu, May 30, 1967

Solano County S.O.

Miss Betty Jensen/Mr. David Faraday, December 20, 1968

Vallejo PD

Mrs. Darlene Ferrin/Michael Mageau, July 4, 1969

Napa County S.O.

Cecelia Shepard/Bryan Hartnell, September 27, 1969

San Francisco PD

Mr. Paul Stine, October 11, 1969

Signature Crime Linkage

SIGNATURE CRIME: (noun) any of two or more crimes that involve the use of a method, plan, or modus operandi so distinctive that it logically follows that the crimes must have been committed by the same person

Merriam-Webster's Dictionary of Law

M.O. is a very broad term and it is oftentimes mentioned in very general nonspecific terms when it comes to criminal investigations.

The squad-room roll call sergeant, when reading off crimes from the previous week, might say, "The suspect is a hot prowl burglar and his M.O. is to enter upscale private residences during daytime hours."

That said, there are signature crimes and *signature acts* within those crimes that are so specific that they become extremely important in attempting to link serial crimes and serial killers.

In my *Most Evil* investigation, there are many such acts that I believe not only link the suspect from crime to crime, but from city to city. As relates to the potential for "Touch DNA" let's examine what I consider to be one of George Hodel's most significant SIGNATURE ACTS—that being:

Bringing with him and use of *pre-cut clothesline* to either strangle or bind his victims.

Chicago's "Lipstick Killer," Los Angeles's "Black Dahlia Avenger," Manila's "Jigsaw Killer," and San Francisco's "Zodiac" *EACH BROUGHT AND USED PRECUT SECTIONS OF CLOTHESLINE WITH THEM AND USED IT IN CONNECTION WITH ONE OR MORE OF THEIR CRIMES.*

"Lipstick Killer," "Avenger," "Jigsaw," and "Zodiac" all used precut clothesline to commit their crimes.

In the 1967 Manila, Philippines surgical bisection murder of victim Lucila Lalu, the suspect used that country's version of clothesline rope. He bound her with "abaca," commonly known as Manila hemp. The photo seen above is a depiction and not the actual rope used in the Lalu crime. The other three photos do show the actual clothesline rope used in those murders.

Touch DNA processing could potentially result in obtaining suspect DNA skill cells on any or all of these ligatures.

Do LAPD and Riverside PD Letters contain Zodiac's full DNA profile?

In 2010, LAPD and DOJ teamed up to connect and solve a series of cold case murders that occurred in Los Angeles over a twenty-two-year period. [1985-2007]

The suspect, Lonnie David Franklin Jr., who the LA press named, "The Grim Sleeper" was arrested on DNA evidence which allegedly connected him to multiple victims. As of 2011, LAPD believes he may be responsible for as many as twenty separate rape-murders over twenty-years in the South Central Los Angeles area.

Based on my now eleven-years of investigation and the new evidence as reported in *Most Evil* and now in this 2012 follow-up, I would suggest that George Hodel, also resumed his serial killing in California some twenty-years after the commission of his "Black Dahlia Avenger" crimes.

Setting aside for the moment the twenty or more Northern California Zodiac letters and evidence, let's just focus on the letters he sent to the police and press in the LA area.

There are four letters: Two mailed in Riverside in 1967, one to the *LA Times* in 1971 and one to the KHJ-Television station in 1978.

Do these four (4) untested Southern California evidence letters contain suspect's DNA?

[Top] Killer mailed notes to both victim's father and Riverside PD in 1967
[Lower left] 1971 Zodiac letter mailed to *KHJ TV* booked into LAPD as evidence
[Lower right] 1978 Zodiac letter mailed to *LA Times* booked into LAPD as evidence

1971 Zodiac Letter to *Los Angeles Times*

"I do have to give them credit for stumbling across my riverside activity, but they are only finding the easy one, there are a hell of a lot more down there."

ZODIAC

I believe *this letter offers the highest probability of yielding actual suspect DNA.* It is recognized as being a legitimate letter written by Zodiac. In it, he acknowledged and took credit for the 1966 Cheri Jo Bates murder, and informed the public that he had killed a lot more victims "down there." [Southern California]

1971 *Los Angeles Times* Zodiac Letter

Mailed: March 13, 1971
Postmarked: Pleasanton, Calif
Sent to: Los Angeles Times

This is the Zodiac speaking
Like I have always said
I am crack proof. If the
Blue Meannies are eveve
going to catch me, they had
best get off their fat asses
+ do something. Because the
longer they fiddle + fuss
around, the more slaves
I will collect for my after
life. I do have to give them
credit for stumbling across
my riverside activity, but
they are only finding the
easy ones, there are a hell
of a lot more than there.
The reason that Im writing
to the Times is this, They
dont bury me on the back pages
like some of the others.
SFPD —0   ⊕— −17+

1978 Zodiac Letter to KHJ-TV

When I first viewed this letter, I had mixed reactions as to whether this was/is a legitimate Zodiac letter. The handwriting in the body of the letter—though apparently disguised—when compared to other known writings, seems a bit off. However, the handwriting on the envelope is much more consistent with known Zodiac samples. In the past few weeks, while focusing my attention on this letter, I have discovered what I believe to be new information that may well strengthen the case for the letter having actually been written by Zodiac. [My apologies if some of the information has been referenced elsewhere by other researchers/investigators. If it has been, I have not come across it.] Here's what I've discovered:

This letter was received by KHJ-TV in May 1978, and turned over to the LAPD as evidence. It contains death threats against five individuals: LAPD chief of police, Darryl Gates; Ex-LAPD chief, Ed Davis; singer, Pat Boone; Black Activist, Eldridge Cleaver; and Manson Family member, Susan Atkins. Specifically relating to Susan, "Zodiac" writes:

> **"And Susan Atkins—the Judas of the Manson Family. Shes gona get hers now."**

The Envelope

On the outside of the envelope where the return address should be were written some backward letters and numbers. The top line reads "CIA" with the letter "C" reversed

Original 1978 envelope booked in LAPD custody

Below I have mirror reversed the original printed information which now reads:

"1,2,3,4,5,6,7" (7 reversed)

A.G.C.G.T.H.!"

Helter Skelter—Bugliosi/Manson

Based on "Zodiac's" reference to the Manson Family in the text of his letter, it becomes obvious that the source of the enigmatic message on the outside of the envelope is also a direct reference to Charles Manson.

Further, it is my belief that the person who wrote this letter had also read and was familiar with author Vincent Bugliosi's, *HELTER SKELTER: The True Story of the Manson Murders*, published four-years earlier. [1974]

Why?

Read this excerpt from Bugliosi's bestseller, page 294:

> On May 25, I was going through LAPD's tubs on the LaBianca case when I noticed standing against the wall, a wooden door. On it was a multicolored mural, the lines from a nursery thyme, "1, 2,3,4,5,6,7—All Good Children Go to Heaven"; and, in large letters, the words "HELTER SKELTER IS COMING DOWN FAST." Stunned, I asked Gutierrez, "Where in the hell did you get that?"
> "Spahn Ranch."
> "When?"
> He checked the yellow property envelope affixed to the door, "November 25, 1969."
> "You mean for five months, while I've been desperately trying to link the killers with Helter Skelter, you've had this door, with those very words on it, the same bloody words that were found at the LaBianca residence?
> Guiterrez admitted they had. The door, it turned out, had been found on a cabinet in Juan Flynn's trailer. It had been considered so unimportant that to date no one had even bothered to book it into evidence.
> Guiterrez did so the next day.

Photo of the Spahn Ranch door booked in evidence at LAPD Property

Writing on door reads, "1, 2, 3, 4, 5, 6, 7—All Good Children (go to heaven)

I believe the enigmatic reference on the 1978 envelope is classic Zodiac. He preferred to write it backwards and in code—another of his cat-and-mouse games. A new taunt from the "master criminal." Let the cops try and connect these dots.

I know for a fact that my father had read and was familiar with Bugliosi's bestseller, *Helter Skelter*, because during that time period, he expressed an interest in the investigation, and, on one of his regular visits with me in LA, told me he had read it and asked me directly, "What did you think about the book?" My response back then was, "Sorry, Dad, I haven't read it."

John Walsh—*Anderson Cooper*—More Zodiac Letters and DNA?

CNN Anderson Cooper 360 "Notorious Crimes"—July 22, 2011

2011 John Walsh and Anderson Cooper discussing Black Dahlia and Zodiac cases

On his July 23, 2011 CNN show, *Anderson Cooper 360*, Cooper aired an updated segment devoted to various "Notorious Crimes."

In September 2006, Anderson had interviewed me on the Black Dahlia Murder, and, on that show, I eliminated the one photo in my father's album as *NOT BEING ELIZABETH SHORT*, and discussed the posing of the body and various signature connections of my father's crime to SURREALISM.

In the 2011 segment, Anderson updated my investigation and introduced the viewers to one of my most important new discoveries— the linking of physical evidence from my father's Sowden/Franklin house to evidence found near the body at the Thirty-Ninth and Norton vacant lot.

He presented the photographs and original receipts I had discovered at the *UCLA Special Collections Department*, linking the cement bags from the house to identical bags that LAPD determined were used to transport Elizabeth Short's body to the vacant lot. [All previously detailed in Chapter 5 of this book, "Scene of the Crime."]

In his update, he also mentioned the important fact that Dr. Hodel had fled the country BEFORE detectives were able to arrest and interview him regarding the tape recorded admissions and confessions he made to killing Elizabeth Short and his secretary, Ruth Spaulding, as well as personally admitting to "performing abortions at his VD clinic and to making payoffs to the police."

In the interview, John Walsh of *America's Most Wanted*, expressed a strong conviction and belief that, "in my heart and in my gut from doing this for so many years, I believe it was the doctor." [George Hodel]

Here is the excerpted exchange between Walsh and Cooper regarding the Black Dahlia Murder:

AC: The Black Dahlia case. This is a case that has been fascinating Hollywood and the country for decades.

JW: Bestselling book, movie all that spin. But I do believe who killed the Black Dahlia, the main suspect they had. The doctor who is now deceased. I believe he got away with that case. They never charged him. He was a stalker. He was the main suspect. [Dr. George Hill Hodel] They never had enough to indict him. She was dismembered by someone who had great knowledge of anatomy and skills in surgery. He was the logical suspect, but back in those days, they didn't have the tools that we have now.

AC: They obviously sensationalized the case not because she was beautiful, but because of the gruesome way that she was killed.

JW: The way that he displayed her. He displayed her as a trophy, like lots of serial killers and horrible narcissistic murderers do. He displayed her in the field for the whole world to see his work.

In my heart and in my gut from doing this so many years I believe it was that doctor. [Emphasis mine]

After discussing the *Black Dahlia* case, the program then reviewed the ZODIAC murder. Here is an excerpt from that discussion where John Walsh described personally receiving multiple letters and death threats from a man identifying himself as "Scorpion," but who had identical handwriting and codes and ciphers to "Zodiac."

...

AC: The Zodiac killer's probably the most famous cold case in the US. Why do you think there is so much fascination with it?

JW: Because he terrorized and held San Francisco captive for so long. They locked down that city when he said, "If you keep looking for me, I have a sniper's rifle, I will kill the kids getting off of the buses." He claimed to have killed multiple victims. They believe he killed seven people. It actually paralyzed a city. A United States city. One low-life coward paralyzed that city. People were fascinated. He always sent this cryptic code around, and everybody analyzed it. *When I first profiled the Zodiac killer, I got a letter sent exactly like his code. Sent to me in exactly the same kind of envelope that he sent others. I had to give it to the FBI. It was signed in blood. In human blood. He said, "I will kill you. You will be the ultimate victory. I got away with it. I've committed mayhem since I murdered those other people. You will be my ultimate prize. I still have the ability to kill people.* It's fascinating. We don't know if it was the Zodiac killer? Nobody knows. It fascinates people when somebody gets away with murder and they brag about it.

AC: The Zodiac killer had seven confirmed victims. Five of them died. But he's suspected possibly to have dozens more.

Several years prior to this interview, John Walsh had published the actual letters on his *America's Most Wanted* website, informing the public that the letters and ciphers containing the death threats were sent to him in 1990. The suspect signed his letters "Scorpion." [That is the same year that George Hodel relocated from Asia back to San Francisco.]

Both the hand printing and ciphers are similar to those of the original "Zodiac" and John Walsh in his Anderson Cooper interview informed us "that the envelopes were the same kind he [Zodiac] sent others."

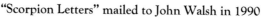

"Scorpion Letters" mailed to John Walsh in 1990

Clearly, based on Walsh's information, these letters should be examined and processed for potential DNA.

John Walsh has been a dedicated fighter for victim's rights for twenty-three years and his success as the host of *America's Most Wanted* has resulted in more than 1,200 "solves." He has been a major force in helping law enforcement take so many vicious criminals "off the streets." His crime fighting efforts have also resulted in an incalculable number of CRIMES BEING PREVENTED.

He has my highest respect and personal congratulations for an OUTSTANDING JOB IN STANDING UP FOR VICTIM'S RIGHTS AND HIS LONG YEARS OF ASSISTANCE TO LAW ENFORCEMENT.

ZODIAC- San Francisco Paul Stine Murder—Shirt and Gloves

In my opinion, the best potential for hard physical evidence in the unsolved ZODIAC murders can be found in the physical evidence booked in connection with the San Francisco, Paul Stine cabbie shooting.

The suspect's bloodstained gloves and the section of shirt torn from the victim's body by his killer and mailed to SFPD both REMAIN UNTESTED. Both items are highly likely to yield a full Zodiac profile—IF TESTED.

The gloves, men's size 7, apparently containing the victim's blood splatters, were inadvertently left behind and very likely fell out of Zodiac's pocket prior to the shooting. The 1969 police and DOJ reports confirm that law enforcement believes that they were owned and worn by Zodiac.

In addition, there remain some fifteen to twenty notes mailed by Zodiac that could be retested using today's much more sophisticated techniques.

I find it incredible that NO CONFIRMED ZODIAC DNA has yet been obtained. There is NO ZODIAC DNA entered into any state or national CODIS data banks.

The last report I am aware of from law enforcement sources dates back to 2002 and that sample reportedly is highly suspect and *contains only a partial DNA profile which is insufficient to include or exclude anyone. That sample only contains three (3) out of the thirteen (13) loci found in a full DNA profile.*

California DOJ Meet and the Zodiac DNA Evidence

In November 2009, two months after the publication of my book, *Most Evil*, I met with two agents from the California Department of Justice.

The agents, I'll call them, X and Y, flew down from the DOJ San Francisco Regional Office to Los Angeles for a morning meet in which I presented them with a PowerPoint summary of my overall investigation.

I focused on the ZODIAC connections and what I believed were the best potential sources for obtaining Zodiac DNA with special emphasis on the size 7 gloves left by Zodiac inside the murder victim's [Paul Stine] taxi.

Both Agent Y [a retired SFPD detective] and Agent X, his supervisor, seemed impressed with my findings. Agent X said she would "be back in contact with me after they had a chance to review the various written materials I had provided them."

Six months later, in May 2010, I contacted Agent Y by e-mail and inquired if he had been able to test the gloves? He responded that the SFPD homicide commander "had given him permission to have them tested, and he was in the process of attempting to locate the evidence."

I recontacted Agent Y in August 2010, and he indicated that he was hoping to meet with the SFPD detective and "track down the gloves and get the process going."

My last communication with Agent Y occurred in November 2010. In that exchange, he said he was "still trying to make contact with his contact at SFPD and continue the search for the gloves," assuring me that "at some point, this will all come together." [As a side note, Agent Y advised me that their DOJ handwriting expert "had examined and compared George Hodel's handwriting to known Zodiac documents and *was unable to include or exclude him as the author of the Zodiac letters.*" Their Questioned Document Expert requested through Agent Y that I provide them with some additional samples of George Hodel's "lower-case handwriting." Unfortunately, I have no additional samples in my possession as my father rarely wrote in lower-case. I am currently attempting to locate additional writing samples. Despite the "inconclusive" finding, *the fact that the DOJ expert could not eliminate, or rule-out George Hodel as the writer of the Zodiac notes and letters–is, by itself –significant.*]

It has now been *two-years* since my original meet with the two DOJ agents. It is unknown if the gloves have been found or tested, or still remain missing? In criminal investigations, "No news is bad news." We can only hope that in Agent Y's optimistic words, "this will all come together."

Have the SFPD Stine Gloves been located and tested for DNA or is the evidence still missing?

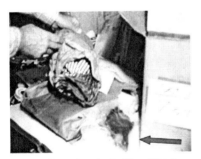

SFPD evidence photo showing Stine shirt and men's black leather gloves ("Size 7") at the bottom of the frame in clear plastic evidence bag. (red arrow points to gloves)

George and June Hodel Rosario Retreat, Orcas Island, Washington 1995.

[Left] SFPD Paul Stine Evidence—Suspect's bloodstained gloves and victim's shirt [Right] George Hodel, putting on his size-7 gloves on a visit to me on Orcas Island in Washington State in 1995.

471

Bottom Line:

I believe that the potential for obtaining the suspect's DNA on many of the 1940s unsolved *Los Angeles Lone Woman Murders* does exist.

I believe that analysis of those samples will, like they did in the GRIM SLEEPER MURDERS—prove linkage.

Once DNA is obtained, cold case detectives can enter the samples into state and federal CODIS data-banks and very possibly identify a suspect and clear many of the cases.

At the very least, detectives should make the attempt to obtain DNA from the Los Angeles area Zodiac letters booked in evidence at LAPD and Riverside to see if they can *be linked to a killer already entered in CODIS.*

With the recent advancement of "Touch DNA," I am extremely confident that the forty-year-old unsolved Zodiac serial murders CAN BE SOLVED.

All that it requires is just one dedicated cold case investigator in any of the many jurisdictions to *take the initiative and make a first step forward!*

That detective may now be assigned to any of the following departments or agencies: Riverside PD, LASD Homicide, LAPD Homicide CCU, Long Beach PD, San Francisco PD, Napa, or Solano Sheriff's or Vallejo PD.

The solution is there, just a simple phone call away. As an old-time homicide detective who has been there and done that, I strongly urge that detective to pick-up the telephone and make the call to his or her crime-lab.

I'll close with a quote from SFPD Zodiac inspector, Mike Maloney, who was one of the last detectives actively assigned to work Zodiac. He died in 2005, believing that DNA would one day solve the case.

In an open letter to the public, written shortly before his death, he said:

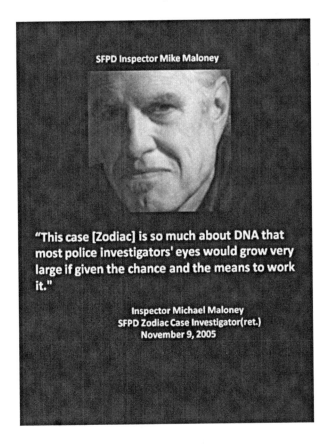

I believe Mike's assessment was absolutely correct!

REST IN PEACE MIKE!

Epilogue

With this updating of the investigative findings as presented here in *Black Dahlia Avenger II*, I am going to "close the homicide book" on my father's serial crimes in and around the Southern California area *in the 1940s*.

As I indicated in my "Touch DNA" chapter, the ball is now in law enforcement's court.

Only time will tell if a detective from one of the multi-jurisdictions will decide to take a look and see if their cold-case evidence still exists, *and then test it*. If they do, I believe that the chances are exceptionally strong that they can obtain a positive match to my father's existent DNA.

As for myself, I will, after taking a short "break" of a month or two, not "move on," but rather-MOVE BACK.

It is my full intention to continue my investigation and present the additional evidence much of which I have been compiling as part of my "ongoing investigation" over the past decade.

I anticipate *Book IV—George Hill Hodel–The Early Years* will complete my criminal investigations into the life and crimes of my father, and hopefully will provide some new light and additional closure to yet unsuspecting family members whose relatives were slain long long ago.

Respectfully,

Steve Hodel
Los Angeles, California
December 2011

ADDENDUM

A

1950 Los Angeles DA Hodel-Black Dahlia Bugging Transcripts [146-pages]
[February 15 – March 27, 1950]

B

1950 Dorothy Hodel DA Jemison transcript/interview [6 pages]
[March 22, 1950]

C

Historical American Building Survey
National Park Service
Sowden House, 5121 Franklin Avenue, Los Angeles, 1969
[Text and Diagrams]

Addendum A

HODEL FILE
FEBRUARY 18, 1950 10:00AM
SPOOL #1 Intermittent recordings while set was being installed.

HODEL

Spool Time		
0-3½	10:05A	Hodel talking to Ellen about lawyer.
3½-5	10:15A	Talking to Ellen about marrying Susie.
-5½		Unable to understand.
	10:20A	Telephoning - unable to hear conversation.

BROWNSON

10:45A	7 minutes - telephone conversation pertaining to medical work
11:00A	11 minutes - telephone call Dr. Hodel makes appointment for 3:00 to 4:00 PM with Mr. Betty? Conversation with housekeeper.
11:45A	Trouble developed on phone line. Stop over - mostly did clicks - some occasional cross talk. Occasional dial tone. Trouble developed suddenly. Mikes still hot. Recording made at 24 minutes.
12:10N	Tone line cleared.

IRWIN
FRANK HRUBLK
February 26, 1950 12:00 noon
Spool #1 Log

12:31	Moving around the house.
12:36	Phone rang - answered - conversation at 5:30 PM-see someone
12:59	End of conversation.
12:54	Very bad reception
12:56	Moving around the house.
12:59	Typing

HODEL FILE
February 18, 1950
Spool #1 Log

Spool Time	
1:07	Calling someone - hello this is George Hodel.
1:09	End of conversation
1:11	Typing
1:13	Typing stopped - just moving around
1:18	Dialing - asking for at 66403 HI 3477 7A 9000 Trying various numbers.
1:32	End of conversation - calling someone use - Betty
1:35	End of conversation
1:38	Moving around
1:43	Received call
1:45	Made call
50-55 1:47	End of conversation
1:50	Typing
55-58 2:00	Called someone
2:03	End of conversation
2:04	Talked with Ellen

HODEL FILE

FEBRUARY 18, 1950

| TIME | SPOOL # 1 | OFFICERS ON DUTY Crowley - LAPD |

12:30A Radio plane. Lady sobbing. Hodel asked, "Do you know Charles Smith. Did you know Mr. Usher?". Hodel mentioned something about during the trial. Mentioned what housekeeper knows. "Did you know ? committed suicide"? "Does your husband know your here. Where were you going? (He was questioning her and it sounded like he was repeating her answer as if writing down her answer)

1:15A Lady reciting poetry. Hodel says something about an affair with Dr. Hodel. "Relax. Let's finish these two." Joe comes in room. Sounds like objects dropping on floor. Crashing noises.

1:45A "Good night Joe".

2:00A All quiet.

SPOOL # 2   OFFICERS ON DUTY
                 F. Hronek-D.A.'s Office

2:10P In bathroom.

2:50P Out of bathroom.

3:26P Phone ringing four times. Picked up - not answered.

3:27P Answered.

3:31P Conversation with some lady about the house.

3:51P Conversation with the lady.

                 J. McGrath-D.A.'s Office

4:00P Noise around the house. Woman asking for Operator several times!

4:20P Sounded as though she was crying.

4:22P No sound.

OFFICERS ON DUTY
HODEL CASE - #   J. McGrath-D.A.'s Office

4:25P Woman asking for operator again. Said something not heard.to operator.

4:26P No noise.

4:35P Someone walking around.

5:18P Man and woman talking. Could not understand.

6:05P Man and woman talking for a few minutes. (Approx. 2) Could not understand. They then left the room.

6:15P Man and woman talking. Garbled.

6:30P "Is Joe here. Joe is here, wait outside".

6:50P Man and woman talking. Woman asked the man a question. Unable to understand. He answered, "Haven't been able to find it yet. Must be around somewhere".

7:07P Someone using a typewriter.

7:08P Phone rang - Hodel said, "OK, right away, good".

7:15P Someone typing.

7:35P Conversation between two men. Recorded.

Hodel and man with a German accent had a long conversation; reception was poor, and conversation hard to understand. The following bits of conversation, however, were overheard.

Hodel to the German - "This is the best pay off I've seen be- tween Law Enforcement Agencies. You do not have the right connections made." Hodel states,"I'd like to get a connection made in the D.A's office."

General conversation between the two - "Any imperfections will be found. They will have to/made perfect. Don't confess ever. Two and two is not four.". Much laughter. "Were just a couple of smart boys". More laughter.

479

OFFICERS ON DUTY
J. McGrath-D.A.'s office

HODEL FILE - 4

8:25P Woman screamed.

8:27P Woman screamed again. It should be noted that a woman was not heard before the time of screaming since 6:50PM. She was not in any conversation and not heard of again until the time of letting out these two screams.

NOTE: Officer Crowley, LAPD, arrived for duty at 7:45 PM while the above mentioned conversation was taking place. His log is as follows:

7:45P Hodel talking to a man with an accent, possibly German. telephone men were here. Operator ? Realize there was nothing I could do put a pillow over her head, and cover her with a blanket. Get a taxi. Call Georgia Street Receiving Hospital right away. Expired at 12:39. They though there was something fishy. Anyway, now they may have figured it out. Killed her. Maybe I did kill my Secretary. They must have enough on him to be guilty or he wouldn't have confessed. Time for research (Lots of pounding). FBI were over to see me too, three weeks ago.

8:35P Above man talking - possible German agent. Two years since. regardless of what happens. Police." Much laughter.

8:40P Above man leaves the house escorted to the door by Hodel.

8:50P Hodel makes telephone call (Very plain) "Are you party advertised for the studio. I have the paper here now. If you'll come over I'll be glad to show it to you. On Franklin, near Normandy. Your a Painter ?" I always have a painter, sculptor, or artist of some type here. It's that kind of a house. It's a wing of this house. Phone me just before you come, NO 27464, and I'll be sure to be in. The name is Hodel, 5123 Franklin Ave Your name - Karbert. If you'll call me, I'll be glad to show you the place."

HODEL FILE - 4

OFFICERS ON DUTY
J. McGrath-D.A.'s office

Hodel then-in exact detail- explained to the German about his wife being stopped on Wednesday morning by McGrath and Morgan of the District Attorney's office when they stopped her going up her steps to the house on Franklin. It should be noted that every question asked of Mrs. Hodel was repeated ver-batum by Hodel to this German. He then began to explain to the German about his recent trial - making statements that "There's out to get me. Two men in the D.A.'s officer were transferred and demoted because of my trial." Hodel then explained about his being questioned at the D.A.'s office on Wednesday morning, and told in great detail as to questions perpounded to him at that time. One statement made to the German was as follows:

"Supposin' I did kill the Black Dahlia. They couldn't prove it now. They can't talk to my Secretary anymore because she's dead."

As stated, heretofore, conversation was garbled, and it was difficult to maintain a line of continuity of conversation. Hodel also referred to a woman in Camarillo. Conversation also referred to Communist. One point of the conversation was also "Have you heard from Powers". The man with the German agent then asked Hodel something about smoking. Hodel said, "I can't afford it - don't smoke". The German said, "I can get it for you Does the Name Hernandez mean anything to you". Hodel then talked to the German about a Furniture store on East 5th Street, where the cops come in and buy lingerie for twenty to fifty dollars. There was much laughter at this point.

8:20P Sounded as though the two men went down steps and entered the basement and began digging. Something was referred to "Not a trace". It also appeared as though a pipe was being hit.

HODEL FILE - #
OFFICERS ON DUTY
Crowley, LAPD (Recorded)

9:25P Maid questioning Hodel about her citizenship and what the immigration officers say in regards to her father. Hodel talking about a drunken judge in a pink shirt deciding the technicality of the law as far as her citizenship is concerned. Maids citizenship papers are fouled up (improper entry) Subject to deportation. Going to have a waiver of documents (1947) They'll realize you acted in good faith. Hodel says, "are you hungry to go across the border?"

9:50P Writing on typewriter.

10:00P Turned on radio - unable to detect conversation.

10:45P Walking - opened drawers. Started typing.

10:50P Telephone rang. (Recorded)
"Hello Muriel, how are you dear? I'm not doing anything. (laught I don't know of any amnesia that you have. I have had some since you were here. A couple of princesses dropped in. I took them to the Burbank to a burlesque-they really enjoyed the show. Why don't you drop by and talk to me about it sometime.

11:00P Typing until 11:15 (steady)

11:15P (Put on spool #4)

FEBRUARY 19, 1950 SPOOL #4   OFFICERS ON DUTY Crowley - LAPD

12:12A Typing.

12:17A Conversing with lady few words (Did not get).

HODEL FILE - #
OFFICERS ON DUTY
Crowley, LAPD (Recorded) (Maybe lady caller)

12:25A Walking and conversation with lady.

Spool Time
0-60 -SPOOL #4

12:35A Radio still interfering. Unable to get any of the conversation.

12:40A Lots of laughing and talking. "Don't make my drink too strong".

12:41A Female voice - "Well I'll be darned." "Hodel-They are just trying -----?"

12:55A Still talking to this lady - Recording it but radio too loud to hear conversation.

12:55A George - Yes.

1:20A Still recording conversation - Unable to pick it up over the interference of the radio.

1:21A Girl - "You know my mother doesn't like it one bit".
Hodel - "Champagne creeps up on you".

1:25A Mentions Brown Derby restaurant.
END OF SPOOL #4

SPOOL #5

1:28A (Sounds like friendly conversation with lady friend, and nothing pertinent to investigation) "Lovey Dovey" tone of voice.

1:42A Walking in house.

1:43A Girl in bathroom. She answers "Yes" to another part of the hou: Talking in the distance. Then conversation ceases.

1:45A NOTE: Officer Bretiel who relieved me came past Hodel's reside at 1:45AM. He observed a girl and a fellow (approx. 25 to 30 y leaving Hodel's house. They got in a 1936 Hudson sedan, license 1Y5 804, man driving, went W on Franklin. There is als a Fleetline Chevrolet about a 1946 grey or light green Ill. license 1J03245 parked in front of the house.

HODEL FILE -

OFFICERS ON DUTY
Brechel-LAPD

1:47A	In bathroom.
1:50A	Typing.
2:20A	Hodel says, "You better go to bed". Lady (probably maid) arguing. Hodel says, "you've been here 5 hours - You don't have to go through everything.
2:48A	Typing - He/said, "Just wipe off table by ashtray. I'll move the tobacco (someone wiping desk) more typing.
2:54A	Woman's voice. "I think I'll get everything". Hodel, "Yes please". Woman's voice. "I'll dust here too".
2:58A	Hodel. "You better go to bed Ellen". Typing stopped, radio turned off. Went to Lavatory and urinated.
3:00A-3:30	Whistling, moving around, then all quiet.
3:45A	Snoring.
7:30A	Faint buzzer. Man's voice very faintly, probably outside door opened momentarily. Very loud, street noises. Hodel still asleep.

J. McGrath-D.A.'s Office

8:00A	
10:20A	A.M. phone rang - talked to someone (personal) about coming over later in the day.
11:50A	Hodel up and around, noise in bathroom.

Jemison-D.A.'s Office

12:00P	
12:45P	Answered phone. "How long you going to be in town. I'm busy this P.M. How about this evening. Let me get in touch with Dorothy first".
12:50P	Typing 10 minutes.
12:55P	Hodel on phone says "This is Hodel I'm going to stay around" and hangs up. "I'm listening to music" to woman's voice inquir "The soloist is up at Camarillo".

HODEL FILE -

OFFICERS ON DUTY
Jemison-D.A.'s office

12:55P	"Do we have any extra blankets Ellen--"No we have sheets only". Hodel - "Oh we haven't".
1:06P	Hodel on phone - "We'll work it out some way. Do you get off in Hollywood or Beverly Hills?" Balance not distinguished.
1:10P	Hodel-"He will be here tonite and may stay until tomorrow. You'd better make up a bed for him anyway".
1:45P	Phone rings - No conversation. ALL QUIET.
1:50P - 1:55P	Phone rings - Recorded. Hodel - "Where are you now. Sunset & Cornel. Then come to 5121 Franklin". Yes, sure I'll do it". Hangs up.
2:00P	Hear conversation in distance or Hodel quoting poetry.
2:05P	S.M. 42421. Hodel asked for this number. "Hello Kenny, let me talk to Mrs. Hodel.
2:05P to 2:08P	Recorded. Conversation. Hodel and Mrs. Hodel. "Hello dear. How's everything. Kids everything. How's everything else? Oh, yes dear, I thought I'd come down and bring that to you that you asked for. Kenneth Rexrall called me today, your friend. Should I bring him down to your house this evening. Have you a snack for us. I'll be there at 6 or 6:30 with Kenneth. We'll leave here at 5 or 5:30.
2:12P	Sit down and relax "Kenny". But you can't pin that on me. So you come down to see Hyder. He's a collector that guy. He works for N.B.C.
2:14P	Recorded. Mr. Ryder is sure queer. Hodel-are you addressing a mass meeting or what You'll have to sleep in the housekeeper's room. She's about this high. Laughter. "Oh we've had some dillys. Discusses chiropractors. "I don't think Dorothy cares. She has a great big living room.

HODEL FILE -

OFFICERS ON DUTY
Jemison-D.A.'s office

2:25P Jimmy Fitzimmons made notes. "Where are these things? What's the name of the poem? Sounds of auto crash in street.

Off 2:29P Both leave and return. Kenny - Exflcius immortality. Hodel- "What have been doing besides writing. Kenny - "Traveling".

On 2:31P Hodel - "Did you get to Cine and the Orient."
Kenny - "No, went to England."
Unable to hear - laughter.
Kenny - "You can make a lot of money in Paris. I was in Western

Off 2:35 Europe about 1 year.

2:38P Hodel - "Did they pay your expenses". Laughter. "Hodel was it hard making ends meet". Kenny-"No, not so bad", Hodel- "He's a sexual character. Probably decayed bodies caused the rancid odors and back ground setting in the orient, in Hongkong" Hodel discusses Chinese food.
Peter Chang on Sunset Strip has the best. Was big shot in China

2:40P Kenny-"You can't believe the terrible food situation in England".

2:45P Hodel-"They gave a banquet and I had an interpreter and the American Guard." Laughter. "It takes a couple months to get thru to Hankow. Kenny-"I always wanted to see Central Asia, but the war has been going on since the 30's."
Hodel-"Jean Lamb spent several years in Peiping. His reports would be on desks of Chinese war lords as soon as on the desk of the Ambassador. He was a staff officer. He then was employed by a War Lord. 100's of cases of wrist watches.] was bribery on a big scale. They had internal war. He was ushered in and here was a yellow silk drapery. He spoke Chines

HODEL FILE -

OFFICERS ON DUTY
Jemison-D.A.'s office

2:45P perfectly. He met Prime Minister Hang Chow.

2:55P Jean became a great power and spent 7 years there. He was out here. I tried to negotiate with him. Hodel-"They have a special variety of pictures".
Kenny-"Yes!

Spool Time

3:00P-3:00P Phone rings. Recorded. Hodel-"Yes, I will", and hangs up.

Off- 3:03 Phone rings. No conversation. All Quiet.

3:05P Phone rings. No conversation. All Quiet.

3:15P Walking sounds

3:20P Hodel conversation with Ellen.
Ellen - "Mr. Hodel". Hodel-"Uh kughuh".

3:25P All Quiet.

3:30P Hodel and Kenny? Converse. Hodel-"Will you have tea or sherry?
Kenny - "Tea"
"Sipping of tea" sound.
Kenny-"This man is a heart special. He is Dr. Roth. I was to th doctor in San Diego.
Hodel - "Read thru this, then we can discuss it more intelligent Maximum Hodel laughs. "It has some coverage. I'm selling my art collection Monday and Tuesday, and I'm then taking off for Asia." Kenny-I am in process of breaking up with my wife of 15 years. No children".
Hodel-"I have 3 boys. You'll see them later. Dorothy lives here a while, and then takes off". Kenny-"What about M".
Hodel-"She is on staff of San Francisco Chronicle. Art Editor. Had a serious operation.

483

MODEL FILE - 1S

OFFICERS ON DUTY
Jemison-D.A.'s office

Spool Time		
On 3:45 -3:40P	Laughter.	

Hodel-"How were they? They had great masses of hair those whores. He was a

Hodel-"Rosey at 555 Hyde St., San Francisco, was a whore but a honey."

Kenny-"I knew a tall one-black hair like Hollywood Blac hair, pale pale gray eyes. I took her home. I thru her in the bath tub - she was drunk. I massaged her. rubbed her under the belly. I got 2 or 3 phone calls. She got mixed up with some bad people. She called and said the Psychiatrist was treating her. I guess I

| Off 3:52-3:52P | am spoiled (Sounded tight) Damss I know all turn out to be psychiatrists with pale gray eyes. |

K. "Dr. Burns would object to your help but he gave 400 to 600 penicillen, but the real help will come from

| On 3:50 | you." Hodel-Wouldn't he object to you coming to my ca: |

K. "No, as you specialize in heart and you are my friend. (Recorded)

| 4:00P | Hodel-"Well alright. |
| 4:00P | |

Hronek-D.A.'s office

32-40	4:16P	Conversation with the patient.
40-44	4:31P	Another conversation with a man.
44-46	4:36P	Phone ringing - Hodel answers.
46-47	4:38	Very bad reception of conversation (3 men)
47-48	4:50P	Someone came in - a woman - Let's go in the other room talking about the house.

MODEL FILE - 2X

OFFICERS ON DUTY
Hronek, D.A.'s office

Spool Time		
48-52	4:54P	Talking with a man about some special treatment apparently syphilis and marital troubles.
SPOOL #6 0-6	5:20P	Continuation of previous conversation.
	5:37P	The man leaves with the instructions to call Wednesday.
	5:45P	Typewriter at work. Looking for something in the desk.
6-15	5:49P	Another man came in - talking about some girl.
15-21	6:03P	Phone rang - answered - continuation of conversation.
21-24	6:11P	Making a call - no answer.
24-33	6:27P	Conversation with his buddy. Mostly females.
	6:30P	Everything quiet.
	7:22P	Phone rang 9X No answer.

Crowley-LAPD

	7:45P	All quiet.
	8:45P	Dog barks.
	9:15P	Someone enters. Walking and noises in house.
	9:30P	Dog barking.
	9:35P	Walking in house - dog barking.
	9:36P	Lady talking in the distance.
	9:37P	Walking near "Mike".
	10:05P	Dog barks.
	11:00P	Telephone rings 4 times (No one answered)

FEBRUARY 20, 1950

BRUCKEL-LAPD

| | 2:00A | All quiet from 11 PM until 2 AM. |
| | 2:00A-8:00A | All is quiet. |

HODEL FILE - Page [##]

SPOOL #6 — OFFICER ON DUTY
J. McGrath, D.A.'s Office

FEBRUARY 20, 1950

Spool	Time	
	8:00A	No noise at all around house.
	9:30A	No noise or activity.
	9:40A	Phone rang 12 times - no answer.
	9:41A	Phone rang 12 times - no answer.
	10:40A	Someone enters - walking and noises in house.
	10:48A	Phone rings 3 times - answered by Ellen. Took message - stated Hodel will be in 2 PM.
	11:20A	Ellen enters - turns on radio - Mexican program.
	11:35A	Much noise in room - sounds like sweeping - no conversation

Sullivan, D.A.'s Office
12 noon

Spool	Time	
	1:00P	All quiet.
	1:15P	Telephone - 4 times - answered by maid - "You his father? He went to beach last nite - said he'd be here early today". No further conversation.
	1:35P	Phone - 3 times - answered by maid - no conversation.
	2:00P	Quiet.
	2:20P	Walking around - maid singing - banging noises.
	2:23P	Quiet.
	2:35P	Phone rings - 2 times.
	2:45P	Someone entered - walked around very fast.
33-42	3:00P	Door bell rings - answered by Hodel. Talking to unknown woman - Dials phone - Asks for some woman - Unable to hear name - Talk about renting rooms over phone - Attempting to get this one party to take both rooms - Hung up - Made another phone call - Wrong number.

HODEL FILE -

Spool	Time	
	3:10P	Walks around house - water running.
42-44	3:12P	Phone rings - answered by Hodel - Unable to identify who he was talking to.
	3:14P	Whistling and rustling of papers.
	3:25P	Phone rings - answered by Hodel.
44-45		Looks for phone # TR 1252.
45-45½	3:28P	Phone rings - answered by Hodel - Unable to connect conversation.
45½-46	3:30P	Phone - Answered by Hodel. Called person on other end "Baby Doll".
	3:45P	Stanton - Crime Lab here; working on set to eliminate hum.
	4:00P	Talking to maid - something about post office, unintelligible - typewriter going.
	4:01P	Machine off - being worked on by Stanton.
	4:08P	Machine back in operation - typing.
	4:09P	Phone rings - "Rex Kane mentioned - Mr. Butlers name mentioned "What 2 boxes represent - Will get a little more information - Will call back".
46-50	4:15P	Walter Morgan - D.A.'s office relieves
	4:20P	Conversation - 27464 - gave number of his phone.
	4:21P	Telephoned - conversation unintelligible - airplane passing over.
	4:22P	Talking to maid - "Close to Mexico".

HODEL FILE - 16

Spool #7

Spool	Time	
	4:25P	Spool #7
	4:30P	Typewriter noise.
	4:35P	Unintelligible conversation with maid.
	4:48P	Telephone rang - was answered by Hodel - short conversation about price of tea.
	4:58P	Began typing.
0-1	5:05P	Conversation with maid - Typing.
1-3.5	5:08P	" " " "
3.5-5	5:14P	" " " "
5-6	5:16P	" " " "
6-8	5:18P	" " " "
8-11	5:28P	Telephone rang - answered by Hodel - conversation about "Units".
11-27.5	5:45P	Telephone rang - answered by Hodel - conversation about crime prevention; Delinquent accounts; Dr. E.W. DeLong's October 1948 account; Blood and spinal fluids; employment of Collector; Hodel's stock ownership in a company - maid entered conversation about time; Hodel stated that it was six o'clock, that he had to leave at seven, that he would be back at twelve - begins to type.
27.5-28.5	6:13P	Noise like writing on paper.
28.5-29.5	6:18P	Hodel asked maid to close door.

HODEL FILE - 17

Spool	Time	
29.5-30.5	6:20P	Telephone rang - answered by Hodel - asked what the score was - ended with goodnight.
30.5-34	6:27P	Hodel asked for Sycamore 60647 (Unrecorded) - Gave operator Olympia 3476; Asked for Cris; Conversation about taking place; Hodel has another party anxious to take place - ended with "So Long".
34-42	6:23P	Dialing of phone - Hodel asked for Mrs. Montgomery - conversation about getting place in one or two days, "Just a minute, hold on", pause in conversation- Desk noise - continued conversation - ended with "Good Nig
	6:52P	Hodel said "Already, O.K."(Not Recorded)
42-44.5	6:53P	Hodel said "Get some from ___
	6:55P	Hodel said, "O.K. be right with you" (Not Recorded)
44.5	6:56P	Desk noise - Hodel walking away - door slams.
45		
	7:20P	Stanton changed recorders.
	7:30P	Shower noise
45-45.5	8:00P	Crowley, LAPD, on duty, relieves Morgan, D.A.
	8:10P	Walking in house.
	8:18P	Walking - door slams.
	8:30P	Walking in house.
	8:35P	Loud noises in desk.
	8:40P	Someone turns radio on.
	8:45P	Crowley and Morgan note that phone # OL 3476 that Hodel charged call to at 6:27PM this date differed from # HO 27464 which he gave at 8:50PM, on 2-18-50. (He gave # 27464 to the party who was inquiring about renting the

HODEL FILE - #?

Spool
Time

studio, gave the address as 5121 Franklin Ave.) Morgan dialed the above OL 3476 from this telephone, and Hodel answered "Hello". (Morgan can positively identify the voice). Morgan asked, "Is this OL 3746", and Hodel answered, "No, this is OL 3476, to which Morgan replied "I'm sorry, I have the wrong number". Crowley was unable to hear any sound whatsoever from Hodel's residence during this conversation - Crowley then called Lt. Hale at Business Office, and was informed that OL 3476 is a non published secret number, registered to Dr. George Hodel at 5121 Franklin Ave.

9:00P — Alls quiet except for radio (playing classical music).
9:07P — Door closes.
9:10P — Lady talking in distance (sounds like maid's voice) It sounded as though she said "are there any more cops around". Heard no answer. (Not Recorded) End of conversation.
9:49P — Walking - door closes.
9:55P — Walking - other noises.
10:07P — Radio - stops playing.
10:25P — Door closes - walking - turns radio on - changes stations then turns it off.
10:40P — All quiet.
10:47P — Someone moving around. Doors open - close. More walking.
11:00P — Sound of someone's movements in house.

HODEL FILE - #?

Spool
Time

11:24P — Door slams - someone's movements in house - goes to bathroom-urinates.
11:45P — Walking in house - radio turned on.
11:55P — Minneapolis Symphony orchestra playing. Station KFAC.
12:30A — Door closes - radio still playing.
12:55A — Walking in house.
1:05A — Radio stops playing.
1:07A — Loud noises in desk - walking.
1:25A — Walking in house.
1:45A — All quiet.
1:49A — Walking in house.
1:50A — Brechel, LAPD on duty, relieves Crowley
45.5-49.00 | 2:15A — Loud noises. Hodel talking to maid. Hodel-"I never found your keys. Have you looked for them?" Maid, "Yes".
Off | 2:20A — Hodel at desk going thru papers, cusses, to himself. Sorting of papers in desk.
2:30A — Still sorting papers. Closes drawer. Opens other drawer. Searching for something in desk.
2:35A — Hodel goes to lavatory. Urinates.
2:40A — Hodel in bedroom with someone, probably Ellen. Hodel - "No use working hard". Other whispered conversati unable to make out. Hodel goes in bathroom - runs water.
2:45A — Conversation with Ellen.
49.00-51.25 | 2:45A — Whispered conversation - recorded. Loud noises. Unable to make out conversation.

HODEL FILE - 28
FEBRUARY 21, 1950

Spool
Time

51.25-54.00	2:55A	Noises at desk. Hodel speaking, unable to make out due to pounding noise.
	3:10A	Sounds of numerous drawers opening and closing in different parts of the house.
	3:25A	Sounds of walking about the house.
	3:30A	Movements in house cease.
	3:45A	Alls quiet. Snoring (Hodel in bedroom)
	4:50A	Snoring ceases - alls quiet.
	5:00A	Some disconnected noises. Hodel tossing in bed or reading.
	5:45A	Hodel yawns and resumes snoring.
	6:05A	Snoring ceases - alls quiet.
	6:45A	Snoring resumes.

HODEL FILE - 28
FEBRUARY 21, 1950, 8:00 AM

J. McGrath, D.A.'s offic
on duty

Spool
Time

49-50	10:55A	Telephone rang - answered by Hodel - said "Hello" then began to walk around and make a lot of noise.
50-55	11:00A	Conversation - sounds like Ellen arguing - unable to hear while recorder on.
	11:10A	Changing wire - doubt if conversation was recorded.
	11:10A	No conversation - just loud noise in house.
SPOOL 9		Started 11:15 AM
	11:20A	Conversation between Hodel and Ellen - unable to understand - not recording - can't tell if recorder is working.
	11:30A	Conversation - Hdel and Ellen.
0-4	11:30A	Telephone answered by Hodel - gave directions to other part Attempting to rent room
4-7	11:40A	Telephone - answered by Hodel - unable to identify other party.
	11:50A	Telephone conversation - garbled.
7-9½	11:50A	Sullivan - D.A.'s office on duty
	12:00noon	Hear Hodel muttering to himself.
9½-10	12:15P	Testing by Nebio Crime Lab.
10-11½	12:50P	Conversation with Ellen - unintelligible - "I like potatous".
	12:55P	Moving around - noises
	1:00P	Bad hum in set - Ellen talking but unintelligible.
10½-19		Words between Dr. and said, "I would call American Counsel if I had money. Discussing her citizenship problems. Mal doing considerable talking - unintelligible.

MODEL FILE - 2?

Spool Time

	1:10P	Typewriter operating.
19-22	1:15P	Conversation by maid - much noise.
to	1:20P	Conversation by maid with Hodel.
22½	1:30P	Noises in room - considerable hum on receiver.
24½-26	1:31P	Conversation between Hodel and Maid - regarding Mexico.
	1:40P	Sounds like water running for past 4 or 5 minutes. Can hear Hodel's voice in background but unintelligible.
	1:55P	Hodel muttering, and water running.
	2:20P	Typewriter.
26-33	2:21P	Phone - Doctor answers - talks about architecture - talking about selling house.
33-35	2:25P	Typing
	2:55P	Conversation between Hodel and Maid. Complaining of havin to do housework.
	3:05P	Typing.
	3:15P	Typing continues.
	3:30P	Hear maid talking in background - hum in set continues.
35-38	3:35P	Hodel and maid talking. Unintelligible due to hum.
38-39	3:38P	Conversation with maid (Recorded).
		Ended recording - nothing being said.
39-40	3:40P	Hodel and maid talking.
	3:48P	Typing
	4:00P	Crime lab boys here - working on hum.
	4:00P	Hronek - L.A.'s office relieving Sullivan

SPOOL 9

| | 4:20P | L.A.P.D. lab men left. |

MODEL FILE - ?

SPOOL TIME

0-4	4:36P	Phone rang - Hodel answers (Patient)
	4:40P	Starts typing again.
4-16	4:44P	Phone rang - Hodel answers.
	4:55P	Starts typing again.
	5:32P	Typing stopped
	5:45P	Typing resumed
	6:15P	Typing stopped - Hodel moving around in the background.
	8:00P	Lewis (LAPD) relieving Hronek (Spool time 16)
	8:17P	Phone rang twice - no one answered.
	8:50P	Radio playing - station KFAC
	9:30P	Radio - still playing - classical music.
	10:45P	Radio off
16-22	10:47P	Maid on phone wants to talk to American Counsel in Mexico. Gave OL phone (Recorded)
	11:10P	Someone went toilet - No further talking on phone. Call never completed.
	11:15P	Radio started playing.
	12:10A	Radio turned off.
	12:35A	Someone walking about house.
	12:50A	Heard Hodel voice first time tonite - "Said leave that on".
	1:15A	A lady gave big "Ho-Hum" also lots of noise like slaming drawers and prying lids off of Wooden boxes. Also sawing.
	1:45A	Hodel told Maid she had better go to bed.

5 minutes - wire used - 2 PM end watch for Lewis

489

HODEL FILE -
FEBRUARY 22, 1950

Spool
Time

Spool	Time	Description
	2:00A	
	2:10A	Brochel, LAPD on duty. Hodel and Ellen enter room.
	2:12A	Hodel - "Will you leave that light on there, I'm just a little nervous". Hodel- "I suppose its asking a little too much". Conversation with Ellen recorded.
22-40		Hodel - "What that you got there". Whistling. Hodel- "Thats a lot of nonsense". Ellen talks back. Water running. Hodel has conversation with Ellen - asks if something is too difficult. Hodel says he is worried. Hodel - "You don't need this rasor". Ellen - "Maybe you better leave it".
	2:20A	Conversation regarding cutting garment and sending it to laundry. Recorded.
	2:23A 2:24A	Hodel asks if red coat is still at cleaners. Ellen thinks she sees it (apparently both are searching a closet). Conversation recorded.
	2:25A	Hodel is asking Ellen if she can stitch. Ellen replies she knows well enough. Ellen admires a chinese box. Hodel says a manchurian princess gave it to him. He says he is going to sell it. Ellen asks for taste.
Off	2:27A	
	2:29A	Ellen wants to stay with him, he tells her to go to bed, she can stay with him tomorrow.
	2:32A	Movements around room. Low conversation unable to make out
	2:35A	Deep breathing. Hodel and Ellen probably having intercourse.

HODEL FILE -
FEBRUARY 22, 1950

Spool
Time

Spool	Time	Description
40-43	2:40A	Ellen says she wants to go now. Hodel says she should have gone to her room. He is pretty well tired. Sounds indicates movements on bed.
off		
43-49.5	2:45A	Deep breathing. Movements on bed. Definite sounds of climax of intercourse. Hodel sighs loudly and passionately.
	2:49A	Hodel and Ellen talking. Ellen wants him to stay with her all night. She begs him. He says no, he is tired.
Off	2:51A	Alls quiet.
	3:10A	Sounds of light snoring. Not Hodel.
	3:40A	Sounds indicate someone moving about.
	3:45A	Alls quiet.
49.5 to 51.5	7:55A	Phone is dialed. Hodel does not speak, but a female voice on phone is not distinct (recorded). This may be Ellen using Kitchen phone as Hodel not up yet.
off	8:10A	Hodel arises, goes to lavatory.
	8:00A	J. McGrath - D.A.'s office on duty.
	8:33A	Phone rings - Hodel answers - told someone to write to Consumers Research, Washington New Jersey, Hung up.
51.5-53.5	8:35A	Conversation with Ellen - could not understand (recorded)
	9:08A	Very heavy breathing or gasping by Hodel as if a nervous dream. About 6 times.
53.5-56	9:55A	Phone rang - Hodel answered - recorded. Said will borrow some money and send you $10.00. Said he would try to come down and get the fish.

HODEL FILE - 26
FEBRUARY 22, 1950
SPOOL 10

Spool	Time	
	10:30A	Put on Spool #10
0-10.8	10:47A	Phone call - Hodel answered - recorded - Hodel did little talking - just kept stating, "Uh-huh" "Uh-huh" Did you see Dr. Burns since I've see you. Does he feel I'm interfering? hope he does not resent - talking to Theodore - said when reports comes at 1 PM today or tomorrow will contact you - When we won't be disturbed.
	11:00A	Hodel urinated - took shower.
	11:23A	Hodel typing.
	11:50A	Hodel said "Let's see the phone is CR 5527 or 5537 Ellen phoned and said, are you open tonight. "Oh after 6" Then Hodel said to Ellen you go tomorrow night, at 9 PM.
	12:00noon	Morgan on duty.
	12:10P	Unintelligible conversation between two men (Hodel and ?- 2 minutes).
	12:21P	Hodel - "There must be something" Ellen - "There isn't anything" Hodel - "I'm pretty sure there is something". Recorded.
	12:26P	Hodel - "Straighten up that room in there - just the way it was before".
10.8-14.6	12:35P	Telephone rang - Hodel - "Oh yeah Power - are you in town - good - things are sort of busy right now for the next ten days - we're tapped now again - well there is pretty much going on regarding yourself and me - I was questioned about you and so forth - maybe you can find out - Don't you know

HODEL FILE - 27
FEBRUARY 22, 1950

Spool	Time	
	12:35P	someone up there? Maybe you can find out what the hell is going on up there. I would like to see you in person when we get a chance - what's your phone? That's your new phone? (Ends) "OK - so long".
14.6-16.8	12:58P	Telephone rang - Hodel - "Hello, yeah, yeah, yeah". Pause - "yeah, yeah, that's the only thing to tell em - don't say a single thing - who was it? - Sullivan? be polite, be very nice but say you can't tell em a thing without your lawyer's advice. O.K.".
16.8-17		Blank.
17-18.5	1:10P	Conversation between Hodel and Ellen (unintelligible) Noise - airplane noise.
18.5-19.5	1:36P	Conversation between Hodel and Ellen (partly unintelligible Hodel in bathroom - running water.
19.5-24	2:00P 2:32P	Telephone rang - Hodel - conversation about sales "what sort of a place did you find? In Santa Monica? Conversation about $1320. "I already sent him a letter - see you maybe over the week end" (Ends "O.D. Dad")
24-25	2:54P	Telephone rang - Hodel - I can't call you back? Can you call me from an outside phone? Call you back where you are now in about ten minutes.
	4:00P	only sound is from radio playing, station KFAC. Not recorded. BROWNSON on duty, 4:00 PM Occasional sound of a person moving about the room.

491

HODEL FILE - 28

FEBRUARY 22, 1950

Spool	Time	
25	8:00P	Lewis on duty - radio playing
25-27.5	9:00P	Hodel come in room - talks to maid "Low" She wants to know what happened - he did not answer. Radio still playing (Recorded)
27.5-30.6	9:24P	Phone rang - maid answered - said Chris is here. (Recorded) No word yet. "Could not hear someone whistling. Radio real loud. Could not make out what else was said.
30.6-35.8	9:40P	Phone rings 3 times - maid said call half hour - no more talking - someone in toilet - flush same. Some one walking heavy and fast - radio - still playing.
35.8-37.5	10:10P	Phone rang - maid answers. (Recorded) What was said - but could not make it out as radio still very loud.
	10:34P	Hodel yelled - is that door locked. Maid answered, "No do you want to come in" Maid said, "Why did you want to know" (No answer)
	11:28P	Radio turned off - everything quiet.
	1:45A	Hodel walk about house-finally goes to toilet - after using toilet he flushes it, then walks about house again. Slams a door and is talking real low to himself (unable to understand him)
	2:00A	Lewis - end of watch.

Brechel, LAPD, on duty

	2:00A	Hodel walking about the bedroom.
	2:30A	Hodel asleep. Snoring. Alls quiet.

HODEL FILE -

FEBRUARY 23, 1950

SPOOL #10

Spool	Time	
	8:00A	Jim McGrath-D.A.'s Office on duty
	8:55A	Phone ringing - Hodel snoring. Hodel did not wake up to answer - still snoring.
	9:07A	Someone (sounds like womans footsteps) enters room (probably living room).
	9:35A	Phone rang - no answer.
	10:10A	Phone ringing - 8 times - no answer.
	10:12A	Someone walking around - sounds like Hodel - conversation between Hodel and Ellen about going to store. Not recorded.
37-40	10:23A	Conversation with someone by Hodel. Phone did not ring, and he didn't dial, but sounded like phone conversation. (Recorded) Said she is my maid - you know she is peculiar - talked like he was asking for medical help.
40-41	10:27A	(Recorded) Hodel talking - it appears to Telephone Co. complaining about maid making long distance phone calls.
41-44	10:28A	Recorded. Hodel phoned someone asked for $1000.00 cash advance - said he was short of ready cash.
44-44.5	10:35A	Dialed phone - asked for a number - sounded like Insurance #451651.
44.5-48.5	10:41A	Telephone rings - said, "How are you Miss Montgomery - talk about getting a house. Read note he said he found on his desk. Said he will call tomorrow.

HODEL FILE -

Spool Time		
SPOOL #11		
48.5-57	10:47A	Phone rings - answered by Hodel - asks about a letter - talk about architecture - says he has been selling some antiques - says he will send some money.
SPOOL #11		
0-2	11:05A	Conversation with Ellen - says, "I haven't any money." I will have to sell everything".
2-12	11:09A	Hodel and Ellen (recorded) in a conversation. Regarding Ellens phone calls to the Mexican Consulate. Hodel gave her hell - said to write letters instead of phoning - raised hell about the bills from the Phone Company - also xxixixxxx told her to never talk over the phone.
12-14	11:23A	(Recorded) Hodel phones someone (Neebs) Neebs not in.
14.5	11:27A	Phone rang - Hodel answered, said Yes, I'll be there at :
14.5-16	11:33A	Hodel and Ellen - talk regarding a form she received about a street car accident - told her to say she did not see anything - throw the form away. (Recorded)
	11:55A	Hodel typing.
	12:Noon	Snyder-Sullivan. D.A's office on duty.
	12:15P	Hodel still typing.
16-18	12:50P	Hodel calls Ellen (recorded) Unintelligible.
	12:52P	Quiet.
	12:55P	Typing.
18-23	1:00P	Phone rings - Hodel answers (recorded) tables and chairs to go - asks for address - expects to give someone money by Wednesday - selling tea.

HODEL FILE -

Spool Time		
	1:09P	End of telephone conversation.
23-24	1:10P	Talking to Ellen (recorded)
	1:11P	Hodel typing.
	1:20P	Phone rings - Hodel answers - short - wrong number.
	1:25P	Phone rings - apparently in remote part of house. Could barely hear it.
	1:30P	Hodel talks to Ellen - unintelligible - very few words.
	1:33P	Someone moving furniture around - hell of a racket - (P.S. not recorded)
24-25½	1:42P	Someone climbing down and up stairs. Hodel talks to someone (Recorded)
25½-27	1:45P	Order a suit of blue - talk by a Charlie China type 5121 - conversation by Hodel (recorded) Delivery in about a week.
27-28	1:48P	Hodel calls Department of Commerce - calls information.
	1:50P	Hodel calls on phone (recorded) Will be out 5 or 6 PM (Recorded)
	1:52P	Hodel dials phone - calls Mr. Neeb - wants to go to office Will not be able to this week (not recorded)
28-32	1:55P	Hodel dials phone - Department of Commerce (recorded) in regards selling car in Mexico.
32-33	2:05P	Hodel dials phone - car to Mexico City - talks to F.B.I. (recorded)
33-35½	2:07P	Hodel dials phone - in regards purchase of Packard car (recorded) (P.S.-he wants to go to Mexico City) No 2-7464.
35½-37	2:12P	Phone rings - Hodel answers - in regards Packard car. (recorded)

493

HODEL FILE -

Spool Time

37-49 2:15P   Phone rings - Hodel answers - Hodel dials phone - talking to "Dear" (Recorded) Want to meet at 4 PM., at Holly and Sycamore - Garden Grove Apts.

49-52 2:30P   Hodel talks to Ellen - in Regards Ellens citizenship. (recorded).

SPOOL #12

0-1 2:40P   Conversation Hodel and maid (recorded) Money for maid. "I don't want any".

  2:50P   Water running - conversation in background.

  3:00P   Plane passes over.

1-1½ 3:05P   Phone rings - Hodel answers "I will call you back on the other phone (recorded)

1½-4½ 3:06P   Dials phone - "Is Dr. Hussey there". (recorded) "Are you holding some lot reports for me?"

4½-7½ 3:10P   Quiet.

  3:11P   Hodel talking - "What's happened" (Recorded)

  3:12P   Phone rings - no one answers phone. Hodel still talking. "Have you got some sheets and blankets?"

  3:25P   Quiet for past 10 minutes.

  4:00P   All quiet on the Hodel front.

  4:35P   Someone walking around.

  5:15P   Movement around including walking.

  5:18P   Jemison on Duty, D.A.'s office.

    All quiet.

  6:40P   Hronek, D.A.'s office on duty

  6:45P   Hear movements, footsteps in the house.

  7:35P   Radio on, very loud.

HODEL FILE -

Spool Time

26-28.5 10:36P   Someone knock - Hodel said, come in - some man entered unable to understand conversation.

28.5-59.5 10:44P   Hodel and some man sounds like talking about going fishing or about pictures of fish - lot of noise. Talking about fastest bird - animal and fish and has fast they are.

Hodel - "Were going to try to get the big house out here. skid-row - Pasadena - case of Bowron - Bug out - don't stay forever. Don't know - Well "Town" - Police Department My moving from house - 3 very large bedrooms - There are twelve bedrooms. Pasadena - Santa Monica - (Talking about houses) 25,000 - 30,000. The grounds are kind of deteriorated. I have to use the car.

  11:30P   Radio playing.

  12:05A   Walking-noises at desk.

  12:35A   Typing - radio playing.

  12:45A   Hodel and maid speak a few words - cannot understand.

  1:02A   Radio turned down. (Volume)

  1:15A   Walking - Hodel and Ellen in conversation (distance)

  1:25A   Walking

  1:45A   Hodel and Ellen talking (unable to hear) Something about a model.

  1:51A   Typing.

HODEL FILE -

SPOOL #13

Spool Time		
0-1.5	1:55A	Lewis, LAPD on duty.
	2:15A	Hodel and maid talking. Hodel asked, "Did you look in the little box in there.
	2:20A	Hodel using typewriter - radio playing.
1.5-3 wire broke	2:25A	Phone rang - Hodel -"Yes Dear, How are you, what trouble Tell me all about it. I can't understand it. I guess the finishes it, impossible, see you later".
new wire	2:30A	Hodel says to Maid - You going to bed dear. Hodel now typing.

SPOOL #14

0-1	2:50A	Hodel to maid, "Come on - you better go to bed". Hodel still typing.
	2:55A	Hodel - "You had better go bed now." Maid said, "OK" Hodel said, "Good night sweet". Everything quiet. No more typing.
	3:10A	Door opened - Hodel says "Aren't you going to bed for Chri sake - Hodel yells "O Mamale Now quiet again.
	3:45A	Hodel snoring.
	6:00A	Everything still quiet.

HODEL FILE - 37

FEBRUARY 24, 1950

SPOOL #14

Spool Time		
17-19	1:20P	Sullivan, D.A.'s office on duty Dials phone (recorded) asks for a new car salesman. What is that car for $1587.00 - How much more with seats in back - $75.00. I've got a 1936 Packard Sedan to trade in. Want to make Packard down payment No chance - Will see you Mr. Shingleton.
	1:25P	Talking to maid - having lunch - maid talks about fi Hodel asks for lemons.
19-20	1:30P	Phone rings - Hodel answers (recorded) "I'll be ther in 15 minutes. Let me come anyway".
	1:31P	Phone rings. Hodel answers (No conversation)
	1:34P	Talks to maid "I got to leave right away".
	1:46P	Phone rings - maid answers - Hodel tells her to tell party he just left.
	1:55P	Phone rings - maid answers - "He will be back in abou 1½ hours".
20-24	2:35P	Someone enters - sounds like maid - answered phone - unable to hear conversation.
	2:38P	Ellen dialed information - asked for number of immigration office - dialed phone - asked to speak to Mr. P------ Apparently out - asked person on phone to have him call her back on NO 27454.

HODEL FILE - 38

Spool	Time	
	3:15P	Quiet.
	3:25P	Phone rings once - answered apparently in some other part of house.
	3:40P	Phone rings several times - hear no answer.
	3:41P	Phone rings several times - hear no answer.
	3:50P	Phone rings twice - hear no answer.
24-28½	3:55P	Hodel and maid talking - (Recorded). About her citizenship.

Hronek, D.A.'s office on duty

	4:00P	
28½-30½	4:02P	NU 9077 - Hodel dials over - Is Marian there. Hello dear.
31-34	4:05P	Tries to dial - phone rings - Hodel answered
34-35½	4:07P	Phone rings - Hodel answered. I'd love to have you when it'll be - around 9 or 10? Operator AT 66402
35½-36½		This is CL 3476.
	4:11P	Hello, Mrs. Clark?
	4:20P	Hodel starts typing.
36½-51½	4:25P	Phone rings - Hodel answered - Ellen took over - still talking about the citizenship, Ellen, didn't I tell you not to tell people things over the telephone. Hodel ordered Ellen not to answer any questions over the telephone - Hodel calls MO 27464. Ellen argues with Hodel that lots of people cross the border without papers. Hodel orders the maid not to let anybody in the office. Then starts typing again. Ellen said something about the FBI investigating us.

HODEL FILE # 39

Spool	Time	
	4:44P	Hodel dials xxx out to some Mr. Blumfield.
	4:50P	Start Spool #15
	4:50P	Typing
	6:14P	Phone rings, stops before Hodel lifts the receiver.
0-1	6:26P	Hodel dials - asks for Lynn report.
1-2½	6:28P	Hodel - Hello Margaret - are you with the patient. I would like for you to stop by - Maybe next week.
2½-8½	6:32P	Hodel dials - What's the number of Boims & Cutie 7100 Beverly Blvd? Talks about car. What's your name? Anderson - That's easy to remember.
	7:10P	Hear Hodel moving around the house.
	8:00P	**Meyer, L.A.P.D. on duty**
8½-9½	8:58P	Phone rings. Ellen answers - unable to understand wh or what she says.
9½-31	10:18P	Some girl introduced Hodel to some girl named Mickey talking unable to understand, said something about China tea, two drinks, another man around.
	10:28P	Phone rings - Hodel answers - couldn't understand too well. Come over tomorrow - call before you come after supper some time - have a pencil handy. OL 3476. Good - so am I - will you do that? I will try to keep tomorrow open. (Hangs up) Hodel talks- She graduated from school in Detroit with top honors- what did I have for desert?
	10:35P	Phone rings - Hodel answers - Yes, Why? I would say just forget it all - put some Hillbilly music on - left room, radio on.

SPOOL #15

Spool Time		
31-32½	10:45P	Taling about records - put more records on.
32½-33¼	10:49P	Phone rings - Hodel answers - yes, sure, absolutely. I don't really care - just forget the whole thing.
33½-34.2	10:51P	Talk about records again. Put more on.
34½-35	10:55P	Talk about records again. Put more on.
35-36½	11:04P	Girls talking - I only had a glass of tea.
36½-41	11:06P	Girls talking - Hodel talking to girls - lot of noise - radio on loud.
41-42	11:11P	Talking - Radio on too loud - can't hear.
42-44½	11:22P	Hodel asks girls if want fire on - turns fire on - girl asks, haven't heard anything further, have you? Someone typing.
44½-45	11:31P	Hodel - reaching for something? Radios on very loud.
45-50	11:40P	Hodel - come here a second. Hear opening desk. Othe girl enters. Girl-"Is this a private conversation? Hodel-"Boy, it is a juicy conversation, what do you want to know". Girl-"I like to be exposed gradually" Hodel-"How many did you have"? Girl-"52"
	11:51P	Spool ran out on 56. Meyer changed spool - just small talk. couldn't hear too well.

SPOOL #16

1-10	11:57P	Hodel and girl talking - unable to understand. Radio is all can hear.

HODEL FILE - 41

Spool Time		
10-11	12:08A	That is Shirley's work.
11-21½	12:10A	Hodel-"Did you ever hear this record?" Played recor sounded like home made, something about humanity??? Played some records of poems. Hodel had recorded.
21½-22½	12:22A	Hodel and girl talking about poems, one girl starts reading poems. Hodel says she is pretty good. Then Hodel reads a poem.
	12:30A	Still reading poems. Hodel and girl. talking about poems as read to each other.
22½-27	12:39A	Still talking about poems - one girl says she read better then Hodel. One girl read them finish
27-32	1245A	Hodel said "Yes - H - Chrisy" then Hodel said, "I can read better setting by a beauty - noise - then Hodel reads poem.
32-32½	12:51A	Talk about poem he just read, reads some more.
32½-47½	12:58A	Hodel finishes. Girl says - "It is a morbid poem," talk about poem. Hodel says - "you read next one". Talk about records. Hodel says he has some. Girl says "go get them" Sounds like someone leaving. Talk about some congetting a divorce. Starts reading again. Hodel - "I own 51% of the stock - talking about Asia - more small talk - played Chinese soundir music.

40

41

HODEL FILE - 42
FEBRUARY 25, 1950
Spool
Time

47½-48½	1:16A	Talking about records - play some - sounds like a cat fight - or a bunch of wash tubs.
48½-50	1:19A	Hodel says something about a sweater looking nice. More music - unable to hear talk.
50-56	1:24A	Talk about "Carrey Grey"? Hodel says, "who is that?" Bath room and radio on at same time - music - so changed spool - then talk about music.

FEBRUARY 25, 1950
SPOOL 17

0-27	1:36A	Talking about some place ideal - people from 48 stat come - a wonderful opportunity - Santa Barbara one ti I waited two years (Hard to hear them) some other man talking - "I was guest artist one time". Girl - "you can't worry about that". Talking about China - Man - "married 4 months. That was enough". Hodel comes back in - talk about drawing. Hodel says for a beginner is pretty darn good.
27-39	2:00A	Lewis, L.A.P.D. on duty Big party going on - several girls and men talking. Hard to understand but being recorded. Some girl sa "Good night Jerry". Party seems to be breaking up as everyone is saying Goodnight.
	2:12A	Everything quiet - outside of one person walking about room.
39-62	2:14A	Hodel and another man talking about a girl - use to be attorney for Barba Sherman. She is wonderful dancer - she married a Swiss Counselor. Hodel talki about taking girls to South America 3 months - they be ready for singing - light opera. I have a way ab

HODEL FILE - 43
Spool
Time

me. I can arrange ti with there folks. I have so many girls I like to have a rest for awhile. Seem as though Hodel and this other man are talking about Traveling with these girls. Hodel said he like to see parent of each girl and get permission in writing from them to allow girls to travel. Made arrangemen to meet again Sunda, and talk further on agreements. Would like to give it a trial in Mexico City. If you have girls over Sunday have them bring photograph of themselves. Talking about they could stay in best hotels and make at least 2500 per week. Hodel- "hard job is talking to parents". Hodel says - I will be the tough guy and you be the great guy. Hodel says - I will have arias. They laugh and Hodel says- let's go to bed. They leave room and everythings qui Hodel snoring "And loud".

End Spool 17
2:35A

SPOOL #18

	3:30A	
	6:20A	Someone up - walking about house. go into bathroom and use toilet - then flush same. Then sound like knocking on a door. Person is Mr. Hodel. Identifie by his cough.
	6:30A	Everything quiet.
0-5	6:50A	Hodel knocks on Ellen's door - ask "are you up". She answers "You want in?" He states, "No, I won't start nothing now - how about 12 o'clock. Huh?" (part talk recorded)

HODEL FILE - 44

Spool Time

0.5	7:40A	Dog barking as if it had someone cornered.
	8:00A	Lewis, L.A.P.D. off duty
	8:00A	J.McGrath, D.A.'s office on duty
	10:17A	Noise around house - sounded as though someone made a phone call from rear of house. Hodel is up.
	10:28A	Hodel made phone call - asked for "Andy Anderson".
	10:40A	Some man said to Hodel - "Andy Anderson called you". Hodel said to this man - "Tell him I'll call him back
0.5-1	10:42A	Hodel phoned Andy Anderson (recorded) about a car deal of some kind. Hodel said, "Oh no, just send me back my check and I will start fresh".
1-2	11:24A	Hodel phoned (recorded) someone asked if Dr. Bussey there. Gave phone, OL 3476, to call back.
2-4	11:27A	Hodel made phone call - asked for the Simmons Co. Wrong number - said, is this (something) 7778.
	11:28A	Made another call - no answer.
	11:45A	Sullivan, D.A.'s office on duty
	1:20P	Phone rings - unable to hear conversation. Can hear talking in background.
	1:30P	Phone rings 4 times - hear no conversation. Can hear some men talking in background.
	1:48P	Phone rings - sounds muffled - rang one - record no conversation.
	2:00P	Someone walking around. Maybe Hodel.
	3:20P	Phone rings 4 times - No answer.
	4:00P	Bronek, D.A.'s office - on duty

44

HODEL FILE - 45

Spool Time

	4:30P	No movements
	5:00P	No movements
	5:30P	No movements
	6:00P	No movements
	6:19P	Phone rings 7 times. No answer.
	6:30P	No movements
	7:00P	No movements
	7:01P	Phone rang 10 times - no answer
	7:17P	Phone rang 10 times - no answer
	7:30P	No movements
	7:51P	Phone rang 9 times - no answer
	8:00P	No movements
	8:00 PM	All Quiet Meyer, L.A.P.D. on duty
	8:22P	Phone rings 6 times - no answer
	9:00P	All Quiet
	9:17P	Sounds like Hodel and someone returns home. Hodel says he has a lot of work to do - moving around.
6-11½	9:20P	Hodel and woman talking and moving - woman talking about a skirt - Hodel says, leave it here Girl - "Have to use bath room - (and she did to)
11½-13	9:35P	Hodel and Ellen talking quite low - unable to understand sounds as though Ellen is crying.
13-13½	9:47P	Phone rings - Hodel answers - will try to make it over later - it will be a latish party wont it? Will look at it from a distance, yes, later. Good bye - then Hodel dials phone, but no answer.
	10:05P	All quiet - sounds as though Hodel is reading or going over papers of some kind.

45

HODEL FILE - 46

Spool
Time

13½-14½ 10:10P — Hodel dials phone - Hello, I just got back to town, hate to bother you so late, do you have report for me? 224, yes, yes, thank you very much. Hodel then uses typewriter.

10:30P — Hodel moving around house.

11:09P — Hodel moving around house.

11:15P — Ellen turns radio on. Hodel asks, can't you do any better than that? Quiet ----

11:30P — Hodel dials phone - no answer - uses typewriter.

11:35P — Hodel turns radio up not too loud - Are you tired. Ellen-"no" Hodel sounded as though he said he was going to start packing.

FEB. 26, 1950

14½-20 12:01A — Phone rings, Hodel answers - Yes, Harry, how is par asks about party, says he had people over - asks if one o'clock is too late - talks to "Baby Doll" about party. says he will be over. Hodel tells Ellen he is going out to stay up and leave Coline (See news article in Times 2-27-50, page 13, Part I) in. I want to talk to him, will be back in an hour or so. Oh hell, they are all "baby dolls" to me. Uses typewriter again.

12:13A — Hodel -"Leave Coline in tell him to wait here for me Goes out.

20-21 1:00A — Phone rings - Ellen answers - he isn't here now. Call back in 1½ hrs. will be here in morning.

1:30A — All quiet.

LEWIS ON DUTY, L.A.P.D.

HODEL FILE - 47

Spool
Time

21-22 2:00A — Phone rang - maid answered, said Mr. Coline is not in. Repeated 3 times. I don't know (sound as if she was talking to Mr. Hodel) "As he had told her he was expecting Mr. Coline when he left house.

22+23.5 2:40A — Talking by Hodel and maid - Hodel says, I am very ti I am going to sleep, and you had better go to bed to. No: No, I am very tired, I am going to sleep.

2:45A — Radio is now playing soft music.

3:26A — Radio - turned off. Everything quiet.

4:00A — Hodel sleeping and snoring.

6:45A — Still quiet - no sounds.

7:45A — Lewis off duty
Lt. H. Dreebin - P.A.'s office on duty.

23+5 8:30A — Hodel snoring very loudly - no other movements.

9:40A — Hodel moving around - seems to be awake.

10:00A — no movements

23.5-24 10:40A — Telephone rings - awakened Hodel - said "I'll call you back". Answered by grunting - also "Yes, I'll be there".

24-25 11:35A — Telephone - answering "Yes, yes", Mentioned "Carlos" said "I'll get it" apparently went back to sleep.

12:00noon — Dreebin off duty.

MODEL FILE - 48

12:00 noon — Cuncino, D.A.'s office on duty

12:15P — Hodel coughed loudly - turned radio on to concert program - New York Symphony orchestra. KMX

25-37½ 12:30P — Toilet flushes. Water faucet is turned on. Concert music makes Hodel's movements difficult to discern. Sounds like he's shaving now. Completes toilet at approx. 12:40.

12:45P — Girl enters. Hodel calls her "Helen, of "Ellen" and asks her to take (something) out of the room. She returns. Conversation concerns the music (Beethoven's) Hodel asks for more tea.

1:00P — Phone rings - Ellen tells Hodel it is Dr. C----- calling. Hodel answers "Yes. Right About what time I'll see you there. Right. Good bye".

1:30P — Hodel dials phone number - gets busy signal. Turns radio off.

2:05P — Hodel dials number - gets busy signal. Conversation Hodel asks girl whether she likes the smell. Girl replies "No". Sounds like he's reading newspap(er)

2:45P — Hodel dials - gets Miss Montgomery Tells her the xx artist is moving out by end of Mardi. (Recorded) Ends conversation with series of yesses. Olympic 3476 is an unlisted number he gave Miss Montgomery. ended 2:40P

2:45P — Is apparently talking to maid. Difficult to understand conversation. Tells her to count his woolen sox.

MODEL FILE # 49

Spool Time

3:00P — Seems to be working in a room alone. Mumbles to himself. Sounds of running water, glasses tinkling, small motor is turned on and off at intervals. Off at 4 PM.

1 4:00PM — Hronek, D.A.'s office on duty
87½   Hodel moving around the house.

4:12P — Hodel taking a bath, splashing and humming to himself.

4:30P — Movements around the house.

5:00P — Movements around the house and starts typing.

37½-40 5:26P — Hodel dials the post office - wants to know if there is a letter pickup today at Hwd. & Western Post offi(ce) Hodel instructed Ellen to take it out (the letter) and moving around.

40-42 5:53P — Ellen returns - tells Hodel mail goes out-one at 6:30, one at 9:30. (recorded) Sends her to Wilcox Post Office

42-43 6:52P — Hodel dials Operator, asks for SU 33419 - This is OL 3476. Is Harry there. Call NO 27454.

7:00P — Hodel moving around the house.

43-44 7:26P — Ellen answered - Hodel apologized for being rude and told her he is expecting some important people 7:30 or 8:00 PM - now let's have some dinner.

44-46½ 7:40P — Phone rings - Hodel answers - recorded.

46½-47 7:55P — Phone rings - Hodel answers - "Yea, I'll be right out Hodel returns.

8:10P — HRONEK OFF DUTY

501

HODEL FILE - 50

8:00P Crowley, LAPD, on duty

8:12P Maid says "hear are the matches".

Maid, "Isn't that away—How miserable I was".

8:20P Hodel answers - unable to hear, Maid "Did you have a good lunch". Hodel-"Tried eggs, and ---- These are check slips.

47-60 8:23P Hodel talking to some man. Man "I made six programs you can try out. Talking about germicides and quantities grams 10/1000 etc. Hodel-"what is the effect of 1/10000? Let's go ahead and run our tests Man-"it will take about 50 days to do that". Hodel-"Organic material that a small percentage of the people are allergic to" Man-"we won't mention that" Hodel-"And these are used for restaurant sanitation? Man-"no as for couches, clothing, etc." Hodel-"Well, how do I get it. How much per lb is------". Man-"35¢ per lb. I think it is-/----". Hodel-And the other detergent than you use?"

Man-(unable to hear) (recorded)

8:35P End of Spool #18 during conversation.

8:3?P Unable to get much of conversation except talking about detergents. Hode. is very much interested and getting the names of all the manufacturers. Hodel-"what are these detergents normally used for". Man-washing, car shampoes? Hodel-"Is there any dang of them conflicting with the other barbitrates?" Lady-"I could take a bath". Man-"what are you so interested in taking a bath for? "Hodel-would you like a drink? Man-no thanks.

HODEL FILE - 51

8:44P Hodel-"Let's build a fire-I'll get some wood".

Leaves.

8:45P Installed Spool #19

8:45P Man-"Do you want the first". Hodel-"You don't know of any othe possibilities or the key answers??

SPOOL #19

0-60 8:50P Hodel-of course you get much more lasting effects from the bath. (Something about 27¢ lb detergent wholesale) Man-but when you take a mixture like "made" which is a mixture of ----, and cost per lb of the ingredients. Man-when you consider the millions of packages they sell it not too much. (apparently the man is a chemist who has been doing and syndiatics research work in detergents/for Hodel.)

Man-most of the perfume they have in this stuff is—
Lady-what was that dish with mushrooms in it—
It was on the Blvd. and it wasn't very far. Hodel-
I don't remember". Lady-if he didn't have legal representation, he wouldn't even be a Doctor.

16 9:05P Hodel-I don't think I have to worry anyway, at least not this year". Lady-"It's necessary to protect your "Career" Hodel-in other words----? Lady----
Hodel-"Any felony periods. Lady-bookmaking doesn't count? Lady-How about moral turpitude. Hodel-something about medical profession. Something about tea. Lady-George, you know how I talk to Joe and you weren't home Saturday. I said to Joe, your

MODEL FILE - 52

24

friend in the "booby hatch" He said she not so bad.

I said, how do you know. Lady-you don't go to
Camarillos unless your dangerous to others. Model-
or yourself. (Something about alcoholics) Lady-
Oh goody---I'm going to get a bath after all. I smell
awfully now.

9:15P   Lady-we should have brought towels along.
9:20P   Water running in bathroom, and lady says something
        about bath tub.

9:25P   Model-Thats almost as good as? in this tub. Lady-
        I'll take a bath in it. Man-no you won't.
        Lady-Why the only reason I came along was to take a bath.
        Man-you wouldn't want to take a bath in an
        experimental deal. Model-It might eat all your skin
        off. Lady-I wouldn't worry with a doctor around.
        Model-wisecracks. Model-a peculiar people, the
        Persians, the country produces no virgins. They xxxx
        xxx fuck all day in a violent way, and at night
        they practice sexual perversion.

        Model-these walls are so thin.

9:30P   Water running in bathroom again. Model and man
9:33P   talking about the ingredients (evidently experimenti
        with soap in bathroom) Man-what I've seen in your
        bathtub and my bathtub----? mentions sodium sulpha

9:36P   xxxx Telephone rings. Model answers - I hope he do
        call because she discussay any information will be
        helpful to me. I'd appreciate any information today
        I have to make this decision immediately. Thanks
        Harry.

MODEL FILE - 53

53

9:40P   Model-do you want to give me the name of this
        domicide man. Man-Mr. Morrison.
9:45P   Model-your telephone. Man-OL 4373?
9:46P   End of Spool #19
9:47P   Lady talks about making reservations to go to
        Santa Barbara tomorrow.
9:50P   Model mentions something about murder.
9:51P   Model - place on the strip. Lady mentions Barbara
        and a Japanese place.
9:52P   Lady-Joe is very friendly toward her. I thought
        he'd be very unfriendly became----Model-Joe is a
        little"punchy" you know. How much does it cost to
        Santa Barbara. She'll get in about 6:00. Lady-
        It would be so much nicer to go by car , then we
        would go straight to Court house.

        Put on Spool #20

9:55P   All quiet - all leave for approx. 5 minutes.
0-3   10:00P   Conversation again with same lady and man. Something
3-38 10:05P   about having made call. Alimony for her. Lady-
        I don't want to get involved, I know the poor man wil
        have to pay the cleaning bill.
      10:09P   Telephone rings - (Hear no telephone conversation)
      10:15P   Talking about tea 40% or 50 lb. Model-the
        difference between green tea and black tea is----
      10:17P   Lady-If we go to Santa Barbara, are we going to see
        Usher? Model-He opened up in the county. He's a
        x xx - Model-something about probation.

503

HODEL FILE - 54
54

10:20P — Telephone rings twice. Hodel-hello, yes I'm home, just fine, Mr. Sheldon. Very good, anything new with you? I'll give you a ring next week. Have you bought a car yet? (Lady whispering something about Joe and Mexico) Hodel-I have some people here, I'll call you tomorrow. Hodel-She's subject to deportati..

10:25P — However, they'll never the fact about the papers. Hodel-I can't know where she'd go. Lady-Are you planning on leaving here by any chance. Lady-Did she ever mention it to Bob Adams. Lady-

ALL RE-COR-DED — ~~Historaxxxxxxxxxxxxxxixxxxxxxxxxxx~~ Did Bob say he would (continuous conversation. Able to pick up only bits) All recorded.

10:3GP — Talking about insuring something, value $76,000. If you want to sell it you would get $750.00 Trinkets. Hodel-Had it insured for $10,000. Alimony payments $300 month. Getting it reduced.

10:35P — Hodel-She looks sick - Lady-Why aren't you selling it, all over the country. Man-Says something "Could not hear" Lady-Well, you'd have to make up

38 — your mind if want to go. Will you pay 10.00 for a ? Hodel-I can get a car. Lady-Then, you dont have to worry.

10:38P

10:40P — Lady and man left house. (This lady seems to know an awfully lot about the legality of matters, possib of alimony) All of foregoing conversation,

10:44P — movements in house.

10:55P — Hodel typing.

HODEL FILE - 55
55

10:57P — Hodel arguing with Ellen - unable to understand. Hodel-I didn't think you'd want to talk to her in front of her husband. Ellen-I'm no more than a dishwasher to you. Hodel-I'm sorry. Noises in the distant part of house.

11:30P — Hodel-I'm adding Maid ?-----Hodel-a little later.

11:31P — Hodel-working at desk.

11:45P — Hodel-That's right. I don't car to ~~extraxtoxxx~~ discuss it any further with you. Take it up with the immigration. Maid talking (unable to hear)

11:55P — Hodel-Was anybody else there. What do you think of me. Hodel typing.

FEBRUARY 22, 1950

Spool
Time

12:00A — Door bell rings. Ellen goes to door. Hodel say - Co in. Turns radio on. Hodel-Did you have a pleasant time in Palm Springs. Unable to hear other parties answer. Radio loud. Mentions "Chicoski".

12:10A — Hodel - You made the headlines today or tomorrow.

38-40 12:10A — Man-I made the headlines?

12:11A — Hodel-like Hitler said.

40 12:11A — Hodel-your a rich man. Hodel-I can see you beating her up. Hodel - Don't bother me. You won't bother me. Man-?(Laughing) Suspicion. Nah. In one place I am a composer of poetry or opera, a hot tempered eurotic woman - leve got to get out of here and get ...

MODEL FILE - 56

Spool Time		
54-60	12:25A	Hodel-"Well anyway, she hasn't said she'd committed incest or killed the Black Dahlia. (other man has an accent - talking about this country) Man-"She said look what you've put in the paper. I hate you." Man-"I've been chased around so much." Hodel-"Whose your Doctor". Man-"On Vine Street. Hodel-"What was the date of your premarital ----- When was your treatment started? When are you going to see him next. End of Spool #20.
	12:30A	Something about 6 units. Hodel-you may be tapering off. Mentioned 4 units.

SPOOL #21

0-27	12:35A	Hodel-"It wouldn't do any harm to wait another month. There are other type of penicillin you are more apt to get the rash on the second---". Man-"She was Queen of Burbank. I'm warning you because I've known you 4 years" (cannot hear most of conversation).
10	12:45A	Hodel-Would she ride the girls and make them work? How do you spill it. Man-"LaCOX. I'll tell you the whole story. About a year ago ---- 4 dias-they live across from the Catholic church on Argyle. I he a group . also heard ... Hodel-Right now in Mexico they the value of the dollar in pesos. Secretarys work for ---- pesos.
20	12:50A	

MODEL FILE - 57

	12:50A	$500 will buy? pesos. Hodel-"You don't think that the girls try their ----- (Juvenile officers observed a 41 cream 4 door Buick parked in front of Hodel's residence at this time. license #7S1014 registered to Etoyle E. Bennett-Legal owner-Hollywood Citizen News).
	1:05A	Man-"A girl called named "Ceva" wanted to know about "Rence"/ (See Times article, page 13, 2-2-50) Hodel-"You and the girls do solo numbers to Man-"Acrobatic numbers, dances, etc.". Hodel-"Something about a streamlined pussy". Man-Those girls are French, they love to travel. I asked one girl and she said of course. Coleen or Colee. Hodel-"They are all unmarried, aren't they?" Man-"Yes". Hodel-"The legal matters are minor. They can get married at 18. I would merely be the backers represen tative. It would look better.
27-48	1:14A	Man-"This is a crucial time for both of us. I told "Renee" several times she is the center of all my hope Hodel-"Well really have to ride herd on them. 4 young chicks in a strange country. Man-"Ha - 4 girls and we two. - what a combination. I will be the musical director. Someone mentions Dr "Colee". Hodel-"I had a friend named Prince ----- who ---- Hodel-"I'm the only person who knows where all these
48	1:30A	things fit into the picture.
	1:32A	All quiet except for radio.
	1:35A	Hodel-"You better take a generous supply of penicilli (Talking to same party)

HODEL FILE - 58
FEBRUARY 27, 1950

48-52	1:45A	All quiet except for radio and someone moving around.
	1:57A	Typing;
		Frechel, LAPD on duty
	2:00A	Typing - radio playing - working at desk.
	4:05A	Turned off radio.
52-55	4:07A	Hodel tells Ellen to go to bed, she has to get up early as they have a lot of things to do, but he wants to sleep late. He tells about getting a lot of work done tonight. She says she won't sleep good.
off		She is nervous.
55-56.5	4:13A	He tells her, come on lets go to bed. They discuss turning on heater.
56.5-61.5	4:15A	Discuss having socks in morning. They talk of his having a cold. She is helping him to undress. She wants some love tonight, but he refuses her. He wants to sleep alone.
off	4:22A	Hodel tells Ellen not to argue with him while Dorothy is around. Tells her how to act in company of Dorothy as Ellen then goes to her room, she appears to be angry with Hodel because he sent her to her room without allowing to have any love.
	4:30A	Change spools - put #22 on. Hodel retires - alls quiet.

HODEL FILE - 59
SPOOL #22 - FEBRUARY 27, 1950

Spool	Time	
	8:00A	J. McGrath, D.A.'s office on duty
	9:03A	Phone rings 7 times, no answer. Hodel snoring.
	9:12A	Phone rings 8 times, no answer.
	9:15A	Ellen goes into Hodel's room, wakes him up.
	9:18A	Phone rings 3 times (if answered was in a rear room could not hear)
	11:12A	Phone rings, 12 times, Hodel finally answers but could not make out what was said.
	11:40A	Hodel at desk - typing.

FEBRUARY 27, 1950
12:00Noon Sullivan D.A.'s office on duty

0-2½	Next 12:10P	Hodel dials and then flushes toilet (recorded) but barely intelligible due to water running-talks about taxes.
2½-3	12:15P	Phone rings - Hodel answers (recorded)
3-3½	12:32P	Phone rings - Hodel answers, "Yes" - (recorded) write to them in Washington".
3½-4½	12:45P	Water running.
	12:50P	Hodel dials phone "Is Mr.? there? (recorded) Will he be in soon? This is Dr. Hodel speaking." Something about account being worked out.
4½-5	12:52P	Hodel dials phone "Is Mr. Meet there? Dr. Hodel speaking: Will you be around this afternoon?"
5-6	12:55P	Talking to maid - Cannot make out conversation (recorded
6-8	1:00P	Hodel dials phone (recorded) No one answers-finally hangs up.
8-13	1:12P	Phone rings - Hodel answers "Oh yes, Al" (recorded)

MODEL FILE - 60

Spool Time		
	1:12P	"Series of yeses agreeing with party on other end. "That sounds pretty good. Wonderful, and his name is Morrison?"
13-14	1:40P	Phone rings - Model answered (recorded) "Unable to make a cash outlay at this time".
14-15	2:05P	Model dials phone (recorded) "I have some business in Detroit for a few days".
15-15½	2:38P	Model dials phone (recorded)
	2:45P	Model typing.
	3:15P	Quiet since 3 PM. Model apparently out of house.
	3:55P	Still quiet.
	4:00P	Kronek, D.A.'s office on duty.
	4:22P	Phone rings - 16 times, no answer
	4:27P	Phone rings 7 times, no answer.
	4:52P	Phone rings 5 times, no answer.
	5:00P	All Quiet.
	5:30P	All quiet.
	6:00P	All quiet.
	6:12P	Phone rings 10 times, no answer.
15-17	6:20P	Someone named Joe used the phone, hear him moving around (Recorded)
17-18	6:45P	Someone with German accent talked with Ellen - hard to understand.
	6:51P	Ellen talking to someone about something.
18-20	7:00P	All quiet.
	7:30P	All quiet.
	8:00P	All quiet - Off Duty.

MODEL FILE - 61

Spool Time		
	8:00P	Binson, LAPD on duty
	8:20P	Someone enters - no conversation - typing.
20-34	8:35P	Typing very fast - strange shuffling noises unable to identify - recording conversation believe it's between Model and Joe. Mostly unintelligible. Model says there is a possibility of a place near Washington and Normandy.
	8:45P	Mentions Finlays - says somebody started from San Francisco, should be here in a couple of days. Talking about some woman, says she needs cheering up, Model say I'll be going up past Santa Barbara and if you want a lift to Camarillo and back I'll drop you off and pick you up a couple of hours later.
	9:30P	Waid entered - short conversation - unable to understand.
34-38	9:40P	Scuffling noise and conversation between a man and woman - unable to understand.
38-55	11:10P	Conversation between Model and Ellen - Model asks her what she plans to do if he manages to raise some money says she has several alternatives - they are arguing Sounds of dishes and eating - Model tells her she can collect $10. per week social security for 26 weeks - tells her if any lady asks to tell them she has only been getting $50. per mo. instead of $100. to avoid income tax. Sounds like Ellen is crying. Model is explaining how she can beat tax - sounds like she is on her way out soon.
End of Spool		

HODEL FILE - 62		
SPOOL #23		
Spool	**Time**	
0-3	11:30P	Install Spool #23
	11:45P	Sends night letter to George Hodel - 249 So. Harvard. night letter sounds like double talk.
3-33	11:52P	Company arrives—Hodel says "come in Theodore " talking about a woman by the name of Renee. Theodore says all this woman can talk about is how much she loves him. Sounds very theatrical. Talk about $10,000. and why he married her. He repeats time and again that she said "This is a trap". Talking of attorneys. Then reads Hodel what sounds like a divorce paper. Hodel and friend talking and laughing at Courts and legal procedu Sounds as if Hodel is putting Theodore up for night. Turns on radio - resumes typing.
FEB. 28, 1950		
33-	1:40A	Hodel says to Ellen "Why do you have your coat on? I'm buring up in here". Can't hear Ellen answer.
60	1:55A	Conversation between Hodel and Ellen, sounds like writing on desk. Ellen says "How will they treat me". Brechel, LAPD relieves Simson. Hodel quotes prices of ten. He speaks Spanish with Ell Hodel recites poetry.
off	2:20A	Turns radio off. Walks around. Checks doors. Goes to lavatory.
0-13	2:35A	Hodel and Ellen in bedroom - not much conversation mostly whispered. Sounds indicate both in bed, probably making love.
	2:50A	Sounds indicate Hodel reading in bed.
	3:30A	Hodel snoring.

HODEL FILE - 63		
FEBRUARY 28, 1950		
Spool #23		
	8:00A	Morgan relieves Brechel
13-16	8:20A	Telephone rang - Hodel "I've been working pretty hard father", etc. - Hodel "Do you know when these people will be there for the furniture?" etc. - ends - "OK Dad fine, goodbye".
16-17	9:25A	Typing
	9:30A	Hodel (on telephone) unintelligible conversation about rates - ends "Thank you".
17-19	9:35A	Hodel (On telephone) "Uh-huh - I'll appreciate it, otherwise I'd have to buy more blankets you see, et I phoned you for the last six or eight weeks - etc. Ends "Alright thank you, goodbye".
19-21¾ 21½	9:45A	Hodel (On telephone) "Pretty good, thank you" etc. Maybe we could finish - etc. When would be a con- venient time for you? Thursday I may be going to Santa Barbara - I have things pretty well worked ou already - I'll have to make a breakdown on expenses etc. I have that all tabulated - we could sit down an hour and work it out - etc. Ends - "Alright fin Very good, goodbye".
21½- 21 3/4	9:55A	Telephone rang - Hodel - "yes, etc. You just want one pound - ends "Alright, goodbye".
21 3/4- 22½	10:08A	Typing
	10:10A	Desk noise
22½- 23½	10:42A	Hodel - conversation with Ellen - unintelligible.

Hodel File - 65

	1:30P	Sounds of pounding or hammering - Hodel has few wor with Ellen. Unintelligible -flushes toilet and breaks wind at same time. Ye Gods - what a racket (not recorded)
32-33	1:40P	Phone rings - Hodel answers - (recorded) states someone is coming to see house.
33-33½	1:50P	Phone rings - Hodel answers - very short (recorded)
	2:15P	Plenty of noise from passing cars and trucks.
	2:20P	Hodel dials phone twice - no answer. Continued hammering and pounding (not recorded)
33½-34½	2:25P	Phone rings - Hodel answers - so much noise from outside could not understand (recorded)
	2:35P	Hodel talking to himself, but hardly above a whisper
	3:00P	Hodel does a bit of typing - no talk - not recorded
34½-35	3:15P	Hodel dials phone - recorded
35-46	3:35P	Hodel talks to someone in regards to house - (this party is female) also talks about Chinese art (recorded) conversation faded out due to Hodel and party going to some other part of house.
	4:00P	Snyder over to ~~xxxxxx~~ McGrath, D.A.'s office
	4:02P	Phone rang 8 times, no answer
46-48	4:10P	Phone call - not able to understand all parts - said he ~~kx~~ Mrs Hodel divorced - also something about children - Hodel became very angry, said "I do not like your question-is none of your business. I do not desire to deal with you." Hodel hung up phone (recorded)
	4:13P	Hodel typing.

HODEL FILE - 64

	10:45A	Airplane noise
23½-24	10:50A	Unintelligible conversation - Hodel and Ellen
24-24½	10:55A	Unintelligible conversation - Hodel and Ellen
24½-25	11:05A	Telephone rang - no answer
25-27½	11:12A	Telephone rang - no answer
	11:13A	Ellen - "Your phone rang" - Hodel - "Find out who it is" Ellen-"Just a moment - Jimmy?" Hodel-what's the name?" Ellen-"It's Jimy (something)" Hodel-"Tell him, I'll be with you in just a minute. Just leave it there". (Toilet noise - Hodel (unintellig ible conversation) ends. "Yes-Goodbye".
27½- 27 3/4	11:30A	Telephone rang - Hodel - "Hello, yes, between 10:30 and 11:00? Does she know where to meet him? I'll tell him - bye".
27 3/4- 28	11:35A	Hodel - (on telephone) "Will he be in tonight? I'll call him".
28-28½	11:55A	Telephone rang - Hodel "hello, no we don't need any help now, your welcome".
	12:00	Hodel in bathroom - filled tub.
	12:00noon	Bill Snyder relieves Morgan
28½-29	12:30P	Phone rings - (recorded) Not much ~~xxxxxxxxxxxxxxx~~
29-29½	12:35P	Conversation with Ellen - (recorded)
29½-30½	1:00P	Hodel talking to Ellen - (recorded) unintelligible Hodel climbed up or down some stairs - sounds of digging or something similar.
30½-31½	1:05P	Hodel talking to Ellen - asks for blanket or something (recorded)
31½-32	1:10P	Hodel continues talking to Ellen (recorded)

HODEL FILE - 66

48-55   5:06P   Phone call (recorded) could not understand (lots of noise and static.) Sounds like trouble in receiving set - said something about 75¢ a hour al- see you 12 to 6 - come on out and try it.

Spool #24

0-1.5   5:40P   Changed to Spool 24

        5:40P   Funny sounding noises (recorded) for a couple of minutes.

        5:45P   Typing

1.5-4   5:46P   More funny noises (recorded)

4-7   5:47P   Phone rings (recorded) Hodel answers "Hello dear." Things are very much status quo". Conversation som what unintelligible due to noises in background. "Well definitely try to see you this week-end." Dorero. (his ex-wife)

        5:55P   Funny noises continue since telephone conversation then some typing.

        6:10P   Lt. Frank Jaminson phoned, said Hodel moving furnit out - if Bug is found or all furniture moved phone him at CR 14917. His name is pronounced (JAMINSON) any time, day or night.

7-23   6:50P   Hodel in conversation - could not make out too much noise. May have been on phone - (tried at 6453 to record some of the conversation). "Expense along that line - tell you where I see you - what date wi this be "Sat". right, shall I come alone or bring another girl - do you have enought? Also talked ab. going somewhere Sat. 2 blks So. of Colorado, 6 Bl. E of Verdugo - the West end of Eagle Rock "I'll just call her Jill" Have you met some of my friends - se

HODEL FILE - 67

        6:50P   you Saturday how are you fixed for girls? I'm too old now - it does not make any difference to me now Did you decide to take the other room? (it seems th person may be renting or buying the house.)

        8:00P   Bimson, LAPD, on duty.

        8:10P   Hodel moving around - no conversation

        9:30P   Hodel enters - heavy rasping noise lasts approx. 30 minutes, can't identify - no conversation-heavy breathing.

23-54   10:20P   Someone writing at desk.

        11:40P   Conversation - talk about selling something for $60 Sounds like a car - conversation very low. Lots of interference - talking about art - believe Hodel is talking to Chris. Talking about houses and somethi about Monday the 6th. Hodel says he needs $16,000. says there is $15,000. against his house.

54-54½   1:20P   Hodel makes phone call - asks if he should come bac now or in the morning.

        1:25P   Hodel typing - company gone.

Spool 25   1:30P   Change spool - put on #25

                  Brechel, LAPD on duty.

        2:00A   Hodel working around. No conversation.

        2:50A   Hodel retires. Snoring. Have not heard Ellen talk since on duty.

HODEL FILE - 68

March 1, 1950
SPOOL #25

Spool Time		
0-1	8:00A	Morgan relieves Brechel
	9:10A	Hodel(Telephoned) "She can come over about one - have her call me - ends "Alright thank you, goodbye".
1-2	9:27A	Telephone rang - Hodel, "Yes Sir" - conversation abou cold tablets - "Follow directions - I hope it breaks up right away". Ends "goodbye".
2-2.6	9:35½	Telephone rang - Hodel "Yes, I'll call him, will you wait just a moment please - Mr. Phillips would you mind calling the number again, and he'll answer it - I won't answer it you see".
	9:55A	While in bathroom, Hodel said to himself "I wish I hadn't done that" (Probably blew his nose too hard - or something)
2.6-4	10:08A	Telephone rang - Hodel "Hello - etc (water running in tub makes voice unintelligible)
4-6	10:12A	Conversation (with unidentifiable man) Hodel "Are they both looking good?" (Water isn't running during conversation; however, conversation is held out of bathroom and hard to understand) Hodel "I was surprised" "Thanks" (went back to bathroom and turne water back on).
6-7.5	10:24A	Doorbell rang - conversation between Hodel and Ellen (something about breakfast)
7.5-8	10:25A	Hodel and Ellen, very short conversation.
	10:26A	Hodel "He already left" (at front door)
8-12	10:30A	Hodel, "Say Ellen", etc - conversation about t-a Hodel - "Go where" (Scraping noise)

HODEL FILE - 69

(This spool #25 and following should be checked with federal income tax man in the future as Hodel's income tax is computed with this man, and it looks like they about to "take" Uncle for a few bucks.)

12tcend	10:35A	Conversation between Hodel and Ellen (Unintelligible) doorbell rang - Hodel answers - talking to some man - Hodel and man enter library - Hodel "Your fault or mine" - Conversation about radio announcer - man (probably Mr. Hagan), "She moved to San Francisco". Conversation about a wealthy man who owned five gasoli stations - Hodel "Is he a good guy". Hagan, "Yes" etc., conversation about auction-something about FBI Hodel "I had an offer in Hawaii" - conversation about tea (men sat down at desk - everything clearly records hereon) Conversation about making out Hodel's income tax - conversation about Mrs. Hodel, alimony, support children - conversation about exemptions - conversatio about inventory - about chinese international export company - about corporations - about five hundred dollar debt owed Hodel - about corporation books - about Hodel's books - Hagan "We have no choice in the matter", etc. Hodel asked operator for Atlantic 66403 Hodel "Well alright, will you ask him to call me pleas No, this is Doctor Hodel" (End) Men check figures (Hagan reads and Hodel checks) conversation about total income-about asking for money back - Hodel - "You accountants and auditors sure make things complicated". Hagan, "No, we don't" etc - about stock.

511

HODEL FILE - 70

	11:20A	Telephone rang - Hodel, "Hello", etc (unintelligible because of loud filing noise) Conversation with Hagan about goodwill being capital gain (long pause) conversation continues about stock - about "Showing it as an advance".
SPOOL 26	11:22A	Wire changed to Spool #26
	11:30A	Morgan requested Bimson to check cars parked in front of Hodel residence.
0-end	11:32A	Hagan, "people call me Mr. Gahagan" - laughter - conversation about income tax. Hagan "Are you married now"? Hodel-"No".
	12:00	Walter Sullivan relieves Morgan
	12:01P	Telephone rang - very short conversation (Bimson reports that there were two cars parked in front of Hodels #1 - HR392, a '47 Pontiac Convertab Sedan, registered to Floyd Hagan - 3208 Montezuma Ave. Alhambra. #2 - 9P3 938, a '47 Chevrolet Coupe, regis tered to Willie Wheeler, 4461 Town Ave., L.A.)
	12:05P	Hodel still in conversation with his acct. (being recorded) (Spools 25 and 26 and 27 will prove very interesting to income tax investigators)
	12:10P	Phone rings - Hodel answers "Yes, whose calling". Conversation regarding house (sale).
	12:12P	HO 93311 - (This conversation may be OK on recorder)
	12:17P	Phone rings. Hodel answers (recorded)
	12:35P	Discussing and checking figures with acct.
	12:45P	Hodel reading off figures and acct. either putting the in adding machine or typewriter.

HODEL FILE - 71

	12:50P	Changing to Spool #27 - Hodel still reading off figures.
Spool 27	12:55P	Started Spool 27. Still with acct. Tabulating figures.
0-22	1:10P	Recorder stops for about 1 min. Found tiny piece of wire which seemed to be shorting recorder.
	1:11P	Working OK now.
	1:15P	Trouble on recorder. Intermittent shipping - called crime lab. and reported to Stanton.
	1:17P	Recorder off. Airplane noise. No further conversatio Apparently account left premises while recorder was giving us trouble.
22-23½	1:25P	Some conversation (recorded) Could not distinguish voices.
23½-24	1:27P	More conversation. Believe with acct. (being recorded
24-28½	1:30P	Conversation (recorded) on figures.
	1:35P	Recorder stops at about 28½
29-33½	1:36P	Started recorder again. After moving reel forward.
	1:37P	Phone rings. Hodel answers "I don't know. Unable to refer you to anyone". Much noise in background.
33½	1:38P	Phone rings. No conversation. Continues talking to acct.
	1:39P	Recorder stops again at 33½
35-36	1:45P	Started recorder again. Still jumping.
	1:46P	Tabulating figures, lots of noise.
	1:55P	Sullivan called to telephone. By Morgan-Recorder on the blink - further tax computations are discussed between Hodel and Hagan.

HODEL FILE - 72

	2:00P	Telephone rang - Hodel "Helo, just a moment".
		Telephone apparently for Hagan - Hagan "Been busy uh-huh". Conversation related to income tax problem made date for Tuesday at 4:30 o'clock - at 35 North Arroyo (not recorded) Conversation ended 2:04 PM.
	2:05P	Hodel telephoned "Hello Beek", "Albert Band who was John Huston's assistant called you this morning - call him at Hollywood 93311 - He asked for Dorothy". End 2:07P
37-39½	2:10P	Turned on recorder at 37. Still discussing income ta with acct.
	2:11P	Phone rings. Hodel answers (recorder still working. Stops at 39½ but starts again). Unable to get any
to		of phone conversation. Recorder stop at 41.
	2:13P	Starts again. Recorder starts and stops.
51	2:20P	"I don't want to specify. I don't want to call it to their attention that such things are going on". (Acct. makes above statement).
	2:21P	Phone rings. Hodel answers.
	2:25P	Spool runs out reading 51.

Spool #28

#/8	2:26P	Conversation between Hodel and acct.
	2:30P	Start, spool #28. (Started recording).
0-3	2:32P	"Ok, George, will see you later". Hodel-"How much will this cost? Good bye."
3-4	2:41P	Conversation with Ellen (recorded) unintelligible.
	3:15P	Telephone rings answered by Hodel - said, "Hello, I'll be down right away".
	3:25P	Radio is turned on

HODEL FILE - 73

	3:30P	Radio off.
	3:35P	Conversation with Ellen.
	3:45P	Phone rings. Hodel answers. "He's already left". (Apparently refers to accountant).
4½-5	3:46P	Phone rings. Hodel answers "He just left, I'll see if I can get him". No further.
5-7	3:48P	Conversation with Ellen. (recorded) Noise in background.
7-7½	4:00P	Conversation with Ellen (recorded)
	4:00P	Frank Hronek, D.A.'s office on duty.
7½-10	4:10P	Conversation with Ellen. Much racket. (recorded).
10-22	4:27P	Hodel invites some lady in, discussing the house and furniture - sounds like a couple of women.
22-26	4:45P	Returned from examination of different rooms and furth discussion.
26-29	4:53P	Hodel talks with Ellen.
	4:59P	Hodel starts typing.
29-33	5:32P	Hodel talking with a man.
	6:00P	Moving around and typing.
	6:30P	Typing.
	7:00P	All quiet.
	7:30P	Hodel starts typing again.
	8:00P	Meyer, LAPD, on duty.
33-34½	8:10P	Hodel calls someone on phone - asks where Michigan State College is - East Lansing - Thanks them - hangs up - starts typing.
	8:27P?	Hodel phones - "Is Slim there. Have him call me when he comes in."

HODEL FILE - 74

Spool
Time

34½-35   8:37P   Ellen enters - asks if can turn radio on - Hodel says, "Sure". Hodel says something about helping Ellen bring in the table. Radio on - Hodel typing.

9:10P   Hodel still typing.

9:30P   Hodel around - all quiet.

10:00P   Hodel around - all quiet.

10:30P   Hodel around - all quiet.

11:10P   Hodel dials phone - no answer - still typing]

11:30P   Phone rang - Hodel answers. Didn't say anything. Ellen turned radio on again.

35-40½   11:37P   Phone rang. Hodel answered - Whoever he was talking he said, "Don't say anything over the phone - it is k tapped - said he had there phone number, and would ca tomorrow - said he would have to go out to call - checked but would not repeat number on phone. Said it is WE 1670 and he knew name of Street. Would have phone people check - said if he said phone numbe "They" would be out and bother them - that is what "They" always do. When Hodel hung up, Ellen asked hi how he knew-Hodel said he was just talking. Still typing.

MAR 2   12:05A   Hodel still typing.

12:45A   Hodel still typing.

1:15A   Hodel still typing and talking to Ellen - unable to understand.

1:45A   Hodel still typing and talking to Ellen - unable to understand.

HODEL FILE - 75

Spool
Time

2:00A   Brechel, LAPD on duty.
Hodel still typing.

2:20A   Hodel stops typing. Tells Ellen to put things away exactly as she finds them. Hodel goes out. All quiet except for radio.

2:27A   Hodel returns - goes to desk - resumes typing.

3:45A   Typing - stops - radio turned off.

4:05A   Hodel retires - All is quiet.

HODEL FILE - 76
March 2, 1950
Spool #28

	8:00A	Morgan relieves Brechel
	9:10A	Door-bell rang (someone walking)
4.5-42	11:32A	Typing Begins
42-42.2	11:40A	Hodel, "Ellen, if you get any mail you'll have it with-out an instants delay".
	12:00 noon	J. McGrath, D.A.'s office on duty
42-43		Someone phoned - Hodel said "are you here now - yes, it just came ½ an hour ago.
	12:07P	Ellen and Hodel talking about some woman. Hodel said, "Tell her to wait, maybe she will leave it at the door.
	12:10P	Door bell rang - Hodel said to Ellen, "Be nice to her, she is an old lady." Hodel still working at his desk.
43-45	12:12P	Hodel makes phone call - (recorded) to a Mr. Overton. Hodel to Mr Overton "I was wondering about RE 4279, it is disconnected".
45-49	12:13P	(Recorded) Hodel makes another phone call - talks abou RE 4279, and WE 6128. Also about some tests of some ki
49-54	12:14P	Hodel phones the Phone company - asked to have NO 27464 disconnected. Had talk with Phone company.
SPOOL 29-12:30P		Spool No. 29 put on
0-1	12:32P	Hodel makes phone call (recorded)
1-3.5	12:34P	Hodel phone call to a Mr. Arnell (recorded) Talked about running something down - a piece of machinery or something.

HODEL FILE - 77

	1:15P	Someone comes to the door - talks about 3 keys and phones.
	1:55P	Hodel asks for phone number of Dow Chemical Company.
3.5-15		Hodel phones - asks for Mr. Morrison - talk about chemical for a bath soap. Asks questions regarding various chemicals.
	2:16P	Reception getting bad, also appears Hodel now using pho in rear of house - hard to hear - other phone pulled ou by Telephone Company.
	2:40P	Hodel makes phone call - no response.
	2:41P	Phone rings - Hodel answers - says "Hello" then hangs up and dials - phone rings again. Hodel says "Hello" then hangs up.
15-21	2:42P	Called Dr. Hussey regarding atest of some kind (recorde Also said something regarding CR 15258 - could be a phone CR 15258.
	4:00P	Hodel typing. -(Hronek, D.A.'s office on duty)
21-23	4:07P	Phone rings - Hodel answers.
23-28	4:24P	Hodel dials operator"BR 20666 - OL 3476. Mr. Lock, thi is Dr. Hodel------" Something about microscopes - abou how much do they sell for - suppose you send me some literature - can you get us a reasonable price - about 300 or 3:30PM.
	4:32P	Starts typing again.
28-30	4:39P	NO 27464 - Interior Decorator.
30-31	4:49P	Hodel talked with Ellen - walked around.
	5:00P	Starts typing.

HODEL FILE - 78

31-33	5:16P	Phone rings - Hodel answers - saw some notice in the paper - "I have a house which I am willing to rent - one wing anyway - (recorded) "I'll be in and out - suppose you call on me tomorrow or Saturday".
33-34	5:50P	Hodel dials - (recorded) couldn't understand.
34-35	6:12P	Phone rang 8 times. No answer. Hodel apparently out for supper.
	6:30P	All quiet.
	7:00P	All quiet.
	7:30P	All quiet.
	8:00P	All quiet - Hronek off duty.
	8:00P	Meyer, LAPD, on duty
	8:30P	All quiet.
	9:00P	All quiet.
	9:10P	Phone rings 18 times, no one answers.
	9:30P	All quiet
	10:00P	All quiet
	10:30P	All quiet
	10:50P	Sounds as though Hodel and Ellen returned home. Some one moving around.
34-40	11:00P	Hodel calls someone - tells them had other phone disconnected and changes phone from time to time - was on phone 15 min., but didn't say much - asked what happened today and just listened.
	11:30P	Hodel still around, but quiet.
3-3-50	12:00A	All quiet.
	12:30A	Hodel and Ellen moving around, talk a little.
	1:10A	Hodel starts typing.
	1:30A	Hodel still around.

HODEL FILE - 79

MARCH 3, 1950

	1:30A	Brechel, LAPD on duty
	2:00A	All is quiet.
	2:10A	Hodel enters den probably from patio. Obtains something from desk - then leaves room via patio. Hodel probably in studio.
	2:30A	Hodel enters lavatory - runs water - urinates - talks to himself "This is too hot". Goes to desk - writes with pen.
	2:40A	Begins typing.
	3:00A	Typing stops - Hodel leaves room.
	3:05A	Hodel returns to den - works at desk.
	3:15A	Hodel leaves room. All is quiet.
	3:20A	Very faint noise of phone ringing 5 times.
	3:25A	Hodel returns to desk in den. Mumbles to himself. Seems to be reading.
	3:40A	Hodel leaves room.
	4:00A	Hodel returns with Ellen - she goes to lavatory. Hodel - "Did it come off alright?" Answer not readabl
40-44.5	4:03A	Hodel speaks Spanish to Ellen. She answers in Spanish. She then tells him the words in English. She seems to be coaching him on Spanish. They enter lavatory. Hod says "You didn't come in here to wash your hands dress in that thing". She whispers an answer. He sends her out of room "to avoid hard feelings".
off		
44.5-46	4:10A	Hodel and Ellen have conversation in Spanish. They are in bedroom having sex intercourse or something, probably perversion. Sounds like he got another blow-job.

HODEL FILE - 80

4:30A	Snoring begins. Hodel asleep.
8:20A	Hodel arises, goes to lavatory.
8:25A	Hodel and Ellen talking. Not much conversation. Coul[d] not make out.
8:30A	Ellen goes to lavatory.

HODEL FILE - 81
Spool #29

	3-3-50, 8:00A	Bimson, LAPD, on duty
	10:00A	Hodel gets up - says "come in Joe" says "There is a not[e] on the phone".
	10:30A	Hodel walking about - washes
	11:00A	Hodel still walking about - muttering to himself
	11:30A	Phone rings - Hodel says "About how soon Mr Kesler" "Very well, I'll be here".
46-47	11:35A	Woman knocks on door, says "George, may I use your bathroom". Hodel says, "Sure come on in". Conversation between this woman and Hodel - they both leave bathroom
47-55		xxxxxxxxxxxxxxxxxxxxxxxxxx conversation - phone r[ings] answered by Hodel, says, "That's all right - tomorrow after 11", hangs up - sounds like he is making a medical exam. Hodel leaves - goes into library.
55-65	11:45A	Conversation between Hodel and woman - typing - conversa-tion regarding branch library - pounding in background. Conversation regarding a play.
Spool 30-12:00P		Changing reel - Sullivan, D.A.'s office on duty.
	12:00P	Phone rings, Hodel answers, "Let me look and see".
0-6	12:07P	Lady talking (recorded) "I owe 4 times 75.00, that's 300.00 (Possibly his wife) "I have to pay my rent or get out".
	12:15P	Conversation with woman continues. Relative to her ex-penses and the childrens.

517

HODEL FILE - 82

6-10	12:16P	Conversation continues (recorded)
	12:19P	Quiet.
10-12	12:21P	Conversation with wife resumed (recorded) He talks about a job.
12-24	12:28P	More conversation (recorded) Hodel "I've lost money every year". Talking about what money she's earned. Hodel discusses his losses "$6000,00 in 1946, "I sold the clinic to pay for the losses of that year. Now, I must sell the house. Hodel-something about penitentia Noises in background.
	12:40P	Quiet.
	12:41P	Conversation resumed. Much racket Hodel-"I can give yo 2 or 300.00 a month."
24-28	12:42P	Started recording "What would you advise me doing?" Static - hard to understand conversation.
	12:45P	Conversation fades. Apparently parites went to some ot Fart of house.
	12:50P	Phone rings. Footsteps, but hear no answer.
	12:51P	A man talking to Hodel - "Anxious to get located in thi area. I have my own firm. We sell yardage. Office at 610 S. Broadway. Negotiating for another office on La Cienega". "Bamboo blinds of various kinds".
	12:54P	Conversation fades.
	1:08P	Conversation with unknown man resumes. "I think I'll t the place". Man leaves.
	1:10P	Conversation with woman (wife?)
28-38	1:11P	Started recording. She's talking about the children. "I'm not too happy about Kelvin". Much racket. Hodel talks about having wife and children with him again.

HODEL FILE - 83

	1:21P	Conversation continues. Low tones.
38-48	1:28P	Started recording. Can't make out conversation, but hope recording is getting it. Hodel reading from Mexic paper about jobs in Mexico.
	1:38P	Hodel reading to wife from some sort of manuscript.
	1:40P	Hodel threw reading. resumes conversation.
48-49	1:44P	Dials phone (recorded) Wrong number.
	1:45P	Dials phone-No conversation.
49-50	1:51P	Dials phone - "Is he there? This is Dr. Hodel. You ha n't typed my report yet? Have him call me".
	1:55P	Hodel and wife continue conversation. Talking about ek their income tax. Man arrives "Dr Hodel - We'll be thr here in a few minutes". Man replies, "I'm going back to see Ellen".
	1:56P	Typing.
	2:00P	Working on her income tax.
	2:10P	Wife talking on phone. Sounded like she called party, Carol.
	2:12P	Wife to Hodel - I won't be able to go today. I'll probably see over the weekend". Much racket and typing
50-55	2:17P	(recorded) Conversation between wife and Hodel "She get some cash and hide it somewheres".
	2:24P	Max Much interference in receiving. Man talking to Hod Unable to recognize voice or he conversation very clean
55-61	2:26P	"When I came in at 6 AM, I parked the car. It was all quiet". (recorded)
	2:28P	Phone rings - Hodel answers "Yes, I know who it is". Apparently talking to tax expert. "I'm very anxious to see the flower shop. I'll see you today.

2:30P Resumes conversation with man.

2:31P Out of recording wire. Crime lab has been notified by Belle.

2:32P Conversation continues. Man talks about displaying the product to a woman. She finally agreed in about 30 to 60 days she'd put thru a 7 or 7 fifty order. "I had 2 - 6.00 tins, 2 - 12.00 tins, and 12 - 3.75 tins." This man is apparently a tea salesman for Hodel. "Our firm is like the Rolls Royce Firm. It's small but it's the best".

2:49P Phone rings. Hodel answers. Again discussing his incom tax. "Take 101.00 out of the commission. That will sat her a few dollars".

2:50P Salesman again talking. "I had 45.00 to make the trip. If you had sent me the 25.00 sooner, I'd have done a better job. The tires are only good for another 60 day: Blew 2 tires on the trip, one out of Modesto; one out o Fresno. (Lots of bull).

3:20P Salesman still talking, nothing from Hodel. All about the tough breaks on the trip. "I'm supposed to report to Presidio Monday AM for active duty. I got .21 in my pocket and I got to get tack up there. I'll work from 8:30AM to 4:30PM, and will have Saturday and Sunday off I can still handle the tea on weekend trips.

3:25P This guy has talked continuously since 2:25PM.

3:26P Phone rings - Hodel answers "Whose calling?" "200 toda is that it? Why don't you talk to her about that?" (water running) Can't hear no more.

3:26P Salesman again talking. Talked about selling some ash-trays. "They found my blood-pressure at 160. They gave me some pills. Will you take my blood-pressure". Both men walk away.

Quiet.

3:35P Phone - "I just thought you might know something".

3:45P Hodel talking to some one. "Radiator 10.00.

3:50P Phone being dialed. "Is this Mrs. Gomez. This is the China? This is the salesman talking. The little electr stove. We got to get rid of this stuff within the next 24 hrs. Have some ply wood and some lumber. We have 3 windows and odds and ends of lumber. We need the space. Could you call this evening. No matter how late. You can sell this stuff. There is 650.00 worth of merchandi We'll take $110.00 for everything. We don't have time t run an ad. You'll come at 8 o'clock and the boss and I will be waiting for you. 8 o'clock tonight." Hung up and then Hodel and salesman had a good laugh.

4:00P "We'd better go-to be back here by 8 o'clock, but I want you to take my blood-pressure first". Hodel, "it's 164." "What are these pills". Hodel-"They look like phenob.

Belle here with more wire.

4:01P Phone call. Unable to hear conversation due to noise.

4:05P Hodel- "HO 91234" (salesman dials) Asks about ad in papers of March. Shangarala - unusual studio rooms or apartment in luxurious modernistic home for artist writer. $46.00, 90.00, Ph. OL 3476, put it in tomorrow' paper $1.52 Dr. Geo. Hodel.

4:10P

HODEL FILE - 86
SPOOL 31

4:20P	Hodel and salesman leave.
4:23P	Fire Department passes Hodel's home.
4:24P	Hronek, D.A.'s office on duty
4:46P	Hodel dials, Mr. Oherley - he can be there in 20-25 min
0-2	Has a conversation with someone
5:00P	All quiet
5:30P	All quiet
5:50P	Phone rang 2 times, no answer
6:00P	All quiet
6:30P	All quiet
7:00P	All quiet
7:30P	All quiet
7:49P	Phone rang 3 times, no answer
8:00P	All quiet, Hronek off duty
8:00P	All quiet - Meyer LAPD, on duty
8:30P	All quiet, sounds as though Ellen is running the vacum cleaner.
2-3 8:48P	Phone rang, Ellen answered, party must have asked for Hodel. Ellen said he wasn't home yet.
3-4 9:01P	Phone rang, Ellen answered, says she will give Hodel the message. He should be home soon.
4-5 9:07P	Phone rang. Ellen took a message for Hodel. Didn't repeat anything.
? 9:10P	Hodel and some man came in - talk in other part of house. Vacum cleaner going - can't hear anything.
5-6 9:15P	Hodel and man talk about arranging something.
6-12 9:23P	Hodel calls "Nickey", and asks her over - says he will bring some drinks - bring some girl along, asks her if she will read some poems - a friend is with him.

HODEL FILE - 87

12-17½ 9:26P	Hodel tells man some girls are coming over - one is 26, a legal secretary to some lawyer. Man asks if girl is going along to Santa Barbara. Talk about 3 girls coming over in about 30 minutes.
9:47P	Hodel trys to phone 3 times, no answer - tells man no one answered.
17½-18 9:50P	Hodel and man talk about a phone number. Hodel said he wasn't sure-repeated number. HO 94142. Wasn't sure about the 2.
18-19 9:52P	Man trys phone - asks for Miss Jackson - says HO 94140 Trys again - says HO 94142 - then repeats 24376-trys another number - no answer.
10:01P	Radio on
10:16P	Hodel asks operator number of some theater - then repeats HO 93131. Calls and asks if anyone is at ticket agency desk.
19-21 10:20P	Man asks Hodel about mailing a letter - wanted her to get it tomorrow - Man asks Hodel for a complete physica check-up. Hodel checks man's blood pressure - talks ab that - Hodel tells him he couldn't get insurance.
21-23½ 10:30P	Girls arrive - unable to understand - are in another ro Lot of laughing.
11:00P	Still in another part of house.
11:13P	Other man comes in. Hodel introduces girls as Mickey-Shirley-Judy. Talking about a deoderizing bath salt, Hodel said he just used.

HODEL FILE - 88

	11:45P	Playing some kind of guessing game.
3-4-50	12:15A	Still playing same game
	1:45A	Playing a new guessing game
23½-24½	1:27A	Phone rang, Hodel answered - didn't say anything.
	1:30A	Meyer off duty.
	1:50A	G.I.Wean, LAPD, on duty
	2:20A	Playing cards
	3:30A	Playing records, can't hear conversation
	8:00A	Visitors left - Hodel apparently gone to bed. Morgan relieves Wean
24½-25	9:30A	Telephone rang - no answer
25-32	9:37A	Telephone rang - man in xxx house woke up Hodel. Man-"Telephone, George". Hodel-"Hello" - conversation unintelligible- Hodel went to bathroom - returned to phone - Hodel "I don't know where he is. I'll be here today".
32-33	11:35A	Hodel and Ellen - unintelligible conversation.
33-33½	11:50A	Hodel and Ellen - unintelligible conversation.
33½-34½	12:00P	Hodel and Ellen - unintelligible conversation.
	12:00P	Sullivan relieves Morgan
	12:35P	Hodel to Ellen "You got crumbs all over my bed. Will you get them off without getting them on the floor.
34½-36	12:42P	Hodel dials phone (recorded) MY 2064 (?) hangs up and dials again. No response.
36-38	12:50P	Phone rings, Hodel answers (recorded) "How are the kid and fishing". Apparently talking to his wife, Dorothy. "I'll come down this evening, around 8 o'clock.

HODEL FILE - 89

38-41½	1:01P	Phone rings. Hodel answers (recorded) Water running a... conversation is unintelligible. Sounds like talking ab... sale of house. Will show by appointment only. Call about 1:45 PM.
41½-44	1:21P	Phonerings. Hodel answers (recorded) "Your's talking over a tapped line. Oh yes, it's been tapped for a lon... time. I'll be home for the next hour. Be sure and com...
44-45	1:26P	Hodel dials phone (recorded) Asking for theater seats.
45-46	1:27P	Hodel dials phone (recorded) "I want Gittleson's. I want 2 front centers for Martha Graham." He got them at $4.80 each.
46-46½	1:28P	Hodel dials phone (recorded) Asking about seats for Martha Graham.
46½-47	1:38P	Hodel dials phone (recorded) Asks for medical desk.
	1:44P	Ellen advises Hodel party there to see house. Hodel tells Ellen to take her back and show her the rooms on other side, that he will be out in a few minutes (from bathroom)
	1:58P	Hodel talking to lady about sale of house.
47-48	2:10P	Talking to Ellen (recorded) Not intelligible.
	2:25P	Quiet.
	2:35P	Man talking in some other part of house. sounds like t... salesman who talked all thru yesterday p.m.
	2:41P	Man still talking.
48-60	2:45P	Men still talking (recorded) talking to Hodel about s... woman. Mentions Barbara Sherman. Dorothy Black (?) Som thing about Santa Barbara. Hodel - "She called me this morning. She's coming over this P.M." Man-"You had pretty good success with some of those dames I fix...

HODEL FILE - 90

90

2:55P   Spool #31 runs out.

2:55P   Man continues talking about his blood pressure and goin
        into army.

3:05P   Phone rings. Hodel answers - "It's on Franklin near
        Normandie". Talked about renting apt. or apt. and a
        single studio room available. 75.00 for room. Wire
        breaks while xxxxxxin xxxit rewinding spool 31 at
        time 32.

3:10   Phone rings - Hodel answers "giving directions as to ho
        to get to his home".

3:25P   Phone rings-Hodel answers "Thank you for calling".

3:26P   Hodel to man "In about 2 or 3 weeks I'll probably be on
        way abroad.

3:27P   Man and Hodel still talking about man getting into serv
        Hodel tells him if he can get even as a private she sho
        He asks Hodel if he got back in and continued to handle
        tea around bay area if it would make his blood pressure
        worse. Talks a lot about "Corky" apparently wife or
        friend of salesman. Hodel tells man he would pay him
        1000.00 if he'd sell Hodel's house. They leave to walk
        around the house.

3:40P   Man and Hodel again talking about blood pressure.

3:44P   Phone rings 2 times, answered in some other part of the
        house.

3:50P   Phone rings 2 times - answered otherpart of house.

4:00P   Quiet for past 15 minutes.

4:06P   Jim McGrath, D.A.'s office on duty.

4:00P   Salesman and Hodel talking again. Something about a
        $15.00 check the salesman wanted Hodel to give him - ma

HODEL FILE - 91

91

4:00P   out to a Joe. Which the salesman wants to show his
        landlady. The check - also salesman told Hodel he was
        broke - told Hodel how this AM he went into a restauran
        he always eats at and had breakfast for 55¢ - then walk
        over to the magazine section - looked at some magazines
        and left without paying - both not a big laugh out of t

Spool 32

4:14P   A Mr Rappart phones Hodel regarding house.

5:27P   Salesman leaves

4:44P   Spool 32 on

4:57P   Someone calls (a girl) re. a room for 2 - Hodel explain
        house.

5:05P   Hodel shows house to some woman - said"I've rented one
        the rooms since talking to you."

5:35P   Phone rings 2 times, answered in another part of house.
        Not able to hear conversation.

5:55P   Hodel in conversation with the man with the German acce
        trying to record, however reception is very poor.
        (tried 2 min. of recording, but shut it off - can't
        understand)

5:58P   Conversation ends - not heard anymore.

6:02P   Hodel receives a phone call regarding the house - could
        not xxxxxxx make out (racket and noise is xx loudest ïve
        heard) Sounds like he rented the other room - said "let
        me have your phone, yes 27829 - No, since there are 4 of
        you, it would add too much of a load on the phones."
        It appears 4 girls are moving in - one by the name of
        Miss Maxwell it sounded like.

HODEL FILE - 92

92

6:40P   Phone rang - Hodel to some woman (recorded) no info. obtained.

6:55P   Some man in conversation with someone on phone - not

Hodel (recorded) the salesman who had dinner with Hode. got some phone number 89561. Prefix not mentioned - th is the phone number of another girl - Hodel came back

phone rang - someone calling re. the house - the addres of the girl is Santa Monica Blvd and Cahuenga. Motion Picture Industry PBX operator.

7:22P   Phone rings once - no conversation - must have been answered on extension.

7:25P   Hodel in conversation with one of the girls who was goin to move in-her phone number is HU 27289 - some indicati they may not take the room. Hodel is to phone in the A could not ascertain her name.

7:35P   Hodel phones party named Mickey - said he would like he to read him some poetry tonight - asked how her energy was. Started talking very low - could not make out. "I'm a easy listener". (Presume it he's talking to a s can't hear clear - said would she like to be observed - frustration and umrlexes-mentioned something about relationship with me - I'm sure of myself - told her 2 stories.

8:00P   Meyer, LAPD, on duty

8:30P   Talking in some other room.

8:40P   Hodel talking to two women who he is trying to sell or rent house - said he would rent for $90.00 month. Two unmarried sisters-sounds as though one can't speak Engl Said he had the studio rented to some woman painter.

HODEL FILE - 93

93

8:40P   One other room to some other woman, asks them to come back and look tomorrow. He won't be home, but house-keeper will change spool.

Spool 33 9:03P   Other man came in - women still there. Hodel introduce man as his business manager - women leave. Hodel goes other part of house.

9:12P   Hodel and man talking - man has accent. Hodel takes hi to bedroom and talks in low voices - said something some case being cold - seemed to talk about tex or sale of clinic - can't hear to well. (Recorded-hope can hear better) Hodel gave man Two phone numbers, his OL 3476 some office TR 1252. PBX operator comes back and other man who has been around for awhile. All three ta about some business deal - can't figure it out - say something about China.

9:40P   Phone rang - Hodel answered. Didn't say anything. Talking about selling something.

9:50P   Sounds as though 2 men left. Hear one person around.

10:00P   All 3 back. Hodel says he knows 4 girls in Burbank Two are 19 and two are 20, who are practising oriental dances and are going to Mexican and Latin America. Hodel asks man with accent if he thinks they would go o down there. Hodel talks as though he has a contract an will go along.

10:37P   2 men talking - one telling about place he lives, but i leaving other can have it. Didn't mention any address.

10:45P   Two people talking in one room, and a lot of racket in another room. (recorded) but couldn't understand.

HODEL FILE - 94

	10:45P	2 men leave. Hodel says he won't be home tomorrow.
	11:15P	Quiet, Hodel and Ellen around.
	11:45P	Hodel typing.
2-5-50	12:12A	Phone rings. Hodel answers, "Yes honey. I am painting some furniture. I am a great lover of honesty." Talks about car other party bought. Said he would like to get one but couldn't pay cash. Asks about taking th car someplace. Break car in andyou in at same time. Talks about a poker game.
	12:45A	Quiet. Hodel still moving around.
	1:15A	Quiet. Hodel still moving around.
	1:30A	All quiet. Think Hodel want to bed in another part of house.
	1:45A	LAPD Wean, relieves Meyer.
	2:00A	Apparently still in bed, no movement of any kind.

Spool 34

0-	8:00A	Hronek, D.A.'s office on duty
	8:30A	All quiet.
	9:00A	All quiet.
	9:30A	Phone rang 2 times, didn't hear anyone answer.
	10:00A	All quiet.
	10:30A	All quiet.
	10:40A	Hear child's voice in background - very faint
	11:19A	Phone rang 3 times, child's voice in background - must answered in another room.
	11:59A	Hear Hodel humming and moving around the desk.
	12:00P	Relieved by Jack Egger, D.A.'s office.
	12:05P	Bathroom noises - woman humming in background.

HODEL FILE - 95

	12:06p	Woman greeted someone at front door, could not pick up conversation.
	12:15P	Conversation in background, cannot pick it up conversation between Hodel and other man.
	12:20P	Turned on radio, playing symphony music.
	12:22P	Typewriting can be heard over the symphony - man coughi
	1 PM	Radio still on (symphony) typewriting still going on.
	1:25 P	Phone rang, cannot hear conversation because of radio.
1½	1:35P	Phone rang - recorded - conversation with some one whom he told to "come over after work tomorrow".
	1:40P	Typewriting resumed by Hodel.
	1:50P	Knock on door, Hodel let woman in-Conversation ensued
3½		(tried to record but it was background)
	2:00P	Hodel seems to be opening and closing drawers. Typewri resumed.
63-7	2:10P	Hodel in conversation with man and woman, but cannot pi it up very well. Too far in background - seem to be talking about photography of a surrealistic nature. Hod shows some xxx pictures of his to the two people - also talking about renting some suites of rooms in his place Man has a definite Spanish accent, asked Hodel about Spanish doctors in this area. Hodel mentioned leaving in a "couple of months" Attempt to record this convers tion proved futile because it was too much in background Hodel again started talking about photographs with the people - part of conversation is recorded.
11½	3:00PM	Pictures seemed to be of Japanese girls.
	3:03P	The two people left.

MODEL FILE - 96

3:05P — Another man came in - talked to Hodel far about a red headed girl who may live there with her mother.

Both seemed interested in if the girl was over 18 or not. Man asked Hodel if when he went to Santa Monica if he was going to stay there or not.

15 3:20P — Hodel called up a girl named Carol, asked herabout buyin a couch from her.

16 — Hodel bought the couch from her for $35.00 and said it a deal, now you only owe $50. and said goodby and hung up.

3:25P — Phone rang - must have been answered in other room.

3:25P — Hodel left the room - radio still on in background.

3:33P — Hodel back in room, some typing and moving about.

4:00P — No conversation. Relieved by Jim McGrath, D.A.'s office.

Spool 35

5:30P — J. Egger had trouble with other spool No. 34, it had br took same off and replaced with #35, lost some of the s in removing.

5:30P — Hodel and salesman in conversation. "Can't make it" Salesman said, it's down in the basement locked up. Th salesman talked about his blood pressure.

6:35P — Hodel and Eilen in conversation - not understood - mumb

7:30P — Hodel and Eilen in conversation - mumbling faint - can' hear.

7:50P — Phone call to Hodel from Pat, said, "Wait a minute, I'l be with you. Hudson 27829, is her phone. Hodel to cal her in A.M.

8:00P — Meyer on duty, LAPD

HODEL FILE - 97

8:40P — Hodel called Joe, asked him if he didn't want the room. Hodel had a chance to rent it to two "sweet"young girls one goes to U.S.C., and the other is a Secretary for Prudential Life Insurance Company.

8:45P — Calls some woman and talks about renting part of house to her - says he is going abroad soon - makes appointmen for 12:45 tomorrow to show house.

9:15P — All quiet.

9:45P — All quiet.

10:15P — All quiet.

10:45P — All quiet.

11:15P — All quiet.

11:45P — All quiet.

3-6-50 12:15A — All quiet.

12:45A — All quiet.

1:15A — All quiet.

1:45A — All quiet.

2:00A — Brechel, LAPD, on duty, all is quiet.

2:20A — Several odd sounds in background, sounds like trumpet o an elephant.

2:45A — Noises in background indicate someone working around, probably in studio.

3:10A — Hodel enters from rear, part of house, goes to lavatory urinates.

3:15A — Hodel goes to bed.

HODEL FILE -
Spool 35
3-6-50
97-A

5:10A   Hodel gets out of bed. Goes to other part of house for a minute, then returns to bed.

8:00A   J. McGrath, D.A.'s office on duty.

9:40A   Hodel up - talking to Ellen - said come on let's get up. Going. Many Gave her hell for being in room for 10 minutes times.

9:55A   Phone rings - Hodel answers-about renting room.

10:15A   Ordering blankets from Broadway Hollywood.

10:35A   Hodel asking for phone number of owner's Realty's Servic

10:50A   Hodel kadik and Spanish man talking about "refiguring a job" of some kind in the house.

11:30A   Hodel phones Manlo 46516 - did not hear any conversation

12:03A   Joe phoned - Hodel talked about callers in the house.

12:00noon   Snyder - D.A.'s office on duty

12:40P   Hodel calls regarding houses for sale - hangs up and raises hell with Ellen over nothing.

12:55P   Shirley Tarochmoyen - student - calls - talks to Hodel regarding being student in Hodel's class (whatever that is) both move to part of house where talk is un-intelligible - both return and Hodel suggests they sit in his car and talk - to which Verty agrees.

HODEL FILE - 98
3-6-50
No wire
No recording
Snyder, D.A.'s office on duty

1:40P   Both return to room - talk on medical problems.

1:45P   Hodel answers phone regarding Miss Davis - xx on positio with some Dr. 1/31/50 date mentioned by Hodel.

1:50P   Resumes conversation with prospect - possibly partners j business - talk re. 2 party phone as to costs, etc. - apparently selling "lady" bill of goods.

2:30P   Phone rings - Hodel answers - not important.

2:30P   Resume talk with lady suspect "W" or prospect.

3:10P   Gal still there - conversation unintelligible. (Belle and Bimson playing back recordings)

3:25P   Hodel phones - wants specimen picked up at 3684 7th Ave.

3:30P   Gal leaves - will return.

3:55P   Hodel does some typing - also talks to Ellen - gives her some more hell for free.

4:15P   Hodel still typing - (monotonous, isn't it?)

4:25P   Phone rings - Hodel answers.

4:30P   Snyder, off duty, Eggers on, D.A.'s office

4:45P   Hodel typing

5:00P   Hodel still typing

5:05P   Hodel goes out of room - all quiet.

5:15P   Hodel back, has another man with him - background conversation cannot pick-up.

5:25P   Woman enters - still in background.

5:30P   Everyone leaves room - all quiet.

5:35P   Hodel returns to the room-opens some drawers and leaves again - all quiet.

MODEL FILE - 99

5:40P   All quiet.

5:50P   Hodel back, with woman - woman talking about Painting he Kitchen.

Hodel talked about a woman named "Tracey Racapore" who attends UCLA who is renting rooms from him. Stated that "she is about 22 years of age, very nice girl who studie most of the time".

6:00P   Conversation continues - woman talking about renting roo

6:02P   Another man enters, conversation very much in the background.

6:05P   Hodel and girl talking - girl said she "would be afraid to live alone". Hodel said he would "protect her to the best of his ability". Girl said that she "would get ove being afraid, O.K."

6:15P   Hodel shows the girl some pictures of his; they seem to portraits of an abstract nature, conversation turns to photos.

6:15P   Man with accent, apparently spanish, comes into conversation.

6:20P   Everyone except Hodel leaves.

6:22P   Another woman comes in. Hodel tells her "to sit down ar take it easy for a minute".

6:30P   Hodel in background, conversation with woman.

6:35P   Woman leaves - Hodel alone working at desk, can hear occasional dog barking in background.

6:45P   Another woman enters, she and Hodel talk about renting rooms. Woman said she will call Hodel between 11 and 1:

6:55P   tomorrow, and leaves.

MODEL FILE - 100

7:05P   Hodel alone - working at desk - typing

7:30P   Hodel still alone - moving about room. Hodel called Menlo 46517 from operator - no answer. Hodel called another number - could not get it, told the girl his new phone number would be OL 3476, and that he was "keeping it secret". He asked the girl if she and "Will would come over soon.

7:47P   A woman comes into Hodel's room; he asked her "when her mother was coming over". The girl said, this event She said her mother is Mrs Alica De Varora, and her name is Villa De Varora. Hodel stated that his type of work is Administrative Medicine, and at present he has a laboratory and has done a lot of work for the government overseas, etc.

8:00P   Egger, D.A.'s office off duty.

8:00P   Woman, LAPD, on duty.

8:10P   Hodel moving around, no conversation.

8:20P   Woman talking to Hodel. Can't understand.

8:25P   Woman leaves - man enters - talks with Hodel about moral of spanish girls. Hodel tells man he should have seen his Chinese collection which was worth $100,000.

8:30P   Man calls woman on phone and tells her he is going out with Hodel - to have some drinks.

8:35P   Hodel suggests they go to a Chinese place. They leave.

9:20P   Someone enters - then could hear woman crying. Phonograph turned on. No conversation.

10:45P Phonograph. Still playing and someone typewriting.

10:50P Phone rings - unable to hear with music.

11:05P Hodel tells Ellen to pack everything in a box and

HODEL FILE - 62

11:50AM	Hodel working around desk
11:55AM	Hodel said to Ellen "Take the suitcase down and have it fixed".
11:55P	Hodel started typing
12:00noon	Hodel still typing
12:00noon	Sullivan, D.A.'s office relieves Eggers
0-1	
12:15P	Hodel talking to Ellen - unintelligible
12:30P	Hodel dials - asks for number of Santa Fe - then dials (recorded) much racket
1-4½	
12:32P	Hodel dials S.P. Rwy. - (recorded) wants info on trains, sounds like to Arizona, to Gila Bend, Ariz. Leave 8:30 at night - asks for fare - $12.04
12:45P	Typing
12:55P	Hodel dials phone - asks about OPA regulations in LA "Does rent control still cover L.A. House was built in 192_ Place has never been registered. Well, it's a big house, a I thought I'd divide it up into rooms and apartments. The name is Harvey; Owner George Harvey; 5121 Franklin.
12:59P	Hodel dials phone - asks for American Red Cross - Call me a OL 3476
1:05P	Hodel typing
1:12P	Hodel talking to Ellen - "I can take that package down and mail. Also Tomar's. Is Tomar's ready. I got to take a trip in the car and can mail the package.
1:15P	Hodel talking in a low voice to some girl. Said something about talking something to her mother. Conversation continued for about 5 minutes, but unable to get any of it due to low tones.
1:26P	Conversation resumes, but still unintelligible.

HODEL FILE - 63

1:55P	Typing
2:00P	Radio on. Hodel and woman talking. Cannot understand due to radio and racket. Sounds like someone interested in house.
2:12P	Emergency vehicle passing. Conversation with woman continues. Still unintelligible.
2:21P	Hodel talking to a woman - radio in background and conversation unintelligible
2:22P	Started recording. Believe woman to be Ellen
4½-6	
2:25P	Conversation with Ellen continues.
2:28P	Phone rings - Ellen answers "Whose calling - Just a moment" can't hear anything further.
2:30P	Hodel talking "I would like a check on OL 3476 - when can you get a service man out".
2:40P	Typing - and radio still playing
2:50P	Phone - Hodel answers - He gives his name and address
3:15P	Quiet
3:25P	Hodel talking, unable to understand
3:45P	Hodel to Ellen - something about reservations. Sounds like Ellen to go to Arizona
4:00P	Kronek, D.A.'s office on duty
4:30P	All quiet
5:00P	All quiet, only water running in the bathroom
5:10P	Conversation in the background, impossible to understand
7-12	
5:30P	Hodel talking with some woman (recorded) too much disturbance to understand.
6:00P	Hear Hodel moving around - talk in the background
6:30P	All quiet

HODEL FILE - 84 103   104

	6:57P	Hodel starts typing
	7:00P	All quiet
12-13	7:08P	Hodel dials - gets wrong number - tries again (recorded)
		Hodel leaves the room
	7:30P	All quiet
13-14	7:31P	Phone rings 5 times - answered by Ellen in another part of the house - couldn't hear at all
	8:00P	Hronek off duty - all quiet
	8:00P	Wean, LAPD, on duty
	8:10P	Talking in background - can't understand.
	9:05P	Talking in background - can't understand.
	10:00P	Hodel messing around in toilet - no conversation
14-30	10:30P-11:25P	Man enters - they talk, can't make out too well (recorded)
30-34	11:40P	Hodel talking about some plans, but can't make out (recorded)
3-8-50	2:00A	Brochel, LAPD, on duty - All quiet. Hodel probably in bed can hear snoring.
	3:00A	All is quiet
	4:00A	All is quiet
	5:00A	Male voice in background, too far away to understand. Sound lasted about a minute then all quiet again. Hodel still snoring.
	6:30A	Ellen moving around.
	8:00A	J. McGrath, D.A.'s office on duty
	8:30A	Phone rings - Hodel answers - about the "Packard jalopy" starting hard talking to some mechanic about fixing up the car. Said "I will see you later - about 10:30A or 11 AM regarding the car - having it fixed".

HODEL FILE - 85 104   105

	10:30A	Conversation over phone with his wife Dorothy - she was complaing about money-he said he is broke - can't pay mortgage on the house this month - has no money coming in' from sounds of conversation bad feelings may be developing
		Also spoke of going to see a Mrs. La Cour. Hodel was to write her.
	12:25P	Called Lou regarding the Packard - said would be down in five minutes.
	12:36P	Called Postal information for information regarding pxu postal service with the capital of Tibet.
	12:36P	Snyder, D.A.'s office on duty
	12:36P	All quiet - Hodel is having car repaired - apparently no or in house at all.
	2:30P	Phone rings 9 times - no one answers.
	4:00P	Hronek, D.A.'s office on duty
	4:19P	Telephone conversation with someone (recorded)
34-39		
39-40		Phone Company to disconnect the extension OL 3476 - should have been disconnected today, tomorrow expects to work only 12-2 PM - or Friday, he'll stay home himself.
	5:10P	Hodel starts typing
40-42	5:30P	Hodel carries a conversation with another man - phone rang and unkn man left.
	6:15P	Hodel dials, asks to have someone call him.
42-44	7:15P	Hodel dials - asks for Dr Friedner, dials another 3787 So. Vermont - Friedner's address
	7:30P	Hodel typing like mad.
	8:00P	Hronek off duty.
	8:00P	Mayer, LAPD, on duty

HODEL FILE - 86 /03/

8:10P	Hodel phones someone and asks name and exact title of Chief of States of Burma and Tibet - wants to know how they are addressed. Name of Minister Public Health of Burma - goes back to typing.
8:45P	Phone rang 3 times, didn't hear anyone answer - has been quiet for past 20 minutes.
8:54P	Phone rang 3 times, didn't hear anyone answer.
9:30P	All quiet
10:00P	All quiet
10:15P	Hodel typing
10:45P	Hodel still typing
11:15P	Hodel still moving around
11:45P	All quiet
2-2-50	
12:15M	All quiet. Hodel snoring.
12:45M	All quiet. Hodel still snoring
1:15M	All quiet. Hodel still snoring
1:45M	All quiet. Hodel still snoring
2:00A	Brechel, LAPD, on duty. All is quiet except for Hodel snoring.
6:10A	Woman - may be Ellen moving around house
8:00A	J. McGrath, D.A.'s office on duty
9:15A	Someone knocking on a door 3 times
9:35A	Phone call - couldn't make much out. Hodel asked "if you were going to pick that up".
9:50A	Hodel phoned Telephone Company to have extension of OL 3476 disconnected.

HODEL FILE - 87 /06/

10:00AM	Hodel has a male patient - gave him Methrolate to put 3 drops in each eye, one time a day. Hodel is talking with man with German accent - talking about going to the auction and buying and selling things - talking about buying paints
10:03AM	Phone call - Hodel answered - nothing said - just "yes,yes"
10:07AM	Another phone call. Hodel talks to someone about selling lumber - pressure cooker, and odd and ends.
10:40AM	Hodel makes phone call - for Repair Department - complained about a condensor - sputtering.
10:55AM	Officer Simson and Sgt. Belle checked Hodel's residence for license plates to find out who man with German accent is - the following plates were in sun in front of Hodel's house 75 P 519 - 35 Packard F.E. Mattoon - 251 S. Lucerne, L.A; 9 P 3938 - 47 Chev. Willie Wheeler, 4461 Towne Ave., L.A. 8A5 420 - 41 Ford Conv. Violet Jean Mallen - 2055 N. New Hampshire, L.A. 6GA6 150 - 36 Packard, Marie L. Valia - 2212 N. Nella Vista L.A.
11:30AM	All quiet around house.
12:03PM	Hodel calls a Mr. Kurst or Kurst - talking about photostats - said Mr. Good has pictures - also the photographers name is Ackerman.
12:15PM	Phone rings - Hodel says "I love you very much. I'm at the house" or something like that. "Will see you at 1:15."
12:16PM	Hodel phones - a Margaret said she has a 2 PM appointment.
12:20PM	Sullivan, D.A.'s office on duty.
1:15PM	Phone rings. No one answers. Quiet since 12:25.
1:30PM	Phone rings - no one answers.
2:05AM	Someone walking around.

HODEL FILE - 68-10 7

2:20AM Hodel talking with some man. Conversation unintelligible (much static and noise in machine).

2:25AM Water running.

2:39AM Hodel dials phone "asks for Mr. Kurst(?) "Kurst not in? I'll call back".

2:50AM Hodel talking to someone by phone about an inlay china box. Apparently trying to sell some China piece he has.

2:51AM Hodel phones. "Hello, brother, good. I'll have some of those special manhattans for you. Take my new number, OL 3476. Give me a ring and drop by around the cocktail hour. I gave it to Mr. Kirsh. (?)

3:00AM Phone rings - Hodel answers "Sure, I'll be here." Conversation in very low tones.

3:17PM Hodel asks for number at 5101 Hollywood Blvd. Then dials number. "Are my trousers and shirts ready? I'll stop by for them".

3:50PM Hodel phones someone - states he is calling for a Mrs. Chajud who wants to share a luxurious apartment with some girl. He gives this party his phone number, and address.

3:51PM Hodel calls. Gives a rental listing to share an apartment. "Calling for Mrs. De Chajud(?) Mrs. C. has a 19 yr. old daughter, and she wants some one-preferably a young college student-to share apartment. Someone xxxx who wants an artistic setup. Mrs. C. is just here from Costa Rica, but speaks good English. Mrs. De Chajud - 835.00, 5121 Franklin by appointment.

HODEL FILE - 89-10 f

44-51

3:55PM Hodel dials (recorded) - (very interesting) repetition of above about Mrs. Chajud and daughter sharing a luxurious apartment in a $150,000. house. 4:00-8:00A - Bronek on duty, D.A.'s office. A woman comes in. Hodel - "How are you". Much static.

4:02PM Unable to understand. Hear Hodel again on phone talking about apartment.

4:20PM Hodel dials phone - again talks to a rental agency. Repeats his Mrs De Chajud pitch about sharing an apartment. Wants a 19 or 20 yr. old girl. Some hammering and sawing in background.

4:25PM Hodel dials phone - another rental agency.

4:30PM Call to another agency

4:35PM Another one

4:38PM Hodel dials - gets another agency

4:41PM Hodel dials - Gets another agency

4:42PM Hodel calls another agency about a girl to share the apartm

4:50PM Phone rings - Hodel answers - something about a box he could use over the weekend

4:57PM Phone rung - Hodel answered. "The sooner we have that audition the better. Sunday will be a good time. Do you know of any place where I could make arrangements?"

5:05PM Talking to some woman (new housekeeper) about showing her the secret of the lock, and about going out for awhile.

6:00PM All quiet.

7:00PM All quiet.

7:30PM Phone rang 3 times - no answer

7:55PM Hodel moving around the house and bathroom.

HODEL FILE - 9-10-50

110

51

5:00PM Meyer, LAPD on duty

5:02PM Hodel turns radio on - low talking - unable to hear - is on phone talking to someone about a sore throat. Said something about Mexico - if she was OK - could probably leave tomorrow night

8:20PM Hodel calls Orchid 22032 - asks for Marian - then talks to someone about Marian - going to Frisco.

8:23PM Hodel calls Sunset 16510 - asks for Harry.

8:24PM Hodel calls Sunset 33419 - talks to Harry - asks if he knows where he can get in touch with Jonathin Usher? Says he is a ham radio operator, and Hodel wants to receive a message from Tibet in about 2 to 4 weeks.

8:55PM Hodel talks to Harry again - same subject

9:45PM Hodel still typing and moving around

10:45PM Hodel still moving around

3-10-50 12:15A One or two men and about same amount of women - Talking to Hodel. Hard to understand - something about a place in Mexico not too far from Arizona - good roads - something about a Whore House, or sanitarium. One man seems to be a doctor. Talking about she at Camarillo. Hodel - "She was going to shoot me and commit suicide "Tamara" (way it sounded) Talking about fishing trip to Mexico 228 miles from Phoenix, Arizona - seem to be looking at map-mentioned Sonora, Mexico - other party leaves 1:15A - says he will leave Hodel know about noon tomorrow - Friday - about trip.

HODEL FILE - 9-11-50

111

2:00A Wean, LAPD, on duty

2:15A Hodel apparently gone to bed. All quiet.

6:15A Hodel getting up - moving around house.

8:00AM J. McGrath, D.A.'s office on duty. All quiet.

8:45AM Phone rang 2 times - could not hear an answer

9:00AM Phone rang - Hodel said, "Hello - yes - how's things" hung up. Hodel is up and around.

9:10AM Hodel and some woman in short conversation - could not understand - then they went to rear of the house.

9:15AM Hodel makes phone call - asks for extension 372 - Mr. Holley or Ragey - about his export business - about an order Hodel had placed - nothing else mentioned as to products, e

10:10AM Phone call from Ted. Hodel asked "do you know a Dr. Donald, L.A. Terry, or L.A. Perez at a mission - address may be 56 Marian or Mariana Rd. Not in private practice - asked how many siamanese practitioners there were. Told Ted first chance he has to phone him to have dinner - as he wants to talk tohim

10:20AM Phone call to Mabel - asked if Irwin was working - asked her to have him come by - also said would like to see you some-time - asked her about pains in her stomach.

10:25AM Phoned Telephone Company to pick up some old telephone directories.

10:27AM Phone call - something about a short stocky man picking up a deposit.

10:32AM Hodel phones someone to pick up something - could not make out what.

HODEL FILE - 92 ///
112

10:33AM — Phone call received by Hodel - said maybe going away for the weekend - said to phone him at 4 PM - he would know

11:07AM — Phone call received - Hodel answered - sounds like planning a trip - asked when can you get away - will phone you prefixes not obtained-numbers are 84435 and 81831

11:27AM — Hodel phones Orchard 22033 - no answer

11:30AM — Phone call received - something about dropping off some clothes - said again he may leave town - also asked for a book containing names and addresses

11:35AM — Hodel makes phone call-too much static and Hodel too far away to make out.

12:25P — Sgt Belle - said he has found out the man with the German accent is one Baron Herringer - a supposed ex-German - Baron. The two new girls are Vilma (age 19) and Sonia (age 15) Said had moved in with their mother. 2 sisters.

1:15PM — Burns, D.A.'s office on duty

2:00PM — Hodel returned to house.

2:20PM — Hodel talking to man about income tax with-holding, etc.

2:35PM — Hodel talks on phone (received call)-too much static.

2:45PM — Hodel received phone call "She's coming over. Does she know the name. I'll have her call you as soon as she gets here.

2:48PM — Resumed talk of income tax, withholding-with man (unnamed)

4:10PM — Hodel called OR 27023, No answer.

4:15PM — Income taxconsultant left.

4:20PM — Hodel received call from patient about stomach.

4:25PM — Woman entered house - no conversation with her.

4:45PM — Hronek, D.A.'s office on duty.

HODEL FILE - 92 //2
113

51½ 4:55PM — Phone rang 2 times - answered in a whisper
5:05PM — Conversation with a woman - distant - hard to understand - toilet being flushed 3 times in a row

41½-52 — Spool ran out just when Hodel talked with Joe. Joe still talks -"that's one of the conditions of my probation." A woman present.

SPOOL #16
0-14 4:20PM — Mixed conversation - Hodel answered the phone. Hodel called Superior 84425 - Superior 81831 - conversation about a plane trip over the weekend.

14-17 5:59PM — Seems to have a woman patient. Woman - ST 45442 - seems like Hodel and party are leaving for Mexico tonight.

17-53 6:40PM — Hodel called Charles about cancelling the trip to Mexico because he can't line up 4 reliable people. Going out for supper - woman called another party - who was willing to loan his car for the trip. Finally decided that they'll leave Wednesday night. Hodel showing the map and pictures the woman.

6:50P — The phone rang - Hodel answered "Hello Betty"- Toilet being flushed - can't understand

7:05P — Hodel dials information "What's the number of 5101 Hollywoc Blvd.

7:20P — Phone rang 7 times - no answer.
7:32P — Phone rang 4 times - no answer
7:57P — Phone rang 5 times - no answer
8:00P — Meyer, L.A.P.D. on duty. All quiet.
8:32P — Phone rang 3 times - didn't hear anyone answer - sounds as though someone talking in another room.

HODEL FILE - 94

113

	10:05P	Phone rang 3 times - no one answered.
3-11-50	1:00A	Hodel comes home - sounds like a woman with him - can't understand them - in another room. Sounds like it may be his ex-wife. Can't understand what talking about.
	1:35A	Sounds as though Hodel is at his desk.
	1:45A	Hodel starts typing.
	2:00A	Wean, LAPD, on duty.
	2:15A	Hodel moving around - no conversation
	2:45A	Hodel apparently gone to bed - can hear snoring.
	7:40A	All quiet.
	8:00A	J. McGrath, D.A.'s office on duty.
	8:10A	Phone call to Hodel - who said "OK will see you at 9 AM".
	9:30A	Phone call - Hodel said "See me Monday or Tuesday. I'm going fishing over the weekend.
	10:07A	Woman phoning Santa Monica 42421 - asked how the children were, said "I went to the doctor's yesterday and I did not feel good so I stayed with George last night. He is driving down later, and I'll be down then. (Sounded like Dorothy-Hodel's exwife)
	10:40A	Hodel and German in conversation. Can't understand as woman in bathroom - running water and making all kinds of noises.
	10:50A	Hodel and German talking - Hodel wants to rent a 26 room lo near Mexecali in Mexico. Where President Comanche of Mexico built to have conference with Roosevelt. He wants to make a rest home 300 air miles from L.A. 500 by car.

HODEL FILE - 95

115

10:55A	Phone rings 2 times - answered in rear of house - could not hear the German talking to Hodel about a man with nervous troubles (the German talks as though he is a doctor i.e., in medical terms)
11:45A	Sullivan, D.A.'s office on duty. Hodel and woman talking in background. Believe his ex-wife, Dorothy.
12:10P	Mrs. Hodel doing a lot of talking, but apparently in some other part of house. Sounds as though she might be reading from a book or script. She's been talking for the past 10 minutes.
12:15P	Woman stops her reading or talking.
12:35P	Phone rings 3 times - possibly answered in some other part of house.
1:30P	Hear woman talking in background. Sounds like a woman and child.
1:40P	Man talking in background. Sounds like the talkative tea salesman.
1:43P	Typing.
1:55P	Typing by someone - not Hodel - Not as adept as Hodel. No conversation
1:59P	Woman dials phone. Sounded like she said, "This is Elsie". Talked about Vincent Price. Also, about M.G.M. Talked abou John getting her a job. "Say Bob", I found a story. A stor of a black saint, a negro. Do you know John Farrow? I thought of him because of his Catholicism. I met him years ago. I have the babies down at the beach. But, I'd love to see you. (t must be Dorothy talking) You're at home all day. Oh, wonderful darling" then "I'll get to see you"
2:05P	End of conversation.

HODEL FILE - 96

2:15P — Hodel talking. Unintelligible

2:25P — Typing

3:15P — Hodel and Dorothy conversing in background. Getting ready to leave.

3:55P — Quiet reigns supreme.

3:55P — Littleton, D.A.'s office relieves Sullivan

SPOOL 37

4:00P — Hodel typing

4:11P — Hodel calls "Come in" Undistinguishable conversation with woman. Typing stops.

4:13P — Woman out, Hodel walking around.

4:20P — Undistinguishable words from woman. Heavy banging sound like wood being wrenched loose, then typing resumed. More wrenching sounds after typing stops.

0-10

4:24P — Woman patient apparently. Short professional conversation. Phone call regarding flight by plane. Asks if party would

10-21

4:35P — "like to go down there tonight". Puts a woman on phone for conversation with caller. Hodel says he can "go tonight" on a flight. Woman tells caller that prospect of trip is "wonderful". Apparently a flight to Mexico. Undistinguishable chatter with woman after phone hung up.

— Phone rings. Woman answers. Undistinguishable conversation because of loud wrenching noises. Bathroom sounds - running water, flushing toilet. Hodel says "we drive (or ride) all night". Her answer undistinguishable.

4:45P — Phone bell (?) rings twice. No one answers. Undistinct mummuring between Hodel and woman. Woman calls, "Doctor!" General moving around in background. Undistinct conversatio Hodel and woman over wrenching sounds. He tells her that

HODEL FILE - 97

— something "is in her closet". More indistinct conversation with woman in background.

5:05P — Typing. Asks some woman (patient?) "let me have your address and phone number, please". Answer undistinguishabl He leaves, then apparently returns after indistinct chatter with a "Merl" (?) in background.

5:10P — Goes to background and calls "Ferrero12(?) followed by indistinct chatter like some kind of instructions. Returns and typing is resumed.

5:15P — Calls "Come in, Rose (?) and get out there". Woman's voice indistinguishable, receding to background. Child's voice indistinct in background. Child's voice - indistinct.

5:25P — Typing. leaves foreground, urinates, and flushes toilet. Undistinct talk in background - Hodel and woman. Hodel say "Next week - maybe make it Friday". Apparently woman patient. Hodel returns to foreground. Talk with woman undistinguishable.

5:35P — Typing, whistling as he does. Someone else moving around in background. Apparently he is not typing because he is talking indistinctly in background on phone. Says, "I'll be there and get it Tuesday night. I'll be looking for you". Rest of conversation not distinguishable because of typing. Says, "That's the only reason I'm going".

5:42P — Typing continuing in foreground. Outside traffic noises also interfering with conversation. Hodel and woman in background. Hodel says something about "Calexico". Woman says "Is there a road?" Hodel says, "The only road there is Typing stops.

5:53P — Indistinct conversation Hodel and woman.

6:00P — Moving about. No conversation.

MODEL FILE - 94(?)

Time	Entry
6:05P	All quiet, except outside traffic and possible very faint conversation in background.
6:08P	Conversation - man and woman in b.g. very faint and undistinguishable. Some faint movement around background.
6:14P	All quiet except outside traffic.
6:37P	Steady, rushing noise - possibly bath water or shower?
6:44P	Noise continues
6:50P	Noise continues. Vacuum cleaner?
7:05P	Noise may be defect in receiver, but if so, cannot determine same. Phoned Lt. Jemison, CR 14917, but no answer.
7:20P	Noise continues. Phoned Technician Braison at OL 9807. While talking with him, noise stopped.
7:22P	All quiet. Normal signal of outside traffic noises coming through. Dog barking.
8:00P	Littleton off duty.
8:00P	Meyer, LAPD, on duty
8:20P	Sounds like someone moving around.
10:20P	All quiet.
3-12-50 2:00AM	Brechel, LAPD, on duty. All is quiet.
3:50AM	Someone moving around for a few minutes.
8:00AM	Egger, D.A.'s office on duty.
8:15AM	All quiet.
8:20AM	Someone walking around, possibly upstairs, no voices.
9:30AM	All quiet.
10:00AM	All quiet.
11:30AM	All quiet.
12:00noon	Cimino, D.A.'s office on duty.
12:05P	All quiet.
1:00P	Radio is turned on. Someone is walking.

MODEL FILE - 99(?)

Time	Entry
1:10P	Voice in background is unintelligible. Radio is still on - music can hardly be heard.
1:15P	Man and woman are talking, but reception is bad - can't understand.
1:30P	Radio off - all is quiet.
1:45P	Bathroom sounds - footsteps. Woman talks - unintelligible.
3:00P	All quiet.
4:20P	Cimino off.
4:20P	Morgan, D.A.'s office, on duty
5:45P	Telephone rang - no answer
7:00P	Woman talking (unintelligible)
21½-23 7:30P	Man and woman conversing (about rooms in house)
8:00P	Wean, LAPD, on duty
8:15P	Telephone rings 2 times - stops - no conversation
8:30P	Telephone rings - 2 times - stops - no conversation
8:45P	Radio playing - someone moving around
2:00A	Brechel, LAPD on duty. All is quiet.
6:30A	Someone moving around house.
6:00A	J. McGrath, D.A.'s office on duty
9:40A	Phone rings 8 times - no answer
11:45A	Phone rings 9 times - no answer
12:05P	Phone rings 8 times - no answer
12:05P	Snyder - D.A.'s office on duty
12:50P	Phone rings - 7 times - no answer
1:20P	Phone rings 6 times - no answer
1:45P	Phone rings 6 times - no answer
1:55P	Phone rings 8 times - no answer
2:10P	Phone rings 6 times - no answer
2:10P	Phone rings 6 times - no answer

HODEL FILE - 109 //9

2:15P	Phone rings 5 times - no answer
2:15P	Phone rings 12 times - no answer
2:22P	Phone rings 9 times - no answer
2:50P	Phone rings 6 times - no answer
3:00P	Phone rings 10 times - no answer
3:40P	Phone rings 4 times - no answer
4:05P	Phone rings 6 times - no answer
5:00P	Snyder off duty
	Wann, LAPD on duty. Someone moving around.
5:15P	Phone rang 6 times - no answer, though some women are talking in the background and moving around

23

7:00P	All quiet
8:00P	All quiet

3-11-50

2:00A	Brecheel, LAPD, on duty, all quiet.
5:00A	Someone enters. Sounds indicate it may be Hodel. Goes to desk, rustling of paper, probably going thru mail. Nope, I was wrong. He was on the car, reading and grunting, then flushes toilet.
5:30A	Hodel walking around house.
6:00A	All is quiet.
6:20A	Female footsteps and voice in background
6:50A	Hodel is snoring
8:00A	J. McGrath, D.A.'s office on duty
8:15A	Using a pretext - determined Hodel is back from Mexico.
9:55A	Hodel receives a phone call - can't understand too much noise and mumbling.
11:45A	Hodel up and moving around in the bathroom.
12:00noon	Sullivan, D.A.'s office on duty
12:05P	Water running. Apparently Hodel in bathroom.

HODEL FILE - HMV //10

12:25P	Phone rings - Hodel answers - about a rental.
1:10P	Bell ringing - sounds like alarm clock turned off.
1:15P	Man talking with Hodel - low tones - unable to understand. Conversation about 2 minutes and man leaves.
1:45P	Door bell rings. Man talking to Hodel. They apparently go to some other part of house.
1:46P	Phone rings 3 times - hear no answer. Possibly in some oth part of house.
1:55P	Hodel pays man. Gives him a check for $18.25 on a $16.50 till. Man gives Hodel change and thanks him very much and is sorry he bothered him.
2:50P	Man talking in background.
3:00P	Someone hammering.
3:05P	Phone rings 2 times. Hodel answers, but unable to hear any conversation.
3:30P	Hodel typing.
4:00P	Kronek on duty.
23-30 4:13P	Hodel answered over the phone about his fishing in Mexico and dropping Ellen off in some town. Hoping she won't have enough money to return - (recorded) Resumes typing.
30-33 6:17P	Joe cam in - (recorded)
6:33P	Hodel makes a call to SUnset 16510 - no answer.
33 7:17P	Hodel calls SUnset 16510 again - no answer.
8:00P	Meyer, LAPD, on duty. All quiet.
8:30P	Phone rang 2 times, didn't hear anyone answer.
9:00P	Hodel and some woman came in. Can't understand conversation.
9:15P	Radio on. Hodel didn't turn it on, not his type of music - too loud.

HODEL FILE - 102 /3/

122

9:36P	Hodel plays some records in Spanish - says were recorded during bombing of Barcelona, Spain - in spanish.
9:53P	About 3 more females enter - sounded like Mickey or Mickey and her bunch, all talking or reading spanish.
10:20P	Phone rang - Hodel answers "Hello Harry, I have been trying to get you". Females making too much noise - can't hear Hodel - said something about fishing in Mexico - radio on again.
11:00P	Females and Hodel just talking.
11:20P	Hodel telling about the place in Mexico - he talked about before - said he look.d at it when he was down this last time - shows a picture of the place - showing onthe map location of place.
11:26P	Some man came in - seemed to know girls.
11:30P	Hodel and man go in back room and talk. Couldn't hear too well - probably receiving order - will pick it up - sounded like will see each other 4 PM tomorrow. Man leaves - man's name "Chris".
33-35½	Lot of talking and laughing.
11:40P	
11:44P	Phone rang - Hodel answers - talks about place in Mexico. Said he had a mexican doctor friend down there, females making lot of noise - tells about fishing in Mexico. Say property will be for sale or lease in two months which about right time. Climate is perfect. Says money is in fishing, about 160 miles by road. Says will try to see him before he goes down to Mexico. Sounded like said "Bob".
3-15-50 12:05A	Hodel says he can get a plane - holds 4 people beside pilot can't hear too well.
12:15A	Women left - Hodel moving around.
2:00A	Brechl, LAPD, on duty. All quiet except for Hodel snoring.

HODEL FILE - 102 /2/

123

6:30A	Female moving around house.
8:00A	J. McGrath, D.A.'s office on duty.
9:30A	No noise, all quiet to present time.
9:50A	Phone call - Hodel answers. Say's wait a minute - sounds like he is looking for some papers. Gave someone a phone number 32341 - could not get prefix.
10:02A	Charlotte, phones Hodel - said to phone him around 6 - just general conversation.
10:55A	Hodel and some man talking about colors. hard to understan talking low. Also talking about plastic bottles, tops, also colors of the caps in bottles. Talking about putting liquid in caps to test them. $16.00 a 1000 for plugs. 2 oz bottles - $27.50 a 1000. $20.00 a 1000 for caps. Non breakable bottles. Hodel going to Bullocks this afternoon - he tells salesman - Hodel talked to the buyer at Bullocks.
11:20A	Salesman leaves - all quiet.
11:45A	All quiet.
11:47A	Hodel called a Mr. Ramey - not in - left a call.
12:00noon	Hodel makes phone call - asks for Department #403 - said CX - thank you, Sullivan, D.A.'s office on duty.
12:45P	Phone rings 2 times - no answer heard. Possibly answered in some other part of home.
12:47P	Hodel talking on phone regarding Sero-logic Laboratories and bills against it. Hodel claims some mistake in bills.
1:05P	Phone rings 2 times - Possibly answered in some other part of house.
1:06P	Hodel on phone - it just got back yesterday - It's 65 miles across the border from Arizona - Sonita (?) Fishing is

HODEL FILE - 104/23

2

good. Talked to Dr. Ignacio Renal (?) much interested in making a sanitrorium out of the place. Cost 1,000,000 pesos to build. I'd just as soon lease it. Are you a Mexican citizen? You're not. I got some photos. Come on over and talk about it. Another Dr., an associate of mi went donthere today to look at it. Would clean about 5000.00 a month. When you come in from Upland the next time, bring her with you so I can meet. Upland 024277 is h phone number. She is a nurse.

1:16P Phone rings - Hodel answers - caught 27 sea bass - may go down next weekend. Talks about his trip. Fine climate, etc.

1:20P Hodel starts typing.

1:22P Phone rings. Hodel answers, "Yes father. I was in Mexico trying to work up a business down there. There have been some new developments that I want to tell you about. OK, Dad, I'll be seeing you.

1:26P Hodel dials phone, mail me my slip for my deposits last month.

1:29P Phone rings - Hodel answers. Oh Joe (?) "They're working on your phone right now. How soon can she come over. I'll wait for her. I'll be glad to have her in here. Does she do day work? How much do you pay her. Oh, she's just a friend.

1:56P Phone rings - Hodel answers. Talks about repairs to garage

2:04P Phone rings - Hodel answers "Pretty good, Pat. I'm just going out - can you be here in 45 minutes. Maybe to-morrow then.

2:05P Hodel dials - Inspector 372 - Mr. Mandy (?) No - I'll call him back.

2:06P Hodel dials - no conversation.

2:07P Hodel dials - Is Dr. Barrett there. This is Dr. Hodel. I just got back from Mexico. I went on a fishing trip. We drove down. I notice we got no business on the Research Maybe on account of phone disconnections. Discusses effort to build up Laboratories business.

2:15P Hodel dials - no conversation.

2:20P Phone rings - Hodel answers - unable to make out conversation.

2:25P Hodel dials - asks for Mr. Rockey - 2All the letter does is to confirm that he is an independent contractor. Relative to unemployment payment to someone.

3:00P Talking to some woman. She said something about doing some work for Hodel. Took her to some other part of house.

3:02P Hodel starts typing.

3:15P Hodel dials phone "Is Mr. Ed Wilcox there". Something about Ed being able to receive a message from Tibet. "I'm expecting a message from Mr. ? of Tibet. (Ed is apparently a ham short-waver)

3:20P Hodel dials phone - no answer.

3:28P Phone rings - Hodel answers. "Hello, dear. How are the children. Did you find your suit-case? I'd love to come down but I can't get away from here. Can't you come in. Try and do it.

3:34P Hodel - "Will you see if PR 8086 is actually busy"?

3:45P Hodel has been trying to reach this number ever since he talked to Ed Wilcox. I believe it is the phone number of another ham.

4:00P Norgac, D.A.'s office, on duty.

HODEL FILE - 105 /∧∿

126

5:10P	Telephone rang - no answer
6:35P	Telephone rang - no answer
8:00P	Meyer, LAPD on duty. Some one moving around.
9:20P	Phone rang 6 times - didn't hear anyone answer.
9:55P	People moving around making lot of noise.
10:05P	Some girls around talking - phone rang - no one answered. Hodel don't seem to be around.
10:13P	Phone rang 35 times - girls still around - no answer.
10:23P	Hodel enters - says he is tired - says something about getting something to eat - all go out to kitchen.
11:00P	Hodel and girls go out to eat.
11:20P	Phone rang - no answer.
12:30A	Hodel and girls return.
1:00A	Girls talking about having babys and how to keep from having them
2:00A	Weaw, LAPD, on duty. Several women talking.
2:30A	Some women leave - Hodel now talking with two women. Radio playing too loud to hear.
3:15A	One woman leaves.
3:30A	Hodel apparently gone to bed. All quiet.
8:00A	Phone rings twice. Hodel answers - a patient with a sore said he would come see him today.
8:00A	Egger, D.A.'s office on duty
8:30A	All quiet.
9:00A	All quiet.
9:00A	Can hear snoring - apparently Hodel.
9:30A	All quiet.
10:00A	All quiet.
10:30A	All quiet.

3-16-50

HODEL FILE - 107 / 24

127

11:00A	All quiet.
11:25A	Phone rings - Hodel answers talking about Mexico. Apparently with some woman - says he will meet her at 3 PM today.
11:30A	Hodel moving around
11:45A	Hodel still moving around - some bathroom noises.
11:55A	Hodel still moving around
12:15P	Some desk noises - Hodel leaves room
	Snyder, D.A.'s office on duty.
12:55P	Hodel calls Sears-Roebuck on Santa Monica Blvd. in regards to mattress covers. Who knows, might be a sale, eh? Also calls Broadway-Hollywood-same subject.
2:10P	Hodel typing, and mumbling to himself.
2:45P	Still noise of typing, among various and sundry other noises.
3:30P	Phone rings 5 times - no answer
3:50P	Female voice in distance - unintelligible.
4:00P	Phone rings - Hodel answers - some chatter regarding personal loans - also some chatter about someone having personal cards printed - talks by selling tea wholesale. $12. per/retail- 40% off - 2% ten days
4:10P	Phone rings - Hodel answers - someone coming right over Snyder off duty 4:15PM

3-17-50

MODEL FILE - 108
3-16-50
SPOOL 37

Time	Entry
4:20P	Model dials Rompage Hardware Store on Hollywood Blvd. about some delivery.
4:35P	Someone called at suggestion of Ed Wilcox - conversation pertaining to Ham station W6CMB (CMB?)
5:05P	Some man, woman and a little boy arrived - adults discuss th CFS
6:03P	Model answered the phone and promised to be right over.
6:10P	Model makes call to OL 5851 - couldn't get his party. Dials another number - "Hello Mabel - is Erwin there?" Talk about sending Erwin a check (Erwin Hough) for digging some thing.
7:44P	Examination of a woman patient, who is coming back Tuesday.
7:50P	Model is typing.
8:00P	Meyer, LAPD, on duty. Model dials phone - asks operator OL 5851 - no answer - hangs up.
8:45P	Model left - all quiet.
9:18P	Phone rang 6 times - no answer.
11:00P	Phone rang 8 times - no answer.
11:40P	Phone rang 5 times - no answer.
2:00A	Model apparently sleeping. Can hear snoring.
3:00A	J. McGrath - D.A.'s office on duty
9:30A	No activity
11:00A	Model up
11:30A	Around bathroom
12:00noon	Eggar, D.A.'s office on duty
12:30P	Model moving around room.
1:00P	Model made phone call regarding sewage disposal or some digging on his property. Model said that he was in a hurry to get the work done, and he would wait for the workmen this afternoon.

MODEL FILE - 109

Time	Entry
1:15P	Model moving around. Phone rings 3 times, must have been answered other room.
1:20P	Model out of room - can hear him talking to several men in background.
1:25P	Called Miss White about placing an ad in the paper - said th ad is in the name of E.L. Marsh in the category of furnished rooms and apts. "Shang-ri-la" is at top of ad. Model wants to change ad to read; Artists and writers preferred.
(Re-corded 1 min to 36:)	
1:30P	Model typing at desk.
1:45P	Model leaves room.
2:10P	Can hear some machine noises - sounds like an electric hand drill. No conversation, drill keeps going on and off.
2:20P	All quiet.
2:35P	Phone rings 4 times - no answer.
2:45P	Machine noise - off - whistling in background - some moving around.
2:50P	Can hear talking, two or three men in background, sound like they might be in basement; cannot make out conversation.
3:00P	Can still hear muffled conversation with occasional machine noises; sawing, etc.
3:30P	Model or someone moving about desk - same background noises men and machines working
3:45P	Same as above
4:00P	Still some background noises as stated above.
4:15P	Same as above
4:20P	Phone rings 6 times - no answer - can hear walking around however.
4:25P	Model called SY 9490 - asked for Fritz. Fritz not there.
4:25P	Hronek, D.A.'s office on duty.

541

HODEL FILE - 110 / 2-7

5:04P	Phone rings 7 times - no answer.
5:25P	Phone rings 5 times - no answer.
6:19P	Phone rings 1 time - must be answered in another room.
7:20P	Hodel returns and starts typing.
7:45P	Phone rings - Hodel answered - talked to someone about his trip to Mexico.
7:55P	Meyer, LAPD, on duty. All quiet.
7:57P	Hodel and some woman came in-talking in another room.
8:00P	Phone rings. Hodel answers - talking to someone who just got back from Frisco.
8:15P	Still talking to female who came in with him-can't make out what they are saying.
8:40P	Radio on - still talking.
8:45P	Hodel on phone - radio too loud to hear - said something about 1735 No. La Brea.
11:10P	The guy with the accent came in - radio on too loud - two women, one don't seem to understand English, other translates to her (mother and daughter)
11:25P	Hodel telling about his fishing in Mexico.
36-491 11:30P	Women leave - Hodel and man with accent - talking recorded - hard to hear. Hodel says probably they are watching me, talk about selling some of his stuff at an auction - says someone don't know anything to tell. Hodel said something about getting married again - talks about place in Mexico. Says it will clear about 4 or 5,000 a month. Hodel talking about Tibet and a letter he wrote there, says it is quite a job getting a letter sent there. Radio still on - talk world aff

HODEL FILE - 114 / 3 ○
2-18-50

12:40A	Hodel - "Do you think those "Bastards" will try to bring action because I am renting rooms". Hodel says "Do you think we could hire some girl to find out what they are doing".
12:45A	Talking about women.
1:00A	Man with accent left - Hodel turned radio off - should have done that a hr. ago.
1:15A	Sounds like Hodel going to bed.
2:00A	Brechel, LAPD, on duty. All is quiet.
6:00A	Radio turned on (Sta KMW) must have been left turned on as there was no one up to have turned it on. The program is first of the day.
6:20A	Radio still playing - Hodel still snoring.
7:30A	Radio still playing.
8:00A	J. McGrath, D.A.'s office on duty.
9:30A	No activity - radio now off.
10:30A	Phone rings - answered in rear of home.
11:45A	Phone rings 2 times - answered in rear.
12:50P	No sound
1:00P	Egger, D.A.'s office on duty.
1:15P	Seems to be moving around in other sections of the house, but otherwise All quiet.
1:25P	Hodel in background - conversation with woman.
2:00P	Woman's voice in background.
2:30P	Phone 1 time, but could hear no one answer - all quiet.
3:30P	All quiet.
3:45P	Background noises - Hodel and woman talking.
4:00P	Morgan, D.A.'s office, on duty.
4:50P	Someone opened and closed all the drawers in the desk

HODEL FILE - 112 /3/
4:40P
4:50P MORGAN ON DUTY (?)
(hurriedly) also sounds of paper shuffling and scrambling in another part of the room.

49½-50½ 4:55P Telephone rang - Hodel answered - conversation regarding room rental - Hodel turned party down.

50½-54½ 5:05P Hodel telephoned - conversation regarding rental or room wherein Hodel suggested that some part time work around place could be applied on Rental of rooms - made appointment for tomorrow about 11 AM to show place - Hodel leaving tonight at 7 PM.

5:13P Telephone rang - no answer.

54½-55 5:20P Telephone rang - Hodel "Yes, yes" What did you say your name is - Madeline Smith - Oh, suppose you call me tomorrow at 12". Ends "Alright goodbye".

5:23P Hodel (I guess) dialed phone several times - no answer.

5:30P Going through drawers again - sounds of dog whining (?)
Typing noise.

55-55½ 5:32P Hodel and woman (sounds like Mrs. Hodel) conversing about some medical term - Hodel "There's about a millionth of an ounce in the human body", etc. (?)

55½-56 6:12P Hodel dialed phone - Hodel "What time does the owl show go on
What time does the whole show end?" Ends, "Thank you".

56½-
563/4 7:00P Telephone rang - Hodel "She left/about ½ hour ago
my place
She should be there about now". Hope you can keep it under control". Ends "Goodbye".

7:15P Hodel conversing with another woman, who he called Gladys about some engravings they were looking at. They discussed h
cursing sounded in French, Spanish, and Chinese.

HODEL FILE - 113 /3/
563/4- 7:43P Telephone rang - Hodel "Hello Jill (or something) How's
60 everything? Under control? Etc. Are you a tea lover?
I have some tea for you - some very special tea - I am abou
to take off for the evening now, etc. something about an
eighteen year - answering the phone, etc.

8:00P Mean, LAPD, on duty.

9:10P Phone rang once, no one answered.

9:25P Phone rang 3 times - no one answered.

9:50P A man enters house, and asks for Hodel - some woman tells hi
he is gone. He leaves.

10:55P Hodel returns - phones andasks someone if they would like to
hear some music. Says OK, and hangs up.

11:15P Hodel talking with eighteen year old girl - radio too loud
to understand.

11:40P Hodel typing.

2-12-50
2:00A Brechel, LAPD, on duty. All is quiet except Hodel is snorin
9:30A Jamison, D.A.'s office - all quiet.
10:00A voices - not distinguishable.
11:20A All quiet.
11:30A Tapping sound.
11:55A Hodel - in bathroom - flushes toilet.
11:58A Hodel takes a bath - says "poor fish".
12:00noon Egger, D.A.'s office on duty.
12:15P Hodel walking around desk noises.
12:20P Hodel turns on the symphony on radio.
1:00P Symphony still on - no other noise.
1:30P Symphony still on; can hear Hodel talking to woman in background.

HODEL FILE - 114/3 3

	1:45P	Hodel answers door bell, lets in woman - he talks to her about renting her a room in return he will knock off the rent - at work she does for him such as cleaning and taking care of his quarters. Negro woman has her minor daughter with her.
	1:50P	Phone rings - Hodel says "Mrs Hodel is out - I can take message. He said he is going down to the beach about 4 PM today - talks about renting room.
	2:00P	Hodel again talking to negro woman. Hodel asks her daughter where she goes to school - the girl says-a catholic school.
	2:10P	Colored woman and child leaving. woman is going to think it over - about renting room. Woman then starts talking about Doctor's-Hodel tells her about his clinic at 1st and Central Woman said she had a curettement (curettement ?) in 1944. Hodel said he has done lots of them. Hodel and woman continue to talk about doctors, sickness, and other medical subjects. (Hodel seems to be acting overly nice to this woman He must be trying to talk her into renting the room, or ?) Hodel tells her that Dr. Hill, a colored doctor, lives next door.
	2:30P	Woman leaves
	2:50P	Phone rings 2 times, must have been answered in another room Hodel moving about desk.
	3:15P	Hodel leaves room - all quiet.
	3:45P	All quiet.
SPOOL 38	4:00P	Hronek, L.A.'s office, on duty.

HODEL FILE - 115/3 4

0	5:00P	Sounds like someone uses the vacuum cleaner.
	6:00P	No sound
	7:00P	No sound
	8:00P	No sound. Wean, LAPD, on duty / Woman's voice in background.
	10:30P	Phone rings 3 times, can't hear anyone answer.
	11:00P	All quiet.
3-20-50		
0-1	12:30P	Hodel typing.
	2:00A	Brodel, LAPD, on duty
	2:08A	Phone rings. Hodel answers "Hello, hes yes". Short conversation is recorded. Apparently is receiving instructions, and agrees to it. "Yes, I'll do it", or "Yes, I'll be there". Hodel was in bedroom when he received call and must have been waiting for it as phone rang once only.
	2:09R	Hodel went out of room after the call.
	2:48A	Hodel returns to room.
	3:25A	Hodel moving around room.
	3:45A	All quiet.
	8:00A	J. McGrath, D.A.'s office on duty
	9:30A	All quiet, no activity.
	10:15A	Phone call received - can't hear-too much racket - Hodel has dinner engagement tonight. Going out of town Wednesday. Hodel talking about selling the house.
	10:17A	Hodel makes phone call - too much static to hear.
	10:21A	Hodel makes phone call - cannot hear.
	10:23A	Phone call received - lots of static
	11:54A	Phone call received by Hodel - talks low - can't hear.
	11:55A	Hodel makes phone call - can't make out.

HODEL FILE - 116 / 3 J

12:00noon Snyder, D.A.'s office on duty

1:10P Phone rings - inquiry regarding rooms or house - Hodel tells her to call back between 3:30 and 4:00. Says he is going out for afternoon.

1:15P Hodel call UCLA - seeking information re. Burrel Ives. Reserves 2 seats, 13th row, near aisle - did not get date.

1:50P The doctor Hodel is taking a bath.

2:15P Hodel leaves house.

2:50P Phone rings 8 times - no answer.

4:00P Kronsk, D.A.'s office on duty.

6:55P Two women and a man carry on a conversation about books and poetry - the fellow is apparently an actor - talks about himself mile a minute.

7:05P Moved to another part of house - conversation unintelligible.

8:00P Meyer, LAPD, on duty. Hear people talking, but unable to understand.

8:40P Man and woman talking, not English, can't understand.

9:00P Hodel talking to some man with an accent (not same) sounds like a photographer talking about taking pictures. Hodel shows some pictures he took.

9:12P Radio on - not Hodel's music.

10:00P Still playing Chinese - music worse then Hodel's music.

10:25P Sounds like Hodel around by himself - radio off.

10:50P Hodel and some guy with accent talking, and looking at map of Mexico. (The photographer).

11:05P Talking about going (to Mexico) want to leave tomorrow night, Hodel says don't tell anyone. Hodel says he has to be back Wednesday. He is going to Santa Barbara, and won't be back until Sunday. Sounds like they are going to take pictures until Sunday. Sounds like Hodel is trying to pull a fast one of some kind

HODEL FILE - 117 / 3 G

11:05P This other guy seems to know the country.

11:25P Guy with accent leaves, says will call tomorrow and make arrangements about going if they go

11:30P Hodel moving around by Himself

12:00A Sounds like Hodel has gone to bed - all quiet.

3-21-50
2:00A Brechel, LAPD, on duty. All is quiet. Hodel must have slep in another part of house. There were no snoring noises all morning. Music in the background all morning till 6:30A coming from rear part of house.

8:00A J. McGrath, D.A.'s office on duty

8:45A Phone call received - could not hear in back room

8:57A Phone call received - zznkit can't make out - ended conversation at 9:22 - could not hear anything-too much noise and static.

9:25A Hodel made phone call - hard to hear - said something about fishing - also a test on a patient named Woman.

9:35A Insurance inspector calls to inspect some belongings of one of the tenants.

9:40A Hodel makes phone call to some doctor - sounds like Barrymore

10:45A Phone call received for someone els - Hodel said "I will have her call you".

10:47A Someone phoned - Hodel said "I will get hold of you as soon as the stuff is here."

10:55A Hodel phones someone about $50.00 a month he paid some woman "Said I'm in trouble" want some advice - do you have a farm.

11:00A Phone call received - Hodel ran to back of house-answered could not hear.

HODEL FILE - 118 /37

11:01A Hodel makes phone call to some one.

11:05A A woman comes to see Hodel - sounds like Dorothy-they go to rear of the house - can't hear.

11:45A Sullivan, D.A.'s office on duty. Can hear Hodel and woman talking but unable to understand as they are in some other part of house.

11:55A Hodel typing

12:05P Dorothy asks Hodel for telephone number - he gives her HO 93311 - Albert Van. She apparently called from some other part of house.

12:12P Dorothy Hodel dials phone - asks for Mr. Holser (Said she was Dorothy Hodel) No conversation.

12:14P Dorothy dials more - asks for Rollin Brown - talks to him "I went down to Mexico and had a nice time fishing, that's why I haven't seen you. Fell off the pier. Told him he should have picked up some of the weights we had dropped dow there. Talks about meeting Doctor in Mexico and about the place in Mexico. Talks about how George and he fly down the: It's in Sonora County. It's near Otho (?) About 400 miles from here (George is prompting her) There are whore houses there, and we visited one. George was seeing rashes all over the place (She's sure giving this guy a sales talk) Hodel is typing and hence unable to hear Dorothy's conversation.

12:26P Dorothy finished conversation.

12:27P Dorothy dials phone - HO 93311 charged to HO 984.85 - This Dorothy Huston. Is Mr. Bangs (?) there. Please have him call me at CI 3476, or Santa Monica 42421. George tells Dorothy John won't call her and won't

HODEL FILE - 119 /38

12:40P Hodel dials - "Is this Miss Machie?" How is Dr. Nicholas? Shall I write him? I'll write him?

12:42P Hodel is typing and hence conversation unintelligible.

12:47P Hodel dials (Tu 4826) asks for medical desk.

1:00 to 1:15P Hodel and Dorothy engage in a little loving

1:16P Water running

1:20P Hodel typing

1:55P Dorothy phones asks for : This is Mrs Rogal (?) Tell him I called.

1:56P Hodel dials - Water running - conversation unintelligible. He's talking about a job. "I prefer part time. Is it hospit or clinic. What pay is he offering. Talks about his work as chief of staff at clinic. I'm medical director of a local laboratory, but I have ten much time. Send me your contract form.

2:02P Talking about their children.

2:10P Phone rings. Hodel answers "I'll call you this evening about 7 or 8 o'clock. Maybe we'll go tomorrow Joe".

2:35P Quiet.

2:55P Phone rings 6 times - no one answers.

4:00P Still quiet.

4:05P Wronek D.A.'s office on duty

4:33P Phone rang 15 times - no answer

4:45P " " 10 times - no answer

5:52P " " 4 times - no answer

7:40P " " 6 times - no answer

8:00P Meyer, LAPD, on duty. All quiet.

9:20P Phone rang 3 time, didn't hear anyone answer.

HODEL FILE - 120

3-21-50

SPOOL 38

11:25 P	Sounds like Hodel just came home - at his desk moving papers.
11:40P	Phone rang - Hodel answers "Hello, Tracey - any calls for me? That was all.
12:30A	Hodel snoring
3-22-50 2:00A	Brechel LAPD on duty - All is quiet
7:25A	Sounds like Hodel getting up - running water in bathroom
8:00A	M. McGrath, D.A.'s office on duty
8:30a	All quiet
10:40A	Phone rings 6 times - no answer
12:00P	Sullivan, D.A.'s office on duty
12:00P-4:00P	Bisson, Belle, and Sullivan listening to past recording: as Hodel has been out for the entire day.
4:00P	Egger, D.A.'s office on duty . Hodel still out.
5:00P	No noise-Hodel still out
5:00P	Woman enters, but no Hodel
5:05P	Phone rings 10 times - no answer
6:00P	All quiet.
6:10P	Hodel comes in - works at desk
6:30P	Can hear Hodel and Woman talking in background - Hodel still working around desk.
6:35P	Hodel phoning, says "This is Dr. Hodel returning your call". Too much background and line noise to make out most of conversation - something about records. Also talking about urine specimens and venerial disease. other party seems to be doing most of the talking. Conversation is along medical lines.

HODEL FILE - 121

6:45P	Woman comes in and calls "Doctor" Hodel is still on phone, can hear the woman walking around, humming, then leaves.
6:50P	Hodel still on phone (not talking much).
7:00P	Conversation has now turned to corporations, stocks, and bonds with Hodel doing very little talking.
7:20P	Conversation over - Hodel moving around desk.
7:30P	Hodel still moving around desk.
7:55P	Hodel still at desk - no conversation. Hodel leaves room - then comes back.
8:00P	Meyer, LAPD, on duty. All quiet.
8:22P	Hodel and some girl come in - talking - can't understand too much other noise.
8:35P	Radio on.
9:40P	Hodel by himself - typing.
10:30P	All quiet except radio on.
10:47P	Radio off - all quiet.
3-23-50 2:00A	Brechel, LAPD, on duty. All quiet.
3:00A	Hodel makes visit to lavatory, returns to bed.
8:00A	J. McGrath, D.A.'s office on duty
10:15A	All quiet.
12:00noon	All quiet.

HODEL FILE - 122
3-23-50

4:00P-8:00P Hronek, D.A.'s office, on duty

4:10P Occasional movement in the background

4:30P All quiet

5:00P All quiet

5:20P All quiet

6:00P All quiet

6:30P All quiet

0- 7:00P Hodel comes in and makes a call - about some compound takes the address, 60E 42nd St., New York 17, N.Y. "I'm writing myself". Serms of yea, yea, yea, alright, yea, yea, that's from the U.S. Chemical News - USI Chem News, Feb 1950 - I know, yea, yea, they have written - OK thanks, Good night.

7:15P Phone rang 5 times - no answer.

7:25P Door bell rang - some woman comes in - conversation in the background.

0-6 7:45P Hodel came in with Dorothy - phone rang (recorded)

8:00P Meyer, LAPD, on duty. Radio on.

8:02P Phone rang - Hodel answers - said Exbrook 32473, about a phone number.

9:30P Radio turned on - don't hear anyone.

10:30P Some woman just came in - Hodel asks if she ever saw a certain book - talking about "Matches" (The woman is) sounds like she designs match covers.

11:20P The dame is still talking, boy she is sure wound up.

HODEL FILE - 123
3-24-50

12:15A Woman left, had been talking since 10:30P

12:40A Dame back again and still talking

12:45A Dame left again.

12:55A Hodel typing - radio off

1:15A Hodel called and sent a nite letter to a Mrs. Barbe 1543 Valejo St., San Francisco. Something about birthday wishes. Message read "My birthday wishes must go to you. I hope each year will make ------?------? Am doing my best and will continue trying. Please leave me know how things are going".

2:00A Brechel, LAPD, on duty. Hodel typing.

2:10A Typing stops - goes to lavatory - urinates then all quiet.

2:15A To bed - all quiet.

8:00A J. McGrath, D.A.'s office on duty

9:45A All quiet.

10:10A Phone call received. Hodel answers - says "Oh yes; fire yes, yes. Well, all right, that's good, as soon as you know, yeah, yeah, good." Hangs up.

10:50A Phone rings 2 times - answered in rear of house.

10:52A Hodel typing at his desk.

11:30A Phone call received - Hodel answers - for someone else.

12:20P Phone call received by Hodel "Yeah, yeah, oh that's swell. Yeah, yeah, oh that's good, uh huh. He will give you some good advice anyway -" Talking about a $1000.00 order now, of some kind. Interested in a merger - "all right Tom, goodbye".

144

MODEL FILE - 125

3-24-50

	4:00P	Hronek, D.A.'s office on duty--All quiet.
	4:30P	Hodel starts typing.
6-8½	5:00P	Call out by Taylor MU 2165, one of Hodel's associates.
8½-11	5:10P	Same person making a call and talking
	6:18P	Hodel starts typing again
11	6:41P	Hodel comes in with another guy -"sit down, let me fix us a drink -" They talk about foods and drinks of different nations - girl comes in. Hodel call Churchil 92146.
	8:00P	Meyer, LAPD, on duty. All quiet.
	8:40P	Phone rang 4 times - too much background noise - couldn't hear anyone answer.
	9:50P	Hodel comes in with some man, talking about Mexico - lots of noise in background.
11-19	10:20P	Radio on playing records - some girl around
nothing	11:15P	Radio off - Hodel staying talking to man, hard to hear.
	11:18P	Phone rang - Hodel answers - sounded like talking to someone in other part of house - man left.
	11:50P	Hodel comes back in - starts typing
3-25	12:05A	Radio on again.
19-20	12:30A	Phone - xHodel answers - radio on - said something about having money by then.
	12:36A	Radio off - sounded like Hodel left.
	1:00A	Mean, LAPD, on duty. Someone moving around and typing
	1:30A	Hodel returns.
	2:00A	All quiet - not sure if Hodel left or is in bed
	3:30A	Phone rings 3 times - woman calls Hodel - no more conversation.
	4:30A	All quiet.

143

MODEL FILE - 124

26
5 to 9 - talk of trial
9 to 40 much talk of juggling figures.

27
13 to 15 - talk about deducting some money as repayment of loans to father and son.
18 to 22 - wire bad Skip - listen from 40 on to
46 to 48 - very interesting (cut this spool off at 50 the end is loose).

Spool #37

3-5   Conversation regarding tax case and Dahlia
5-17   Conversation regarding code and mailing - have to be careful - income tax starts at 15 on Spool 25

145

HODEL FILE - 126

8:00P   Meyer, LAPD, on duty. All quiet.

20-61 11:10P   Hodel and Baron (man with accent) came in talking low - can't hear (recording) only stays few minutes and leaves. I was wrong - was in bathroom. Sounded like Hodel said something about Black Dahlia. Baron said something about F.B.I. Then talked about Tibet - sounded like Hodel wants to get out of the country. mentioned passport - Hodel giving Baron dope on how to write to Tibet. Hodel talking about Mexico - going down and take pictures and write a story. Hodel seems afraid about something. Hodel says his Sanatorium - if he got it started in Mexico - would be "Safe".

Spool 39
12:00A
Mar 26 1950
0-50 12:07A   Spool ran out - changing - talking about woman.
Not much talk - still recording. Hodel says he wants money and power - talking about China - talking about selling some of Hodel's paintings or something. Hodel talking about picture police have of him and some girl - thought he had destroyed them all - wire quit at 50 - new one going on - not much talk.

Spool 40
3-37 1:00A   Had trouble with one spool. Had to use another - still talking about selling paintings.

1:50A   Sounds like Baron left - don't know if there is anything on these records or not.

2:00A   Hodel at his desk - all else quiet - Good night.

3:00P   Hodel having party - about 8 people - someone listening to radio programs. Meyer, LAPD, on duty.

3:30P

5:00P   Woman and Hodel talking, but radio too loud to hear.

146

HODEL FILE - 127

37-49 6:20P   Hodel talking with woman.

6:35P   Recorded

49-50 8:00P   Phone - Hodel answers - recorded - couldn't hear too well. Meyer, LAPD, on duty.

50- 10:15P   Hodel and some man came in - not sure if Baron or not -
60   guess it is (recording) talking about paintings and etc. And Asia - Change records

Spool 41
0-1½ 11:15P   New wire on-guess both left.
1½-23 11:55P   Hodel-some woman come in - also the Baron. Hodel and Baron talking low - guess woman left. Woman back. Guess same gabby woman that was there other nite. About watches. Advertising woman left again. Gabby is back - all looking at pictures and etc.

3-27 1:00A   Everyone left.
2:00A   All quiet. Good nite.

147

Addendum B

Bk 49
Pg 14

STATEMENT OF DOROTHY HARVEY HODEL TAKEN AT 410 SANTA MONICA
PIER, SANTA MONICA BY LT. FRANK B. JEMISON AT 1:15 P. M.
ON MARCH 22, 1950.

File No.:   Present:
Charge: Murder   Questions by: Lt. Jemison
Title: Reported by: Dorn A. Perisho
Deputy:

Q What is your full name?
A Dorothy Harvey Hodel.

Q What is your residence address at the present time?
A 410 Santa Monica Pier.

Q What is your phone number here?
A I don't have a phone. There is a fishing renting place
downstairs, SM 42421.

Q What is your present occupation?
A Housewife. I do a little writing, but I'm not working
at the present time.

Q Were you formerly married to Dr. George Hodel?
A Yes.

Q Are you now divorced from him?
A Yes.

Q How long have you been divorced from him?
A The interlocutory decree was in 1944 and the final was
in 1945.

Q Do you have any children from him?
A Yes, I have three boys.

Q Are you acquainted with Tamara Hodel?
A Yes.

Q And is Dr. George Hodel the father of Tamara?
A Yes.

Q Are you acquainted with her mother?
A Yes.

Q What is her name?
A Dorothy.

-1-

1 Q Where is she living now, what city?
    A I believe San Francisco, but I'm not sure.

2 Q You are familiar, are you with the trial that Dr. Hodel
3 just went through in connection with Tamara?
    A I know about it, but I didn't attend it.

4 Q Do you know Lillian Lenorak?
5 A Yes, I do.

6 Q When did you first become acquainted with her, about what
year?
7 A I think it was about 1940. Let me see, say '46. I'm
not really sure.

8 Q When did you last see her?
9 A Just before she went to Camarillo and just before her mother
came for her. Anyway, after she was ill over there at
10 George's.

11 Q Do you know her mother?
    A No.

12 Q When you last saw her did you feel she was a mental case,
13 is that what your information is?
    A I felt she must be. The little boy was running around
and was very distressed. Poor little kid.

15 Q I will now show you a photograph of Beth Short, Santa Barbara
No. 11419 and ask you whether or not you have ever seen that
16 young lady in your life?
    A No, I never have.

17 Q Did you have a conversation with Dr. Hodel about the
18 murder of Beth Short?
    A No, unless we mentioned it when it was in the papers, but
19 I don't like to read about things like that. I can't say
for sure that I have never mentioned her name to him, but it may
20 have been in passing.

21 Q Did he ever tell you, "They can't pin that murder on me?"
    A No, to the best of my knowledge he didn't and doesn't
22 know her.

23 Q On or about the date of her murder, January 15, 1947
do you remember being out until 4:00 in the morning with George
24 Hodel and coming in slightly intoxicated? Now, that's three
years ago.

25 A Well, I think I explained before we never went on
drinking parties because I don't drink because of certain
tendencies to drink too much and particularly if I were near

-2-

1   him I would not drink because from a medical point of view
2   he does not approve of my drinking and I don't know that I
    understood that question.
3 Q Well, the information that I have is that he was quite
4   intoxicated himself and at that time of that occasion stated
    that they couldn't pin the Black Dahlia murder on him.
    A No. No, that isn't true.
5 Q Do you remember ever telling Tamar that?
6 A No.
7 Q Did you ever tell Tamar that Dr. George Hodel was out
    the night before the murder with Beth Short at a party?
8 A No, I was living at my brother's house at the time. We
9   were not living at the same house. I wouldn't know what he was
    doing.
10 Q What was your brother's address at that time?
11 A 2121 Loma Vista Place.
12 Q Has anybody ever told you that Dr. George Hodel had Beth
    Short over to his home?
13 A No.
14 Q Nobody has ever told you that?
15 A No. No one has ever told me that.
16 Q For your information her photograph has been identified by
    certain persons as resembling the young lady that was over to
17   his house prior to the murder. You never heard anything about
    that?
    A I never did.
18 Q As a matter of fact you are on quite a friendly relation
19 aren't you, with Dr. George Hodel?
    A We are friends.
20 Q And at the time of this murder, which was so publicized
21 and made headlines in the newspaper at that time, weren't
    you on pretty friendly terms with him?
22 A We have always been on friendly terms.
23 Q That was January 15, 1947 three years and two months
    ago.
24 A I'm trying to relate it to when he got back from China.
    Was that before or after he got back from China?
25 Q It was sometime after he got back from China. It was
26 at a time when Dr. George Hodel had a medical clinic on East
    First Street, near Central Avenue.
    A He had the clinic for a long time before he left.

-3-

1 Q Let's go back to the time and do you remember at that
    time of Dr. Hodel having noon lunch or dinner at the Biltmore?
2 A No.
3 Q Did you ever have lunch with Dr. Hodel at the Biltmore?
    A I imagine so.
4 Q Would you know it to be a fact that Dr. Hodel did eat
5 lunch or dinner on occasion at the Biltmore?
    A He has taken me to lunch there once or twice and we have
6 had dinner there perhaps.
7 Q For your information we know of other women that have had
    lunch with him at the Biltmore Hotel and dinner.
8 A It's a central location.
9 Q There is further information that Dr. Hodel stayed at the
    Biltmore Hotel on a few occasions. Do you remember those?
10 A I believe when he was between apartments when they had that
    three-day law in effect, he stayed I believe. I'm not sure.
11 I think the Biltmore was among them. He made a tour of the
    hotels and stayed three days in each while he was finding
    an apartment.
12
13 Q You understand that a very serious crime has been
    committed here and the District Attorney would not like it
14 if you were to withhold any information in connection
    with a murder of this type and we would like to have you
15 give us any and all information you may have in connection
    with this murder on this suspect George Hodel. If there is
16 anything you have to tell us, tell us.
    A I have nothing to tell you that would bear out any idea
17 you may have that he did this. All I know is that he is not
    the sort of man that would psychologically be the kind to do
18 it. He has a fine record as a doctor and is a dedicated man.
19 He has never had a fashionable practice. He could have had.
    He is a man that really cares about medicine, not of earning
20 money, but it is incredible to me that he should be in
    any way connected with it.
21 Q You know that Dr. Hodel has had practice with surgical
    tools?
22 A I know he has neverpracticed surgery. His branch of
23 medicine is V. D. generally and Administrative Medicine.
24 Q I show you Sheriff's Photograph B 119364 and will ask
    you if you recognize that?
    A Yes.
25 Q Who is that?
26 A Dr. George Hodel.

-4-

-5-

1 Q Now in view of the fact that the District Attorney's office
2 is interested in contacting all persons that might know something
  about whether or not Dr. Hodel had anything to do with this
3 murder, I now show you a photograph of a nude girl and ask
  you if you recognize who that girl is. In other words,
4 we went to know her name and where we can contact her?
  A There is something familiar about her face. I think she may
  have been some model or something.

6 Q Would you say she is a colored girl or half Indian, do you
  know?
  A No.

7 Q Would you know who the photographer might be in connection
8 with this picture?
  A No.

9 Q I show you another photograph of the same girl with a
10 man. Do you recognize that man in that photograph?
  A I would say that was Dr. Hodel.

11 Q Do you know the person who owns the cat that they are holding
12 between them?
  A No, I don't.

13 Q In other words, I am sincerely interested in contacting
14 this girl for information.
  A No, I don't know her. I have seen her face. I have seen
15 photographs that George has of her.

16 Q Would you have any idea where we could find her?
  A No.

17 Q I show you the third picture. Dr. Hodel and the colored
18 girl. You still can't place any person that might know where
19 I can find her?
  A No, I don't know. I can't think.

20 Q Did you ever hear Dr. Hodel say anything more about
21 the details of this murder of Beth Short about the body or
  anything about it?
  A No, I never heard him discuss it at all.

23 Q Well, if you look back on the events that took place
24 about the time of the murder, did you have any reason to
  suspect that Dr. Hodel might have had something to do with it?
  A None whatever.

25 Q Let me advise you that we do have information that he did
26 associate with Beth Short and as you know the last place she

-6-

1 was seen alive was at the Biltmore Hotel in the evening
2 of January 9, 1947.
  A I didn't know that.

3 Q You are positive at this time that you never met that girl?
  A Very very sure.

4 Q What is the name of your attorney?
5 A Robert Butts.

6 Q And what is his address?
7 A It's the Bank of America Building at Hollywood and Iver.
  I forget the number.

8 Q Did he advise you to give a statement to the District
9 Attorney's office?
  A Yes.

10 Q He did request however that you get a copy of the statement
11 is that right?
  A That's right.

12 Q And as I have stated before, that's something the District
13 Attorney has never done in connection to giving copies to any
  witnesses at any time.
14 A I didn't know.

Addendum C

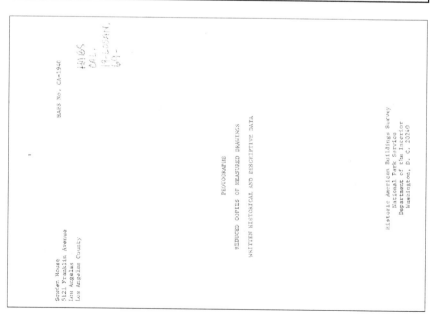

HABS No. CA-1940

2

HISTORIC AMERICAN BUILDINGS SURVEY

SOWDEN HOUSE

Location: 5121 Franklin Avenue, Los Angeles, Los Angeles County, California.

Present Owner: Mrs. E. G. Mazur, 6626 Franklin Avenue, Los Angeles, Dr. and Mrs. Harold Mazur, 4621 Los Feliz, Los Angeles.

Present Occupant: Unoccupied.

Present Use: Residence.

Significance: This house, designed by Lloyd Wright in 1926, is built around a central court which originally contained an elaborate fountain. The house is entered through a cavelike opening whose textured concrete units create a striking contrast to the planar surfaces flanking it. These blocks are repeated in the central court.

PART I. HISTORICAL INFORMATION

A. Physical History:

1. Date of erection: 1926.

2. Architect: Lloyd Wright.

3. Original and subsequent owners:

   1926   John Sowden

   1930   Ruth Rand Barnett

   1936   Milton Blazier, Jr.

   1944   Romayne Goldsmith

   1945   George H. and Andree Hodel

   1950   Helen Fitzpatrick

   1951   The Mazurs

   Legal description: Book 5589, page 3, Parcel 1, Lot 20, Tract 3369; and 25 feet on E. end of Lots 4, 5 and 6 of Tract 2099 (Site is 100 ft. by 175 ft.)

4. Builder, contractor, suppliers:

   W. W. Moore, Contractor

   Chevy Chase Staff and Stone Co.: textured concrete block, under direction of Mr. Paolio.

1

HABS No. CA-1940

Sowden House
5121 Franklin Avenue
Los Angeles
Los Angeles County

PHOTOGRAPHS

REDUCED COPIES OF MEASURED DRAWINGS

WRITTEN HISTORICAL AND DESCRIPTIVE DATA

Historic American Buildings Survey
National Park Service
Department of the Interior
Washington, D. C. 20240

SOWDEN HOUSE
HABS No. CA-1940 (Page 3)

3. Wall construction, finish, color: 2" x 4" stud wall construction with members 16" o.c.--carried on 4" x 6" wood sills on concrete foundation. Metal lath and plaster. Exterior stucco finish in brownish tone. Reinforced concrete structural frames form the "cathedral" ceilings of studios and living room.

4. Porches, stoops, bulkheads, etc.: Entrance slab at the southern front to the house, 39'-4" away from the front of the house. Stairs up to the south front, which has an impressive cavern-like entrance passage. The entrance is on axis, but the path of entry beyond that point is indirect to the right.

There is a terrace in the central court.

5. Chimneys: A 14" x 16" flue is located on the west wall near the south corner of the house; it is finished flush with the parapet. An 8" x 12" flue is also located on the west wall just north of the midpoint. It also is finished flush with the parapet.

6. Openings:

a. Doorways and doors: Entrance passage is controlled through the use of a copper gate which has chevron-like plates on vertical bars. The front door is located atop the stairway, which is to the right upon passing through the gate. This door measures 3' x 6'-8" and has a glass light.

Sliding doors provide for passage from the courtyard to the corridor and also into the rooms of the house. They have 5 lights by 2 lights and are the same as those mentioned for interior doors.

There are sliding doors to the rear court in the northeast corner of the house. They have screen panels.

The side door (west) is 2'-8" x 7'-8".

b. Windows: Casement windows (on east side of house), double hung, and hopper type windows are used. On the east and west side of the house the windows were originally covered with trellis screens. Skylights provide light into some of the interior spaces. There are large glass walls on the north and south sides of the living room, and on the south side of the studio.

SOWDEN HOUSE
HABS No. CA-1940 (Page 2)

5. Original plan and construction: Rectangular plan (64' by 125' court) with a rectangular court at center, with all rooms opening directly or by way of a corridor onto the court. Originally, there was 32' long pool in the court, now filled in. In the pool were a pair of concrete-block pylons forming a water organ. The material is reinforced concrete block and stucco over a lathed wood frame. Originally, colored stones filled the openings in the concrete blocks in the court; these have been removed.

6. Alterations and additions: 1969. Removal of some of entrance steps with widening of Franklin Avenue. No architects, dates unavailable; planter box on stairs from street removed; pylons and pool removed in court; colored stones removed from plaster and concrete block. Changes have been made in the kitchen and in the bathroom.

Prepared by: Esther McCoy
July 1968

PART II. ARCHITECTURAL INFORMATION

A. General statement:

1. Architectural character: The Sowden House, designed by Lloyd Wright in 1926, is a city residence built around a central court which originally contained an elaborate fountain. The house is entered through a cavelike opening whose textured concrete units create a striking contrast to the planar surfaces flanking it. These blocks are repeated in the central court. The two principal rooms terminate the major axis of the house—the living room at the front, the studio at the rear.

2. Condition of fabric: Fair. The house is structurally sound although there are areas revealing deterioration of the materials, especially with regard to the textured concrete units. The interior court has been neglected and has become overgrown with vegetation. The fountain mentioned above has long since disappeared.

B. Detailed Description of the Exterior

1. Overall dimensions: 64' east to west; 125' north to south. There is one principal level. At the front (south) of the house there is a partial basement. The plan is basically rectangular, with the rooms situated around the courtyard.

2. Foundations: 8" reinforced concrete; concrete footing 1'-4" wide.

SOWDEN HOUSE
HABS No. CA-1940 (Page 4)

7. Roof:

a. Shape, covering: Hip roof behind parapet walls. It is constructed of 2" x 4" rafters with 1" x 6" bracing. The red sand composition roofing is laid atop 7/8" sheathing.

b. Cornice, eaves: There is a plaster parapet rising about 2'-0" above the roof at the wall. 4" downspouts are used.

c. Dormers, cupolas, towers: Skylights are the only forms to rise above the roof except for the forms of the living room and studio, which peak above the primary roof level.

C. Detailed Description of the Interior:

1. Plans: Entrance is at the south end of the building on axis. After passing through the front gate, a sharp right turn is made to the stairs. Entrance is atop that stairway.

The main floor is composed of a central courtyard with the living room at the southern end and the studio at the northern end. Corridors flank the court, providing passage to the rear of the house and also providing access to the rooms opening off of them. Both corridors are single-loaded with the rooms between the passage and the exterior walls. The inner side of the corridor opens onto the court. The entrance door is at the south end of the corridor on the east side of the court. Down the corridor, opening to the right are bedroom #1 with its private bath, bedroom #2, bathroom, bedroom #3, bedroom #4, and bedroom #5. A darkroom terminated the corridor. A small courtyard is located on the north side of bedroom #5 and is accessible from it.

In the southwest corner of the house, adjacent to an opening from the living room, is the library. To the north of that room is the western corridor begins at the northern side of this room. Adjacent to the dining room is the pantry, followed by the kitchen and the screened porch (the side entry). The corridor continues past the servants' quarters to the garage. The servants' quarters has a hall paralleling the main passage and provided access to the two servants' rooms and bath.

There is a partial basement below the living room on the south and in the southern portion of the eastern wing. Neither is finished as a useable space.

2. Stairways: 23 risers provide access to the front entrance gate of the house. These stairs are presently being altered due to the widening of Franklin Avenue and some of them are being removed. Beyond the gate, 28 risers in a scissor type stairway provide access to the front door at the upper level. Both these stairways are composed of concrete tile treads.

SOWDEN HOUSE
HABS No. CA-1940 (Page 5)

There are six 4" risers from the patio to the studio floor level, and two 4" risers all around the court. In addition, stairs are located at the ends of the corridors on the north side.

3. Flooring: 1-1/2" oak flooring is used in all rooms except for 5-1/4" oak flooring in the living room, library, dining room, and studio; and asphalt tile in the kitchen and pantry; and concrete tile in the two major corridors (15" square with the corners off).

4. Wall and ceiling finish: Plaster; the bathroom has yellow ceramic tiles.

5. Doorways and doors: Solid wood doors in wood frames without face moldings. They are 2'-5" to 2'-8" x 6'-8" x 1-1/3" thick.

Sliding pocket doors with 5 x 2 lights (13-1/2" x 14-1/2") are used for access into the major bedroom (#2) as well as between the corridor and the courtyard.

6. Special decorative features, trim and cabinet work: The master bedroom (#2) has wood paneling on the west wall and has a heavy wood cornice. There are built-in shelves and cabinets in the library, as well as built in shelves and bureaus in the closets.

The doors have strap hinges and brass door knobs and lock plates. The front door thumb latch is also of brass.

A major decorative motif in the textured concrete block units. They are employed on all the courtyard piers and in the studio and living room. They are also used on the exterior of the house around the main entrance. The pylons in the courtyard stood 25'-4" high and also used the textured blocks.

There is a decorative skylight in the bathroom and in the dining room.

7. Mechanical equipment: There is a forced air furnace in the basement which is reinforced throughout the house by unit heaters.

There is a working fireplace in the library, on the west wall. An incinerator is located on the screen porch near the west center of the house.

The bathroom fixtures are standard, with the exception of the built in tub in the bathroom between bedrooms #2 and #3.

Lighting--coffered lighting in the living room, light panels are used in conjunction with the skylights in the dining room, bathroom and around the library fireplace.

SOWDEN HOUSE
HABS No. CA-1940 (Page 6)

7

D. Site and Surroundings

1. General setting: The house is located on the north side of Franklin Avenue, somewhat elevated above the street level. The main entrance is centered on the south facade. This, and the living room cavern-like form above it, are the only penetrations on the south facade. The house is inwardly oriented.

2. Historic landscape design: Originally, there was a planter box on axis with the house, with stairways on either side and merging behind it.

The hillside was covered with ivy.

Prepared by: Robert C. Giebner
Project Supervisor
Southern California Project II
August 1969

PART III. SOURCES OF INFORMATION

A. Primary Sources:

Lloyd Wright, architect, 855 N. Doheny Dr., Los Angeles; original drawings in his possession; information on changes in house.

Dr. and Mrs. Harold Mazur, owners, 4821 Los Feliz Blvd., Los Angeles, California; some information on change of ownership.

Hall of Records and Assessor's Office, Los Angeles Civic Center; legal description.

B. Secondary Sources:

"Lloyd Wright," Esther McCoy, Arts & Architecture, Los Angeles, October 1966, Vol. 83, No. 9, pp. 22-26.

Guide to Architecture in Southern California, Gebhard-Winter, Los Angeles Co. Museum, 1965.

1868-1968: Architecture in California, David Gebhard, U.C. Santa Barbara, catalogue, 1968, p. 75.

PART IV. PROJECT INFORMATION

This project was undertaken by the Historic American Buildings Survey in cooperation with the Southern California Coordinating Committee for Historic Preservation. This is the HABS-Southern California Project II, and was undertaken in 1969.

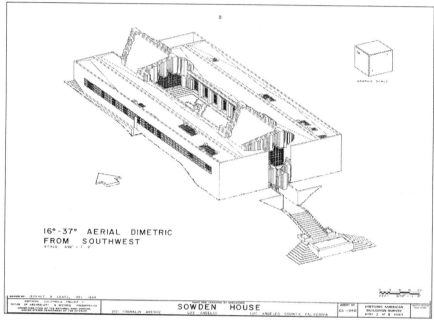

16°-37° AERIAL DIMETRIC
FROM SOUTHWEST

SOWDEN HOUSE
LOS ANGELES — LOS ANGELES COUNTY, CALIFORNIA

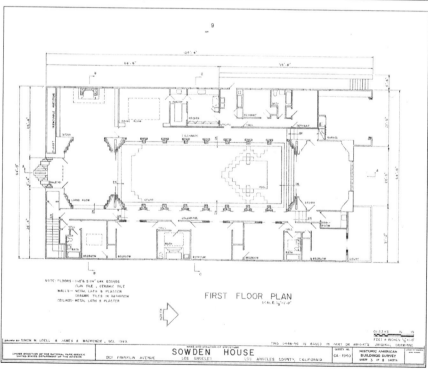

FIRST FLOOR PLAN

SOWDEN HOUSE
LOS ANGELES — LOS ANGELES COUNTY, CALIFORNIA

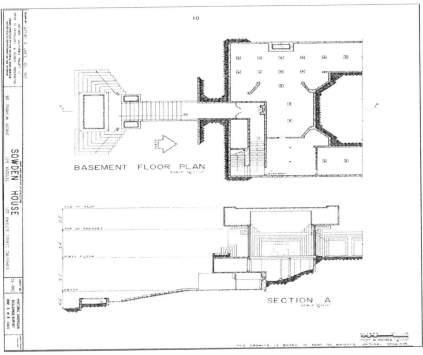

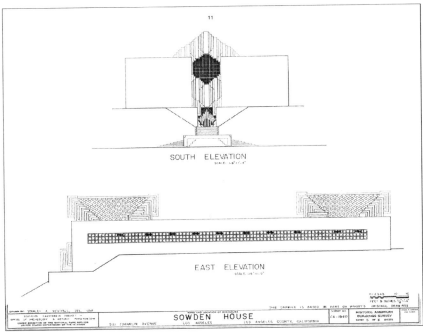

559

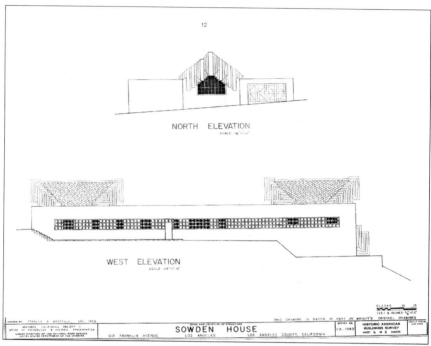

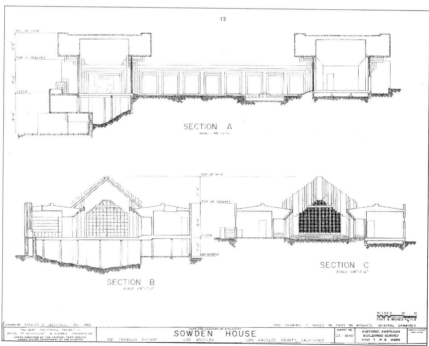

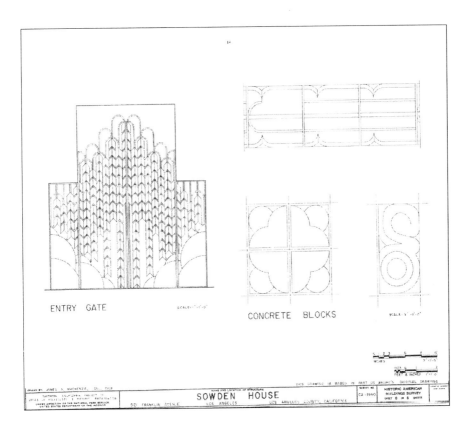

ENTRY GATE

CONCRETE BLOCKS

SOWDEN HOUSE

HISTORIC AMERICAN BUILDINGS SURVEY

15

HISTORIC AMERICAN BUILDINGS SURVEY

INDEX TO PHOTOGRAPHS

HABS
CAL,
19-LOSAN,
69-

Sowden House
5121 Franklin Avenue
Los Angeles
Los Angeles County
California

HABS No. CA-1940

Marvin Rand, photographer 1971

CA-1940-1   FRANKLIN AVENUE FACADE

CA-1940-2   ENTRANCE, OBLIQUE VIEW

CA-1940-3   ENTRANCE, AXIAL VIEW

CA-1940-4   ENTRANCE GATE

CA-1940-5   ENTRANCE GATE - DETAIL VIEW

CA-1940-6   LIVING ROOM, DISTANT VIEW, LOOKING WEST TO STUDY

CA-1940-7   LIVING ROOM, CLOSE VIEW LOOKING WEST TO STUDY

CA-1940-8   STUDY, FIREPLACE

CA-1940-9   GLAZED OPENING, LIVING ROOM, LOOKING TOWARDS COURT

CA-1940-10   COURT, LOOKING NORTH FROM LIVING ROOM TERRACE

CA-1940-11   ENTRANCE TO STUDIO AT NORTH END OF COURT, FROM COURT

CA-1940-12   CLOSE VIEW, ENTRANCE TO STUDIO AT NORTH END OF COURT

CA-1940-13   VIEW IN COURTYARD, LOOKING SOUTH TO LIVING ROOM

CA-1940-14   LIVING ROOM, CLOSE VIEW FROM COURTYARD

CA-1940-15   COLONNADE, LOOKING THROUGH DOOR

CA-1940-16   COLONNADE, BEYOND DOOR

CA-1940-17   BATHROOM, TUB

CA-1940-18   BATHROOM, SINK

Bibliography

Anger, Kenneth. *Hollywood Babylon.* San Francisco: Stonehill Publishing, 1975.

——. *Hollywood Babylon II.* New York: NAL Penguin, 1984.

Bonelli, William G. *Billion Dollar Blackjack.* Beverly Hills: Civic Research Press, 1954.

Blanche, Tony, and Brad Schreiber. *Death in Paradise: An Illustrated History of the Los Angeles County Department of Coroner.* Los Angeles: General Publishing Group, 1998.

Breton, Andre. *Manifestoes of Surrealism.* Ann Arbor: University of Michigan Press, Ann Arbor Paperbacks, 1972.

Bruccoli, Matthew J., and Richard Layman. *A Matter of Crime,* Vol. I. San Diego: Harcourt Brace Jovanovich, 1987.

Carter, Vincent A. *LAPD's Rogue Cops.* Lucerne Valley, Calif.: Desert View Books, 1993.

Chandler, Raymond. *The Blue Dahlia: A Screenplay.* Chicago: Southern Illinois University Press, 1976.

Cohen, Mickey. *In My Own Words.* Englewood Cliffs, N.J.: Prentice-Hall, 1975.

Cox, Julian, *Spirit into Matter,* J. Paul Getty Trust, Los Angeles, 2004

Demaris, Ovid. *The Last Mafioso.* New York: Times Books, 1981.

De Rivers, J. Paul, M.D. *The Sexual Criminal: A Psychoanalytical Study.* Burbank, Calif.: Bloat, 1949; rev. ed. 2000.

Domanick, Joe. *To Protect and to Serve: The L.A.P.D.'s Century of War in the City of Dreams*. New York: Pocket Books, 1994.

Douglas, John, and Mark Olshaker. *The Cases That Haunt Us*. New York: Lisa Drew Books/Scribner, 2000.

——. *Mind Hunter*. New York: Lisa Drew Books/Scribner, 1995.

Ellroy, James. *The Black Dahlia*. New York: Mysterious Press, 1987.

——. *My Dark Places*. New York: Alfred A. Knopf, 1996.

——. *Crime Wave*. New York: Vintage Crime/Black Lizard Vintage Books, 1999.

Fetherling, Doug. *The Five Lives of Ben Hecht*. Toronto: Lester & Orpen, 1977.

Finney, Guy W. *Angel City in Turmoil*. Los Angeles: Amer Press, 1945.

Fowler, Will. *The Young Man from Denver*. Garden City, N.Y.: Doubleday & Company, 1962.

——. *Reporters: Memoirs of a Young Newspaperman*. Malibu, Calf.: Roundtable, 1991.

Giesler, Jerry, and Pete Martin. *The Jerry Giesler Story*. New York: Simon & Schuster, 1960.

Gilmore, John. *Severed: The True Story of the Black Dahlia Murder*. San Francisco: Zanja Press, 1994.

Goodman, Jonathan. *Acts of Murder*. New York: Lyle Stuart Books, Carol Publishing Group, 1986.

Granlund, Nils T. *Blondes, Brunettes, and Bullets*. New York: David McKay, 1957.

Gribble, Leonard. *They Had a Way with Women*. London: Arrow Books, 1967.

Grobel, Lawrence. *The Hustons*. New York: Charles Scribners's Sons, 1989.

Halberstam, David. *The Powers That Be*. New York: Alfred A. Knopf, 1979.

Hall, Angus, ed. *Crimes of Horror*. New York: Phoebus, 1976.

Halleck, Seymour L., M.D. *Psychiatry and the Dilemmas of Crime*. New York: Harper & Row, 1967.

Harris, Martha. *Angelica Huston: The Lady and the Legacy*. New York: St. Martin's Press, 1989.

Henderson, Bruce and Sam Summerlin. *The Super Sleuths*. New York: Macmillan, 1976.

Hecht, Ben. *Fantazius Mallare: A Mysterious Oath*. Chicago: Pascal Covici, 1922.

———. *The Kingdom of Evil: A Continuation of the Journal of Fantazius Mallare*. Chicago: Pascal Covici, 1924.

Heimann, Jim. *Sins of the City: The Real L.A. Noir*. San Francisco: Chronicle Books, 1999.

Hodel, George Hill. *The New Far East: Seven Nations of Asia*. Hong Kong: Reader's Digest Far East, 1966.

Hodel, Steve, *Black Dahlia Avenger: A Genius for Murder*, Harper, New York, 2006

Hodel, Steve, with Pezzullo, Ralph, *Most Evil: Avenger, Zodiac, and the Further Serial Murders of Dr. George Hill Hodel*, Dutton, New York, 2009

Huston, John. *An Open Book*. New York: Alfred A. Knopf, 1980.

——. *Frankie and Johnny*. New York: Albert and Charles Boni, 1930.

Jeffers, Robinson. *Roan Stallion, Tamar, and Other Poems*. New York: Boni & Liveright, 1925.

Jennings, Dean. *We Only Kill Each Other: The Life and Bad Times of Bugsy Siegel*. Englewood Cliffs, N.J.: Prentice-Hall, 1967.

Kennedy, Ludovic. *The Airman and the Carpenter*. New York: Viking Penguin, 1985.

Keppel, Robert D. *Signature Killers*. New York: Pocket Books, 1997.

Klein, Norman M., and Martin J. Schiesl.*20th Century Los Angeles: Power, Promotion, and Social Conflict*. Claremont, Calif.: Regina Books, 1990.

Knowlton, Janice, and Michael Newton. *Daddy Was the Black Dahlia Killer*. New York: Pocket Books, 1995.

Lane, Brian, and Wilfred Gregg. *The Encyclopedia of Serial Killers*. New York: Diamond Books, 1992.

Martinez, Al. *Jigsaw John*. Los Angeles: J. P. Tarcher, 1975.

Morton, James. *Gangland International: An Informal History of the Mafia and Other Mobs in the Twentieth Century*. London: Little, Brown & Company, 1998.

Mayo, Morrow, *Los Angeles*, Alfred A. Knopf, New York, 1933

Nelson, Mark and Bayliss, Sarah Hudson, *Exquisite Corpse,: Surrealism and the Black Dahlia Murder*, New York, Bulfinch Press, 2006

Nickel, Steven. *Torso: The Story of Eliot Ness and the Search for a Psychopathic Killer*. Winston-Salem, N.C.: John F. Blair, 1989.

Pacios, Mary. *Childhood Shadows: The Hidden Story of the Black Dahlia Murder.* Downloaded and printed via electronic distribution from the World Wide Web. ISBN 1-58500-484-7, 1999.

Parker, William H. *Parker on Police,* Charles C. Thomas Publisher, Springfield Illinois, 1957

Parrish, Michael. *For the People.* Los Angeles: Angel City Press, 2001.

Phillips, Michelle. *California Dreamin': The True Story of the Mamas and Papas.* New York: Warner, 1986.

Rappleye, Charles, and Ed Becker. *All American Mafioso: The Johnny Rosselli Story.* New York: Doubleday, 1991.

Reid, David. *Sex, Death and Gods in L.A.* New York: Random House, 1992.

Reid, Ed. *The Grim Reapers: The Anatomy of Organized Crime in America.* Chicago: Henry Regnery, 1969.

Richardson, James H. *For the Life of Me: Memoirs of a City Editor.* New York: G. P. Putnam's Sons, 1954.

Roeburt, John. *Get Me Giesler.* New York: Belmont Books, 1962.

Rothmiller, Mike, and Ivan G. Goldman. *L.A. Secret Police: Inside the L.A.P.D. Elite Spy Network.* New York: Pocket Books, 1992.

Rowan, David. *Famous American Crimes.* London: Frederick Muller, 1957.

Sade, Donatien-Alphonse-François de. *Selected Writings of de Sade.* New York: British Book Centre, 1954.

Sade, Donatien-Alphonse-François de. *The Complete Justine, Philosophy in the Bedroom and Other Writings.* New York: Grove Press, 1965.

Sade, Donatien-Alphonse-François de. *The 120 Days of Sodom and Other Writings*. New York: Grove Press, 1966.

Sade, Donatien-Alphonse-François de.*120 Days of Sodom, or the School for Libertinage*. New York: Falstaff Press, 1934.

Sakol, Jeannie. *The Birth of Marilyn: The Lost Photographs of Norma Jean by Joseph Jasgur*. New York: St. Martin's Press, 1991.

Seaver, Richard, Terry Southern, and Alexander Trocchi, eds. *Writers in Revolt: An Anthology*. New York: Frederick Fell, 1963.

Sjoquist, Arthur W. *Captain: Los Angeles Police Department 1869–1984*. Dallas: Taylor, 1984.

Smith, Jack. *Jack Smith's L.A.* New York: McGraw-Hill, 1980.

Starr, Kevin. *Inventing the Dream: California through the Progressive Era*. New York: Oxford University Press, 1985.

———. *The Dream Endures: California Enters the 1940s*. New York: Oxford University Press, 1997.

Stevenson, Robert Louis. *The Strange Case of Dr. Jekyll and Mr. Hyde and Other Stories*. New York: Barnes & Noble, 1995.

Sterling, Hank. *Ten Perfect Crimes*. New York: Stravon, 1954.

Stoker, Charles. *Thicker'n Thieves*. Santa Monica: Sidereal, 1951.

Stoker, Charles. *Thickern'n Thieves*, Los Angeles: Thoughtprint Press, 2011.

Tejaratchi, Sean, ed. *Death Scenes: A Homicide Detective's Scrapbook*. Portland: Feral House, 1996.

Terman, Lewis M. *Genetic Studies of Genius*. Vol. 1. Stanford: Stanford University Press, 1925.

Terman, Lewis M., and Melita H. Oden. *The Gifted Group at Mid-Life: Thirty-Five Years' Follow-Up of the Superior Child.* Stanford: Stanford University Press, 1959.

True Crime—Unsolved Crimes. Alexandria, Va.: Time-Life Books, 1993.

Tygiel, Jules. *The Great Los Angeles Swindle.* New York: Oxford University Press, 1994.

Viertel, Peter. *Dangerous Friends: At Large with Huston and Hemingway in the Fifties.* New York: Nan A. Talese/Bantam Doubleday Dell, 1992.

Viertel, Peter, *White Hunter Black Heart,* New York, Doubleday, 1953

Underwood, Agness. *Newspaperwoman.* New York: Harper & Brothers, 1949.

Waldberg, Patrick. *Surrealism.* New York: Thames & Hudson, 1997.

Walker, Clifford James. *One Eye Closed the Other Red: The California Bootlegging Years.* Barstow, Calif.: Back Door Publishing, 1999.

Webb, Jack. *The Badge.* Greenwich, Conn.: Fawcett, 1958.

White, Leslie T. *Me, Detective.* New York: Harcourt, Brace & Company, 1936.

Wilson, Colin. *Murder in the 1940s.* New York: Carroll & Graf, 1993.

Woods, Gerald, *The Police in Los Angeles,* Garland Publishing Inc. New York, 1993

Wolf, Marvin J., and Katherine Mader. *Fallen Angels: Chronicles of L.A. Crime and Mystery.* New York: Facts on File, 1986.

Weintraub, Alan. *Lloyd Wright: The Architecture of Frank Lloyd Wright Jr.* New York: Harry N. Abrams, 1998.

Work Projects Administration, *Los Angeles: A Guide to the City and its Environs*, Hastings House, New York, 1941

Man Ray Research–Related Books

Foresta, Merry. *Perpetual Motif: The Art of Man Ray.* New York: Abbeville Press and the National Museum of American Art, 1988.

Man Ray. *Self Portrait.* Boston: Little, Brown & Company, 1963.

——. *Man Ray Photographs.* New York: Thames & Hudson, 1991.

Penrose, Roland. *Man Ray.* New York: Thames & Hudson, 1975.

Robert Berman Gallery. *Man Ray: Paris–L.A.* New York: Smart Art Press Art Catalog, 1996.

Butterfield and Dunning. *Fine Photographs.* Catalog, November 17, 1999.

——. *Fine Photographs.* Catalog, May 27, 1999.

Newspaper Sources

San Francisco Chronicle: 1969-1978
San Francisco Examiner, 1969-1970
Vallejo-Times Herald, 1969
Los Angeles Record, 1925
Riverside Press Enterprise, 1966-1971
Los Angeles Times, 1941-1972
Los Angeles Mirror, 1947
Los Angeles Herald Express, 1945-1951
Los Angeles Examiner, 1947-1950
Chicago Daily Tribune, 1945-1950
The Manila Times, 1967

Miscellaneous:

F.B.I., FOIA Files on Elizabeth Short
Los Angeles District Attorney, Bureau of Investigation, "Black Dahlia and Dr. George Hill Hodel Files"; Electronic Surveillance Files on George Hodel, and Investigative summaries on Black Dahlia by DA Lt. Frank B. Jemison; 146-page Hodel-Black Dahlia transcripts; Frank Jemison/Dorothy Hodel 6-page interview transcripts.
Sowden House, Historic American Survey, National Park Service, Department of Interior 1969

Websites:
www.stevehodel.com
www.zodiackiller.com
www.lapl.org
www.lmharnisch.com

Black Dahlia Avenger Television Documentaries & Shows:

Dateline NBC, "Black Dahlia" Josh Mankiewicz (2003 twenty-minute segment)

Court TV, "Who Killed the Black Dahlia?" Josh Mankiewicz (2003 one-hour)

CBS 48-Hours Special, "Black Dahlia Confidential" (2004 one-hour)

A&E Bill Kurtis Cold Case Files, "Black Dahlia" (2006 one-hour)

NBC Universal (France), The Truth about the Black Dahlia (2006 one-hour)

CNN Anderson Cooper-360, "Black Dahlia" (2006 eight-minute author interview)

Discovery Channel, "MOST EVIL" (2007 one-hour)

ABOUT THE AUTHOR

Photo by Ed Evans

Steve Hodel was born and raised in Los Angeles, California. He served four years as a medic in the U.S. Navy, and then joined the Los Angeles Police Department in 1963. After six years in uniform patrol, he transferred to Hollywood Division Detectives where he worked all of the "tables": Burglary, Robbery, Auto-Theft, Juvenile, Crimes against Persons and was then permanently assigned to the Homicide Detail.

During his career at Hollywood Homicide, Steve promoted to Detective II and in 1983 was the senior field homicide detective. During his years of service he received more than 75 commendations and handled over 300 separate murder investigations and had one of the departments highest "solve rates. " Steve promoted to Detective III (the highest attainable rank in detectives) and retired from LAPD in 1986.

Steve's first book, *Black Dahlia Avenger: A Genius for Murder* published in 2003 with new updated investigative chapters added to the *HarperCollins* paperback edition in 2004 and 2006. *Black Dahlia Avenger* is a *New York Times* Bestseller, a *NYT* Most Notable Book and was nominated by the Mystery Writers of America for an Edgar Award in the Best Fact Crime category.

Harper Collins 2006

"Hodel's investigation is thoroughly and completely convincing. So too is this book. As far as I am concerned, this case is closed."

MICHAEL CONNELLY
Bestselling author, Harry Bosch novels

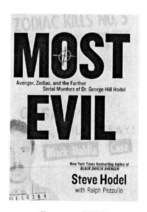

Dutton 2009

When veteran LAPD homicide detective Steve Hodel discovered that his late father had known the victim in the infamous *Black Dahlia* murder case in 1947 Los Angeles, the ensuing three-year investigation became the New York Times bestseller *Black Dahlia Avenger*. Publication led directly to the discovery of a cache of hidden documents, covered up for decades, that confirm George Hodel had long been law enforcement's number one suspect in Elizabeth Short's grisly death. A lurid murder mystery that had endured for more than fifty years was finally solved.

But for Steve Hodel, that revelation was only the beginning. With twenty-five years of experience investigating homicides as an LAPD detective, Hodel's instincts told him that a man capable of bisecting Elizabeth Short's body, arranging it in a gruesome and public tableau, and taunting the police and the public with notes and phone calls, did not begin or end his killing career with the Black Dahlia. A chance encounter in the wake of Black Dahlia Avenger's publication led Steve to consider a question as preposterous as it is compelling.

Twenty years after shocking the world in Los Angeles, could Dr. George Hill Hodel have returned to terrorize California as the killer known as Zodiac?

Author website: www.stevehodel.com

Thoughtprint Press

THOUGHTPRINT PRESS RECOMMENDS:

THICKER'N THIEVES

By

CHARLES STOKER

Foreword by Steve Hodel

Available on-line in print and e-book formats

www.thoughtprintpress.com

CPSIA information can be obtained at www.ICGtesting.com
Printed in the USA
LVOW101719180413

329856LV00016B/237/P